AFTER LIFE

AFTER LIFE

EUGENE THACKER

THE UNIVERSITY OF CHICAGO PRESS
CHICAGO AND LONDON

EUGENE THACKER is associate professor in the Media Studies program at the New School.

The University of Chicago Press, Chicago 60637
The University of Chicago Press, Ltd., London
© 2010 by The University of Chicago
All rights reserved. Published 2010
Printed in the United States of America

19 18 17 16 15 14 13 12 11   2 3 4 5

ISBN-13: 978-0-226-79371-9 (cloth)
ISBN-13: 978-0-226-79372-6 (paper)
ISBN-10: 0-226-79371-0 (cloth)
ISBN-10: 0-226-79372-9 (paper)

Library of Congress Cataloging-in-Publication Data
Thacker, Eugene.
  After life / Eugene Thacker.
    p. cm.
  Includes bibliographical references and index.
  ISBN-13: 978-0-226-79371-9 (cloth : alk. paper)
  ISBN-13: 978-0-226-79372-6 (pbk. : alk. paper)
  ISBN-10: 0-226-79371-0 (cloth : alk. paper)
  ISBN-10: 0-226-79372-9 (pbk. : alk. paper)   1. Ontology.   2. Life.   I. Title.
  BD311.T43 2010
  113'.8—dc22

                                        2010007700

♾ The paper used in this publication meets the minimum requirements of the American National Standard for Information Sciences—Permanence of Paper for Printed Library Materials, ANSI Z39.48-1992.

CONTENTS

If philosophy begins in a certain perplexity towards the world, then perhaps this perplexity is resolved in life. However, in philosophy (as in the world . . .), "life" is never a simple affair. More often than not, life is understood to be something that, though it is not *lived* exclusively by human beings, is, however, *thought* exclusively by human beings. In fact, it could even be said that it is this capacity to think that which is lived—sometimes to the point that the two coincide—that has come to traditionally define the task of philosophy.

"Life" is a troubling and contradictory concept. Its metamorphic quality is witnessed in the essentialist concept of "life itself" as information, in the twofold approach to life as at once scientific and mystical, in the return of vitalisms of all types, and in the pervasive politicization of life. Today, in an era of biopolitics, it seems that life is everywhere at stake, and yet it is nowhere the same. The question of how and whether to value life is at the core of contemporary debates over bare life and the state of exception. At another level, in our scientific worldview, it seems that life is claimed of everything, and yet life in itself is nothing. While biologists continue to debate whether or not a virus is living, the advances in genetic engineering and artificial life have, in different ways, deconstructed the idea that life is exclusively natural or biological. We also live in a time in which events at the micro-level are also events at the macro-level: the increasing frequency of global pandemics and the prevalence of natural disasters are events that are at once local and global, molecular and planetary. While human beings or human groups are obviously involved in such events, there is also a sense in which such events are beyond human comprehension. In short, life is human-centered and yet unhuman-oriented.

In each of these cases, thought and life approach a horizon of absolute incommensurability; the thought of life becomes increasingly disjunctive with the vague set of phenomena we call "life itself." Where, then, should one begin such an inquiry? Too often the concept of life is understood to be a specifically modern one, resulting in a rather predictable stratification: the foundation of biological life, and above it, the ascendant layers of human ethical, social, and political life. Such stratified thinking is a direct descendant of Aristotle, who organizes life in an ascending pyramid of plant (nutritive; growth and decay), animal (sensate and mobile), and human (reason, consciousness) forms of life, adding to this the famous "political animal" that is political life. Against this stratification one can ask simple but far-reaching questions: What if life is not reducible to biology— but also not reducible to "consciousness," "spirit," or "intellect"? What if life is never self-evident in lived experience? However, once one entertains these questions, a whole host of other questions present themselves. The very concept of life itself begins to dissolve and dissipate, while still remaining in use and in circulation. What if life is not assumed to reach its pinnacle in human life? What if life is only incidentally, and not fundamentally, an anthropocentric phenomenon? And what if life actually has very little to do with the presumed self-evident nature of the living?

After Life is a book that addresses the ontology of life in Western philosophy. It does this not in order to formulate a new or an alternative theory of life, but in order to begin articulating a *critique* of life. That critique begins with a proposition and an observation. The proposition is the following: *Every ontology of "life" thinks of life in terms of something-other-than-life.* As we will see, that "something-other-than-life" is most often a metaphysical concept, such as time and temporality, form and causality, or spirit and immanence. From this follows an observation, which is really the core of this book: *"Life" is not only a problem of philosophy, but a problem for philosophy.* In other words, life is not only inscribed by regional discourses (for instance, theology or biology), but in many instances it effects a reversal whereby it describes fundamental ontology, shoring up its limits and internal contradictions. Tracing the twists and turns of how this happens in philosophy is one of the book's aims.

Needless to say, undertaking such a project is daunting. There are, to begin with, historical and disciplinary issues to consider—the concept of the "life-principle" in Aristotle is markedly different from how it was understood by Aquinas, and the entire understanding of life and nature dramatically changes when one moves to adjacent fields such as natural theology or natural history. There are also formal issues to consider, in the continuities and discontinuities between any two thinkers, be it in terms of a debate (for example, the debate between Aquinas and Duns Scotus on the concept of the creature), or in terms of influence (for example, the role that Duns Scotus and other Scholastic thinkers play in Gilles Deleuze's philosophy). Finally, there is the issue of periodization to consider. Should a book that attempts to unpack philosophical reflection on life also be a history of the concept of life? If so, how should one avoid the undue amassing of names and books that such a summary necessarily demands? If historical continuity is not an issue, then how should one approach the issue of continuity without assuming that a given concept such as life has a universality?

These questions are questions of method. And, while this book does not answer all of them definitively, a number of decisions have nevertheless been made. The first is that philosophical questions often take precedence over historical ones; this means, simply, that in tracing the ontology of life priority has been given to the morphology of that concept as it shifts historical and philosophical contexts. While this book does not aim to construct a history of the concept of life, it does focus on several major threads that emerge from Aristotle and reach a point of culmination in Kant, while passing through early modern philosophy.

In this way, this book approaches the ontology of life as being shaped by the premodern context of what I will be calling post-Aristotelian Scholastic philosophy. This is a broad and uneven tradition in which the concept of life is situated in a zone that is neither quite biology nor quite theology, with something called "philosophy" often playing the role of mediator. I will be using the terms "Scholastic" and "Scholasticism" in a number of ways. In a more conventional, stricter sense, the terms refer to the philosophy produced by theologian-philosophers in the twelfth- and thirteenth-century European university. In a less conventional and broader sense, the terms "Scholastic" and "Scholasticism" will also refer to a range of speculative modes—from the poetry of mysticism to the analytical rigor of the commentary—that take up the conceptual framework set out by Aristotle's *De Anima* and the various forms of Aristotelianism that follow upon it (some of which are indistinguishable from forms of Neoplatonism or mystical theology)—and, in particular, those speculative modes that reflect on a cluster of concepts that themselves are constellated around the idea of "life" (e.g., "soul," "creature," "nature").

The implication that runs throughout this book is that any attempt to construct an ontology of life must confront the challenges put forth by the long tradition of post-Aristotelian Scholasticism. One of the cen-

tral questions raised by this tradition is the following: to what extent is
it possible to formulate an ontology of life that is neither reducible to biology nor sublimated within theology? As we will see, the terms of this
are set out by Aristotle, particularly in the *De Anima*, and are taken up
in a variety of ways by Neoplatonic, negative theological, and Scholastic
philosophies—and in ways that frustrate the veneer of modernity's distinct disciplinary boundaries of biology, theology, and philosophy. These
challenges in thinking "life" reach a certain pitch in Kant, who both re-
vives Aristotle while attempting to resolve the antinomies that the concept of "life" evokes.

If choosing a place to start is difficult, choosing a place to end is even
more challenging. To open with Aristotle and to close with Kant would
seem to foreclose a whole host of philosophers and ideas that have come
to define modernity. This is, to be sure, an unavoidable pitfall. Suffice it
to say that one of the conclusions of *After Life* is that a fundamental shift
occurs in the ontology of life after Kant—a shift in which the Aristotelian
framework still remains but the responses radically change. This has necessitated a separate study altogether—entitled *Darklife*—could be viewed
as the "sequel" to this book.

At its core, *After Life* isolates two traditions that address the ontology
of life: the first is the dominant thread of post-Aristotelian, Thomist Scholasticism, which constructs an ontology of life that is superlative, analogical, and governed by transcendent emanation. The second tradition is a
more radical, "heretical" orientation in which life is defined by negation,
univocity-equivocity, and the concept of pantheistic immanence. In this
eclectic strain of heretical Scholasticism, we will examine the thought of
philosophers such as the Pseudo-Dionysius, John Scottus Eriugena, John
Duns Scotus, Nicholas of Cusa, and Benedict de Spinoza. Along the way,
these Scholastic thinkers will be situated within the framework of contemporary philosophy, including treatments of Gilles Deleuze's own engagement with Scholasticism and biophilosophy. Additionally, the book
also contains three short "ellipses" that consider the ontology of life in
comparison to Arabic, Chinese, and Japanese philosophies of the twelfth
and thirteenth centuries. These should be read not as fully worked-out arguments, but as initial attempts to think the concept of life across very
different philosophical trajectories.

After Life is organized into three chapters. Each discusses a philosophical concept of life in terms of something other than life: life defined in
terms of time and temporality ("Superlative Life"), life defined in terms
of form and finality ("Univocal Creatures"), and life defined in terms of

spirit and immanence ("Dark Pantheism"). Each culminates in a tension between orthodoxy and heresy, dominant and minoritarian conceptions of life: in the "Superlative Life" chapter, life as nothing (*nihil*) is poised against the dominant concept of life as generosity or gift; in the "Univocal Creatures" chapter, life as univocal or equivocal is poised against life as analogical; and in the "Dark Pantheism" chapter, life as "dark" or empty immanence is poised against life as transcendent emanation.

In each chapter, an ontology of life is followed to its conclusion, whereby a contradiction is revealed that is fundamental for that ontology itself: life as affirmation and negation (life as time), life as additive and subtractive (life as form), and life as interiority and exteriority (life as spirit). What results is a set of fundamental contradictions inherent in the concept of life, contradictions that are logically coherent, and yet ontologically necessary. Thus one of the main questions we will consider in this book is the following: in what way does the Aristotelian ontology of life actually necessitate a set of logically coherent contradictions?

Arguably, we are still under the spell of this conceptual framework. If the question of Being was the central issue for antiquity (resurrected in the twentieth century by Heidegger), and if the question of God, as alive or dead, was the central issue for modernity (Kierkegaard, Marx, Nietzsche), then perhaps the question of "life" is the question that has come to define our contemporary era . . .

Consider the three major modes in the philosophical engagement with "life" today—the affective-phenomenological, the biopolitical, and the politico-theological. It would seem that the classical framework set out by Aristotle, and developed by post-Aristotelian Scholasticism, still informs philosophical reflection on "life" today—life as time (the affective-phenomenological), life as form (the biopolitical), and life as spirit (the politico-theological).

In the first case, there has been a steady loosening of the concept of life in the "new vitalisms" of affectivity, process, and self-organization. On the one hand, phenomenology descended from Merleau-Ponty and Michel Henry has reframed life less in terms of its scientificity and more in terms of its embodiment and affective *époché*, its propensity for "auto-affection." Despite its incommensurability with phenomenology, philosophies inspired by Deleuze and Bergson have pointed to a concept of life that is defined by its immanently dynamic, self-organizing, and germinal qualities. Life is in this case neither a quality that a body has, nor a vital force separate from a thing that is vitalized, but the priority of immanence in itself, a continuum or network of affects in which individuated subjects are more effects than causes.

In the second case, life is politically at stake in Giorgio Agamben's notions of "bare life" and "form-of-life," creating a state of exception in which, as Antonio Negri notes, "all politics is biopolitics." More specifically, the so-called post-9/11 era has reinvigorated the figure of the body politic and, as Jacques Derrida notes, its "autoimmunitary disorders," in which every instance of community is doubled by immunity, or by what Roberto Esposito calls an "immunization paradigm" of boundaries and boundary management. The publication and translation of Michel Foucault's lectures at the Collège de France have prompted new views on biopolitics, foregrounding the role that political economy, war, and technoscience have had on the concept of "population."

But the concept of "life" is not simply about this ambivalent conjunction of biology and politics—today it is also being extended across broad swaths of social, economic, and cultural existence. Building on the prior work on religion by Heidegger and Derrida, philosophers as wide-ranging as Mark C. Taylor, Luc Ferry, Jean-Luc Marion, and Slavoj Žižek have each noted the ambivalent relations between the qualified social life of *bíos* and the religious or spiritual life, be it of the individuated subject or of a community—real, imaginary, or "to come." Furthermore, "life" is first and foremost the experience of living, and this life-experience—once the hallmark of modernity and its existentialist preoccupations with authenticity—is still the center of the experience of life today, mediated, simulated, and virtualized in a range of ways, culminating in the metastability of what Zygmunt Bauman calls "liquid life."

These three contemporary strands find their point of tension in political reflection on "life," where what is at stake is not just the thing or the self, but the qualified life, the life worth living, the life that is part of the body politic. Thus it should be no surprise that the life of the body politic also ascends to, or descends from, the moral, ethical, and spiritual life, be it of an individuated subject or a collectivized community. Beyond this, or outside of this, there is only the nebulous realm of the life-after-life, a negative theology of that paradoxical life that can never be lived. The study of such a life-after-life would seem to require a kind of "supernatural philosophy" adequate to the task—that is, a supernaturalism that would not be a superhumanism. But such a philosophy would have to be as skeptical of the reductionism of the philosophy of biology as of the dogmatism of the various theologies of life; it would have to refuse both organism and spirit as the exemplars of life.

This leads to the two central challenges that this book puts forward for any speculation on "life" today. One of these challenges is to refuse a dichotomous concept of life, as caught between the poles of reductionism and mysticism, scientificity and religiosity, the empirical and the romantic notions of life. Caught between these poles, life appears at once as the exclusive domain of technoscience, and as the privileged domain of an eschatological religious extremism. This opens onto a second challenge, and this is the pervasive anthropomorphism of the concept "life." It is often noted that it is only human beings that worry about the definition of life—the rest of the world simply lives it. This is undoubtedly related to the long-standing tradition in Western thought to regard life specifically as the life *for us* as human beings. Life is, at least from Aristotle onwards, a concept that is highly stratified, the view down from on top of a pyramid of increasing complexity. But if the existence of disasters, pandemics, and nonhuman networks tells us anything, it is that there is another world in addition to the world that is there "for us." This is not simply a world in itself, and neither is it a world that is destined for us—rather, it is a world that presents us with the very limits of our ability to comprehend it in terms that are neither simply that of the "in itself" or the "for us." It is a world "without us" (the life *sans soi*). It is the challenge of thinking a concept of life that is foundationally, and not incidentally, a nonhuman or unhuman concept of life.

A few words of acknowledgment are in order. A research leave from the Georgia Institute of Technology enabled me to make substantial progress on this book, and I am especially grateful to Kenneth Knoespel for his ongoing collegiality and encouragement. At the University of Chicago Press, Alan Thomas's enthusiasm, openness, and support for this project have been indispensable, and the Press's staff has made the publication process an enjoyable one.

A number of the ideas in this book have been presented previously, either in lectures or publication: "After Life: *De Anima* and Unhuman Politics," *Radical Philosophy* 155 (2009); "After Life: Swarms, Demons, and the Antinomies of Immanence," in *Theory After Theory*, ed. Derek Attridge and Jane Elliott (New York: Routledge, 2010); "On Life and the Living," in *Epistemologies of Difference*, ed. Bettina Bock-Wülfingen et al. (Heidelberg: Springer, 2010); as well as lectures given at: Humboldt Universität-

Berlin, the Intermediae-Matadero Center (Madrid); PAC-TAC (the Pacific
Centre for Technology and Culture), SCI-Arc (the Southern California Institute of Architecture), the University of Aberdeen, the University of Ba-
sel, the University of Washington-Seattle, and Wayne State University. My
thanks to all those involved in the organization of these lectures.

Finally, for Prema: "Où la vie se contemple tout est submergé."[1]

CHAPTER ONE

Life and the Living
(On Aristotelian Biohorror)

Nature proceeds little by little from things lifeless to animal life in such a way that it is impossible to determine the exact line of demarcation, nor on which side thereof an intermediate form should lie.
—Aristotle

1.1 SUPERNATURAL HORROR AS THE PARADIGM FOR LIFE

In the early twentieth century a unique literary genre emerged that combined horror, myth, and developments in science and technology. The stories tended to be concept-driven rather than plot- or character-driven, and, though they often utilized well-known motifs such as the mad scientist or alien invasion, more often than not they moved towards a singular affect: the terrifying and sublime conclusions to be drawn from a view of the world as an utterly unhuman world.

Writers such as H. P. Lovecraft, Clark Ashton Smith, Frank Belknap Long, and Robert E. Howard are often associated with this type of writing, which appeared throughout the early twentieth century in pulp magazines such as *Weird Tales*, *Amazing Stories*, and the like. The pulp magazines dubbed this kind of writing "weird fiction," though Lovecraft himself preferred the more literary term "supernatural horror." Its mid-twentieth-century inheritors were TV shows such as *Twilight Zone* and *Outer Limits*, and its contemporary influence can be felt in the Japanese horror boom of the late twentieth and early twenty-first centuries.

I mention this "cult" tradition because many of the stories contain thought-provoking insights into the concept of "life"—and, specifically, into the limits of such a concept when it is thought of in exclusively human-centric terms. Consider the late-period works of Lovecraft as an example. In these stories, one often finds three forms of life: There is, first, the world of the living and the nonliving (plants, animals, human beings), existing within the human-centric world of society, politics, and science. This is a world in which we find characters weighted down by deeply ingrained ways of thinking about the world—rural vs. urban, regional vs. global, civilized vs. primitive, race vs. species, ancient vs. modern, and so on. In the midst of this all-too-human world, Lovecraft's characters discover remnants—often at a distant, furtive archaeological dig—of an advanced form of life that confounds all human knowledge about life as we know it. These types of beings—the "Old Ones"—are often characterized as an advanced race of other-dimensional beings that are discovered to have existed eons prior to the appearance of human beings. This is the life that is so ancient it is alien.[1]

This in itself is cause for horror for Lovecraft's characters. The strange, alien facticity of the remnant throws into abeyance all human presupposition—history, biology, geology, cosmology—concerning the human and its relation to the world. This alone qualifies Lovecraft's stories as science fiction. But there is another element that pushes the works into that intermediary zone of supernatural horror and "the weird." In addition to these two forms of life, there is also a third form of life that appears in Lovecraft's stories. This third form of life often resists easy description, either in terms of the human world, or in terms of the Old Ones. Sometimes this third form of life is given an awkward name, such as "Elder Things" or "Shoggoths." Clark Ashton Smith once used the term "Ubbo-Sathla," while Frank Belknap Long used the phrase "the Space-Eaters." William Hope Hodgson preferred the more menacing and shapeless term "the Watchers." However, while this form of life is often named, more often than not it represents the very horizon of human thought to think this third form of life at all—hence Lovecraft's characters obliquely refer to them as the "nameless thing"—or better, in Ambrose Bierce's phrase, "the damned thing."

This third form of life is, then, the nameless thing that is living, with all the contradictions this implies. It is described by Lovecraft's characters in ways that are poetic and highly articulate. In "The Shadow Out of Time," for instance, the central character not only discovers remnants that this third form of life had actually once been alive, but, to his horror, he also discovers that they are still alive. The narrator begins, in a classically unreliable mode, by evoking the unreality of his situation: "Dream, madness, and memory merged wildly together in a series of fantastic, fragmentary delusions which can have no relation to anything real." But this

is not enough, for what is then evoked is the strange objectivity of these delusions: "There was a hideous fall through incalculable leagues of viscous,
sentient darkness, and a babel of noises utterly alien to all that we know of
the earth and its organic life." Finally, the delusion itself is revealed to be
not only something "real," but, more importantly, something dormantly
alive: "Dormant, rudimentary senses seemed to start into vitality within
me, telling of pits and voids peopled by floating horrors and leading to sun-
less crags and oceans and teeming cities of windowless basalt towers upon
which no light ever shone."[2]

There is more here than the menacing monster of classic creature-
feature films. In these passages, what is horrific is not just that such nameless things are still alive, but, more importantly, that in their living they
evoke in Lovecraft's characters the limits of thought—the limits of thought
to think "life" at all. The very terms of human thought fail to encompass
the nameless thing. In Lovecraft's novel *At the Mountains of Madness* one
of the central characters attempts to describe the Shoggoths—an oozing
hyper-complex form of life composed of mathematically grouped dots and
a multitude of eyes:

> Formless protoplasm able to mock and reflect all forms and organs and
> processes—viscous agglutinations of bubbling cells—rubbery fifteen-
> foot spheroids infinitely plastic and ductile—slaves of suggestion,
> builders of cities—more and more sullen, more and more intelligent,
> more and more amphibious, more and more imitative . . . [3]

Lovecraft's characters are not insane—in fact, the source of their horror
is the realization that they are not hallucinating or suffering from "exhausted nerves." With the requisite melodramatic flair, Lovecraft's characters often express the wish that they were simply hallucinating or dream-
ing, for then they could dismiss what they encounter as pure subjectivism,
and the self-world dichotomy would remain intact. The problem is that
Lovecraft's characters come to verify this third form of life—but in a manner that is incommensurate to any form of rational verification. The very
categories of matter and form, actual and potential, origin and finality,
growth, decay, and organization—all these categories of thought flounder
before a form of life that is at once oozing and mathematical, formless and
geometric.

This third kind of life, the "nameless thing" so often described by Lovecraft, is a paradigm for the concept of life today. The concept of life en-

compasses so much, from the most reductive biological viewpoint to the most open-ended ethical or existential viewpoint. When definitions or criteria for life are given, even these are subject to modification and revision. There is a sense in which the major problem concerning life has to do not with its definition, and whether such a definition is possible, but with the very *plasticity* of life, a shape-shifting quality exhibited in all the different ways in which we use the concept to correlate to the different phenomena that are deemed to be living—the plasticity of all the different ways in which life is thought and shaped, all the myriad ways in which life reflects upon itself and shapes itself, all the forms of existence, resistance, and insistence that life is.

This invites us to consider a more general set of problems concerning the concept of life today. We can briefly summarize some of these. There is, first, the polyvalence of meanings for "life." Here life means so many things that it does not mean any one thing. If the concept of life encompasses everything from the physical organism, to socioeconomic living conditions, to the life that is subject to ethical and legal decision-making, to the entire planet itself, then there is a sense in which almost nothing is excluded from life. This is a synchronic dimension in which, at any given moment, and in any given context, there are such a wide range of meanings for "life" that the term ceases to have any stable meaning at all. The limit of this is, of course, relativism. If life means everything, then life means nothing.

Despite this polyvalence of meanings, some can be viewed as more dominant than others. Here the apparatus of social norms, disciplinary specialization, and institutional legitimacy all come into play. Although everything and anything may come under the term "life," there is also a sense in which some things are more living, or more essentially living, than others. The hegemony of scientific concepts of "life" has had an impact that reaches far beyond scientific specialization. Here "life" is that which fulfills a descriptive list of behavioral criteria in natural systems (Does it contain DNA? Does it display adaptive evolutionary behavior? Does it maintain itself by exchanging matter and energy with its environment?). This is as true of biology historically speaking as it is in current fields such as systems biology, biocomplexity, or even astrobiology. Whereas the polyvalence of meanings of life point to a synchronic dimension, the scientific hegemony of life points to a diachronic one. The scientific grounding of the concept of life obtains a normative power that itself may change over time (from mechanism to vitalism to organization to information, and so on). The limit of this is not relativism but rather reductionism. In some instances this becomes a case of checking off the appropriate boxes.

However, this specialist notion of life is doubled by its opposite, which is the banalization of the term "life" in everyday language. In English, one regularly hears the phrases "lifestyle," "quality of life," "that's life!," "get a life!," and so on. Often this quotidianism points to the central category of experience in relation to life. And experience itself comes to overlap almost perfectly with the concept of life; there is no experience of life, because experience is life. Life is the flux and flow of living in the world; life is the experience of being alive, of living in time and through time. Unlike the above cases, in which the concept of life is distributed along synchronic and diachronic axes, here life obtains a pragmatic quality, as the very phenomenon of life in its being lived. Life is simply the experience of living, and vice-versa. But this too has a limit, and that is universalism. Everything that happens to a person is part of this flux and flow of life. Life becomes everything and anything that can possibly be experienced, and what can be experienced becomes the totality of life.

This leads to a fourth usage of the concept. When life is taken as subjective experience, life is projected from subject to object, self to world, and human to nonhuman. Another name for this process is anthropomorphism. The life that is fully commensurate with experience and the phenomena of living tends to become a life that is rooted in a living, experiencing subject. And, since a reflexive awareness of living is implied in the very idea of life as experience, this also means that life becomes a human-centric concern. Life in this sense really means life-for-me, or life-for-us. This has clear political implications. Life is the privilege of designation and the status that designation accords. Life is granted or taken away, not given. Life is classified or stratified; perhaps it is designated rights, perhaps one speaks for this or that form of life, perhaps some lives are more worth living than others. Life may be named, constructed, instrumentalized, it may itself become a form of power. This is not simply a pragmatic dimension, but a political or biopolitical one. The difficulty here lies precisely in this nexus between "life" and "politics," for if life is not exclusive to the human, or a privilege of the human, then the question becomes: can there be a politics of life in terms of the nonhuman or the unhuman?

These are the contours of any attempt to think the concept of "life." The effects can be seen not just in the cultural expressions of these problems, but in the metamorphoses of the concept itself—its variability, its lability, its plasticity. However, with so many definitions of life, and so much knowledge produced about this or that form of life, the more basic question of "life itself" does not disappear. In fact, it becomes more pronounced. In other words, the various and often competing epistemologies of life in the end point back to a more fundamental question concerning an ontology of life . . . and to what extent such an ontology is possible.

It is for this reason that a return to Aristotle's project is worthwhile. But let us be clear. This is not to suggest that Aristotle provides any new perspectives or alternatives, much less an "answer" to the question of life. What we can suggest is that Aristotle sets out a framework for thinking about life whose influence can still be discerned to this day. That framework is really a limit—and it is a limit that must be "overcome" if we are to continue thinking about our current situation of biopolitics and necropolitics, immunity and community, bare life and precarious life, and so on. And the key to moving beyond the Aristotelian paradigm lies not in the search for an alternative perspective; what is needed is not a new theory of life, and not an undiscovered, forgotten, or underappreciated alternative. What is needed is a *critique* of life. And the key to overcoming the Aristotelian ontology of life lies in the fissures within that ontology. We are jumping ahead a little here, but for the time being suffice it to say that these fissures are not lacunae or lapses in argument—rather, they entail the development of a logically coherent, and yet a necessarily contradictory concept of "life."

1.2 ARISTOTLE'S *DE ANIMA* AND THE PROBLEM OF LIFE

The text given the title *De Anima* occupies a strange position within the Aristotelian corpus. On the one hand, it undertakes an investigation into the principle or essence of life, and thus overlaps with the ontological concerns of the *Metaphysica* and the logical treatises. On the other hand, this ontology is concerned not with "being" or "substance" in itself, but specifically with the phenomena of life, suggesting that the *De Anima* is more a natural philosophy. This aligns the *De Anima* with the so-called biological treatises, such as *Historia Animalium* (*On the History of Animals*), *De Partibus Animalium* (*On the Parts of Animals*), *De Motu Animalium* (*On the Movement of Animals*), *De Generatione et Corruptione* (*On Generation and Corruption*), and the various treatises given the title *Parva Naturalia*. This distinction is also played out in Aristotle's biography. Between his time as a student of Plato in the Academy, and his return to Athens later in life to found his own school, the Lyceum, Aristotle spends a number of years in and around the eastern Aegean, where he observes, describes, and catalogs the diversity of natural life. No doubt this period in exile comes to be foundational for Aristotle's natural philosophy. In this way, there are two Aristotles—there is Aristotle-the-naturalist, describing animal anatomy and physiology, and the vital processes of growth and decay, and there is Aristotle-the-metaphysician, developing fundamental metaphysical concepts concerning substance, accident, causality, form, and so on. In the *De Anima* these two Aristotles come head-to-head, resulting in a number of interesting contradictions.

Before delving into this text, a bit of an overview is in order. In its surviving form, the text of the *De Anima*—whose original title is *Peri Psukhē*—is divided into three parts. The first part announces Aristotle's project, which is to investigate the principle of life. The term Aristotle uses here and throughout is *psukhē*, which broadly translates into English as "life-principle" or "vital principle." This sets the stage for Aristotle's own definition of *psukhē*, which opens part 2 of the *De Anima*. It is here that Aristotle also stratifies life forms (plants, animals, humans) according to the type of *psukhē* that is manifested in them. Part 2 goes on to examine specific aspects of *psukhē*, including nutrition, movement, and sensation. This continues into part 3, with comments on imagination, cognition, and *nous*, a difficult term in Greek philosophy that is often translated as "mind" or "Intellect." Part 3 closes with reflections on movement and desire and a summary of the work as a whole. It is thought that the text was intended to serve as a theoretical introduction to a more extended lecture course on natural philosophy.[4]

If the *De Anima* is thematically interstitial in relation to Aristotle's other works, it also has an interstitial position in its complex history of translation and interpretation. The various translations of the *De Anima* during the Middle Ages demonstrate how translation was indelibly bound up with interpretation, especially in an age in which the boundary between philosophy and theology was continually being debated.[5] Arabic philosophy played a pivotal role in both the translation and interpretation of the *De Anima*. From the ninth century onwards, there were at least two editions of the *De Anima* circulating in Arabic. One of these editions would be used by Ibn Sina (Avicenna) and by Ibn Rushd (Averroës), the latter producing the three separate commentaries on the *De Anima*, as well as the compendium *De Animalibus*. One of Averroës's commentaries (the so-called Long Commentary) would be translated by Michael Scotus in the thirteenth century, around the same time that William of Moerbeke also produced a literal, word-by-word translation of the *De Anima* from Greek to Latin. It is this latter edition that is used by Thomas Aquinas, who not

only produces his own commentary but several other works that attempt
to find a compromise between Greek philosophy and Christian doctrine,
while also condemning the heretical quasi pantheism of "Latin Averro-
ism."[6] Translation and interpretation again go hand-in-hand when, in 1277,
the bishop of Paris issues a series of official Condemnations against the
Faculty of Arts at the University of Paris. Of particular concern is the understanding of the Aristotelian concept *psukhē* (as the "active" or "passive" *nous*, or Intellect) as being personal and transcendently immortal, or
impersonal and fully immanent.

All of these factors make approaching a text such as the *De Anima*
exceedingly difficult. There are few texts in the history of philosophy
that are as complicated as this little treatise, originally written as lecture
notes, and belonging neither to metaphysics nor physics, neither to logic
nor to biology. Nevertheless, the *De Anima* remains an important text
within the Western philosophical tradition, primarily because it signals
one of the first, formalized attempts to think an ontology of life. In addition to this, no other text has elicited so much commentary and controversy, from the earliest commentaries by Themistius and Alexander of
Aphrodisias, to the Medieval heretical commentaries of Siger of Brabant,
to such modern commentaries as that of Franz Brentano. And this points
to a final interstitiality concerning the *De Anima*—its complicated reception throughout antiquity and the Middle Ages. While the *De Anima* in
its current form may not have been widely known until the twelfth century, the basic ideas in it were disseminated in a variety of ways. One of
these was, as we've mentioned, via the translations. Another was by way of
compendium books, such as the *Liber de Causis* or the *Theologia Aristo-
telis*. Books such as these, long attributed to Aristotle, were subsequently
discovered to be either an amalgam of Aristotelianism and Neoplatonism,
or wrongly attributed altogether.[7] Thus, when speaking about the relationship between Aristotle's *De Anima* and Scholastic philosophy, we would
do better to think broadly about the nexus of Aristotelian, Arabic, and
Neoplatonic ideas as received by Scholastic thinkers. Let us hazard a
term—post-Aristotelian Scholasticism—to name all these different types
of interstitiality regarding the *De Anima*, bearing in mind that the question of interpretation with regard to this text is never simple or clear-cut.

That said, it is important to note that the approach to the *De Anima*
presented here differs significantly from its previous interpretations. Generally speaking, one can say that there are three main hermeneutic traditions surrounding the *De Anima*. The first is that of theology, in which
the notion of "life" is read in terms of "soul" (in late antiquity) or "spirit"

(in the early Christian tradition).[8] Between the eleventh and thirteenth centuries, the extensive commentaries by Arabic, Jewish, and Christian philosophers deeply influenced this theological reading of the *De Anima*. Here life is understood as a life-spirit, the divine spark of life that emanates or is manifest in all the individual instances of living creatures, by virtue of a sovereign and transcendent divinity. The unfortunate English translation of the *De Anima* as "On the Soul" still betrays the influence of this tradition today.[9]

Added to this is a second hermeneutic tradition, that of biology. While natural philosophers such as Buffon noted the importance of Aristotle for taxonomy and classification, it is with the emergence of a distinct discipline of biology, especially after Lamarck and Darwin, that Aristotle begins to be incorporated into the history of biology.[10] Here life is understood as primarily natural-biological life, endowed with a quasi-vitalistic life force that flows through each living organism. The effect of this is seen in twentieth-century "pop science" books such as François Jacob's *The Logic of Life*; current university textbooks on the "philosophy of biology" routinely begin with a chapter on Aristotle, the "father of biology."

Third, there is the hermeneutic approach of psychology and cognition. This has become the dominant framework for reading the *De Anima* today, though not without some controversy.[11] Arguably, this approach was inaugurated by the work of Franz Brentano, whose *The Psychology of Aristotle* foreground the sections from the *De Anima* dealing with sense perception, emotion, and cognition.[12] This post-Kantian reading of the *De Anima* relegated the question of "life itself" to the background, in favor of an understanding of the human subject and its phenomenal relation to its environment. Interestingly, this approach absorbs the biological interpretation (in terms of the hierarchy of life forms) into a psychological one that remains indebted to Cartesian dualism. A great deal of recent scholarship on the *De Anima* emphasizes this cognitivist approach. In uncanny ways, the debates over this "cognitivist" Aristotle replay many of the debates over the status of the "Intellect" in antiquity.

These hermeneutic traditions are not chronological in relation to each other, and neither are they mutually exclusive. Rather, they form three ways in which the central philosophical question that the *De Anima* poses—the question of "life itself"—is sublimated into a nonphilosophical domain (theology, biology, psychology). In the process, however, the question of philosophy often drops out—and this strange disappearing act is, in a way, the fundamental fissure within the *De Anima* itself. Our aim here will be to recover and to account for this disappearance of ontology within the *De Anima*. Therefore, we will be reading the *De Anima* as a treatise of ontology, but of a particular kind—a treatise on the ontology of life, *insofar as "life" for Aristotle is not simply reducible to or synonymous with "being."*[13] Put simply, in the *De Anima* Aristotle poses a general question concerning the ontology of life, and the question he poses can be put in modern terms: To what extent is it possible to formulate an ontology of life that is not reducible to biology or sublimated within theology?

The *De Anima* is, then, an approach to this basic problematic: whether there can be an ontology of life that does not simply become either biological description or theological sublimation. And let us state up front the core of this problematic, which is this: Aristotle must presuppose that which he sets out to discover. In setting out to discover the principle of life, the "is-ness" of life, Aristotle must presume not only the category of substance, but, more importantly, the distinction between the living and the nonliving.

The problem is deceptively simple. It goes something like this: Aristotle, in approaching the diversity of life forms, observes a set of characteristics unique to what he calls life. These are described in treatises such as the *Historia Animalium*, and they are also summarized in the *De Anima*. These include life as defined by its forms (life as creative, inventive, and productive of different forms of life), life as defined by its temporality (life as characterized by movement, change, and alteration), and life as defined by a spiritual aspect (life as that incorporeal essence that remains the same; life as that immaterial essence that is common among all forms of life). In modern terminology, we might say that life for Aristotle is defined by form (life is the multiplicity of forms-of-life), by time (life is that which comes-to-be and passes-away), and by spirit (life is that which is common to all forms of life).

In spite of—or because of—these characteristics, Aristotle is confronted with a challenge, which is to articulate a concept that is adequate to the diversity of what counts as "life." Such a concept must account for the characteristics of life (life as time, as form, as spirit). It must account for the conditions in which life is possible at all, as well as for the ends of life (*entelecheia*). It must, in Aristotle's terms, be at once the formal and the final cause, and the point at which the two overlap. But this means that such a concept cannot itself be a part of life, cannot be one kind of life, or one among many instances of life. For otherwise this simply begs the question, in an infinitely deferred search for a first principle of life.

Thus any concept of life must account for the principle characteristics of life, without itself being part of them.

But in addition to this, any concept of life must account for life in a way that acknowledges the internally caused, self-animating, and self-organizing capacities of life. The concept of autonomy is important for Aristotle, both in the *De Anima* and in treatises such as the *De Motu Animalium*. The cause of life, and the condition for life, is part and parcel of life itself. For Aristotle, it is this self-maintaining and self-governing aspect of life (often encompassed by the term *kinesis*) that serves as one of the distinguishing characteristics of the living from the nonliving. Any concept of life must be inseparable from actual instances of life—while not being determined or limited by them. Any concept of life cannot simply be a purely transcendental concept, one that lies above and beyond life, for then this would go against Aristotle's commitment to the inseparability of the cause of life and life itself.

This is, then, the Aristotelian problematic: On the one hand, any concept of life must be transcendent to life in order to account for its ephemeral nature and its propensity for change. On the other hand, any concept of life must be immanent to life in order to demonstrate the inseparability between principle and manifestation (or, in Aquinas' terms, between essence and existence). So, while Aristotle-the-biologist observes a set of characteristics unique to what he calls life, Aristotle-the-metaphysician struggles to articulate a coherent concept to encompass all these heterogeneous characteristics of life.

1.3 THE ONTOLOGY OF LIFE

How does Aristotle resolve this problematic? In the *De Anima* Aristotle performs two operations that are crucial for his ontology of life. The first is to propose a reworking of the Greek term *psukhē* (ψῡχή) such that it can function as the concept of "life itself." As we've noted, the complicated tradition of translation and commentary on the *De Anima* has resulted in the English rendering of the term *psukhē* as "soul." However Aristotle certainly had in mind a nontheistic notion of "soul." The term *psukhē* is perhaps better translated as "vital principle" or "principle of life," given the way that Aristotle's text straddles the domains of philosophy, biology, and theology.

Most of book 1 of the *De Anima* is concerned with an overview of how *psukhē* has been used by earlier thinkers, from Anaxagoras to Plato.

For atomists *psukhē* is that principle of motion and energy that makes the individual atoms move, collide, and bind; for the cosmologies of Anaxagoras or Empedocles, *psukhē* is a unifying principle that is constant and itself not subject to change; for the Pythagoreans, *psukhē* is the abstract unity of number, a matheme or mathematical principle governing the universe. In each case, what Aristotle extracts from prior concepts of *psukhē* is an animating principle of the world that is not itself reduced to its own attributes.

For Aristotle, the prior uses of *psukhē* are adequate insofar as they comment on the dynamic properties of the natural world; the presocratic use of *psukhē* successfully accounts for movement, and in particular, the very capacity for movement, change, and development that is characteristic of living beings. But such theories are inadequate for Aristotle in that they do not account for how dynamic change or movement occurs, especially in the cases of living beings. What is it that conditions this very capacity for movement and change? Life, then, becomes the standard for understanding the dynamic and processual aspects of the natural world. For instance, one can simply define "life" not in terms of what it is, but in terms of what it does. In book 2 of the *De Anima* Aristotle notes that, of bodies generally, "some have life ($\zeta\omega\acute{\eta}v$) and some have not; by life ($\zeta\omega\grave{\eta}v$) we mean the capacity for self-sustenance, growth, and decay."[14] But for Aristotle it is precisely this sort of descriptive definition that must itself be explained. Thus *psukhē* must not simply describe but define, and what the term *psukhē* defines is the very idea of "life itself." Aristotle reiterates this equation throughout the *De Anima*:

> The soul ($\psi v\chi\grave{\eta}$) is the cause the first principle ($\dot{\alpha}\varrho\chi\grave{\eta}$) of the living body ($\zeta\hat{\omega}v\tau o\varsigma$ $\sigma\acute{\omega}\mu\alpha\tau o\varsigma$).[15]
> . . . for the soul ($\psi v\chi\tilde{\eta}\varsigma$) is in a sense the principle ($\dot{\alpha}\varrho\chi\grave{\eta}$) of animal life ($\zeta\acute{\omega}\omega v$).[16]
> . . . that which has soul ($\check{\epsilon}\mu\psi v\chi o v$) is distinguished from that which has not by living ($\zeta\hat{\eta}v$).[17]

In these and other passages, Aristotle arranges a number of terms in a constellation with each other. There is, of course, the principal term *psukhē*, which Aristotle equates with the concept of life-in-itself. But this is also distinguished from other terms denoting "life," such as *zoē*, which often implies a biological, naturalistic understanding of life, and *bíos*, which often implies a qualified "good" life.[18] What distinguishes *psukhē* as not just meaning "life" but specifically a "principle-of-life" is the term Aristotle uses again and again, *arché*. This is the key to Aristotle's "raising up" of the term *psukhē* to an ontological principle, the *arché* of life, the life-principle.

In short, Aristotle takes up the way that the concept of *psukhē* explains *that* life is and *how* it is, but he also makes the term account for *what* life is. Aristotle raises up this term to mean not simply the facticity of living beings, but that by which such a facticity of life is possible. If the problematic that Aristotle confronts is how to articulate under a single concept the diversity of life, here we see in the concept of *psukhē* an attempt to account for not just this or that particular living being, but for "life itself." For Aristotle, *psukhē* is the *arché* of *zoē* and *bíos*; it is the principle of life, or the life that is common across every instance of life—even, and especially *if this principle remains empty or unexamined.*

Aristotle's reworking of the concept of *psukhē* allows him to do a number of things conceptually. First, the raising-up of *psukhē* as a principle means that any ontology of life will have to articulate a *principle-of-life*, or that which is the essence of life. But, as we've seen, this essence is often defined in terms of something other than life—life defined in terms of time, form, or spirit. Additionally, the principle-of-life makes possible a number of distinctions, the most prominent one being that between the living and the nonliving. These distinctions serve to establish the categories and boundaries through which one may account for life in terms of species, genera, and so on. We can call these *boundaries of articulation.* Finally, these two aspects—*psukhē* as a principle, and the boundary between the living and nonliving—enable Aristotle to employ a range of concepts in the analysis of life forms. These include the familiar Aristotelian pairs of form/matter and actual/potential, as well as the important concept of finality or entelechy. These serve as the *governing motifs* of the ontology of life, the logical terms that govern any analysis of life.

However, this Aristotelian ontology of life opens onto a further problematic regarding the status of *psukhē* as a concept. From one perspective, *psukhē* is that which conditions change and which itself does not change; a principle of life that is itself not life. But *psukhē* also cannot be totally separate from the actualization of change, or towards that to which it tends—its purpose, its finality, its goal or aim. Here, in a much-referenced passage, Aristotle will use the analogy of the eye: "If the eye were a living creature (ζῷον), its soul (ψυχή) would be its vision; for this is the substance in the sense of the formula of the eye."[19] This in turn implies that *psukhē* is never present in itself, apart from its manifestation in the various forms of life. Aristotle continues with the analogy: "just as a pupil and the faculty of seeing make an eye, so in the other case the soul and body make a living creature. It is quite clear, then, that neither the soul nor certain parts of it, if it has parts, can be separated from the body."[20]

While Aristotle's concept of *psukhē* enables him to unfold an entire ontology around "life" as a principle-of-life, with its boundaries of articulation and governing motifs, there still remains the basic problem of the relation between *psukhē* as this "life-in-itself" and *psukhē* as manifested concretely in physical, biological, living beings. At times Aristotle discusses *psukhē* as if it were a purely abstract, ideational concept, a concept belonging more to the *Metaphysica* than to the *De Anima*. At other moments—as with his numerous biological analogies—the concept of *psukhē* is understood to be inseparable from particular living beings, something inherent within them. While *psukhē* functions well as a principle, the problem that remains for Aristotle is this ambiguous relation between—or indeed within—the concept of *psukhē* itself.

Aristotle's concept of *psukhē* must perform contradictory functions—it must account for life without itself being life, and yet it cannot be separate from life. It must be at once external and internal to life. How does Aristotle smooth over this contradiction?

The clearest statement comes in the opening passages of book 1 of the *De Anima*, part of which we have cited earlier, and which we can now quote at length:

> The knowledge of the soul (ψυχῆς) admittedly contributes greatly to the advance of truth in general, and, above all, to our understanding of Nature, for the soul is in some sense the principle of animal life (ζῷον). Our aim is to grasp and understand, first its essential nature (οὐσίαν), and secondly its properties; of these some are thought to be affections proper to the soul itself (ψυχῆς), while others are considered to attach to the animal (ζῷοις) owing to the presence within it of soul.[21]

Here, at the outset of the treatise, Aristotle is laying bare his aim. But in so doing he is also setting out the parameters for what an ontology of life can possibly mean. He sets out to inquire into what *psukhē* is. Why? Because *psukhē* is the principle (*archē*) of all living beings. Thus *psukhē* is the principle-of-life. But how and in what way is *psukhē* a principle of life? Again Aristotle's original problematic returns, though he is in many ways never far from the forests and fields, and the flora and fauna of Mytilene or Stagira. We look around and bear witness to all the diverse and particular instances of life; how can there be a concept to encompass everything that is life?

Aristotle's reply is that a single principle of life can encompass all the particular instances of life only if that concept is itself internally split, and that split will be between *psukhē* as a life-principle and *psukhē* as a manifestation in living beings. This is a delicate distinction within the *De Anima*—truthfully, it never quite holds, even though Aristotle states it at the outset. But it is also a crucial move, for it allows Aristotle to think both a concept of life-in-itself, not tethered to this or that particular instance of life, as well as a concept of life that is immanent with respect to its manifold variations and manifestations.

But this internal split is not simply a split between an abstract Idea and its attendant, accidental characteristics. There is no universal model or mold called *psukhē*, which then takes on derivative forms as it is incarnated in the world. For, as Aristotle notes, there is no thing called "life-in-itself" that is ever present apart from its formal, dynamic, and temporal instantiations in the variety of living beings. And yet, Aristotle does not dispense with the *archē*-of-life altogether. He seems to imply its necessary existence if one is to think something like "life" at all.

How, then, should one characterize the internal split within *psukhē* that Aristotle puts forth? Quite simply, Aristotle utilizes metaphysical concepts to describe an internal differentiation within *psukhē*. There is a first aspect of *psukhē*, the essence or the "being" of life, as it were—the *ousia* of *psukhē*. Here one is considering not this or that particular living being, but that aspect of life that cuts across all particular instances of life. Then there is a second aspect of *psukhē*, or those attributes that may vary or change, without affecting the principle-of-life itself. In the case of an animal, the first notion of *psukhē* would be that which it has in common with any other living being, that by virtue of which it is living, while the second notion of *psukhē* would be all those attributes that constitute the variables of this particular animal—e.g., the variables that delineate one species from another. Thus, to use an example from the *Historia Animalium*, a giant squid is a living being in the same substantial sense that a human being is living, though there are of course numerous differences between them. These differences can be partially attributed to the first sense of being alive—that is, the way in which *psukhē* as a principle is instantiated in a living form—and partially attributed to variations between two or more living beings of the same kind (e.g., the number of tentacles, coloration, spotted marks of one squid versus another).

It is this partiality—reflected in the citation above—that distinguishes

Aristotle's ontology of life from being ontology pure and simple. Aristotle's familiar metaphysical pair of substance-accident does not quite apply to these two notions of *psukhē*; in fact, they are contained within the second notion of *psukhē*, as both the substance of this singular living being, and the set of accidental attributes of that living being. It is also not like the Neoplatonic "One," a reservoir of energy or spirit that then descends, via a divine gift, into the receptacles or husks of living beings. Though it can be distinguished in concept, the *ousia* of *psukhē* cannot be separated in the manifestation of the living itself.

This means that, while the very idea of *psukhē* as principle may be necessary for Aristotle in order to think "life" at all, it appears to be unthinkable except in its manifestations. On the one hand, the *ousia* of *psukhē* can never be thought in itself, since *psukhē* is never present as one living being among other living beings. But on the other hand, *psukhē* in its *ousia* is also never exhausted in this or that particular instance of a living being. Insofar as *psukhē* exists only in particular instantiations, it also moves outside the individuated living being, always cutting-across and exteriorizing the living being.

How, then, can *psukhē* be isolated or distinguished at all? Not by virtue of any intrinsic characteristics "in" the living being, for then *psukhē* would simply be one among many (accidental) attributes. Perhaps it is not the intrinsic attributes that point to a principle of life, but instead the extrinsic vectors by which *psukhē* cuts across all instances of life. If this is the case, then the distinguishing mark of *psukhē* would be this capacity for always exteriorizing, always cutting-across, always transposing and transforming between one form and another.

Aristotle hints at such an explanation in book 2 of the *De Anima*, when he explains that there is not one, homogenous *psukhē* for all living beings, but several types of *psukhē* that are specific to their functions or their ends—a nutritive *psukhē*, dealing with growth and decay, a sensory and motile *psukhē*, dealing with "movement" in the broadest sense, from physical motion to sensation and affection, and finally a rational and ideational *psukhē*, that deals with thought and spirit.

This capacity for cutting-across—which really implies a principle of immanence—is immediately recuperated within more vertical stratification of life forms. In Aristotle's formulation, the extrinsic capacity of *psukhē* to cut across instances of life is rendered in a highly stratified and hierarchical manner, in an ascending order of complexity. Furthermore, if the uniqueness of *psukhē* lies in its capacity for cutting across living forms, then this would seem to work against a more restricted notion of *psukhē* that relies on intrinsic properties and the stable boundary that defines the living being in its living.

In short, Aristotle bifurcates the concept of *psukhē* into *psukhē*-as-principle and *psukhē*-as-manifestation. Put in different terms, we can say that Aristotle splits his ontology of life into *that-by-which-the-living-is-living* and *that-which-is-living*. We can choose less verbose terms, and summarize by saying that Aristotle's ontology of life depends on a split within the central concept of *psukhē*, and that split is one between *Life* and *the living*.

Here let us insert a terminological clarification. Throughout this book, the word "life" will be used to denote the general *presumptions* about life, be it in terms of biology (the organism), philosophy (existential, ethico-political, or otherwise), or humanism (theories of the subject and its privileged phenomenality). We will use the terms "Life" and "the living" to denote two interrelated *presuppositions* about life: "Life" as this idea of that which grounds and can be manifested only in its particular instances, and "the living" to denote those manifestations or particular instances. Certainly, the presuppositions rely a great deal on a more general, fuzzy backdrop of presumptions (e.g., that "life" is there "for us"). But, in our subsequent discussions, we will also be looking for those moments when the presuppositions turn back on, and even negate, the presumptions altogether. This will have, as one effect, a more radical questioning of the concept of "life" itself, and the degree to which it can be adequately thought within a philosophical framework.

In the *De Anima*, Aristotle bifurcates life between a quasi-ontological notion of Life and a naturalistic notion of the living. Here "Life" is the concept of life-in-itself, the life of the living, the abstract notion of life, while "the living" are any and all the instances of life, the manifestations of life, in some cases even the naturalistic, organismic, and biologistic notions of life. Life is that *through* which the heterogeneous domains of the living are alive; Life is that *by* which the heterogeneous domains of the living can be said to be alive. Aristotle's ontology of life sets out to address both the concept of life and its manifestations; the term *psukhē* signifies that which is held in common among all the living, while the internal distinction between Life and the living accommodates stratifications within life.

It is this bifurcation that serves as the platform for subsequent debates between, for example, mechanism and vitalism. As Georges Canguilhem notes, for there to be a debate over life in itself, there must be a certain "vitalist exigency," a minimal difference between Life and the living. Thus, "vitalism translates a permanent exigency of life in the living, the self-identity of life immanent to the living."[22] This in turn also requires that Life maintain a certain conceptual nebulousness in relation to the living—it is the horizon of what can be thought of Life, by the living.

This means that the vitalist exigency cannot remain at the level of the philosophy of biology, if it is to inquire into "life" as an ontological category. In this way, the Aristotelian split between Life and the living also evokes another conceptual pair—that of the ontological difference between Being and beings highlighted by Heidegger. This distinction is crucial for Heidegger, as it comes to form the basis for any ontological query at all. Heidegger's lecture courses often turn to Aristotle in talking not only about ontological difference, but the pulling-apart of metaphysics from physics (*phusis*). As he notes, it is this latter term *phusis* that encompasses not only "nature," but a whole host of questions for Aristotle concerning the ontology of life: "Questions are asked concerning what life itself is, what the soul is, what arising and passing away are . . . what the emptiness is in which that which moved moves, what that which moves itself is as a whole and what the Prime Mover is."[23]

The obvious question here is whether the Aristotelian Life-living split is simply a variant on the Heideggerian one between Being and beings. This is a complicated question, to be sure, especially since it invites us to examine in greater depth the influence of Aristotle on the early Heidegger. Interestingly, Heidegger argues that this broad usage of *phusis*—covering as it does "life itself" as well as modality, movement, and causality—undergoes a pulling-apart process in Aristotle, in which physics, as the Being of beings, detaches itself from metaphysics, as Being in itself: "We thereby have two meanings of φύσις [*phusis*] that are found together in Aristotelian philosophy: firstly φύσις [*phusis*] as beings as a whole, and secondly φύσις [*phusis*] in the sense of οὐσία [*ousia*], the essentiality of beings as such."[24]

For our purposes here, let us note a few things. First, for Heidegger, the question of Being (and beings) always supersedes the question of Life (and the living), just as the disciplines of biology, psychology, and anthropology must presuppose a more basic set of ontological commitments concerning the existence of their objects of study. A philosophy of life that cannot question the being of life runs in circles (it is, for Heidegger, no more helpful than saying "the botany of plants"). "What strikes us first of all in such a philosophy (and this is its fundamental lack) is that 'life' itself as a kind of being does not become a problem ontologically."[25] So if the Life-living split is a variant of ontological difference, this is less because it is retroactively derived from Heidegger, and more because it is a part of Aristotle's metaphysical system itself. In books Gamma and Delta of the *Metaphysica*, Aristotle is relatively clear on the question of being in itself and its distinction from particular instances or types of beings. What is lacking, of course, is a privileging of the phenomenal life-world of the subject as the ground, or, in Heidegger's term, the "wavering" between these two senses of being.

Another, more important point, is that it is not at all clear in the *De Anima* whether the question of "life" is an ontological one. In other words, while the Being-beings distinction is a question concerning fundamental ontology for Heidegger, and while the same basic distinction is also found in Aristotle's metaphysical works, it remains unclear whether the Life-living distinction is an ontological distinction. This is both a source of frustration and interest in the *De Anima*. In the opening passages of the treatise, Aristotle, as if to express his uncertainty about this topic, throws nearly every metaphysical term into the text—the question of life is discussed in terms of substance and accident, the actual and the potential, formal and final cause, definition and number, and so on. The real question for Aristotle—one that he admits in the opening and closing sections of the *De Anima*—is what kind of a thing "life" is for thought. Should it be considered as an object of metaphysical speculation, empirical verification, or subjective phenomenality? The *De Anima* contains bits of each of these, with "life" being discussed in terms of geometrical systematicity, in terms of natural philosophy, and in terms of affect, imagination, and cognition.

This uncertainty is arguably what separates the Life-living distinction from that of ontological difference. Aristotle remains fuzzy about the degree to which the question of "life" is reducible to the question of "being." For Heidegger, this is not a question at all, since there is no more fundamental question than that of being, and no more basic distinction than that between Being and beings. Heidegger is clear on what ontological difference entails: "The being of beings 'is' itself not a being."[26] Furthermore, this very distinction, for Heidegger, points to a special kind of being (a "being-there" or *Dasein*), one that inculcates a certain priority to the human being: "Da-sein is a being that does not simply occur among other beings. Rather it is ontically distinguished by the fact that in its being this being is concerned *about* its very being . . . The ontic distinction of Da-sein lies in the fact that it *is* ontological."[27] What is at stake for this distinction between Being and beings is the way that the specifically human being hovers between these two terms: "We consider beings as a whole, and thereby think being. Thus, in thinking, we move within the differentiation between beings and being."[28]

Aristotle's fuzziness vis-à-vis the question of life remains interesting, however. For, on the one hand, Aristotle appears to simply apply metaphysical concepts to the question of life, implying—contra Heidegger—that the latter can in fact be adequately thought in terms of, and subordinate to, the question of being. On the other hand, Aristotle repeatedly makes attempts to carve out a niche for the question of life that is not reducible to that of pure metaphysics or to any branch thereof. Yet, what it is exactly that makes the question of life unique proves to be elusive in the *De Anima*. Aristotle sometimes settles on a kind of final causality specific to living beings, *entelecheia*. But even this turns in on itself, since what makes "life" unique is entelechy, and entelechy is simply defined as the manifestation of final causality in living beings. At other moments, Aristotle appears to accord human consciousness—as a particular manifestation of *nous* or "Intellect"—a special place as that which makes life distinct from being. But this runs into the problem of confusing the exemplar with the ideal form—the life-principle *psukhē* does double-duty, at once the most basic and fundamental aspect of life, and also the most developed or highest form of life. In short, Aristotle sets out for himself—and for nearly all ontologies of life that follow—a tautological problem: the *De Anima* attempts to articulate that which makes the question of life distinct from the question of being, but this can only be done through the framework of being. The concept of *psukhē*—as that which distinguishes life from being—is also that which *ontologically* distinguishes life from being.

So crucial is this move that it can be said to be equivalent to the very possibility of an ontology of life itself. Aristotle's original problematic is how to articulate a concept of life that accounts for its plasticity—that is, "life" in terms of time, form, and spirit. His solution is to develop a concept of a principle-of-life, encapsulated in the term *psukhē*. But then this requires a presupposition between something called life-in-itself and the various and manifold instances of life. The problematic then becomes that of explaining the relationship between these two, between life-in-itself and the manifestations of life.

Certainly, this raises more questions than it answers. The principle-of-life (*psukhē*) and the boundary-of-articulation (Life and the living) appear to at once provide a ground for an ontology of life, while also dissolving the concept altogether. To this end, the *De Anima* presents the concept of *psukhē* as an always-receding horizon that is never present to thought in itself. It is as if, in proposing a concept of the principle-of-life (*psukhē*), Ar-

istotle is forced to think "life" in terms other-than-life (time and temporality, form and causality, spirit and transcendence). In the process, these
other-than-life terms eventually come to displace and efface the principle-
of-life altogether. There is a sense in the *De Anima* that what remains of
"life" is this strange animate nothingness, a kind of vitalist void in which
the principle-of-life can assert itself only via that which displaces it. In
Aristotle's *De Anima*, the life-principle *psukhē* is at once ontologically
necessary and yet that which cannot be thought in itself.

Even a cursory examination of this ontology reveals what appear to be
a number of contradictions, a few of which we can list here. To begin with,
while we can point to numerous instances of the living, Life, in itself, is
never existent as such. The only "evidence" of Life is precisely its manifestation in and as the living; Life, or that which conditions the living, is
in itself nonexistent. As we will see, following this line of thought leads
either to an aporia that nevertheless grounds the concept of "life," or to
the acceptance of a negative theology at the heart of the ontology of life.

If Life, as that which grounds the living, is never present in itself, then
this opens onto another contradiction: What is common among the living
is Life, but Life in itself has no properties, attributes, or characteristics.
Thus, what is held in common among the living is itself nothing in particular. While the living is manifested as discrete, "full" presence, Life itself
is never manifested, and can be thought only as a continuum of absence,
or void; while Life is empty, the living is full; and this empty principle
therefore grounds the surplus of its manifestations.

If this is the case, then we are led to yet another contradiction. While
the living is characterized by production, growth, and development, Life,
never being present, is void of any content, biological or otherwise. If
the previous contradiction—Life as common among the living—is one
grounded in a spatialized relation, then in this contradiction—Life as
static basis for the living as dynamic—involves a temporal one. The problem here becomes how to correlate a static, fundamental concept with a
dynamic, regional one.

Although these contradictions appear to point to an incommensurability between Life and the living, it is important to note that, for Aristotle,
Life and the living form an indissociable pair. And this is also a final contradiction that we can mention, one that encapsulates the previous ones:
*One cannot think Life without thinking the living; one cannot think Life
while at the same time thinking the living.* While Aristotle makes a distinction between Life and the living, he is careful to avoid implying that
they are autonomous and separate terms. But, as we've seen, these two

terms point to a number of contradictions, such that it becomes difficult to think their relation at all . . . except in terms of contradiction.

It would be tempting, in this situation, to simply throw out the Aristotelian ontology of life altogether. One could easily dismiss it as outmoded and anachronistic, especially in an era of advanced technoscience, when the question of life itself is disparaged as mere metaphysics. One could also recuperate the *De Anima* within a fairly linear continuum, and call it the "history of biology" or even the "philosophy of biology." In this case Aristotle would be extended and corrected by Descartes, Buffon, Linnaeus, Darwin, and molecular biology ("Aristotle, the father of biology . . . "). In either case, Aristotle and his ontology of life would appear as outmoded or as the point of origin.

We can suggest another approach, which involves neither dismissing nor recuperating Aristotle, and that is to highlight the *De Anima* as presenting an ontology of life, and not simply a theology or a biology, in spite of—or because of—its contradictions. This, as we've seen, points to the two moves that Aristotle makes—the concept of *psukhē* and the bifurcation between Life and the living. Let us neither ignore nor try to resolve the apparent contradictions at the heart of the *De Anima*, and instead preserve them as that which makes such an ontology possible, and that which ultimately undermines it.

What would this entail? To begin with, it would mean thinking about the more general relationships between logic and life that Aristotle's *De Anima* only begins to outline. Such a thought would not simply be that of a commensurability between them (e.g., that life is ordered and thus logical), but rather of a basic incommensurability between them, a kind of vitalist incommensurability between logic and life. Note that this does not simply mean that life is inaccessible to logic, or that the former always remains mysteriously out of reach of the latter. It means, instead, that a different kind of logic—that of contradiction and its own logical coherency—may serve as the ground for the Aristotelian concept of *psukhē*. As we will see in the subsequent sections of this book, accepting this means rethinking not only the relation between thought and life, but the notion that thought *is* life.

1.4 THE ENTELECHY OF THE WEIRD

To get a sense of what this may mean, let us return briefly to Lovecraft's third type of life—the nameless living thing (the Shoggoths, the Elder Things, or the vague and ominous creatures that inhabit William Hope

Hodgson's *Night Land* . . .). This third type of life is different both from that of the profane world of human beings, and from that of the ancient, alien world of the "Old Ones." But this third type of life is not simply that of the "monster," at least in any traditional sense. The monster is a creature of norm and law, a form of life that is defined by its deviation from a norm, its aberration in the order of things, and its transgression of the law. Monsters are also often produced, or are by-products, of this norm or law—be it in terms of a divine Book of Nature, or in terms of the mad scientist playing God. Monsters are always *monstrum*, that which demonstrates, which testifies, and which inadvertently affirms the biological norm or political law.

The third type of life form described in Lovecraft's stories is not a monster in this traditional sense. The Shoggoths or Elder Things do not even share the same reality with the human beings who encounter them—and yet this encounter takes place, though in a strange no-place that is neither quite that of the phenomenal world of the human subject or the noumenal world of an external reality. Lovecraft's characters search for an adequate set of concepts to describe them but ultimately fail—they have material bodies, but not materiality "as we know it"; they have "intermittent lapses of visibility"; they can manifest themselves in our world and yet they have no fixed form.

In Lovecraft's stories the Shoggoths can barely be named, let alone adequately described *or thought*. And this is the crux of supernatural horror, the reason why life is "weird." The threat is not the monster, or that which threatens existing categories of knowledge. Rather, it is the "nameless thing," or that which presents itself as a horizon for thought. If the monster is that which cannot be controlled (the unlawful life), then the nameless thing is that which cannot be thought (the unthinkable life). Why can it not be thought? Not because it is something unknown or not-yet known (the mystical or the scientific). Rather, it is because it presents the possibility of a logic of life, though an inaccessible logic, one that is absolutely inaccessible to the human, the natural, the earthly—an "entelechy of the weird."

This is, perhaps, one definition of what Lovecraft and other writers refer to as "the weird." For Lovecraft, the weird is not the discovery of an aberration, which would place us in the context of law, norm, and the monster. Rather, the weird is the discovery of an unhuman limit to thought, that is nevertheless foundational for thought. The life that is weird is the life according to the logic of an inaccessible real, a life "out of space and time," and life of "extra-dimensional biologies." However this does not mean that life remains mystical and ineffable; life cannot be thought, *not* because it is poetry, the sublime, or even the noumenal. Rather, life cannot be thought because it can only be thought through a logic of contradiction, and contradiction is—as Aristotle reminds us—the very bedrock of rational thought itself.

Perhaps, if supernatural horror is the paradigm for thinking "life" today, it is less because of the way it situates life vis-à-vis the monster and the law or norm, and more because it raises the question of logic, life, and the "weird" relation between the two. Let us restate this idea: supernatural horror provides us with the model for thinking about the Aristotelian ontology of life in terms of its ontologically necessary contradictions. We can, not without a bit of humor (since there is always humor, if not the absurd, in the weird), refer to this monstrous coupling of logic and bio-logic as "Aristotelian biohorror."

From the framework laid out in the *De Anima* one inherits not only a set of concepts, but the contradictions that necessarily follow upon them. This is not just a problem *of* philosophy—in which life is an object of inquiry for, say, the philosophy of biology. What results is also a problem *for* philosophy. Aristotle utilizes metaphysical concepts to describe an internal differentiation within *psukhē*. There is the "being" of life, as it were—the *ousia* of *psukhē*. But this also presupposes an ontology of life that is not simply identical to ontology per se. This involves the basic presupposition that every ontology of life presumes a primary distinction between life and being—but only insofar as it can think of life only in terms of being.

The principle-of-life (*psukhē*) and the boundary-of-articulation (Life vs. the living) appear to at once provide not only a ground for an ontology of life, but also the ground for dissolving the concept altogether. To this end, the *De Anima* presents the concept of *psukhē* as an always-receding horizon—on further examination, "life" simply becomes isomorphic with time and temporality, with form and causality, or with spirit and transcendence. In the *De Anima*, the life-principle *psukhē* is at once ontologically necessary and yet that which cannot be thought in itself, and the *De Anima* is, early on, already insinuating the necessary and yet unexamined void at the heart of philosophical questioning of life: To what extent are all ontologies of life determined within the twofold framework of the principle-of-life and the bifurcation between Life and the living?[29]

CHAPTER TWO

Superlative Life

Negations are true and affirmations are inadequate.
—Nicholas of Cusa

2.1 LIFE WITH OR WITHOUT LIMITS

We begin this chapter with a broad question: To what extent is an ontology of life possible? When one looks at the concept of life in Western philosophy, one sees a duplicity in nearly every attempt to think life itself. In one line of thinking, life appears to be defined by limit—life as defined by that which exists in time, and, as such, is subject to finitude and temporality. Indeed, life is precisely this finitude, the constraints of corporeality, and the limitations of temporality. Aristotle, for instance, dedicates an entire treatise—*De Generatione et Corruptione*—to this idea, describing the dual processes of "coming-to-be" and "passing-away" as central to the Life of the living. And such constraints apply not only to the individuated living being, but to groups of living beings—hence the idea of extinction doubly haunts every instance of the living, as an individualized living being and as a generalized type or form of life.[1] So finite are life-processes that Descartes could, using a notorious analogy, describe the living being as a clockwork mechanism, reducible to its component parts and their discrete interactions. But such an orientation is not limited to vitalistic or mechanistic theories. In the Romantic and *Lebensphilosophie* traditions, this finitude of life (birth/death, growth/decay) is not denied but affirmed, culminating in an organicist philosophy of dynamic change and becoming. Here is Schelling: "So long as I myself am *identical* with Nature, I understand what a living nature is as well as I understand my own life . . . As soon, however, as I separate myself, and with me everything ideal, from Nature, nothing remains to me but a dead object, and I cease to comprehend how a *life outside* me can be possible."[2]

At its limit, the notion of life-as-finitude turns into its opposite—death, decay, and decomposition. In eighteenth-century pathological anatomy, life is seen to be working even in the "vital" processes of tissue decay and the decomposing corpse—the "vital properties" are thus distinguished from the merely "physical properties" by "contractibility," "sensibility," and other attributes.[3] The phenomena of putrefaction and fermentation serve as laboratories for thinking about a kind of necrological vitalism in eighteenth- and nineteenth-century German biology. In a way, biological vitalism begins to overlap with philosophical vitalism. Schelling again: "Life-activity is the cause of its own extinction . . . and so life itself is only the bridge to death."[4] Life-processes, thought of in terms of finitude, begin to turn into their opposite, death-processes.

At the same time, however, it is precisely this emphasis on process that reveals another line of thinking about life, one in which life is associated not so much with the finite, but with the infinite. The infinite is understood here not in the mathematical sense, but rather in terms of duration and continuity. It is precisely because life exists in time, but is not fixed in time, that it is infinite. While the discrete living organism lives and dies, life itself is a continuum that conditions the possibility of the living. No doubt there are influences of Neoplatonism in this regard (as we will see below); but the notion of life as flow, flux, and process is not only a key feature of Darwinian biology, but it is also at the center of early-twentieth-century attempts to think life in a nonreductionist way, be it in the process philosophy of Bergson or Whitehead, the process theology of Chardin, or the renewed "scientific" vitalism of Driesch. In the *History and Theory of Vitalism*, Driesch had identified the "autonomy of the processes of life" as central to any philosophical inquiry into life. Driesch would also bring back a concept posited by Aristotle and redefined by Kant: entelechy, or the immaterial guiding force of life-processes towards particular ends.

Thus, from a general point of view, life is at once finite and infinite, closed and open, discrete and continuous. In many instances the view of life in terms of finitude eventually opens onto the view of life as infinite. Whatever the case, there is a general tendency to characterize life itself in some opposition to limit, at the same time that life is defined in terms of temporality as a kind of de-limitation. We can broadly refer to this dual move as "philosophical vitalism."

What is required of vitalism as a philosophical gesture? First, life must be characterized as something that is generous, productive, proliferative, and germinal. Life is that which flows or pours forth—whether one posits a transcendent source of that flowing, or whether life-as-process simply flows from itself. This implies a second requirement, which is that the generosity of life is itself irreducible and unlimited, though the particular manifestations of life may in and of themselves be constrained. Whether one posits a "life-force," "All-Soul," *élan vital*, or emergent properties, there is something, some Life, that conditions the possibility of the conditioned, or the living—even if this conditioning principle is itself fully immanent within the conditioned. This means that, in addition to it being generous and conditioning, life in philosophical vitalism must fulfill a third requirement, which is that it be distributive, pervasive, and outflowing. This means that life for philosophical vitalism is at once everywhere and nowhere, a pure excess and generosity, and yet in itself not any one, single, individual instance of life.

For philosophical vitalism, a number of questions arise from these requirements. For example, if life is understood as generosity and excess, as something that never "runs out," from what reservoir does it derive this generosity, this propensity? This question leads to others: Must one presuppose a transcendent principle-of-life, from which it derives its excess—a kind of divine reservoir of life? If not, then how can the concept of life be thought at all, without some externally conditioning principle or criterion by which we can think of something as alive? Is a principle-of-life something that is ontologically necessary for thinking the concept of life in philosophical vitalism? If not, how then does one account for the dialectics of identity and difference, or being and becoming vis-à-vis this notion of life as flux and flow?

This is the central problematic that will occupy us here: Life understood in terms of time. Life is understood not only as that which exists in time, but this existing-in-time brings with it a host of questions, questions concerning change and stasis, life-as-productive and life-as-destructive, the reduction of life to nonliving substance (the chemistry of life, the physics of life) and the raising-up of life to phenomenological or even mystical levels (the phenomenon of life, spiritual life).

All of this points to a problematic outlined by Aristotle—the relation between Life and the living, and the way in which both are inscribed in time. For Aristotle, both the particular species of the living, as well as the life-principle (*psukhē*), are often discussed in terms of temporality, change, and movement. Time also becomes a concern in the many debates concerning mechanism and vitalism, whether time be reversible or not, whether the temporality of the organism be different from that of the nonliving. Arguably, contemporary interest in emergence and self-organization takes up the issue of time as well, but, instead of relying on an external organizing principle (divine order or natural law), such research asks how the living dynamically organizes itself internally, from within its own local contingencies. In short, how can one account for the dynamic production and creation of the living, once one subtracts a transcendent principle, once one subtracts an Artificer or Creator?

Thus, our guiding question—can there be an ontology of life that does not become a biology or theology of life?—will take us in a direction that, at first, may seem counterintuitive. Instead of marching through the history of biology, we will consider a few specific moments in Medieval philosophy, by way of Neoplatonism and mystical theology. But if we are not to reduce life to biology, equally must we not reduce it to theology. Philosophy provides a middle path here, though, as we will see, it opens onto its own set of problems as well. Our guiding question will serve to set up a number of attributes by which we can delineate the contours and limits of life as an ontological question. One of those attributes will be the idea of life thought of in terms of time: as generosity, as proliferation, as excess— an idea that we will call *superlative life*. Tracing the development of superlative life will take us, by way of Plotinus, to the works of the Pseudo-Dionysius and John Scottus Eriugena, both of whom make key contributions to the idea of superlative life. But the way in which they think life in terms of time has within it a "heretical" strand, in which superlative life and its positivity is, in turn, thought in terms of negativity and what Eriugena calls *nihil*. The enigmatic turn for these thinkers is, then, a superlative life that is also "nothing."

2.2 LIFE AS TIME IN PLOTINUS

To begin with, let us consider the concept of the superlative. In its most general sense, the concept of the superlative is about transcendence, about that which is fundamentally or absolutely beyond. If we posit, for example, a First Cause that conditions all instances of causality, then we conceive of this Cause as superlative to any particular instances of causality. The same can be said with regard to a Prime Mover. But this being-beyond is also a transcendence that encompasses, that conditions, and that is, ontologically speaking, necessary. The superlative is not only beyond all that is, but its being-beyond fundamentally conditions all that is. This last point also means that, at some level, the superlative is indelibly connected to all that is—the First Cause not only conditions all instances of causation, but is, in some minimal sense, in effect "in" each of those instances of causality. The question that arises from the superlative is precisely how to think the superlative as at once absolutely transcendent and yet minimally immanent.

This question becomes especially prescient in Neoplatonic thinking. Here, the synthesis of Greek and early Christian thought opens onto a set of questions that would preoccupy Medieval philosophers for centuries to come. At the center of Neoplatonism is the question of the superlative as a dynamical concept. And one of the challenges that this concept of the superlative brings with it is the following: between the world—contingent, always changing, finite—and the divine—conditioning, eternal, and infinite—there must be some relation that does not either simply deify the world or naturalize the divine. This means that the superlative is not simply an inaccessible and static transcendence "out there," but that, insofar as it conditions, causes, and forms the world, the superlative expresses a temporality that is specific to creation, generation, and production. However this relation is characterized, it must take into account some notion of the superlative in temporal terms. The superlative is that which is absolutely "beyond" at the same time that it is that which is absolutely "within."

Consider the concept of the One in Neoplatonism. The One is defined in part as that which produces the Many. This means that the One is "first" causally, in terms of it being ontologically necessary for thought to begin at all. But is the One itself produced? This would then mean that the One is produced by something else, a meta-One of sorts. If the One is not produced, then this would imply that it has always existed. But what then guarantees its continued existence, its persistence? That is, the persistence of the One would seem to imply its continued production (but a production that cannot come from outside itself). So, does the One produce itself? If it does, then the One would also seem to take on the attributes of time and temporality. But this time specific to the One would have to be different from the time of creaturely life and the world, else the One would simply be one among many things in the world. The compromise is to suggest that the One is temporal, in the sense that it produces itself as well as producing the world, but that its temporality is beyond any concept of creaturely or worldly temporality. That is, the One persists in a superlative time.

Moreover, the concept of the superlative that is presented, linked as it is to time, production, and process, implies that this superlative *time* is also a superlative *life*, being both the causal source and the principle of animation (*psukhē*) of the world. One of the results of this thinking in Medieval philosophy is the bifurcation of the concept of life between a superlative divine life and a subordinate creaturely life. The Life of the living, the creaturely life, the life of the world, necessitates a grounding concept of a life-beyond-life, a Life that causes and conditions all possible instances of living. Yet, since this Life is by definition absolutely transcendent, it remains inaccessible to thought, lying beyond any possible conceptualization. The conjunction of Life with time in the concept of the superlative conditions any and all possibility of thinking subordinate instances of the living.

Neoplatonism—especially in the version presented by Plotinus—presents us with the basic terms of this idea. *The Enneads* are often described as providing a tripartite metaphysical schema: the One, which is in itself absolutely transcendent and unknowable; the Intellect, which encompasses the primordial causes; and the Soul, which is both the principle of animation and the emanation of the Intellect. *The Enneads* repeatedly describe the procession from the One, through the Intellect, via the Soul, and to the world, as a process of emanation from a source to the multiplicity of things it causes.[5] Not surprisingly, the analogies of the river and the sun are frequently used to describe this relation between the One and the world.

Scholarship on *The Enneads* has raised a number of questions regarding this system.[6] For example, is the relation between the One, Intellect, and Soul a hierarchical or a topological relation? It is, certainly, hierarchical in that the divine "descends" or emanates from the One, which is the source of all things. The Intellect is the point of mediation, the first movement from divine simplicity to earthly complexity. The Soul enacts the movement of emanation from the Intellect. But this priority may also be viewed as an ontological priority, and the relationship actually more topological, akin to concentric circles. Such a relation—from pyramidal strata to concentric circles—would emphasize the pervasive quality of the One within each "level" of emanation (a situation not totally absent in *The Enneads*). This does not, of course, imply that the concept of the One in Plotinus is a fully immanentist concept. It does bring to the foreground the issue of the temporality of the One-Intellect-Soul relation, based as it is on the dynamical and processual acts of creation, emanation, and radiation.

The key term here is Soul (ψῡχή), of which Plotinus has a very particular definition in mind.[7] The Soul is—as it is with Aristotle—a principle of animation or a life-principle. The Soul is not simply that which guarantees that some thing or another exist; it is the dynamic principle by which things are brought into existence, by which the uncreated is created, and so forth. For Plotinus the Soul is also indissociable from the processes of emanation and radiation that distribute the One, via the Intellect, into the world. The Soul is not only a point of mediation, closely associated with Intellect; it is the very continuum between the One (as absolutely transcendent) and the world (as fully contingent). "For the Soul ($\psi\upsilon\chi\acute{\eta}$) is many things, is all, is the Above and the Beneath to the totality of life ($\zeta\omega\tilde{\eta}\varsigma$): and each of us is an Intellectual Cosmos, linked to this world by what is lowest in us, but, by what is highest, to the Divine Intellect."[8]

As that which establishes the continuum between the "Above" and the "Beneath," the Soul is, for Plotinus, internally differentiated as well. In the opening pages of the First Ennead (which was, at one time, given the title "On the Animate" by Porphyry), Plotinus asks "whether a distinction is to be made between Soul and Essential Soul (between an individual Soul and the Soul-Kind in itself)."[9] In the Fourth Ennead, Plotinus returns again to this question, suggesting further distinctions between the individual Soul, the "World-Soul" (the Soul as manifested in and as the world), the "All-Soul" or actively emanating Soul in itself, and the "Hypostatic Soul" (where the Soul in itself becomes nearly indistinguishable from the Intellect).

What all these internally differentiated types of Soul have in common is this principle of animation or vitality, and it is for this reason that the Soul is, for Plotinus, indelibly linked to a concept of life: "we sum all into a collected unity once more, a sole Life in the Supreme . . . thus we know Identity, a concept or, rather, a Life never varying, not becoming what previously it was not, the thing immutably itself, broken by no interval, and knowing this, we know Eternity."[10] On this level, the Soul is a principle of transcendence; it is not this or that particular instance of the living, not this or that particular manifestation in the world. It is that which conditions every possible instance of the living, while remaining itself above and beyond those instances: "Thus we come to the definition: the Life ($\zeta\omega\acute{\eta}$)—instantaneously entire, complete, at no point broken into period or part—which belongs to the Authentic Existent by its very existence, this is the thing we were probing for—this is Eternity."[11]

For Plotinus, the Soul has one aspect that is unchanging (though it conditions change), infinite (though it structures the finite), and eternal (though it is itself a dynamic, temporal principle). It is defined more by its upward association with the One, than it is by the multiplicity of things in the natural, caused world. Plotinus' evocation of the eternal is quite intentional, in that the Soul can be regarded as precisely that which does not itself change: "That which neither has been nor will be, but simply possesses being, that which enjoys stable existence as neither in process of change nor having ever changed."[12]

However, as we've already seen, the Soul in *The Enneads* also has another aspect, one that is intimately tied to temporality, change, and the dynamic emanation or radiation of the world. While Plotinus never states that the Soul is identical with the world, it does, nevertheless, have an important temporal association with the world. But if the Soul is defined in its temporality, how can it remain absolutely transcendent to all that changes? The Third Ennead contains an important meditation on the Soul, Life, and Time, where Plotinus outlines the problem:

> Putting forth its energy in act after act, in a constant progress of novelty, the Soul produces succession as well as act; taking up new purposes added to the old it brings thus into being what had not existed in that former period when its purpose was still dormant and its life was not as it since became: the life is changed and that change carries with it a change of Time. Time, then, is contained in differentiation of Life; the ceaseless forward movement of Life brings with it unending Time; and Life as it achieves its stages constitutes past Time.[13]

The important phrase here comes near the end: "Time . . . is contained in differentiation of Life." The Soul is defined as a principle of animation or life because it is inherently a temporal principle, manifested in the very persistence of the Soul as an emanation that goes on forever and that never ceases. The Soul, then, is a principle of life-beyond-life (or Life with a capital "L"); it is a principle of Life that is at once manifested in the living but which is not reducible to the living. And it is here that Plotinus shifts from the more common notion of the living (ζωή) to the life-principle (ψῦχή). Unlike the particular instances of the living, which are constrained by the finitude of time, the Soul is a Life that is in excess, a "ceaseless" Life operating through an "unending" time.

This would seem to be in conflict with the earlier pronouncement that the Life of the Soul is identical to Eternity, to that which is beyond time. So much does Plotinus link Soul, Life, and Time together in a triangulation that he can ask rhetorically, "Would it, then, be sound to define Time as the Life of the Soul (χρόνον τις λέγοι ψυχῆς) in movement as it passes from one stage of act or experience to another?"[14] His reply is telling, for it becomes indicative of much subsequent thinking on the topic:

Yes; for Eternity, as we have said, is Life in repose, unchanging, self-identical, always endlessly complete; and there is to be an image of Eternity—Time—such an image as this lower All presents of the Higher Sphere. Therefore over against that higher Life (ζωῆς) there must be another life (ζωὴν), known by the same name as the more veritable Life of the Soul (ψυχῆς) . . . [15]

Here again we see Aristotle's split between that-which-is-living and that-by-which-the-living-is-living, between the living and Life. Here we also see an emphasis on the dynamic principle of the creation, causality, and formation of the world. But what Plotinus does is to place this concept of the Soul squarely between a principle of absolute transcendence (the One), and a manifestation of emanation (the world, as caused by the Soul). The Soul is not just a principle of animation or life, but a principle of mediation as well. It sits, nestled between the absolutism of the One and its pervasive spreading-out or emanation in the world. The Soul is, in a sense, Janus-faced, with one side "in repose" and unchanging, turning towards a contemplation of the One, and another side that is actively in operation, emanating the world. In fact, given this bifurcation between the Soul-as-eternal and the Soul-as-temporal, we can suggest something further about Plotinus' concept of the Soul: *the Soul is precisely that which contains the duplicity, if not the contradictions, inherent in the concept of Life.*

For Plotinus, the Soul establishes a continuum between the One and the world; but it is also internally differentiated between many kinds of Soul. This dual movement of a continuum and a differentiation, of a drawing-together and a spreading-apart, raises a number of problems for the concept of the Soul, which Plotinus outlines in the Fourth Ennead[16]: the Soul is everywhere present in all things and yet it still remains singular; the Soul, as the continuum between the One and the world, is both immaterial and material; the Soul, as both a derivation from the One and an emanation of the world, is at once eternal and temporal, infinite and finite:

. . . over against that Movement of the Intellectual Soul there must be the movement of some partial phase; over against that Identity, Unchangeableness and Stability there must be that which is not constant in the one hold but puts forth multitudinous acts; over against that Oneness without extent or interval there must be an image of oneness, a unity of link and succession; over against the immediately Infinite

and All-comprehending, that which tends, yes, to infinity but by tending to a perpetual futurity; over against the Whole in concentration,
there must be that which is to be a whole by stages never final.[17]

With Plotinus we get a concept of Life that is really a life-beyond-life, but
also a life-within-life, insofar as it is dynamically emanative and continuous with all instances of the living. This results in a tension that is especially evident in the meditations on time and temporality in *The Enneads*.
And this tension begins to become formulated in terms of limitation and
negation—albeit tentatively—in Patristic thinkers such as Augustine and
in the early Scholasticism of Anselm. Both hint at a concept of the divine that is at once transcendent and immanent, static and dynamic, and,
above all, as something that cannot be positively thought.

2.3 ON THE SUPERLATIVE

Let us call this life-beyond-life, or really, this Life-beyond-the-living, *superlative life*. It both persists in a continuum that cuts across all instances
of the living, while at the same time existing apart from any particular
instance of the living as its ground or condition. It is a delimited life, a life
that is superlative because it is not finite and never "runs out." While it
is Aristotle who first articulates the distinction between Life and the living, it is Plotinus who gives us a concept of Life that is characterized by a
tension between the superlative perfection of the divine and the dynamic,
processual generosity that is also identical with the divine. Superlative life
is neither the principle of life in itself, nor the concrete instance of the living, but an ontological necessity positing a background excess (Life) from
which manifestations of this excess are foregrounded (the living). Superlative life is, quite simply, an ontology of Life that is thought of in terms of
time, temporality, and process.

But superlative life has several sides to it, a major and a minor key. The
major key is that of positive theology: Augustine, Anselm, and Aquinas.
Positive theology proceeds to think the superlative in terms of affirmative
assertions of divine attributes; its major motifs are light and radiation. It
aims for beatitude, the moment at which reason is superseded by faith. Insofar as it utilizes negation, this negation is always subordinate to affirmation, and always sublimated (the negative statement "God is not-living"
always turns into "God is the most perfect Life"). Positive theology has a
number of political advantages as well. Its motifs of light and radiation not
only reaffirm a single, centralized divine source, but, in its Neoplatonic

variant, it also assures a hierarchy of processes, causes, and distributions, from one circle to the next, from a higher layer to a lower layer, along the great chain of beings.

In contrast to this, we can consider several examples of negative theology, which, arguably, remains the minor key of Medieval philosophy.[18] Frequently, negative theology is interpreted such that it can be brought within the ambit of positive theology. Negative theology also has within it a number of important ambiguities, specifically regarding the idea of superlative life and the role of negation in thinking the superlative. Recently, negative theology has become a central preoccupation of continental philosophy, especially as regards the role of aporia, negation, and limit in the debate over the "post-theological."[19] For our purposes here, the thinkers we will consider are the Pseudo-Dionysius and John Scottus Eriugena. In contrast to the motifs of light and radiation, the motifs these thinkers prefer are those of darkness, shadow, and nothingness. This negative theology does not lead straight to beatitude, but often ends up somewhat lost, wandering amidst divergent paths of doubt, confusion, and even, at times, skepticism. While positive theology always sublimates the negative into the positive, negative theology employs a different strategy, that of contradiction, limitation, and irresolution. Negation in negative theology is not just a temporary "not-X" but an absolute "not-X," a notion that leads both the Pseudo-Dionysius and Eriugena to consider a contradictory "superlative negation."

The point in examining the tradition of negative theology is not to suggest that it is somehow more accurately able to "get at" the divine, much less the concept of life, for both the Pseudo-Dionysius and Eriugena are far from being traditional theologians. But neither is the point to suggest that thinkers such as these are outright heretics or proto-atheists (even though their works were often accused of heresy and later dubbed "pantheist"). The point in examining the tradition of negative theology is that it is unique in the way that it both internalizes classical thinking about the life-principle, while at the same time it displays an acute awareness of the challenges to thought itself that such a concept evokes. Negative theology is unique in that it most clearly articulates the contradictions inherent in any attempt to ontologize Life. It is this conjunction of "life" (as superlative) and "nothing" (as a form of negation) that we will trace in both the Pseudo-Dionysius and subsequently in Eriugena. Bearing in mind the Plotinian framework for the idea of superlative life, we can begin with a consideration of the role of "apophatic life" in the Pseudo-Dionysius, before considering the conjunction of Life and *nihil* in the thought of Eriugena.

2.4 SUPERLATIVE LIFE I: PSEUDO-DIONYSIUS

Mystical writings have a tenuous status in philosophical discourse. On the one hand, a number of thinkers who are part of the Western philosophical canon (Augustine, Aquinas) also wrote in the "key" of mystical discourse, and works such as *The Cloud of Unknowing* or *The Dark Night of the Soul* have established mystical writing as a tradition in its own right. On the other hand, in the public consciousness mystical writing is often regarded as being too close to its uncouth, modern cousins—"new age" spiritualism, occult and paranormal studies, or, at its most banal, religious self-help. However, the flowering of mystical texts in the early monotheistic traditions provides us with a set of texts with which to pose certain ontological questions. It is also worth noting that mystical theology itself is as varied as Medieval philosophy. Mystical theology writings often note how the idea of a principle of life, of a life-beyond-life, even "a life beyond being" (in the words of the Pseudo-Dionysius), is at the same time spoken only through the concepts and language of negation, darkness, and "nothing."

A word should be said about the Pseudo-Dionysius, an author with no name. Four major works are attributed to him: *The Mystical Theology*, *The Divine Names*, *The Celestial Hierarchy*, and *The Ecclesiastical Hierarchy*. The first two are works of mystical theology, the last two deal more specifically with institutional and doctrinal aspects of the Church. The author was originally thought to be one Dionysius the Areopagite, briefly mentioned in Acts 17:34, a convert and follower of Paul.[20] But, as early as the sixth century, the authorship of the texts ascribed to Dionysius the Areopagite were called into question.[21] Part of the reason for the disputation may have been the ideas attributed to Dionysius: he is, along with several other authorities, cited as a monophysite thinker, believing that Christ has only one nature, which is divine (as opposed to Christ having a twofold nature, divine and human). Such topics were intensely debated in the fifth century as early Christianity struggled to articulate a coherent boundary between orthodoxy and heresy. In addition, the works of the *Corpus Areopagiticum* show a marked Neoplatonic influence, which plays a part in the more mystical passages, as well as participating in the ongoing and conflicted synthesis of Aristotelian, Neoplatonic, and early Christian thinking.

Despite the disputed authorship, the *Corpus Areopagiticum* continued to exercise a strong influence in Medieval philosophy and theology—the anonymous author is cited numerous times by Scholastic thinkers such as Aquinas and by late-Medieval mystics such as Nicholas of Cusa. Works from the *Corpus* were translated into Latin numerous times—in the early ninth century, by Hilduin, abbot of a Parisian monastery (reportedly under the patronage of Dionysius), and in the late ninth century, by the Irish philosopher John Scottus Eriugena.

The two works from the *Corpus Areopagiticum* that have exercised the most influence are *The Mystical Theology* and *The Divine Names*. As recent scholarship has noted, they are important not only as documents of the mystical theology tradition, but they also contain innovations in philosophical reflection on the logic of negation.[22] The former is a brief but dense poetic meditation on method. In it the Pseudo-Dionysius makes the important distinction between "affirmative" or "positive" theology and "negative" theology. The latter work, *The Divine Names*, is a more extended, more "philosophical" work divided into chapters with subheadings. In it the Pseudo-Dionysius meditates on a number of topics, including the method of negative theology, the divine nature, creation and creatures, "unity and differentiation," the Neoplatonic motif of light, and the nature of evil. For our purposes, we will look at two specific points: in *The Mystical Theology*, the introduction of the concept of negation, and its development into a concept of "superlative life" in *The Divine Names*.

2.4.1 NEGATIVE VS. AFFIRMATIVE THEOLOGY

The body of work ascribed to the Pseudo-Dionysius raises the issue of the limits of thought. To what extent can the divine be thought as such? When we give names to the divine, referring to it as "One," or "Good," or "Life," to what extent do such names imply a knowledge of the divine or a comprehension of the transcendent? Would not an adequate thought of the divine be tantamount to an experience of the divine itself? Would such a "divine thought" also imply a "divine life"? There is a thread that runs from Neoplatonism through to the high Scholasticism of Aquinas that meditates at length on such questions.[23] One of the central problems in thinking the divine lies in the very act of naming the divine—is naming also knowing, and if so, how can the finite, contingent, human creature make such a claim to know the infinite, unbounded, and transcendent realm of the divine, without actually making a claim for the divinity of the creature itself? Often this conundrum is resolved by a distinction between a statement *that* something is and knowing *what* something is; thus one could safely posit, and even prove, the existence of God without making any undue claims about knowing anything beyond this mere fact of God's existence.

But such resolutions are only temporary, for, even if the "divine name" signifies nothing more than mere existence, this existence in itself has to be accounted for, or at least qualified: if God exists, does this imply that God is also subject to the contingencies of life and death, as are creatures? If not, then one is led into a labyrinth where one has two choices: either one would have to affirm God's existence in a qualified way (e.g., as a "super-existence," "super-eminence," or purely positive existence), or one would have to entertain the idea that the divine or the transcendent is, in a sense, "nothing" (literally, no thing, no existent). In this latter mode, the divine is given a paradoxical name, the name of negation: God is "not-One" (since a numerical notion of One implies that something can be added to it), God is "not-Life" (since there is no life or death in the divine), God is "not-Good" (since the good presupposes a state of falling-away or evil).

The long tradition of meditation on the divine names is often split: those who make positive claims for the divine (the divine can be named, but qualified in a way that places it transcendentally above all things), and those who make negative claims for the divine (the divine can only be named as not-this or not-that). The works of the Pseudo-Dionysius mark an important moment in the latter, negative tradition, and they do so because of the particular concept of negation that they propose, a concept that works against both the positive tradition as well as the negative-privative tradition.

Poetically dense and often enigmatic, the short text entitled *The Mystical Theology* sets out the problematic:

> The fact is that the more we take flight upward, the more our words are confined to the ideas we are capable of forming; so that now as we plunge into that darkness which is beyond intellect, we shall find ourselves not simply running short of words but actually speechless and unknowing.[24]

The more thought reaches upward and outward, the more it increasingly comes up against the limits of thought itself; the pinnacle of thought is its very foundation, precisely that which it cannot think. The author continues, noting that as one works up from the domain of creatures to that of the divine life, "from what is below up to the transcendent . . . the more language falters, and when it has passed up and beyond the ascent, it will turn silent completely," since, at that point, it will effectively be indistinguishable from the divine itself.[25] For the Pseudo-Dionysius, the problem is not simply in finding the adequate words or the most appropriate names for the divine; rather, the problem has to do with the horizon of thought itself. Let us take a modern viewpoint of this problematic, and suggest that, for the Pseudo-Dionysius, the problem of the "divine names" is really a problem of the unthought, a problem of the blind spots of thinking. As with many writers in the mystical theology tradition, the divine not only positively signifies the transcendent or the supernatural, but it also comes to demarcate the very boundaries of thinking itself.

This problematic leads the Pseudo-Dionysius to distinguish between two methods for thinking the divine. There is, first, the "affirmative theologies," by which one positively designates attributes to the divine, usually of the simple form "God is x," where x is most often some attribute found among creatures (especially human creatures), but "raised up" to its most perfect state. This is the *via affirmativa* ($\kappa\alpha\tau\alpha\varphi\alpha\tau\iota\kappa\eta$ or kataphatic). It is the affirmative way, "in which God is described as good, existent, life, wisdom, power, and whatever other things pertain to the conceptual names for God."[26] Thus, if x is "life," then this attribute of being alive is beyond any instance of creaturely or natural life, marred as it is by temporality, decay, and death.

The *via affirmativa* or affirmative theology is dependent on and begins from the creaturely world, from human attributes such as being "good" or "wise," and then attempts to work its way up from there. Such a method invites an anthropomorphic tendency as well, in which the divine obtains the characteristics of the earthly and human domain. In this case, the attributes of the divine are "analogies of God drawn from what we perceive . . . his anger, grief, and rage, of how he is said to be drunk and hungover, of his oaths and curses, of his sleeping and waking, and indeed of all those images we have of him, images shaped by the workings of the symbolic representations of God."[27] Despite this intriguing, rather pagan image of the drunken God, the Pseudo-Dionysius notes the limitations of affirmative theology—all affirmations of the divine and the transcendent must by necessity end up negating themselves in their attempt to posit that which is beyond all positing—indeed, anthropomorphism is this limitation itself.

It is here that, in a characteristically cryptic passage, the Pseudo-Dionysius distinguishes the *via affirmativa* from the *via negativa*, the kataphatic from the apophatic (ἀπόφατιϰη), affirmative theology from negative theology:

> Now it seems to me that we should praise the denials quite differently than we do the assertions. When we made assertions we began with the first things, moved down through intermediate terms until we reached the last things. But now as we climb from the last things up to the most primary we deny all things so that we may unhiddenly know that unknowing which itself is hidden from all those possessed of knowing amid beings, so that we may see above being that darkness concealed from all the light among beings.[28]

There are two movements described here: a movement of ascension and descension, and a movement of affirmation and negation. The Pseudo-Dionysius combines them in a particular way: the *via affirmativa* is, for him, a top-down approach in which one begins from the positive assertion "God is *x*," where *x* is regarded as perfected, and then one proceeds in a Neoplatonic manner from this perfected attribute *x* to its less and less perfect instantiations in the world of creatures. The *via affirmativa* is therefore a method characterized by "descending assertions." By contrast, the *via negativa* is a more bottom-up approach, whereby one successively negates the existing, creaturely world, eventually arriving at a kind of degree-zero of the divine, an absolute minimalism of the divine whose logical conclusion is nothingness and silence. The *via negativa* is therefore a method characterized by "ascending negations." The Pseudo-Dionysius provides another, perhaps more rigorous explanation in the following chapter:

> When we assert what is beyond every assertion, we must then proceed from what is most akin to it, and as we do so we make the affirmation on which everything else depends. But when we deny that which is beyond every denial, we have to start by denying those qualities which differ most from the goal we hope to attain.[29]

The *via affirmativa* operates on the analogy of distance from a center: as one moves further and further away from the divine cause of all things, the divine name or attribute becomes less and less fully identical with the divine itself—the one becomes many, the good becomes acts of goodness, life becomes living creatures, and so on.

2.4.2 SUPERLATIVE NEGATION

But the *via negativa* is more complicated. There are several types of negation presented in *The Mystical Theology*. In the above passage, the Pseudo-
Dionysius follows with a rhetorical question: "Is it not closer to reality
to say that God is life and goodness rather than that he is air or stone? Is
it not more accurate to deny that drunkenness and rage can be attributed
to him than to deny that we can apply to him the terms of speech and
thought?" The second part of the question is asked in the manner of the
via negativa—ascending from the domain of the natural world to the supernatural, one proceeds by successively negating those attributes that are
the most opposed to the notion of the divine (e.g., from abstract attributes
such as finitude, temporality, and death to more anthropomorphized attributes such as desire, fear, or rage). But this type of negation knows no
limits, it has no end, for if there were such an end, one would eventually
reach a point where everything inessential has been negated, and what remains would be—affirmatively, positively—the divine name. Thus the *via
negativa* would become the penultimate instance of the *via affirmativa*,
precisely that which is foreclosed in the very concept of the divine as transcendent and "beyond" all thought.

However, this is not the only kind of negation presented by the Pseudo-
Dionysius. Consider the first part of the rhetorical question: "Is it not
closer to reality to say that God is life and goodness rather than that he
is air or stone?" This is asked in the manner of the *via affirmativa*—
assumedly the Pseudo-Dionysius would prefer to attribute the Good and
Life to the divine, which more closely describe its essence, than to say
the divine is air or a rock (though the latter is certainly more interesting). But the *via affirmativa* harbors within it a movement of negation,
or really, a privation, whereby the greater or lesser proximity to a divine
source dictates what can be positively said of the divine. Thus, even the
lowliest creatures, even the rocks, must be minimally attributed to the
divine, insofar as they are the products and the creations of the divine Creator. But, in true Neoplatonic fashion, it is in the distance of the rock or
the beast from the divine source that the latter is negated—privately—by
the former. The rock or the beast is thus the divine "minus" something, a
privative negation.

Thus far, the *Mystical Theology* presents us with two types of negation.
There is, first, the negation inherent in the *via affirmativa*—"God is x,"
where x is a creaturely attribute minus its imperfections. Let us refer to

this as *privative negation*. Then we have the more active negation in the *via negativa*—"God is not-*x*," where *x* is a creaturely attribute defined by its imperfections. This we can refer to as *oppositional negation*. To these two types of negation—that of the *via negativa* and that which is inherent in the *via affirmativa*—the Pseudo-Dionysius presents a third kind of negation. It comes in the first chapter, where the author discusses the concept of the transcendent:

> What has actually to be said about the Cause of everything is this. Since it is the Cause of all beings, we should posit and ascribe to it all the affirmations we make in regard to beings, and, more appropriately, we should negate all these affirmations, since it surpasses all being. Now we should not conclude that the negations are simply the opposites of the affirmations, but rather that the cause of all is considerably prior to this, beyond privations, beyond every denial, beyond every assertion.[30]

Using the example of creation and causality, the Pseudo-Dionysius proposes a third type of negation that is neither quite that of opposition (in the *via negativa*) nor quite that of privation (in the *via affirmativa*). The passage nearly has the form of dialectic, though it lacks the rigor found in later authors such as Anselm or Eriugena. We begin with an affirmation ("God is *x*," where *x* is qualified), but, as we've seen, even the affirmation holds a negation within it, since the very definition of the divine is such that no term is absolutely identical to it. Thus, "God is *x*," but since *x* is qualified as perfected, as beyond any worldly conception of *x*, the attribute *x* really surpasses itself, and in so doing, negates itself (the *x* beyond all possible instances of *x*). In this regard, we really say "God is not-*x*" insofar as *x* is defined by limitation and finitude.

Importantly, the Pseudo-Dionysius proposes that, even though a negation follows every affirmation, this particular type of negation is not simply the opposite of affirmation. Here the author turns to the more mystical language of that which is transcendent and "beyond every assertion." This is the negation that is neither a privation nor an opposition, but, strangely, a kind of affirmation—or better, a kind of affirmation that is characterized by its generosity, by its germinality, by its being a transcendent sort of negation that precedes all possibility of affirmation. Here one says "God is *x*," where *x* is the negation of every particular instance of *x*. This would mean that the attribute *x* is literally "no thing," because it is never constrained by any particular instantiation—it remains fully abstract. Thus, the statement "God is good" or "God is life" would imply a Good beyond any possible, particular manifestation of goodness, a Life beyond any possible manifestation of the living. The Good and Life are ontologically prior to and condition the very possibility of thinking good acts and living beings—but they are never to be found "in" those good acts or living beings.

In this third type of negation, negation is not privative (that is, not that which is taken away or withdrawn), and not oppositional (that is, not a direct counterpoint or annulment). Rather, it is *superlative negation*, a negation of all finitude and limitation that is, in the same breath, an affirmation of the limit and finitude of thought. In this superlative negation, the divine is defined as being negative because it is defined as being beyond every possible conceptualization, thereby always receding into a sort of dark, opaque nether region that later authors such as Eriugena will simply call *nihil*.

This is an assertion of transcendence—indeed, the language of mystical theology is teeming with the poetics of transcendence. But, unlike the tradition of affirmative theology, with its evocations of beatific light and vision, here we have a contradictory kind of transcendence, one more characterized by shadows, darkness, and the immanent limits of knowledge— the "darkness which is beyond intellect." In addition to the *via affirmativa* with its privative negation, and in addition to the *via negativa* and its oppositional negation, we can say that the Pseudo-Dionysius also presents a *via superlativa*, a contradictory form of negation that is negation precisely because it is superlative.

This is, arguably, the central point of *The Mystical Theology*—that negation is not simply the opposite of affirmation. This insight structures both the negative theology tradition, as well as the possibility of thinking Life in relation to the living. To understand how these types of divine negation operate in the ontology of life, we can now turn from the methodological consideration of the *Mystical Theology* to the theological and philosophical consideration of *The Divine Names*, a longer and more erudite text, where we see the Pseudo-Dionysius develop a concept of life in superlative terms.

In the opening sections of *The Divine Names*, the Pseudo-Dionysius warns against naively applying the concepts of human thinking to the divine realm, since by definition the latter lies beyond the comprehension of the former. One must, the author states, proceed in a manner akin to the textual exegesis of scripture, "in a manner surpassing speech and knowledge," leading to a place where "we reach a union superior to anything available to us by way of our own abilities or activities in the realm of discourse or of intellect."³¹ In short, scripture already outlines the boundaries of the discourse on the divine, beyond which one should not go.

However, the passage immediately following does precisely that, and here the language of negative theology can be detected: "Since the un-knowing of what is beyond being is something above and beyond speech, mind, or being itself, one should ascribe to it an understanding beyond being."³² While the Pseudo-Dionysius is careful to note that this mysti-cal unknowing beyond being itself is still within the ambit of scripture, already the assertion of the indefinite "unknowing," as a kind of negative knowledge beyond all knowledge, begins to reveal the contradictions at the center of negative theology as a method. Put simply, it appears that we can and cannot adequately think the divine and the transcendent.

The Pseudo-Dionysius then attempts to mediate this antinomy by describing the divine as "superlative"—a concept that is, as we've seen, at the heart of the Plotinian philosophy. This comes first by a rather an-thropomorphized, paternal characterization of the divine: "For, if we may trust the superlative wisdom and truth of scripture . . . the divine goodness is such that, out of concern for our salvation, it deals out the immeasur-able and infinite in limited measures."³³ The figures used here are those of mystical theology and the threat or the danger of the concept of the divine itself—the light that is too bright for human eyes, the thought that is too profound for the human mind. The direct, unmediated thought of the di-vine would thus lead to either madness or death. For the finite, contingent mind, the infinite and eternal nature of the divine is thus rationed out in digestible portions, in a kind of divine metabolism. Here it is the textual exegesis and its mediating concepts that negatively point to the superla-tive nature of the divine as surpassing all human comprehension:

> Just as the senses can neither grasp nor perceive the things of the mind, just as representation and shape cannot take in the simple and the shapeless, just as corporeal form cannot lay hold of the intangible and incorporeal, by the same standard of truth beings are surpassed by the infinity beyond being, intelligences by that oneness which is beyond intelligence.³⁴

Using the analogies of dualism (matter-form, sense-intellect, corporeal-incorporeal), the Pseudo-Dionysius here employs a strategy that character-izes the entire text of *The Divine Names*: he uses negation to think the divine, not in terms of something lacking, but in terms of its superlative nature, its "life beyond life," its "being beyond being." This is precisely the function of negation in *The Divine Names*—to point to a superlative affirmation, which is itself another, higher order of negation. Every assertion concerning what cannot be thought is asserted in thought, via a multifarious language of negative terms that point to the superlative.

2.4.3 Negation and Preexistent Life

As we've seen, the text of *The Divine Names* deploys negation in different ways, which we can briefly summarize below:

- Privative terms, in which the divine is regarded as lacking something. These often take the form of assertions about the divine as being without attributes that are specific to the creaturely domain; so the privation here really leads to an assertion of excess and superabundance. In this sense the privations of the divine paradoxically point to its superlative, transcendent nature. Thus the divine is "without cause," since it is the First or Primordial Cause, and "without form," since it is the form-giving principle.[35] It is also, in a phrase that turns back on itself, "the Nameless One."[36]
- Properly negative terms, of which the Pseudo-Dionysius uses both "not" terms ("not-living," "not-caused") and "non-" terms ("non-participation"). Take the example of "not" terms: these are terms in which the divine is described as superlative and transcendent precisely because it is not-x, where x is a lessened or not-transcendent attribute whose derivative form points to a more perfected, exemplary form, or X. Thus, while the divine is described as "Life," it is understood that this divine Life is not the life of living creatures, bound as it is by death and finitude—the divine is "not-living."[37] The same is said of the divine as not-caused or not-willed. Again using the contradictory language of negative theology, any attribution of the divine as X is only posited as not-x (so that X = not-x by exemplarism more than opposition).
- Indefinite terms, in which the divine is, by its ineffable nature, described in proximity to creaturely attributes. These come in several variants, including "in-" terms ("infinite") and "un-" terms ("unchanging," "unnamed").[38] Whereas creaturely life is corporeal, the divine is incorporeal; whereas creaturely life is finite, the divine is infinite; whereas the life of the creature is tangible, the divine life is intangible. Technically speaking, indefinite terms are not negative terms, since they occupy a position that is between assertion

and negation, not-quite-this and not-quite-that. But in the context of *The Divine Names*, the indefinite terms deploy negativity by taking an attribute of creaturely life (finitude, change) and then, by negating the limits of that attribute—without positively naming the openness beyond this delimitation—arriving at the indefinite (infinite, unchanging).

- Hyperbolic terms, which are the most common in *The Divine Names*. These most often take an attribute of creaturely life and append the prefix "super-" to it. The divine is "superabundant" and "supernatural."[39] It is not simply a more perfected Life or Wisdom, but is "superabundant Life" and "superabundant Wisdom."[40] Alternately, hyperbole is also used in a metaphysical sense, in which creaturely attributes are raised up by reference to their essences: "It [the divine] is the Life of the living, the being of beings, it is the Source and the Cause of all life and of all being, for out of its goodness it commands all things to be and it keeps them going."[41] "These and similar terms," the author notes, "concern a denial in the sense of a superabundance."[42]

While there are nuances between these types of negative terms, they are united in the way they assert a negation, which, by its negation, points to an unassignable and unthinkable domain beyond the negation. But there is another way, aside from the use of negative terms, in which negation is deployed in *The Divine Names*. This comes in the second section, where the Pseudo-Dionysius discusses the concept of "divine differentiation."[43] Addressing the problem of how a simple and single divine nature produces the multiple, differentiated aspects of creation (a problem pervasive in Neoplatonism), the author proceeds to describe the divine nature's propensity for *production*:

> if differentiation can be said to apply to the generous procession of the undifferentiated divine unity, itself overflowing with goodness and dispensing itself outward toward multiplicity, then the things united even within this divine differentiation are the acts by which it irrepressibly imparts being, life, wisdom and the other gifts of its all-creative goodness.[44]

The language here is that of Neoplatonism and the proliferative productivity of the divine nature—flux, flow, and emanation from an unlimited source. A number of key characteristics follow from this. The divine nature is, first and foremost, characterized by a *generosity*, as a gift that continually bestows its essence outward towards creation (the passages that follow utilize the geometrical motif of the radii of a circle, as well as the well-known motif of the sun). "It flows over in shares of goodness to all."[45] Insofar as the divine nature is the primordial Cause of all things, it is a superlative cause, one that never ceases and is never totally expended. It produces multiplicity and yet remains unified, "dispensed to all without ceasing to be a unity."[46] The divine nature is, in this sense, defined by being a kind of divine excess, a primal source that knows no limits.[47]

Taken together, these two attributes—excess and generosity—lead to a model of production or proliferation that is both distributive and *pervasive*: "Now this is unified and one and common to the whole divinity, that the entire wholeness is participated in by each of those who participate in it; none participates in only a part."[48] The divine is not simply above and beyond, transcendent and apart from creaturely life. Neither is its sole purpose the cause of all creation. Rather, its very nature is this continual, dynamic process of distribution. It is for this reason that the Pseudo-Dionysius uses the Neoplatonic language of participation (elsewhere describing the divine nature as "nonparticipated"). Passages such as these would be read centuries later by theologian-philosophers such as Eriugena, and the idea of a pervasive, distributive God hints at a quasi-pantheistic understanding of the divine (though the Pseudo-Dionysius never makes such claims without qualification).

This notion of a pervasive, distributive divine also brings with it the same type of superlative negation found in the use of negative terms. A pervasive Source that is everywhere is also one that is nowhere. Each moment of excess turns on another moment of expenditure. Hence the contradictory terminology of a full void, an empty excess, a divine nature that is "full amid the emptying act of differentiation," an "unfilled overfullness which produces, perfects, and preserves all unity and multiplicity."[49] The divine is here not a static, inert, equivocal principle or cause; rather, it seems to be pervasively, even contagiously "in" every instance of creation, while still maintaining its transcendent nature. But, as we've seen, its transcendental nature can be guaranteed only via the forms of negation outlined above, negations that really point to a superlative beyond, which itself remains negative and "unnamed."

This idea, expressed in the poetics of the mystical theology tradition, is significant for thinking about any ontology of life, because it attempts to think the divine as inherently dynamic and processual, while still conserving its conceptually transcendent structure. In *The Divine*

Names there are three kinds of concepts of life at work. There is, first, the creaturely life of the living, which the Pseudo-Dionysius outlines in a descending hierarchy from Intelligences (supernatural beings), Rational souls (human beings), Irrational souls (animals), subsistence (plants), and existence (things).[50] Here "life" is subordinate to a larger concept of either Being or God, these latter concepts superlative to all others.

This in turn requires a larger metaphysical principle for the living, or that-by-which-the-living-is-living. Crucially, in the sixth chapter of *The Divine Names*, the Pseudo-Dionysius uses the name "Life" to describe the ways in which "the divine Life beyond life is the giver and creator of life itself . . . From this Life souls have their indestructibility, and every living being and plant, down to the last echo of life, has life."[51] Furthermore, this Life is both ontologically and causally necessary, since "it gives to life itself the capacity to be life, and it gives to everything alive and to every form of life the existence appropriate to it."[52] So necessary is this concept ontologically that the Pseudo-Dionysius even acknowledges the Life in that lowest of low life forms, the demonic: "So overabundant is its goodness that it reaches down even to demonic life which draws its life and its demonic life from this and from no other cause."[53]

In addition to the creaturely, natural life and its supernatural cause, the Pseudo-Dionysius also hints at a life beyond even this divine Life. "All life and living movement comes from a Life which is above every life and is beyond the source of life."[54] Even the divine Life as the source of all instances of the living, must itself have some ontological ground, one that would take into account the dynamic and process-based production of the living and the self-production of Life. And this is precisely what the concept of superlative life does. That is, in the idea of the processual, distributive, pervasive divine nature, the Pseudo-Dionysius also evokes this third type of life, a superlative life that is transcendent even to the other divine names ("One," "Being," "Good," etc.).

Superlative life is inherently dynamic and temporal, but not in the limiting, finite way in which creaturely life or the living are. What conceptually guarantees the possibility of thinking this type of superlative life, this type of process or pervasiveness, cannot simply be its opposite (being vs. becoming, stasis vs. change, eternity vs. temporality), because one then has to account for the movement from one term to its opposite (thus introducing more mediating concepts). But this superlative life cannot simply be identical with the creaturely life or the living, for this merely begs the question of form and causality (that-by-which-the-living-is-living).

The superlative life can only be beyond-the-beyond if it can at once remain an ontological foundation (without which the concept of the living cannot be thought) while at the same time preserving its inherently processual and pervasive characteristics (as cause, form-giving, and animating). The Pseudo-Dionysius refers to this as the *preexistent* of life, wherein the divine "lives and grants life out of that Life surpassing all life and it preexists in it as the single Cause of life."[55] The concept of the "preexistent" is introduced earlier in *The Divine Names*, where the Pseudo-Dionysius attempts to assert an ontological principle that is prior to all things, and which is a combination of existence (but an existence beyond all existence) and productivity (but an endless, superabundant productivity): "Every being and all the ages derive their existence from the Preexistent . . . The Preexistent is the source and is the cause of all eternity, of time and of every kind of being."[56] Thus the preexistent is what grounds superlative life as a double-transcendence, the superlative life beyond the relation between Life and the living. The preexistent is condition (ontological foundation), cause (form-giving, productive), culmination (completion of the ends of life), and ineffability (by its superlative, equivocal nature).[57] But its curious introduction in the text also seems to dangerously open up an infinite regress. At the heart of the preexistent is thus this tension between the need for a stable ontological foundation in which life can be thought at all, and the corresponding assertion of the superabundantly dynamic and processual nature of the divine. Enigmatically, what the Pseudo-Dionysius provides in *The Divine Names* is a concept of superlative life that is characterized by contrary negations and affirmations—a superlative life that cannot be thought, and a preexistent positivity that affirms a "beyond-the-beyond."

Nevertheless, the concept of superlative life as presented in *The Divine Names* does have discernable contours. Superlative life is, first and foremost, transcendent and beyond all possible instances of creaturely life or the living. But its being "beyond" in no way implies its separation, its removal, or even its differentiation from the living. Hence the Neoplatonic conundrum of a Source that is pervasive, a Cause that is distributed. Superlative life, as pervasive and distributed, never runs out in its expenditures; it is a pure vitalist surplus, characterized by generosity and superabundance. It is (in terms evocative of Georges Bataille's own mystical theology), a superabundant expenditure, a divine negation. This leads to a third aspect of superlative life, which is that its pervasiveness and distribution are at once absolute and yet not total, not exhaustive. This follows from the processual and dynamic aspects of the divine—there is no outside and yet the superlative life of the divine never ceases to produce,

never runs out or is depleted. As the life-beyond-all-life, the concept of superlative life is therefore *preexistent* (transcendently immanent), *generous*
(excess and expenditure), and *pervasive* (absolute and not total).

2.4.4 EXCESS, EVIL, AND NONBEING

These three characteristics come together in an interesting way in the
Pseudo-Dionysius' discussion of evil. The primary—not to mention the
secondary—literature on the theology of evil is vast; nearly every theolo-
gian of the Patristic and later eras commented at length on the problem of
evil. Thus it is no surprise to find an extended meditation on evil in *The
Divine Names*.[58] For our purposes here, this little treatise on evil is of interest because it appears to offer a direct counterpoint to the other passages
in *The Divine Names* that point to a superlative life that is characterized
by its excess and abundance. Taking his cue from scripture, the Pseudo-
Dionysius notes that the problem of evil has to do with how something
can produce its opposite—that is, if the divine is "Good" in a superlative
sense, then how can its opposite, evil, derive from it? This counterpoint to
superlative life is, interestingly, conceptualized in analogous ways to the
divine nature—as being beyond all being, as literally "no thing," and as
thinkable only via a logic of negation. Both the superlative life of the divine and the demonic life of evil appear to present limits to thought—both
the divine and the demonic point to a domain beyond which thought can
proceed only via negation.

In its general outlines, the concept of evil presented in *The Divine
Names* is a fairly orthodox one. Evil is not simply the opposite of Good,
for, inasmuch as the Good is identical with the divine, it can have no opposite (since this would then necessitate a higher being that would encompass both Good and Evil, and so on *ad infinitum*). The Good (as the divine) must be absolutely Good, and Evil must therefore be privative, or the
taking-away of goodness; Evil is thus not a thing in itself, but a defect, an
imperfection. "Nor does evil inhere in beings, for if all beings derive from
the Good and if the Good is inherent in and embraces all beings, then evil
has no place among the things that have being or else it is to be located in
the Good."[59] Following the Neoplatonic cosmology, the further away one
is from the divine, superlative source of the Good, the less one has goodness, and the closer one is to this ambiguous non-state of evil.

But it is this last point that is of particular interest—"evil has no place
among . . . being." The Pseudo-Dionysius repeats this mantra several
times: "Evil therefore in itself has neither being, goodness, the capacity to

beget, nor the ability to create things which have being and goodness"; "So, then, evil has no being nor does it inhere in the things that have being."[60] How can evil, which has, by being named, some minimal being, also not have being? The convoluted dialectics of this question are outlined in the middle of the fourth chapter of the *Divine Names*:

> Evil is not a being; for if it were, it would not be totally evil. Nor is it a nonbeing; for nothing is completely a nonbeing, unless it is said to be in the Good in the sense of beyond-being. For the Good is established far beyond and before simple being and nonbeing. Evil, by contrast, is not among the things that have being nor is it among what is not in being. It has a greater nonexistence and otherness from the Good than nonbeing has.[61]

Let us pause a bit on the twists and turns of this passage. Evil is defined, in the first sentence, as that which is not a being. Already, this moves us away from the more orthodox definition of evil as privation or lack, as a distance from the Source, the Good. For if evil has any degree of being, it ceases to be evil and is merely a defective or derivate instance of the superlative, divine Good. This would seem to imply a concept of evil that is not privation—that is, partial negation—but a negation without reserve.[62]

But in the second sentence, the Pseudo-Dionysius immediately denies this possibility, since nothing can have absolute negation, absolute nonbeing—unless it is the superlative life of the divine itself. Here the author is careful to note that evil cannot simply the opposite of being ("nonbeing"), and in fact nothing can absolutely have nonbeing, unless, paradoxically, it can obtain absolute negation via a superlative means—that is, through the *via negativa*. For the Pseudo-Dionysius, evil is thus not privative, it "has no being," even in the most minimal sense. Evil must therefore be not a partial negation (privation), but an absolute negation. But this is precisely how the Pseudo-Dionysius, in *The Divine Names* and *The Mystical Theology*, describes the divine nature—as that which is absolutely beyond all being and nonbeing, beyond all thought, and therefore "nothing." The only instance of absolute negation is one that turns on itself and becomes absolute positivity, pure superabundance and excess.

If evil is neither partial negation (privation) nor absolute negation (the superlative), then what is it? On a conceptual level, the proximity of evil in this regard to the divine reveals some important tensions in the idea of superlative life. Insofar as both the divine and demonic are "nothing," and insofar as they can be thought only via negation, what then is the

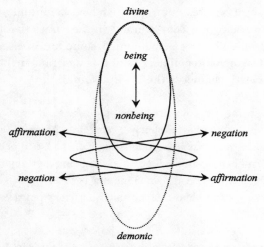

Figure 1. The demonic as superlative negation in the Pseudo-Dionysius.

ontological difference between them? This conundrum is expressed in the sentences that follow in the citation above: in the same way that evil is neither being nor nonbeing, the Good is beyond being and nonbeing. The terms "neither" and "beyond" here merge into a singular but contradictory assertion—that something "is not" because it superlatively "is."

Even so, the Pseudo-Dionysius still attempts to make a distinction between the divine concept of the Good and the demonic concept of evil. Evil, the author notes, "has a greater nonexistence" vis-à-vis the Good than does nonbeing. A group of terms are put into play here, which we can simply diagram as in figure 1. One interpretation, in line with orthodoxy, would be that while the concept of the divine begins with negation, it culminates in an affirmation. By contrast, the concept of the demonic begins with a minimal affirmation (e.g., that evil names something), but then moves towards a full negation (including the negation of being and nonbeing). The Good encompasses both being and nonbeing, and is therefore transcendent, while evil repudiates both being and nonbeing, and is therefore "descendent," or perhaps, a "demonic descendence." Nonbeing is still encompassed within the superlative divine nature, and indeed it must, since by definition the divine (the One, the Good, Life, Wisdom) is a first principle, beyond and outside of which there is nothing more and nothing higher. The divine is, in this sense, a pure interiority—everything and all things are accounted for within the ambit of the superlative life of the divine.

What of the demonic, then? If, as the Pseudo-Dionysius cryptically suggests, evil has "greater nonexistence" than nonbeing, and if nonbeing still lies within the domain of the divine, then would not evil have to be a non-ontological nonbeing, a negation without reserve, an *absolute negation*? If the divine superlative life is a pure interiority, then would not evil have to be a pure exteriority? But surely this only leads to more contradictions—an exteriority without interiority, a negation without assertion, and so on. Again, another turn: is not this dream of a pure exteriority also that of mystical theology itself, with its poetic evocations of a divine "life beyond life"? This is the dream of a positivity that is so great that it appears only as negation, a something which by its very sublimity appears only as nothing. What appears as empty is really the most substantial. Mystical theology is predicated on this stylistic approach—what begins in shadows and nothing is soon revealed to be a light beyond all lights. The Pseudo-Dionysius definitely works in this tradition, but there are as many passages that simply end with shadows and darkness as there are passages that lead to transcendent light. The rather rigorous demands of the Pseudo-Dionysius' concept of evil continually place it in relation to the equally challenging demands of the concept of the divine. Despite the requirements of orthodoxy, they are never as far apart as the author presents them.

This is especially the case in regards to the concept of superlative life. As we've seen, the Pseudo-Dionysius intimates a divine life beyond the naturalistic, creaturely life, a transcendent Life vis-à-vis the living. This is most often characterized in the processual and pervasive nature of the divine. But, whereas the superlative life of the divine is at once processual and "preexistent," pervasive and transcendent, the concept of evil that the Pseudo-Dionysius presents is also an admixture of an ontological foundation and an assertion of something processual, distributive, and pervasive. There is a difference in our reading here, though it is not the one that the Pseudo-Dionysius would like to present. That difference lies in the temporality, processuality, and productivity of the divine versus the demonic. Whereas the superlative life of the divine is a site of pure excess and superabundance (never "running out" or fully expending itself), there is perhaps another kind of superlative life—that of the demonic—that does not follow the oppositions of mysticism (where the negative is followed by the affirmative), but which, instead, follows a different logic. That logic is one of productive negativity, in which each assertion of negation actually germinates another, further negation. In *The Divine Names*, this most often has the form of "not-x . . . not-not-x . . . etc." Thus evil is the negation of being, and also the negation of the negation of being (nonbeing), and so on. This productive negativity is thus counterpoised to the negative productivity of the divine (where negation produces a concept of affirmation, mediated by the negation, often taking the form of "not-$x = y$," where y is defined in purely equivocal terms).

While the superlative life of the divine is "nothing" by virtue of its superabundance and excess (it is literally "no thing," has no bounds spatially or temporally), the more shadowy superlative life of the demonic is "nothing" in a different way, by virtue of a negative transcendence, always pointing to a negation beyond all negation, a nothing without reserve, an absolute negation. Note that both of these are conceptual fantasies—one of being able to think that which is by definition unthinkable, the other of a pure exteriority, the absolutely unthinkable. And both reveal important structures of contradiction that are at the heart of any ontology surrounding Life and the living.

A brief summary is in order: In *The Divine Names*, the Pseudo-Dionysius presents us with the components of the concept of "superlative life." This begins from a negative-theological assertion of a life-beyond-life, or really, a "Life" beyond all instances of the living, a superlative life that is characterized by its being (i) transcendently immanent, (ii) generous or superabundant, and (iii) pervasive or distributive. But this life-beyond-life, lying as it does beyond any particular instance of the living, must be thought of as necessarily preceding any and all instances of the living—in short, the superlative life must be the "Preexistent," a kind of life that is ontologically prior to all instances of life, and, as ontologically prior, which grounds them and conditions them as well. This is the "Preexistent Positivity" at the center of the superlative life concept.

This Preexistent Positivity is, for the Pseudo-Dionysius, necessary in order to condition the very possibility of life—as transcendentally beyond, as generously productive, and as distributive emanation. But we also saw that the Pseudo-Dionysius inadvertently doubles back on all this positivity and affirmation in his short meditation on evil. Here the language of negative theology enters the picture, and the two kinds of "nothing" (demonic and divine) end up highlighting the contradictions in the transcendent concept of superlative life. At the core of the meditations on life is a problem of logic.

In the mystical works of the Pseudo-Dionysius we see an ontological problematic and a vitalist problematic being formulated, both of which culminate in the concept of superlative life. The ontological problematic is that of the transcendent: how to think that which is by definition beyond all

possible thought? The Pseudo-Dionysius suggests that only a negative theology (*via negativa*, the apophatic way) can adequately address this problem. The negation employed here is neither that of privation nor of opposition, but rather a superlative negation, which, in its very act of negation, is
a transcendent "nothing" that lies beyond everything.

But this ontological problematic is, for the Pseudo-Dionysius, indelibly
tied to another problematic that we can call vitalist (using the term in its
philosophical sense). The question of the divine nature is not simply that
of its being as such; rather, the question of what the divine is hinges on
what it does. For the Pseudo-Dionysius, the being of the divine is inseparable from its processuality and dynamics. In true Neoplatonic fashion,
the divine is not simply transcendent, it is superlatively and superabundantly transcendent; it has a processual and pervasive character that is
nevertheless distinct from the temporal finitude of creaturely process and
the pervasiveness of the living. In short, in the concept of the divine-as-
superlative, the Pseudo-Dionysius crucially lays the groundwork for a conjunction between the divine as an ontological principle and the divine as a
vitalist principle.

The term "superlative life" is used here to designate the stratifications
of the divine, from the lowest, most material level of living creatures in
nature to the abstract principle by which they are made alive and animated, to the processual and pervasive nature of the divine, presented via
the language of negative theology. For the Pseudo-Dionysius, the ontology
of life is not simply split between the living and Life, for the latter term
"Life" is itself bifurcated between a principle of formal causation and an
ever further superlative life that is itself "beyond being and nonbeing."
In this way, *an ontological problematic*—a negation that points to a superlative affirmation—*is tied to a vitalist problematic*—a superlative affirmation that is superlative by its generosity, its processuality, and its
pervasiveness.

The two problematics that are outlined by the Pseudo-Dionysius—
ontological and vitalist—push the logic of negative theology to its extreme.
A passage in the final chapter of the *Mystical Theology* gives a sense of
this poetics of superlative negation:

> It [the divine] falls neither within the predicate of nonbeing nor of be-
> ing. Existing beings do not know it as it actually is and it does not
> know them as they are. There is no speaking of it, nor name nor knowl-
> edge of it. Darkness and light, error and truth—it is none of these. It is
> beyond assertion and denial. We make assertions and denials of what

is next to it, but never of it, for it is both beyond every assertion, being the perfect and unique cause of all things, and, by virtue of its pre-eminently simple and absolute nature, free of every limitation, beyond every limitation; it is also beyond every denial.[63]

A negation points to a superlative affirmation, and a superlative affirmation points to a paradoxical "nothing" that is beyond all oppositions, all contraries. At its limit, the superlative life of the divine becomes absolutely inaccessible, culminating in an iterative language of reflexive negation (worthy of the literary wordplay of Alfred Jarry or Samuel Beckett). The strange life of the divine is not even accessible negatively via its manifestations or theophanies, for it is "beyond assertion and denial." What results is a tension within the concept of the superlative, a tension between a concept of the superlative as "beyond" or transcendent, and a concept of the superlative as "within" or immanent. In the works of the Pseudo-Dionysius, this tension is just below the surface; it becomes more explicit in the work of Eriugena—a reader and translator of the Pseudo-Dionysius—who provides the concept of superlative life with a newfound rigor and suggests that superlative life must be thought as actually equivalent to *nihil*.

2.5 SUPERLATIVE LIFE II: ERIUGENA

The basic idea of negative theology—that the divine is, by definition, that which transcends thought—has a great appeal, for it could be read as an affirmation of faith over reason, theology over philosophy (and it would be taken up again centuries later by Aquinas in his own glosses on the relation between theology and philosophy). But there is another tradition influenced by the Pseudo-Dionysius' works, one that was not so quick to turn negation into affirmation, philosophy into theology. One example in this regard is the ninth-century philosopher John Scottus Eriugena, whose major work is known as the *Periphyseon*, or "The Divisions of Nature."[64]

Historically Eriugena is identified with the height of the Carolingian Renaissance, which fostered cultural and intellectual development as key elements of an expanding empire (working during the reign of Charlemagne, Eriugena was also present at the court of Charles the Bald). Having studied in an Irish monastery, Eriugena was familiar with the work of prominent intellectuals such as Alcuin of York, and he would become involved in a number of debates and controversies happening at the time.

In the mid ninth century, one such debate concerned the idea of predestination (that is, whether the divine will is constrained by divine ends). Eriugena was asked to intervene in this debate by the bishop of Rheims. The work he produced—*De Praedestinatione*—did little to resolve the debate, and in fact led to charges of heresy against him. Despite this, around 858, Eriugena was asked by the king to produce a translation of the Pseudo-Dionysius from the Greek into Latin (he also translated other authors, including Maximus Confessor and Gregory of Nyssa). These translations would prove to be deeply influential on Eriugena, not only in terms of their mystical content, but—especially in the case of the Pseudo-Dionysius—in their exploration of negative theology, and the "darkness mysticism" with which it was often allied. Thus it is no surprise to find that Eriugena's writings abound with references to the *via negativa*: "Affirmation is less capable than negation of signifying the ineffable essence of God, seeing that by the former one among the created attributes is transferred to the Creator, whereas by the latter the Creator is conceived in Himself beyond every creature."[65] Or again: "For there is more truth in saying that God is not any of the things that are predicated of Him than in saying that He is."[66]

Sometime around 862–66 Eriugena composed the work he is now mostly known for, the *Periphyseon*. It occupies some four books, and takes the form of a dialogue between a teacher (the "Nutritor") and student (the "Alumnus"). The text became somewhat notorious for what were regarded as its heretical claims—for instance, that the divine nature was immanently "in" all things, or that God was identical to *Natura*—and later thinkers would associate the *Periphyseon* with pantheism, though the text itself never uses this term. As a result, the *Periphyseon* was included in the official condemnations by the Church in 1050, 1059, 1210, and 1225; at the center of the controversy surrounding the *Periphyseon* was whether it had influenced later heretical sects such as the Albigensians, or authors such as Amaury of Bene and David of Dinant.[67]

Several manuscripts of the *Periphyseon* exist, and each differs from the others, as Eriugena himself, or a student of Eriugena's, made extensive annotations, corrections, and edits to the main text. Thus, when the *Periphyseon* was published in 1865 as part of the *Patrologia Latina* series, a definitive edition still did not exist. Modern scholarship has helped to elucidate the genealogy of the manuscripts and their changes, and today there two editions of the work—one by I. P. Sheldon-Williams and John O'Meara (published by the Dublin Institute for Advanced Studies), and another, perhaps definitive edition by Édouard Jeauneau (published by the Pontifical Institute for Medieval Studies).[68] Secondary research on the *Periphyseon*

has also played a part in the resurgence of interest in negative theology
and its relation to continental philosophy.[69]

2.5.1 NEGATION IN THE *PERIPHYSEON*

One of the central concepts of the *Periphyseon* is that of "Nature" (*natura*). But by *natura* Eriugena does not mean the natural or biological
world. *Natura* encompasses this, as later passages in the *Periphyseon* on
natural philosophy illustrate, but *natura* is also more than this. In the
opening passages of book 1, *natura* is defined simply as "all that which are
and which are not" (*quae sunt et quae non sunt*).[70] On this level *natura*
appears to be Eriugena's most basic ontological term. *Natura* is both the
natural world, and the "nature" or essence of something. But *natura* is
also defined as all that can be thought, since "nothing at all can come into
our thought that would not fall under this term."[71] Thus *natura* seems to
be at once the world "out there," thought "in here," and the existence or
non-existence that runs through world and thought. Eriugena's concept
of *natura* is, in a sense, the conjunction of these three elements—world,
thought, and being.

Eriugena states that there are four "divisions" of *natura*, which are introduced early on in book 1, and which can be simply listed as follows: That
which creates and is not created (God or "Universal Nature"); that which
creates and is created (Intellect, Primordial Causes); that which does not
create and is created (the natural world, creatures); and that which does
not create and is not created (God or "Universal Nature"). As is evident,
Eriugena stresses the role of creation and production in the divisions of
natura. The dialectical pairings between "created" and "uncreated" serve
to establish a number of relationships: the first division is the opposite of
the third division, and the second the opposite of the fourth. In addition,
the first and fourth divisions are identical, implying that the divine nature
is at once the source and end of all things, at once the principle of creation
and production, as well as the principle of destruction and return.[72] If the
first and fourth divisions are identical, then the second and third divisions
are also identical as all of creation, including the natural world and its
causal principles (described in Neoplatonic terms as "primordial causes").
The symmetry of Eriugena's divisions of *natura* are that four divisions become two (the divine nature and creation), and two divisions become one
(all things being a part of and return to a single *natura*).

This dialectics of creation and destruction, affirmation and negation,
implies that being and nonbeing are the most basic aspects of *natura*. This

is developed further by Eriugena in what he terms the "five modes of being and nonbeing," which we can briefly summarize here. The first mode is ontological: All that can be sensed or understood exists, while that which eludes sense and intellect does not exist.[73] That which does not exist is taken not in the privative but in the absolute sense. Following this is the second mode, which is categorical. In a Neoplatonic vein, this involves affirmations and negations of lower or higher orders of being, in a similarly dialectical fashion (e.g., the affirmation of a higher order implies the negation of a lower order, the affirmation of a lower order is the negation of a higher order).[74] This leads to a third mode, which follows a broadly Greek orientation: being is actual, and nonbeing is potential; created effects exist, while that which is not yet or hypothetically existent in matter or form, time or place does not exist.[75] This in turn leads to a formal mode, in which those things that can be contemplated by the intellect exist, while those things that change, come into being, or pass away, do not exist.[76] And this opens onto the final mode of being and nonbeing, which is doctrinal: humankind, which through the Fall has lost its originary divine nature, does not exist, and only when it is reunited with its divine source can it truly be said to exist.

Eriugena's *Periphyseon* is dominated by this framework—the divisions of *natura* and the modes of being and nonbeing. Both axes—that of *natura* and that of being (*esse*)—are not simply static grids that lie forever beyond the ambit of human reason. Instead, Eriugena stresses the dynamics that drive each framework—creation/destruction in *natura* and being/nonbeing in *esse*. These two frameworks, of "Nature" and "Being," intersect in some common, dynamic principle that courses through and drives their states.

In the *Periphyseon*, Eriugena refers to this dynamic principle in broad, superlative strokes, as the "life of the world" (*mundi uitam*), as "life-through-itself" (*se ipsam uita*), or, evocatively, as "Universal Life" (*generalissima uita*):

> For as there is no body which is not contained within its proper species, so there is no species which is not controlled by the power of some life (*uitae*). Therefore, if all bodies which are naturally constituted are governed by some species of life (*specie uitae*), and every species seeks its own genus while every genus takes its origin from universal substance, it must be that every species of life which contains the numerousness of the various bodies returns to an universal life (*generalissimam quandam uitam*), by participation in which it is a species.[77]

We have been suggesting that this dynamic principle, also found in the Pseudo-Dionysius, serves as the foundation for thinking about a concept of "Life," or, more specifically, of a superlative life that is, in the case of the Dionysian and Eriugenan works, intimately associated with the divine. Not only do we see a distinction between natural, creatural life (the living) and a transcendent principle of life (Life), but Eriugena, like the Pseudo-Dionysius before him, will go further, and describe this life-beyond-life, this superlative life, in a way that suggests that it is at once excess, generosity, and pervasiveness. In short, Eriugena lays the groundwork for a concept of superlative life that is a conjunction of *natura* and *esse*.

For Eriugena, *natura* applies as much to that which can be thought as well as that which cannot be thought; even nonbeing and the un-thought are encompassed within *natura* (albeit negatively). Eriugena glosses this by suggesting that "all that is" are those things that can possibly be sensed or intuited by the intellect. By contrast, "all that is not" are those things that, by their nature, transcend sense and intellect. This last, negative definition of *natura* implies that it encompasses both the natural and supernatural domains. And immediately questions arise as to the relation between the natural and supernatural, within this overarching concept of *natura*: is God also subsumed within *natura*? Are God and *natura* identical? These and other questions regarding the so-called pantheist readings of the *Periphyseon* will concern us more in later sections. For our purposes here, however, what is important to note is that Eriugena's concept of *natura* not only encompasses the natural and supernatural, but in so doing it makes room for a negative ontology, or that which by definition cannot be thought. This negative ontology will be crucial, as we will see, for Eriugena's development of a concept of superlative life that is related to *nihil*.

2.5.2 THE *QUAESTIO DE NIHILO*: ON NOTHING

As both a translator and careful reader of the Pseudo-Dionysius, Eriugena further develops some key concepts from the *Corpus Areopagiticum*. But there are important differences between them as well. Whereas the Pseudo-Dionysius establishes a relationship between a mystical ontology of superlative negation and a "vitalist" ontology of superlative excess and generosity, Eriugena is not so quick to affirm the divine life-beyond-life in this way. In a sense, the stylistic choices determine much about each thinker's method. Whereas the Pseudo-Dionysius will prefer the more poetic mode of mystical affirmation, Eriugena's *Periphyseon* employs the dialogue format as a means of highlighting a number of ambiguities, particularly surrounding the transcendence and immanence of the divine nature. This is, perhaps, most evident in the lengthy discussion on "nothing" (*nihil*) in book 3, often referred to as the *quaestio de nihilo*. Here the method of negation employed by the Pseudo-Dionysius is pushed to its extreme, to the point where one must *affirm negation itself*. As a method, negation in the *Periphyseon* does not always end on a note of affirmation; instead, the link between "negation" and "life" that was implicit in the Pseudo-Dionysius' works is now made explicit.[78]

Recall that the tension inherent in the Pseudo-Dionysius was how to correlate, on the one hand, a conception of the divine-as-life (the life-beyond-life) based on generosity, excess, and pervasiveness, with a conception of the divine-as-nothing—not in the privative sense, but in the superlative, superabundant, supernatural sense. We have used the term "superlative life" to denote this tension between the dynamic and the static, excess and totality, immanence and transcendence. More often than not, the note on which the Pseudo-Dionysius ends is one of affirmation—not only of the superlative nature of the divine itself, but also of the contradictions inherent in that superlative nature—which, in being contradictory, force a methodological shift from philosophy to poetry or mysticism. The affirmation in the Pseudo-Dionysius' mystical theology is thus a double affirmation—an affirmation both of the divine nature (as superlative), and an affirmation of its inherent contradictions (following from its superlativeness). The Pseudo-Dionysius denies the adequacy of positive theology (of the sort "God is x"), and offers an alternative method of negative theology (of the sort "God is not-x"), but this in turn has as its goal a more superior affirmation, an affirmation of absolute transcendence, of the "beyond" of the divine, filled with contradictions and enigmas. What the Pseudo-Dionysius offers, then, is an *affirmative negation* by way of mystical theology.

Eriugena-the-theologian never denies this superlative aspect of the divine. But the twists and turns of the conversation in the *Periphyseon* don't always lead so directly to this Dionysian affirmative negation. By contrast, Eriugena-the-philosopher, especially in the *quaestio de nihilo*, will focus less on the Dionysian affirmative negation, and more on the absolute limits of the negative in negative theology—that is, on a *negative negation*. In short, by pushing the tension-filled relation between Life (as superlative generosity) and negation (as superlative nothingness) to its extreme, what results is a question concerning logic and thought itself. We are getting ahead of ourselves here, but what we will see in the *quaestio de nihilo* is a concept of Life that is not just related to negation, but a concept of Life that is related to, even isomorphic with, the logic of contradiction, a logic that stems from the extended discussion on "nothing" in the *Periphyseon.*

Let us, as if on a casual walk, proceed methodically through this discussion, highlighting specific points. As pointed out, the *quaestio de nihilo* occupies a considerable portion of book 3 of the *Periphyseon.*[79] While Eriugena does discuss the concept of *nihil* elsewhere, this represents the most sustained and detailed discussion of the topic in the work as a whole. Again, because the *Periphyseon* is written in a dialogue format, this enables Eriugena to utilize the conversants—a teacher or Nutritor and a student or Alumnus—in a variety of ways. The *quaestio de nihilo* can broadly be broken up into an overarching question—"how can something come from nothing?"—and, following this, three replies follow in sequence. Each reply has, nested within it, sub-questions and sub-replies that further clarify or probe into the nuances of the main question. A brief outline of the *quaestio de nihilo* will serve as a guide for our reading:

The *quaestio de nihilo* (*Periphyseon* III):
- Q: How can something come from nothing?
- A_1 (*nihil* as the cause of something from nothing)
  - Q_{1-a} (on *nihil* as privation)
  - A_{1-a} (on *nihil* as both cause and privation)
- A_2 (*nihil* as both eternal and temporal)
  - Q_{2-a} (on contradiction in the divine)
    - Q_{2-b} / A_{2-b} (on diversity in unity; on harmony)
    - Q_{2-c} / A_{2-c} (on temporality and eternity)
  - A_{2-a} (the divine as both eternal and made)
- A_3 (*nihil* as contradiction)
  - Q_{3-a} (on *nihil* as contradiction and shadow)
    - Q_{3-b} / A_{3-b} (on intermediaries—*logos*—as contradictory)
    - First Dilemma (on identity)
    - Second Dilemma (on totality)
  - A_{3-a} (on *nihil* as the divine inaccessible)

Let us first begin with the question, posed by the Alumnus, which frames the entire discussion on *nihil.* After speaking about the relation between Creator and creation in the Neoplatonic vocabulary of "participation," the Alumnus asks how a creating source is able to make something out of nothing:

> But when I hear or say that the Divine Goodness created all things out of nothing I do not understand what is signified by that name, 'Nothing' (*nihil*), whether the privation of all essence or substance or accident, or the excellence of the divine superessentiality.[80]

A rhetorical question, perhaps, for one would not expect a doctrine of the divine as privation or lack to develop from this question. Nevertheless, the Alumnus poses what would become the standard philosophical problematic concerning causality as it was inherited from the Greeks: given that causality structures much of our understanding about the world, must we suppose an originary or first cause? This idea of a first cause can in turn be understood in several ways: either as a temporally first cause, or as an abstract, transcendent principle of causality that is necessary in order to think in terms of cause at all. Whatever the case, such a first cause points to something before or outside this cause-of-causes. Hence the Alumnus' appeal to the scriptural notion of creation-out-of-nothing.

We see that immediately the Alumnus points to two possibilities that the Pseudo-Dionysius had also articulated: that this "nothing" that is before or outside of the principle of cause can either be privative (that which lacks causality) or superlative (that which is beyond causality). In the first reply given, the Alumnus further articulates the question, this time in terms of being and nonbeing. As the Alumnus notes, it would seem that "not-being is predicated of the superessential for no other reason than that true reason does not allow it to be numbered among the things that are because it is understood to be beyond all things that are and that are not."[81]

The Nutritor's first reply is to say that *nihil* in this sense does indeed mean privation, but not privation in terms of lack or incompleteness. Rather, the privation at issue is the privation of the essence of a thing:

> For that word "Nothing" is taken to mean not some matter, not a certain cause of existing things, not anything that went before or occurred of which the establishment of things was a consequence, not something coessential or coeternal with God, nor something apart from God subsisting on its own or on another from which God took as it were a kind of material from which to construct the world; but it is the name for the total privation of the whole essence and, to speak more accurately, it is the word for the absence of the whole of essence.[82]

What *nihil* is in this sense is not the divine nature itself, but the way in which the divine nature governs the conditions of existence of a thing.

In this case, *nihil* is not simply the lack of existence of a thing (that is, the lack of actual existence but not of potential existence), but the absence of its conditions of existing, of its very essence. Thus *nihil* names not just privation as the lack of existence, but the absolute, essential absence of existence—absolute non-existence, "total privation." And here we see something that will recur in each of the Nutritor's replies concerning *nihil*. If we follow the Nutritor's train of thought, *nihil* as absolute non-existence is something that can be identified only *a posteriori*, after a thing exists or has ceased to exist, for otherwise its non-existence would not be absolute, only accidental and incidental. Absolute non-existence implies that its very possibility, its very conditions, cannot be thought. Absolute non-existence is never something that one can think in its non-existence, as it were. Thus, in the first reply, where *nihil* is taken to be the absolute non-existence of a thing, we reach a first limit of thought concerning the superlative. While the Alumnus wants to say that the divine is *nihil* due to its superlatively transcendent nature (more in line with the Pseudo-Dionysius), the Nutritor's first reply is simply that *nihil* means what it says—absolute non-existence, total privation.

Like all of the Nutritor's replies, this one leaves the more inexperienced Alumnus puzzled and disturbed by "dark clouds" of doubt (the motifs of which we will consider below). If *nihil* is simply absolute non-existence, then how do we connect this nebulous zone of nothingness to our understanding of the divine nature as superlative, generous, and an excessive flowing-forth? On the one hand, *nihil* as absolute non-existence seems a bit like infinity or eternity—something vast, boundless, and empty. But on the other hand, the divine nature, as superlative, is also clearly defined in terms of its creative, generative, germinal capacity—always flowing outward, emanating from a central source, down to the most lowly, inert stone. This leads the Alumnus to ask more directly about the act of creation itself:

> For if all things that are, are eternal in the creative Wisdom, how are they made out of nothing? For how can that be eternal which before it was made was not, or how can that which begins to be in time and with time be in eternity? For nothing that participates in eternity either begins to be or desists from being, whereas that which was not and begins to be will of necessity desist from being what it is. For nothing that is not without a beginning can be without an end. Therefore I cannot discover how these opinions do not contradict one another.[83]

This dialectic between that which is made (*facta*) and that which is eternal (*aeterna*) dominates the second reply on *nihil*. The Alumnus proposes a choice: either the divine nature is total and static—and thus defined by being eternal—or the divine is partial and dynamic—and thus defined by the processes of actuality and actualization.

This second reply has, nested within it, two sub-questions and sub-replies. In the first sub-question, the Alumnus asks how contradictory things can come from the divine nature, which is defined as being superlative, simple, and non-contradictory. The Nutritor readily admits the perplexing nature of the problem. How, he notes, "could the unformed come from the Form of all, the variable and mutable from Him Who is immutable and invariable . . . that which admits intervals of places and times and quantities from Him Who is not extended by intervals of places and times . . . the corruptible from the Incorruptible, the composite from the Simple, and other objections of that sort . . ."[84]

The Nutritor's reply involves the use of several analogies, including that of music and cosmology. These hinge on the concept of harmony, and harmony achieved, in particular, through diversity-in-unity and difference-in-identity. Just as a single musical melody consists of a multiplicity of sounds, and just as the unity of the cosmos consists of a multiplicity of bodies, so does the superlative divine nature operate through this harmonic balance of unity and diversity. This follows down through all the levels of the natural world, for, as the Nutritor argues, "the beauty of the whole established universe consists of a marvelous harmony of like and unlike in which the diverse genera and various species and the different orders of substances and accidents are composed into an ineffable unity."[85]

Philosophically speaking, the Nutritor's reply does more to reify the question than to answer it. For any reference to harmony and order must in turn appeal to a source of that harmony or order, and this brings us back again to an inaccessible, superlative kind of law or governance. The artifice of music, like the artifice of the cosmos, must have an Artificer, or at least some transcendent principle by which celestial and musical harmony is made possible. However, this principle can only be posited as such, since by definition it lies outside of the ambit of human thoughts. But already we are seeing a concept of the superlative life take shape around the theme of *nihil*. In the Nutritor's second reply, we can see that it is the exception of the superlative divine to not only govern harmonic order, but, in so doing, to function through contradiction (unity-diversity, form-formless, and so on).

This leads to a second sub-question, which the Alumnus poses with rather crafty specificity. The Alumnus first begins by making a crucial distinction, one that has, up until this time, not been made: that when we speak of "cause" we can speak of either chronological or ontological causality. In a proto-Humean vein, the Alumnus notes that temporal or chronological causality need not imply an ontologically necessary causality, since "it is not in time that formlessness precedes form but in the natural order in which the cause comes before the effect."[86] While one can debate whether or how the divine nature creates and makes things chronologically in time, this cannot be the essence of the divine nature—it must also be causal in an ontologically necessary sense, as that concept without which one cannot think causation itself.

But the Nutritor's previous examples (music, the cosmos, the natural world) seem to point more to the contingent, chronological type of causality. How can these two types of causality coexist in one superlative, divine nature? Hence the Alumnus' second sub-question, which we can quote at length:

> But now I hear differently from you things which disturb me greatly and turn me reluctantly from what I hitherto firmly held to be true as I thought. For the present line of reasoning, as I think, seeks to teach nothing else but that those things which I used to think were made from nothing and were certainly not eternal . . . are at the same time eternal and made, which I think to be surely a contradiction, and reasonably so . . . For things that are eternal never begin to be, never cease to subsist, and there was not a time when they were not, because they always were; but things which are made have received a beginning of their making—for they began to be—because there was a time when they were not, and they will lose the being which they began to possess. For, if right reason be consulted, nothing which begins in time to be is permitted to endure for ever, but it is necessary that it should tend towards the end in which that which has a beginning of its being in time is compelled to perish.[87]

Perhaps the Almnus is truly shaken by uncertainty and confusion; perhaps he senses a real and profound lacuna in the Nutritor's thinking and is furtively undermining it. Whatever the case, the Alumnus here raises the discussion to another level. The issue is no longer simply whether creation is made or eternal, but how such a fundamental contradiction can exist within the divine nature itself.

This contradiction exists on three levels. The first is on the level of temporality: that which is made presupposes a beginning, and that which has a beginning cannot be eternal. The second level is that of teleology: that which is made also has an end, either as cessation or as fulfillment, and therefore cannot be eternal. And the third level is that of mereology: that which is made implies the production not just of parts but of relations between them, the order and "harmony" of which constitutes a unity. But this implies a dynamical, emerging capacity of that which has not always existed, and is therefore not eternal. In short, the Alumnus' two sub-questions concerning *nihil* dovetail on this issue of the contradiction between the made and the eternal—that is, on a problematic that the Alumnus maintains as a philosophical problematic.

This is important to note because, immediately following this, the discussion reaches a dramatic pitch—the Nutritor does not have an immediate, ready-made reply. Instead, he notes the difficulty of the question and enjoins the Alumnus to meditate and say a prayer with him so that they may be able to continue and discover an adequate answer—if ever there was a paradigmatic "prayer to philosophy," this would surely be it.

What the Nutritor comes up with—after the prayer—is perhaps unsurprising. It is mathematics—in particular, the theory of numbers, as it was understood by Eriugena in the ninth century. If treated like a riddle, the Nutritor's reply starts to make sense. Question: what begins but does not have an end, and yet is not subject to the contingencies of created, natural things in the world? Answer: number. Number, and in particular cardinal numbers, begin but need not have an end. Furthermore, particular instances of counting are different, for the Nutritor, from the abstraction of number itself. Citing the work of Boethius on mathematics, both the Nutritor and the Alumnus agree on this basic distinction: "Arithmetic is the science of numbers, not of those which we count, but of those by which we count."[88]

This, in turn presupposes a higher principle by which number is countable, and which encompasses any and all possible instances of numbering. This is what the Nutritor calls the Monad:

[C]onsider carefully those who affirm that unity never had a beginning. If unity, which the Greeks call the Monad, is the beginning and middle and end of all numbers . . . it will not be one unity from which the numbers proceed and through which they move and another towards which they tend and in which they come to an end, but one and the same that is both beginning and middle and end. Therefore, numbers which proceed from their beginning proceed from nowhere else than their end—for their beginning is not one thing and their end another, but they are one and the same unity—, and therefore it must be concluded that if they extend to an infinite end their extension must begin from an infinite beginning. But the infinite end of all numbers is unity; therefore the infinite beginning of all numbers is the same.[89]

The Nutritor's rather dizzying but articulate logic begins from a basic distinction between concrete instances of numbering (x number of things) and the abstract concept of number that makes such instances possible. We can refer to this as a distinction between numbers and Number, the latter providing the conditions of possibility for rendering the former functional.[90] For the Nutritor, the essence of Number is the Monad, the Number of all possible numbers. The Monad is further characterized by the Nutritor in a Neoplatonic fashion: it is the emanative cause of all numbers (instances of counting); as such, it is simple and indivisible; it is at once universal and multiple; it is based on abstract reason rather than sense; and, following from this, it is infinite in reason, but not in sense.[91]

Thus the Nutritor's reply to the second sub-question is by the analogy of mathematics—God, like the Monad, is at once both cause and eternity, both having ontological priority and proceeding to infinity. When the Alumnus persists, the Nutritor nuances the analogy through the use of modality: "Do you then see that the same numbers are eternal there where they are potentially in their cause, that is, in the Monad, but where they are understood to be actually, there they are made?"[92] So the Monad, like God, is eternal when perceived in its potentiality, and made when it is perceived in its actuality. This modal qualification in turn sets up a string of contraries that enable contradiction to be thought: potential vs. actual, eternal vs. made, Monad vs. numbers, Creator vs. creature, Life vs. the living, and so on.[93]

2.5.3 THE *QUAESTIO DE NIHILO*: SUPERLATIVE NOTHING

The two preceding sub-questions—one having to do with temporal vs. causal priority, the other having to do with the analogy of the Monad—dovetail into a larger reply—the second—that the Nutritor gives. Recall that in reply to the Alumnus' overarching question "how can something come from nothing (*nihil*)?" the Nutritor gave a first reply, which was that *nihil* designated a privation, but a privation of the essence of a thing, which in turn implied a notion of a divine nature that was also a first cause. But this only begged the question for the Alumnus, who persisted, questioning the contradiction inherent in this notion of *nihil* as at once eternal and made, nothing and something, negative and positive. The Nutritor's important second reply is that if one is to think the divine nature in relation to the concept of "nothing" or *nihil*, one must affirm the contradiction of the world being both eternal and made: "the things that are eternal are not other than the things that are made but the same things are at once both eternal (*aeterna*) and made (*facta*)."[94] In his second reply, the Nutritor does not try to quell the anxieties surrounding contradiction; indeed, he agrees with the Alumnus that it is contradictory to think of something produced from nothing. Quoting numerous passages from scripture, the Nutritor's reply is that the concept of the divine nature, as superlative, entails a necessary affirmation of contradiction.[95] The contradiction between the world-as-made and the world-as-eternal is, thus, only an apparent contradiction:

> Let us, then, believe and, so far as it is given us, contemplate with the keenness of our mind how all things visible and invisible, eternal and temporal, and the eternal itself and time itself, and places and extensions and all things which are spoken of as substance and accident, and, to speak generally, whatever the totality of the whole creature contains, are at the same time eternal and made in the only begotten Word of God, and that in them neither does their eternity precede their making nor their making precede their eternity. For in the dispensation of the Word their eternity is made and their making eternal. For even all things which are seen to arise through generation at times and places in the order of the centuries were made all together and at once eternally in the World of God.[96]

The divine nature, as superlative, is overflowing generosity or production, and yet still "nothing." The natural world is at once made or produced, and yet, by being made, it also participates in the eternal and infinite. The concept of the divine superlative is, in a sense, based on an affirmation of a contradiction: that God, like Number, is at once transcendent to and immanent within all things:

> If, then, God is prior to the universe which He established for no other reason than the sole fact that He is the Cause while it is the caused, and every caused thing always subsists in its cause . . . then the universe, since it is caused, that is, participates in its cause, is eternal in

its cause. Therefore it is evident that the universe of the whole creation is eternal in the Word of God.[97]

While this is not quite an assertion of pantheism—a term that was, more-over, unknown to Medieval philosophers—the Nutritor is nevertheless pushed forward by the questions of the Alumnus into a consideration of the two contradictory meanings of *nihil*: *nihil* as privation and *nihil* as excess.

Thus, while the Nutritor's second reply does offer a way of thinking the contradiction, what still remains is this troubling concept of *nihil*. Simplifying things greatly, we can see that the *quaestio de nihilo* sets up a relationship between three elements: first, a divine nature that is de-fined by its being superlative and a first cause; second, the created, natural world that flows forth from the superlative divine nature; and third, an am-biguous state before or outside of creation that can only be characterized through the language of negation (as *nihil*). Up until this point, neither the Alumnus nor the Nutritor has addressed the relation between these three elements. Is *nihil* equivalent to the superlative, divine nature? Or does the latter stand transcendently above everything, even above "nothing"?

These relationships are brought to a head with the question that the Alumnus now asks:

> Concerning the eternity of all things and their creation . . . I neither doubt nor think that you were teaching anything else. I only inquire how all things are at the same time eternal and made . . . For it does not, as I think, accord with reason that made things shall be eternal or eternal things made. For there will seem to be no difference between the eternity of the Universe in the Word and its creation if eternity is created and creation eternal.[98]

The Alumnus drives this line of thought to its logical conclusion, adding, not without some skepticism, a challenge to the Nutritor: "Hence there is nothing left, as I think, but either to respect it in complete silence in defer-ence to its excessive profundity or for you to begin your investigation if it seems to you that there is anything about it to be investigated."[99]

From one point of view, the Alumnus is simply being thick-headed and stubborn, asking again the same question about the contradictions in the divine nature. And the Nutritor's frustration is apparent: "I am surprised and very much disturbed that you should seek for reason where all reason fails, or understanding where all understanding is surpassed."[100] What do you think we're doing here?, is the Nutritor's response. Of course reason fails, that's the whole point. The Nutritor chastises the Alumnus for attempting to know the unknowable, but in so doing, he backs out of a philosophical problem via a religious response.

But in the naiveté of the Alumnus there is something interesting. Whereas before, the Alumnus was asking specifically how something made can also be something eternal, here the Alumnus seems to be asking another kind of question, a question about contradiction itself. The Alumnus, step by step, pursues his questioning: "I do not ask for the establishment of the universe in the World and of its eternity, for no one can say how things that are eternal are also made . . . But I do ask for the reason why we are compelled to profess that eternal things are made in the Word of God, if it can be found."[101]

Here again we see the Alumnus ratcheting up the discourse to a higher level. The question is not so much about how one can think both the made and the eternal in a single thought, but how one can think the divine nature at all. "Nothing is left but to ask, not how they are eternal and made, but why they are said to be both made and eternal."[102] We can read the Alumnus' question as asking why, in the above case of the eternal and the made, must the contradiction be maintained? Why does contradiction seem to be a central component of theological—and perhaps philosophical—discourse itself? The Alumnus' question is thus really about why contradiction appears to be at once unavoidable and necessary for thought to occur.

To this, the Nutritor has no direct reply, except once again by recourse to scripture and mysticism (e.g., the references to "divine ignorance").[103] The Alumnus does not seem to so easily accept the reply of mysticism, and he goes even further to articulate two logical dilemmas that illustrate the centrality of contradiction to theological-philosophical discourse.

The first dilemma deals with the relationship, in Neoplatonic terms, between the divine will or volition and the superlative nature of the divine.[104] In other words, is it so much the nature of the divine that it cannot not flow forth into creation? Can the superlative divine nature *not* create? Between the superlative nature and the divine will there appears to be a tension. If they are the same, then God equals creation, since the divine will is identical to that which is willed. If they are different, then God is not simple, since the divine will resides outside of the superlative nature, thus requiring another mediation.

The second dilemma is a variant on the first, and concerns the tension between, on the one hand, the superlative divine nature as rooted in its causality (being the first cause), and, on the other hand, the superlative divine nature as rooted in its teleology (being the final cause).[105] The superlative nature as at once outflowing and inflowing reveals another, similar tension. Does the superlative nature of the divine imply a predestination or predetermination? Insofar as the divine is an absolute cause (the cause of all causes), does this totality imply a limit to causality (that is, the *nihil* that would seem to be uncaused)?

Such contradictions lead the Alumnus to follow a line of thinking that would later be called, rightly or wrongly, "pantheist":

> But if the nature of the Divine Goodness is one thing and what it sees to be made and did make, and saw and made in itself, is another, the simplicity of the Divine Nature (*diuinae naturae*) will be broken when there is understood to be in it that which it is not, which is altogether impossible. If on the other hand the Divine Nature is not other than that of which it sees the making in itself, but they are one and the same nature (*natura*) whose simplicity is inviolable and whose unity is indivisible, it will at once be admitted that God is all things everywhere, and wholly in the whole, and the Maker and the made and the Seer and the seen, and the place and the essence of all things and their substance and their accident and, to speak simply, everything that truly is and is not.[106]

The Nutritor is quick to reply here, using the Neoplatonic notion of intermediary beings (exemplars, causes, *logos*) to avoid any implication of pure immanence between the superlative, divine nature and the created, natural world. But this still does not address the concept of *nihil* and the recurrent presence of contradictions. It seems that, given the Alumnus' questioning, the only avenue left open is to entertain the possibility that *nihil* is, in a sense, equivalent to contradiction itself. It is here that the Nutritor finally provides a definition of *nihil*, one worth quoting in its entirety:

> I should believe that by that name is signified the ineffable and incomprehensible and inaccessible brilliance of the Divine Goodness which is unknown to all intellects whether human or angelic—for it is superessential and supernatural—, which while it is contemplated in itself neither is nor was nor shall be, for it is understood to be in none of the things that exist because it surpasses all things, but when, by a certain ineffable descent into the things that are, it is beheld by the mind's eye, it alone is found to be in all things, and it is and was and shall be.

Therefore so long as it is understood to be incomprehensible by reason of its transcendence it is not unreasonably called "Nothing," but when it begins to appear in its theophanies it is said to proceed, as it were, out of nothing into something, and that which is properly thought of as beyond all essence is also properly known in all essence, and therefore every visible and invisible creature can be called a theophany, that is, a divine apparition.[107]

The divine nature is *nihil* in a privative sense, because what it lacks is the contingency of being caused and created that would make it "some thing." But then this means that the divine nature is *nihil* in a superlative sense, since it is by virtue of its superessential nature that it is literally "no thing," since it surpasses all things. The Nutritor smooths over the contradictions of *nihil* by the intermediary levels of causation: in itself the divine is nothing, but in others the divine is all things; in itself, the superlative life of the divine is *nihil*, in others, it is theophany. While this does repeat the principles of negative theology inherited from the Pseudo-Dionysius, what it leaves untouched, and untouchable, is the relation between the superlative divine nature (as generosity, as excess, as pervasiveness) and this "ineffable" concept of *nihil*.

In the *quaestio de nihilo*, what we see taking shape is a concept of Life—as divine, superlative life—that ends up being closely associated with a concept of *nihil* or "nothing." The central dynamic at work here is that between, on the one hand, a concept of the divine that is superlative positivity, and, on the other hand, a concept of the divine that is negation, nothing, and *nihil*. On the one hand, a concept of Life that is characterized by its generosity, its germinality, its flowing forth, and, on the other hand, a concept of Life that is, in itself, static, vacuous, a nothingness. In these passages from the *Periphyseon*, Eriugena provides us with a central concept for any ontology of life, here understood through the concept of *nihil*. Beyond any particular instance of life in the living, creatural, natural world, there is a concept of "Life" that makes it possible to think life as instances of the living at all.

In the *quaestio de nihilo*, Eriugena ventriloquizes, through the voices of the Alumnus and Nutritor, the contradictions that inhere in any attempt to think an ontology of life-beyond-life. The Nutritor, in replying to the Alumnus' questions, will more often than not opt for a solution that involves mediation and mysticism, with frequent references to scriptural exegesis and the "divine ignorance" of theology above and beyond philosophy. By contrast, if we take the perspective of the Alumnus, with his persistent questioning on the level of philosophy, it would seem that *nihil* implies not just an incidental, but a fundamental connection between "life" and "nothing." If life is *nihil* in this sense, it would not be because it is a privation of some essence, but precisely due to its excess, its generosity, its pervasiveness. That is, while *nihil* can, in one sense, be mediated in the way the Nutritor describes, in another, more furtive sense, *nihil* points to *the antinomial nature of the divine, superlative life as "nothing."*

2.5.4 DARK INTELLIGIBLE ABYSS

Before moving on to consider this relation between Life and *nihil* more closely, a final word needs to be said about the language through which Eriugena most often discusses the concept of *nihil*. At the end of this lengthy definition of *nihil*, Eriugena has the Nutritor add that "the inaccessible brilliance of the celestial powers is often called by theology darkness (*tenebrositas*)."[108] Throughout the *quaestio de nihilo* both the Nutritor and the Alumnus return again and again to the language of shadow and darkness to describe the absolute alterity that *nihil* represents.

A good example in this regard occurs near the beginning of the discussion on *nihil*, where the Alumnus expresses his hesitation: "I feel myself to be surrounded on all sides by the dark clouds of my thoughts (*nebulis ualde tenebrosis cogitationum*)."[109] A bit later on, the Alumnus again expresses himself in a similar way, his confusion described as "the thick clouds of my thoughts (*tenebras densissimas cogitationum*)."[110] Here the language of darkness is used in a rather conventional manner, to express doubt, uncertainty, and confusion. But in other passages, the Alumnus uses the language of darkness in a slightly different way, noting that his thoughts are "daunted by the excessive obscurity, or rather, the excessive brightness, of the very subtle reasons that elude me."[111] Here darkness is not the absence of understanding, but its being surpassed by a superlative kind of knowledge. What is dark and shadowed is such because it is beyond "vision" altogether.

This other use of darkness and shadow is developed at greater length in book 2 of the *Periphyseon*, where Eriugena discusses the divine nature as at once superlative positivity and yet the nothingness of negativity. In Eriugena's Neoplatonic-influenced cosmology, the divine nature is split between its primordial causes, which, through their generosity and germinality, flow forth into the world, and the divine in itself, which maintains its transcendence above and beyond the world. As the Nutritor argues, while the divine in itself is supereminent, beatific light, the divine causes are darkness and shadow, "waste" (*inania*) and "void" (*uacua*).[112] This nebulous and dynamic realm, this superlative life, is described as a "dark abyss" (*tenebrosae abyss*), or, more strikingly, as the "dark intelligible abyss" (*tenebrosa abyssus intellectualis*).[113]

This sort of language points to what is often referred to as "darkness mysticism" in Christian mystical writing, of which works such as *The Cloud of Unknowing* stand out as examples.[114] Eriugena's preference for the language of darkness stands in direct contrast to Patristic thinkers such as Augustine, for whom divine knowledge was obtained through beatific vision and light. The influence for Eriugena is clearly that of the Pseudo-Dionysius, in particular that of *The Mystical Theology*, of which Eriugena produced a Latin translation around 860, prior to his writing the *Periphyseon*. That translation would be amended with commentary and scholia by later generations, and eventually would become a textbook for Dionysian studies during the high point of Scholasticism in the twelfth century, read at the University of Paris, and consulted by theologians such as Hugh of St. Victor and Albert the Great. Eriugena's own edition of the Pseudo-Dionysius' *The Mystical Theology* shows an awareness of the prevalence of darkness and shadow-terms in the text. His translation consistently employs the term *caligo* in Dionysian phrases such as "divine darkness" or the "darkness of unknowing," and *tenebrae* in phrases such as "divine shadows."[115]

Thus, on one level, the language of darkness allows Eriugena to chart a middle path between the poles of either total affirmation (vision, light, beatitude) and total negation (silence, void, death). Darkness, shadows, clouds, and such are not in themselves the divine *nihil*, but they serve a dual function: they delineate the limits of thought, while also pointing beyond those limits to an antinomial site that, in itself, can only be thought in terms of contradiction. The language of darkness allows Eriugena to be able to continue to think beyond the conventional limitations of thought—indeed, it allows him to think the limit of thought itself.

2.6 APOPHASIS

Let us briefly review the ground we've covered thus far. Our opening question had to do with the possibility of an ontology of Life—that is, a concept of Life that, while thought ontologically, did not immediately become a question of Being (metaphysics) or God (theology). This question led to a specific dimension to the ontology of Life—in particular, the ways in which life is conceptualized in terms of time. Life is that which is defined

by change, by dynamic process, by its propensity for creation and production. Life, viewed in terms of its temporality, is always a "superlative life."
But Life, insofar as it is characterized by change and process, is also not
the same as the living, for it variously serves as first cause, transcendent
principle, and ontological necessity for the possibility of thinking about
the living. Thus, an ontology of Life guarantees a minimal intelligibility of the living, for the living. At the same time, however, a distinction
is maintained between Life and the living—even in those instances in
which Life is immanently "in" the living. This minimal distinction arises
out of the temporality specific to Life and the living, be it viewed in terms
of creation, production, emanation, gift, or immanence. Life appears to
be at once the fundamental cause and ontological necessity of all possible
instances of the living, and yet this Life is itself not one of the caused and
is itself not one of those instances of the living.

In short, Life can only be thought via those instances of the living that
Life itself produces. And what this means is that Life, which is conceptualized in terms of its superlative temporality and its generosity, this concept of Life must be thought in terms of negation, or, as Eriugena suggests,
in terms of waste (*inania*), void (*uacua*), and nothing (*nihil*). This is a particular variant on the *via negativa*, the logic of negative theology inherited
from the Pseudo-Dionysius and extended by Eriugena. *The concept of Life,
when ontologized in terms of time, has the structure of negative theology.*

2.6.1 THE APOPHATIC LOGIC

In the Pseudo-Dionysius and Eriugena, we see the concept of life split between the natural, creaturely life of the world, and a superlative life that,
in some cases, appears to be identical with the divine nature itself. It is
this latter, superlative life, that remains both a limit and a necessity for
thought. Life, which grounds all possible instances of the living, is, in itself, nothing. The apophatic logic provides a framework for sustaining this
contradiction, and, in effect, synthesizing reflection on the natural world
with reflection on the supernatural world. We can refer to this synthesis
simply as *apophasis*, the process in which Life is ontologized via the logical framework of negative theology.

But what does it mean exactly, to employ negation in this way to the
idea of life as superlative? One would have to outline a logic of negative
theology, an apophatic logic in which negation always points towards contradiction. In the works of the Pseudo-Dionysius and Eriugena, we can discern an apophatic logic, which we can here put in its simplest terms:

- If A = Life and a = the living, then:
  - Define A as that which conditions a;
  - Define A as that which is beyond a;
- A and a are always correlated in an asymmetrical way;
  - A in itself is never manifest except in instances of a;
  - A in itself can only be thought in terms of a;
- All thought of A must be the thought of a plus or minus something;
  - In any given situation W in which a is embedded, a can refer to A only in terms of not-A;
  - Any statement of not-A is likewise embedded in a given W;
  - Any statement not-A implies a universal not-W;
  - At its limit, not-A = not-W;
- This not-A has as its main function the turning back upon and annulling of every statement about A—even those statements concerning not-A.
- A, which is the essence of a, is in itself nothing (*nihil*).

This is not, of course, a rigorous formalization of negative theology, but even so, what is evident is the way in which a kind of furtive, subterranean notion of *nihil* is fundamental for negative theology's contradictory affirmation of a pure exteriority, a domain of pure excess and generosity. The greatest affirmation requires the greatest negation. It is not only that A can be thought—and is existent—only via the instantiations of a, but the very ontological necessity and ground of a can be thought of only as *nihil*.

In the context of Medieval and Scholastic thinking, this contradiction opens onto a set of interesting issues. On the one hand, the ostensible purpose of negative theology is to end on a note of affirmation—even though this affirmation can never be truly affirmative. Thinkers such as Augustine provide one approach, whereby one takes away the qualifiers "this" or "that," leaving only a pure Platonic essence. Augustinianism thus tends more towards the motifs of beatitude and light. By contrast, we have the apophatic or negative way, represented by the Pseudo-Dionysius. Here one employs negative terms, but this negation is understood not to be a negation based on privation or incompleteness, but a negation based on that which is superlative and in excess of all possible thought. Thus, by saying that God is "not-Life" one is also implying that God is "beyond-Life" or "after life." "Not-a" immediately becomes "more-than-a," or even "other-than-a." Negation, in this mode, implies a "nothing" that is nothing by virtue of being superlatively other than everything. In this sense,

the apophatic way intentionally employs contradiction, both to deny that
there can be any truly positive theology, and to assert the pervasive, distributive, and even immanent existence of the superlative in all things.
For the apophatic way, the only affirmation is the affirmation of negation,
and the only negation is one that employs contradiction.

However, at this point, an impasse occurs, and three options are presented: (i) total silence, (ii) the poetry of mysticism, or (iii) the logic of paradox. While both the Pseudo-Dionysius and Eriugena do suggest the first
two options, it is in the third that their works are the most intriguing.
And because of this, it is in these moments that they also reveal the most
about the ontology of Life. This ontology takes a concept of the divine, and
comprehends it in terms of its superlative nature. This superlative nature
is at once absolutely transcendent and yet, by virtue of its creative and
productive generosity, it is also pervasive and immanent. This temporal,
dynamic, processual notion of the divine nature splits the concept of life
between a subordinate, caused, creaturely life of the world, and a superlative, causing, creating Life. This latter, while ontologically necessary for
the former, cannot, in itself, be thought, except in negative terms. Here
the only affirmation is negation, a negation that can never, by definition,
be superseded by affirmation. This negation, as we've noted, is understood
not to be a negation characterized by privation, but a superlative, excessive
negation, lying beyond all possible conception. The divine or supernatural
is defined as the limit of thought, or that point at which thought cannot
but become contradictory.

2.6.2 Negation in Frege and Ayer

It is important to note that the poetics of darkness, *nihil*, and *tenebrae*
is indelibly linked to the apophatic logic. There is not, beyond the limits
of thought, simply an arbitrary poetry of darkness—rather, what apophasis shows is that darkness, *nihil*, and *tenebrae* are articulated through the
logic of negation. In order to understand this, it is necessary to make some
distinctions concerning the concept of negation itself. This concept has
had a long and complex history within the Western philosophical tradition alone; we will limit ourselves here to three modern distinctions, as
they bear upon the ontology of life, defined in terms of negation.

Negation is a tricky affair; it is a reflex, an echo, an iteration. Negation
is also a shadow; it is always doubled by the fact that it must minimally
assert itself. To state "not-*X*" is to make an affirmation (of a negation) in
the statement itself. Furthermore, "not-*X*" presupposes the prior existence

of an "*X*" and thus requires, prior to the negation, an affirmation of *X* (which is subsequently negated . . . via the affirmation of a negation). Even terms that are not derived from positive terms are compromised by a similar problem (e.g., the term "nothing" must posit or assert nothing).

In a 1919 essay simply titled "Negation," Gottlob Frege suggested that conundrums like these are indications of the untenability of the affirmation/negation distinction.[116] Although the distinction between affirmation and negation has long been a central part of logic, for Frege there exists no definitive way of distinguishing between them, and we should drop the distinction altogether as unnecessary for logic.

Much of this is also demonstrated in our use of language: for example, if you believe in the existence of an ancient, malevolent, and oozing species of Elder deities called Shoggoths, and if I say to you "Shoggoths don't exist," my negation is redoubled by an affirmation (albeit an affirmation of the ideal or imaginary existence of Shoggoths). Furthermore, in response to my statement, you may reply "Yeah, right." If your reply is said in a tone of profound sarcasm, then you would have made an affirmation that is really a negation (e.g., only a fool would deny the existence of Shoggoths). Thus to make judgments based on affirmation and negation makes little sense in cases like these, since a statement is both affirmation and negation, either simultaneously, or sequentially.

Despite Frege's recommendation, the topic of negation was not dropped; in an essay also titled "Negation," A. J. Ayer suggested that negation need not be an absolute concept; more often than not, negation is "partial negation" that leads to another affirmation, that is in turn limited by other negations, and so on:

> The fact is that every significant predicate has a limited range of application. Its correct use is determined both by the fact that there is a set of occasions to which it applies and by the fact that there is a set of occasions to which it does not apply. This being so, it must always be possible to find, or introduce, a predicate which is complementary to the predicate in question, either, in the wide sense, as applying to all and only those occasions to which it does not apply, or, in a narrower sense, as applying to all and only the occasions of this sort that fall within a certain general range.[117]

Thus, for every term *X* it is possible to discover or introduce a term not-*X*. Such a term can even be given an affirmative status while remaining functionally negative. For example, if *X* = Shoggoths, instead of the negative term "not-Shoggoth" we can create a new term, spelling Shoggoth backwards for instance, giving us "Htoggohs." The term Htoggohs would be the negative complementary to Shoggoth. Whereas the term "Shoggoth" would mean "ancient, malevolent, oozing Elder deity," the term "Htoggohs" would have no positive content, but would mean simply "not an ancient, malevolent, oozing Elder deity"—a definition that leaves a lot open.

However, Ayer goes on to make an important distinction. If a negative term is really a complementary predicate to any affirmative term (which is itself defined by the limits, or the negation, of its usage), then there can be more than one way in which a negative term can operate. This Ayer gives at the end of the citation above. There is, first, a negation that applies "to all and only those occasions to which it does not apply." Ayer refers to these kind of negative terms as "not" terms (not-X, not-Shoggoth). But there is also a more nuanced, partial negation, one that applies "to all and only the occasions of this sort." Ayer refers to these as "non" terms (non-X, non-Shoggoth). To say that something is not-X is to say that it fundamentally does not apply, even though one might think it would apply; it is something like a category error. By contrast, to say that something is non-X is to say that it does apply generally, but does not apply specifically. For instance, to say that something is a "not-black" is to say that black, as a color, does not apply to the thing in question, even though one is looking at what appears to be a black painting on the wall. But it is also true that a sound, an idea, or power cannot be black—except insofar as black is used metaphorically. By contrast, to say that something is "non-black" is to still presume that the thing in question can be colored, but just not black (it can be quasi-black, like charcoal grey, or another color altogether). The distinction between "not" and "non" terms can also be stratified. A tiger can be a "non-cat" if the general category of "pet" is operative, or a tiger can be a "non-elephant" if the general category of "mammal" is operative, or a tiger can be "not-Shoggoth" since it has nothing whatsoever to do with Elder deities.

Do Ayer's distinction between "not" and "non" terms apply to the ontology of Life? Earlier, we saw how both the Pseudo-Dionysius and Eriugena develop a concept of superlative Life via negation. For the Pseudo-Dionysius, this was by way of the method of negative theology, whereas for Eriugena this was by way of the concept of *nihil*. In both cases, Life—that by which the living is living—is in itself not some thing. Thus, Life, as that which affirms the living, can be thought only via negation. In both cases, the affirmation of negation itself pointed to a superlative limit beyond the affirmation of negation itself. Both instances of negation—of apophasis—seem to be caught in the conundrums pointed out by Frege.

When we apply the distinction between "not" and "non" terms to the ontology of Life, what is revealed is an asymmetry. On the one hand, Life— as superlative, as pure excess and generosity—remains absolutely beyond the living. If the living are conditioned by being in time, then the superlative Life lies outside the constraints of temporality, while still allied with process, change, and dynamic proliferation. Thus applying the concepts of the living to Life does not apply, except in a negative or superlative sense. We might say, then, that *Life is not-living*. This is only part of the story, however. For, even though Life remains absolutely superlative, beyond comparison, and a limit for thought, it is still related to the living—Life is that by which the living is living, and the living thus retains some thread of Life, be it in terms of creation, emanation, or manifestation. Thus any given instance of *the living is non-Life*. The ontology of life, structured as it is around the Life-living dichotomy, contains within itself the two sides of negation—"not" from the perspective of Life, "non" from the perspective of the living.

2.6.3 NEGATION VS. SUBTRACTION IN BADIOU

Negation seems to pervade the very possibility of affirmative statements. Rather than presume that negative terms are the opposite of affirmative terms, negation—as limit—inheres in the very possibility of affirmative terms and the contingency of their usage. How do we account for this productive, generative aspect of negation? One possibility is not just to consider an internal distinction (between "not" and "non"), but to consider an external distinction, between negation and other similar terms. This is what Alain Badiou offers in his distinction of the terms negation, destruction, and subtraction. For Badiou, negation has both a negative and affirmative side, a "negative negation" and an "affirmative negation." What Badiou calls "destruction" is the negative part of negation, the passing-away of the old, the "eventual concentration which realizes the negative power of negation."[118] But negation also has an affirmative side, one linked to creation: "the very essence of a novelty implies negation, but must affirm its identity apart from the negativity of negation."[119] This is what Badiou calls "subtraction," the affirmative part of negation.

One of the examples Badiou uses is musicological (the other is political): in the early twentieth century, the innovation of Second Viennese School (Schönberg, Webern, Berg) and the twelve-tone system achieved

both a destruction of and subtraction from traditional Western classical music. This new music was, on the one hand, a destruction of the old
forms, the old ways of composing, a destruction in the sense that it posed
a challenge to the traditional system—one could no longer compose music without in some way confronting this challenge. But the music of the
Second Viennese School also achieved a subtraction from the very tradition it was acting against, having developed a new method and a new way
of understanding music: "The point that we must understand is that this
new coherence is not new because it achieves the process of disintegra-
tion of the system. The new coherence is new to the extent that, in the
framework that Schönberg's axioms impose, the musical discourse avoids
the laws of tonality, or, more precisely, becomes indifferent to these laws.
That is why we can say that the musical discourse is subtracted from its
tonal legislation."[120]

Subtraction, then, is indelibly tied to a certain form of creation, a form
of the production of novelty, one that proceeds not by assertions or imposi-
tions of something, but one that articulates novelty by way of receding,
pulling back, withdrawing, maneuvering. "Sub-traction, that which draws
under, is too often mixed with ex-traction, that which draws from out of,
that which mines and yields the coal of knowledge."[121] If subtraction is not
a simple affirmation, if it is not simply the production or agglomeration of
knowledge, then how does it obtain its contradictory affirmative-negative
effects?

Badiou offers four "operations" by which subtraction is affirmative-
negation. These are the undecidable, the indiscernible, the generic, and the
unnameable. We can briefly describe them, using the distinction between
life and death as examples. In a situation in which the evaluation of statements a_1 or a_2 is based on some normative criteria (e.g., of being alive or
dead, etc., that is, of x or y for a statement F), "the undecidable statement
will be the one that subtracts itself from that norm."[122] So the undecidable
is some statement a_n that is cumulatively not-F; it is inapplicable to norms
that are defined as being exhaustive. Something similar happens with the
indiscernible. If our statement $F(x, y)$ has the normative criteria of $x =$ living and $y =$ dead, then the indiscernible is the inability to distinguish, in
a statement F, the difference between $F(a_1, a_2)$ and $F(a_2, a_1)$. "The indiscernible is what subtracts itself from the marking of difference as effected by
evaluating the effects of a permutation."[123] In the case of the generic, the
issue has to do with sets and totalization. If we consider a set U—let's say
it's actually a species of living organism—then each member of U can be
hypothetically listed as $a_1, a_2, \ldots, a_n$. We can then take a statement $F(x)$,

which takes the form "x is more complex than a_1." If we then take $F(a_2)$, we can arrive at a true or false statement (depending on whether the organism a_2 is organizationally more complex than a_1). We can also create a subset U_1 that contains all those instances of $F(x)$ within the larger set U. But what if the statement $F(x)$ actually changes with each instance of $F(a_2)$, $F(a_3)$, . . . ,$F(a_n)$ because $F(x)$ does totally account for each instance of a_2, a_3, . . . ,a_n? What we would have is another type of subset, a generic subset that is "subtracted from every identification," a subset that "contains a little bit of everything, so that no predicate ever collects together all its terms."[124] Thus, "the generic subset is subtracted from predication by excess."[125] Finally, there is the unnameable. If we take again our statement $F(x)$, here its function can be a nominating one, so that, if x is "the last living human being," it names something that gives x a value (as true or false) if it is the only thing that gives a truth-value to x. The unnameable is, by contrast, "the only one in the universe that is not named by the expression."[126] It has the singularity of the proper name, but its singularity lies in its being subtracted from any possibility of naming

Badiou neatly summarizes the operations of subtraction as follows: the undecidable is subtracted from a *norm* of evaluation, the indiscernible is subtracted from the marking of *difference*, the generic is subtracted from the *identity* of the concept, and the unnameable is subtracted from the proper *name*. There is always an antagonism in the creativity and productivity of subtraction. This antagonism is not simply that of being oppositional or "anti-" and neither is it the reactionary mode of either apathy or *ressentiment*. In its "drawing-under," it creates a kind of house-of-cards effect, in which each moment of destruction turns on a moment of subtraction, and vice versa. In fact, it is in the isolation of subtraction and destruction that Badiou sees the stakes of contemporary politics: "That the very essence of negation is destruction has been the fundamental idea of the last century. The fundamental idea of the beginning century must be that the very essence of negation is subtraction."[127]

Let us think about these four operators of subtraction in relation to the distinction between life and death. In our examples, the undecidable is that situation in which the living/dead distinction does not apply (we might call this the crystalline, or even the "elemental"). The indiscernible is that situation in which the living cannot be distinguished from the dead, and vice versa (we might call this "nonorganic life," or even "living dead"). The generic is that situation in which the living can be articulated as a set, but can never be totally accounted for as such (we might call this "germinal life," or even "pathological life"). Finally, the unnameable is

that situation in which the singularity of life or death is such that it is de-
conceptualized, and is contracted into a name (but a name beyond "Robert
Neville" or "the last man," something like "those we do not speak of").

These are all instances within subtraction—but subtraction is more
broadly coupled with destruction, the two forming the process of negation as Badiou theorizes it. This notion of subtraction also pertains to the
relation between Life and the living. On one level, the particular, singular
instances of the living always threaten the coherence of the larger, more
abstract categories of biological species. There are always exceptions to the
rule, marginal cases, unresolved puzzles, oddities, curiosities, and undiscovered creatures. By definition, the monster is that which upsets categories and boundaries, it destroys the coherence of the preexisting sets, in
fact challenging them in their nonapplicability. In this sense, *the living is
the destruction of Life.*

But Life, as an ontological principle, as that-by-which-the-living-is-
living, is not simply a part-whole affair. If it is an ontological principle,
"Life" will obtain its effect not by enumerating all the instances of it in
the living, but by asserting a conceptual necessity—as that without which
the living is inconceivable. As we've seen, the logic of this relation is that
of negative theology—Life that conditions the living but which in itself is
"nothing." Thus *Life is what subtracts itself from the living.* There is one
instance in which this subtraction ceases, and what ends up being affirmed
is the absent center (this is, perhaps, what we see in Plotinus' meditation
on Life and Time). But there is also another instance in which the subtraction of Life from the living opens onto all sorts of cross-pollinations (e.g.,
demonic life in the Pseudo-Dionysius, the shadowy life in Eriugena), and
whose logical endpoint is the dissolving of the concept of life altogether.

2.6.4 NEGATION AND CONTRADICTION IN PRIEST

In this consideration of Life as it is related to negation (Ayer) and subtraction (Badiou), we have forgotten one important thing, which is that these
processes of negation and subtraction often turn on a fundamental logical contradiction. Life is both a something and a nothing, both continuous with the living and absolutely separate from it. The ontology of Life
thus bears within itself an intimate relation to contradiction. This would
seem to undermine the concept itself, since every thought of Life entails
some contradictory dynamic (something-nothing, presence-absence, and
so on). Despite this, the concept of Life and its relation to the living still
functions in a wide array of fields and approaches, from the life sciences,

to bioethics, to medical and patent law, to biodefense applications, to the discourses surrounding climate change and the environment. How then, should one regard the concept of Life, insofar as it is ontologized not only via negation ("not" vs. "non"), and not only via subtraction, but also by contradiction itself?

Part of the dilemma is that our thinking about contradiction can itself be contradictory. This is evident early on in the West, in the form of transition states (Heraclitus' famous formulation—"We step and do not step into the same rivers; we are and are not")[128] and instances of movement (Zeno's equally well-known paradox of the arrow that never reaches its destination). Non-Western philosophies often place contradiction at the center of their thinking, as can be seen in the Zen concept of "unthinking" in the work of Dōgen. There are other, more everyday examples as well: a person entering a room is, at one moment, both inside and outside the room. Legal and political philosophy provides an abundance of such examples (e.g., a person who fits the category of those for which something is legal and those for which something is illegal).

Graham Priest has suggested that, because of examples such as these, we ought to reconsider the role that contradiction plays in logic. In the Western tradition, the dominant attitude was first formulated in Aristotle's *Metaphysica*.[129] There Aristotle proposed that any statement A must be either true or false, but not both—what we have come to know as the law of non-contradiction (LNC). To this Aristotle adds a corollary, which states that, for any statement X, it is necessary that at least one of X or $\neg X$ be true, but they cannot both be true (often called the law of the excluded middle). For Priest, the common arguments for the LNC rest on the assumption that "some" equals "all"—that is, if a statement is in some ways contradictory, or in some instances contradictory, then it must be in all ways and at all times contradictory. This—an inference type known as "explosion"—means that, for all X and Y, the contradiction of X and $\neg X$ entails everything else, or Y. This need not always be the case, however. A contradiction in one domain need not immediately entail all domains. When this is the case, the logical relation of explosion fails, although the logic of the contradiction remains—in such a case one must then consider the logic as "paraconsistent."

One can, then, consider the existence of contradictions as both logically coherent and as actually existent: "The view that the LNC fails, that some contradictions are true, is called *dialetheism*. As we have already seen, one does not have to be a dialetheist to subscribe to the correctness of a paraconsistent logic, though if one is, one will."[130] For Priest the com-

mon arguments against dialetheism, and in support of the LNC, all presume the absolute entailment of explosion: the argument that contradictions have no meaning or no content (when they have all content, total
content); the argument that if contradictions are true, then nothing is true
(when contradictions exclude nothing); the argument that negation sup-
plies the truth conditions for statements, so that ¬ X can be true only if X
is not true (when, as we've seen, negation is more than simply negative);
and the argument from example, that contradictions are not witnessed in
the world (an inductive argument based on selected examples).

Does any attempt to ontologize Life entail a dialetheic approach? On
one level, the suggestion is almost absurd—precisely because we intui-
tively accept it as true. "Life is contradictory" says one person. "I don't
need a philosopher to tell me that!" replies the other:

> We, all of us, discover sometimes—maybe by the prompting of some
> Socratic questioner—that our beliefs are inconsistent. We assert a, and
> then a little later assert ¬ a . . . We are not denying a. We do accept a;
> that, after all, is the problem. Hence, to assert a negation is not neces-
> sarily to deny—and the problem that this objection points to is just as
> much a problem for the classical logician as for the dialetheist.[131]

But beyond this, the way in which an ontology of Life—that is, an attempt
to account for both the very conditions or possibility of thinking "life"—
the way in which this ontology is structured around negation is the key
to understanding Life as dialetheic. That negation has many dimensions,
from the negation of a superlative Life in the Pseudo-Dionysius to the
nearly immanent identification of Life with *nihil* in Eriugena. Hence, one
observation that dialetheism provides on the ontology of Life is that contradiction may be the very mechanism that drives the ontological relation
of Life and the living. *Does the ontological relation between Life and the
living function through a dialetheic logic?* We might even say that, for the
concept of superlative Life, contradiction is fundamental and even necessary, in order for the ontology of Life to be thought at all.

Thus, we have three modern variants on the concept of negation, each
of which offers three further distinctions on the relation between negation
and the concept of Life:

- Life is not-living, while the living is non-Life (Ayer's distinction
  between "not" and "non" terms).

- Life is subtracted from the living, while the living is the destruction of Life (Badiou's distinction between negation, destruction, and subtraction).
- The ontology of the Life-living relation is thinkable through a dialetheic logic (Priest's distinction between the LNC and dialetheism).

According to the apophatic logic, Life—which conditions the very possibility of the living—can never itself be one among the living. Life must always remain superlative, and thus negated from the living. This means, in short, that Life can never be inscribed within the set of all those things that are called the living. But if Life is not part of the set of the living, neither is it the set of the living itself, for this would imply a part-whole relationship that negative theology explicitly avoids (and this is, perhaps, where the Pseudo-Dionysius and Eriugena part ways with Plotinus). These are, for apophasis, the requirements for any ontology of Life: that Life is not itself contained with the set that it conditions, and that Life is also not that set itself in its totality. But neither does this mean that Life is the meta-set, or the set of the set of the living. The problem here is that what results is a logical *mise-en-abîme*. Thus, to the proposition that "Life is not-*a*" is immediately added "Life is not-not-*a*" and so on. These can quickly become logical games, to be sure. But, in the context of the possibility of an ontology of Life, what this apophatic logic leads us to question is the very tenability of the ontological relation between Life and thought itself.

Let us pause on this point for a moment. As we said, the apophatic logic quickly becomes a *mise-en-abîme*, negations "all the way down" in which negation becomes generative and proliferative. We can entertain a number of interpretations of what this might mean. On the one hand, this seems to lead us into contradiction, plain and simple. If it is dialectic, it is one that is never resolved or "raised up," simply continually negated. But because the process can hypothetically go on forever, it actually means that the negativity is, in some minimal sense, a generative one. There are a number of ways of understanding this generativity. In terms of modern logic, this negation—that is, this superlative negation—can simply be understood as a kind of machinic iteration, one which, by its purely formal iteration, actually points to negation that is both denumerable and infinite (the "not-not-*a* . . ." that goes on forever). Thus, insofar as superlative Life can only be thought negatively, this negation-of-Life becomes a kind of denumerable negation.

In another vein, the process of superlative negation in the apophatic

logic can be understood as a Deleuzian process, one in which what is repeated each time is difference itself. Each superlative negation ("Life is
not-not-*a* . . .") is not just a mechanical iteration, but it pushes against the
limit of thought itself, each time actually creating new conditions. This
repetition of difference is not merely the creation of new ideas or even new
possibilities or potentialities (that may or may not become real), but it is,
instead, a sort of phase shift in the very conditions of thought itself ("virtual while remaining fully actual" as Deleuze often states).

However, both of these interpretations presume that something is
added with each negation ("Life is not-*a*" . . . "Life is not-not-*a*" . . . "Life is
not-not-not-*a*" . . .). There is also the interpretation that this iterative negation is not additive but, instead, simply neutral. It is the exact same gesture each time, something like Nietzsche's eternal return, something like
a negative-ontological mantra. The horror of this thought—a horror evoked
in Nietzsche's parable—is precisely its neutralization, its blankness, its
expression of *nihil*. This seems to be more the case with the Pseudo-
Dionysius, as well as with the more "apophatic" moments in Eriugena.
There is only one negation, only a single "not-*a*" that can, despite its singularity, be infinitely repeated. There is, then, no drama of affirmation or
negation, superlative or privative, but rather a pervasive neutralization.

One question that then arises—a question that we will return to in
later sections—is whether this *nihil*-as-neutralization is simply another
name for immanence, but a notion of immanence that is effectively
"empty."

For the time being, what we can note is the way in which negation and
nihil come to play fundamental roles in the articulation of a concept of
Life that is based on its superlative, excessive generosity. While instances
of the living can be directly understood and comprehended, Life can only
be negatively posited—exactly as that which is not-living. Life is beyond
any given instance of the living, but it is also inseparable from the living.

2.7 THE DIALETHEIC VITALISM OF NEGATIVE THEOLOGY

By way of conclusion, we can step back and offer several propositions concerning the concept of Life in terms of time, temporality, and its superlativity. This can also serve as a way of talking about method, since our
inquiries will take up Medieval and Scholastic thinking in a way that is at
once modern and nonmodern. Ultimately, this is also the critical limit of
any ontology of life, when life is understood in terms of its superlativity.

Our first proposition is that, for Medieval and Scholastic philosophy,

God is ontologized in terms of Being. This is our modern "misreading" of the Scholastics: every time we read "God" we should really think "Being." Put differently: what Scholastic onto-theology means by God is what modern ontology means by Being. This is a tactical approach to reading. It is not, of course, to suggest that all theology reduces to philosophy. But it is to suggest that we can understand attempts to think the divine nature in terms of what Kant described as the *ens entium*, or the being of all beings. Furthermore, this is not exclusive to Scholasticism, but can be discerned in classical thought (e.g., Plato's demiurge in the *Timeaus*) and in the Neoplatonic synthesis (e.g., Plotinus and the Primordial Causes).

A second proposition extends from the first: Being is regarded as indissociable from beings via the process of emanation. What modern ontologies—most notably, that of Heidegger—articulate as the ontological difference between Being and beings is established in two phases: first, a classical phase, in which that-which-exists is distinguished from that-by-which-something-exists, either by model, mold, and perfection (Plato), by cause, form, and creation (Aristotle), or by a perfection that is also the cause (Plotinus). With Plotinus, the conceptual hierarchy is maintained, while also allowing for the necessary relation between divine and earthly, supernature and nature. Medieval and Scholastic thought can be regarded as different ways of formalizing the problems that arise from this basic distinction: the divine as at once static and dynamic, the relation between Creator and creature, and the transcendence and/or immanence of the divine in nature.

A third proposition, again extending from the second: Emanation or emanative Being is most often granted a superlative status as "Life." From a metonymic shift of God-as-Being, to the distinction between Being and beings, comes the necessity of mediation between the Being and beings, Creator and creature, Life and the living. Something that conditions everything is at the same time "in" everything. The Neoplatonic notion of an emanative, radiating source must also be thought in temporal terms. But, if it is not to be confused with the temporality of nature and the living, its temporality must be thought of in a superlative, absolute sense. Thus, working from analogy, what the domain of the living is to the temporality of nature, the superlative Life of the divine is to the temporality of emanation and creation.

But there is a problem, for the analogy only begs the question of how this life-beyond-life is different from the creaturely domain of the living. Hence, a fourth proposition: The superlative Life of emanative Being is characterized in terms of its generosity. Superlative Life, if it is not to be constrained by temporality, must also be thought of as pure excess, as generosity, and an endless flowing-forth. This problem is raised by Plotinus, but its true articulation comes in the Pseudo-Dionysius and is later nuanced by Eriugena. That which is pure generosity, pure superlative Life, that which never "runs out," cannot simply be thought positively, as an infinite reservoir or anthropomorphized Goodness, but it must instead be thought negatively, as that which is nothing (*nihil*) precisely because it is superlative.

This gesture towards negation leads us to a final proposition: Life as generosity is negatively articulated in terms of the "divine inaccessible." If superlative Life can be thought only negatively, then this means that the only relation between Life and the living is a non-relation, or a relation of, literally, nothing. How can Life be nothing? There are really two key questions here: First, is Life itself living? On the one hand, Life is not living, because it is not one among the living; on the other hand, Life in its ontologization is itself the principle-of-life, coextensive with each and every instance of the living. This leads to a second, more basic question: Does Life exist? On the one hand, Life in itself is no thing, and does not exist; on the other hand, the concept of Life as superlative not only presumes existence, but it also conditions the ontological modes of what Aristotle called "coming-to-be" and "passing-away." In both cases—the relation between Life and the living, and the relation between Life and Being—a condition of contradiction appears to be fundamental to the very thought of Life. The impasse here has to do with whether or not any attempt to resolve the contradiction sublimates Life into something else: Life as indistinguishable from divine, sovereign Creation (theology); Life as subordinate to Being (metaphysics); or Life as pure description and classification (biology). In each instance, Life dissipates into God, Being, or the living.

Earlier we outlined the logic specific to the concept of superlative life, an apophatic logic. To this we can add the above propositions. They outline the conceptual progression whereby the concept of Life as an ontology surfaces and recedes before thought: from God to Being (first proposition), from beings emanated from Being (second proposition), from emanation to the temporality of life (third proposition), from life to generosity (fourth proposition), and from generosity to the divine inaccessible (fifth proposition). In this process the tenuousness of the concept of Life is revealed, as it surfaces from a discourse that ontologizes the divine nature, and then is submerged beneath contradictions that are resolved in terms of theology or biology.

Our goal here is not to dispense with the general concept of life, but neither is it to defend or conserve it. Rather, in our mode of critique, our goal was to begin to delineate the contours of a concept that appears to mean so many things that it means nothing, a concept that is everywhere formally operative and yet emptied of content. In this section we've outlined one of the dominant attributes of life when ontologized in terms of time, temporality, and process. As our considerations of Plotinus, the Pseudo-Dionysius, and Eriugena have suggested, this notion of life-as-time is not an exclusively modern thought. Rather, it is formulated in a range of premodern discourses, from mystical theology to Medieval natural philosophy. In particular, it is formulated in an inadvertently subversive way, where Life, as superlative, is indelibly linked to negation, darkness, and *nihil*. Thus, a central lesson that we can draw from the negative ontologies of the Pseudo-Dionysius and Eriugena: Superlative Life is defined as the necessary inaccessibility of Life to the living. To this, we can append a note on method: *the ground and the limit of any ontology of Life is negative ontology.*

2.8 ELLIPSES: SUHRAWARDĪ AND THE LUMINOUS VOID

The Aristotelian distinction between Life and the living addresses the problem of ontology in relation to "life," in that it provides both a universal conceptual ground as well as a way of accounting for its manifestations. But this distinction only highlights the problem of the relation between Life and the living. The question is whether Life is, in relation to the living, an essence concept. On the one hand, Life can only be negatively thought in relation to the living, and yet this concept grounds the very intelligibility of the living as such (and, by extension, the "realism" of Life itself). This leads to a dilemma, which is how to maintain the necessity of the Life-living distinction while also allowing for the blurring between the terms, often to the point that they negate each other.

The tradition of negative theology offers one example of an attempt to resolve this dilemma. While the question of life is never simply a question of natural philosophy (or even of natural theology), it is also not simply a question of pure theology. This paradoxical life-beyond-life, what Aquinas obliquely calls "the Life of God," serves as the platform on which philosophy grapples with a concept of Life that is neither that of Aristotelian Being nor that of the Patristic God.

The contradiction at the heart of negative theology relies on a back-and-forth between affirmation and negation: the superlative can be affirmed only in terms of negation. Be that as it may, negative theology is often characterized by a dichotomous split between the rhetorical figures of light and darkness. In this way, the Pseudo-Dionysius shares a great deal with the darkness mysticism of St. John of the Cross or *The Cloud of Unknowing*. But the dichotomy is less theological than it is ontological—in the interplay of light and darkness, like that of affirmation and negation, one serves to continually supersede the other. In fact, negative theology requires this dichotomy, because it structures the inversion that is so central to its philosophical style: affirmation always leads to negation, and affirmative to negative theology. For these thinkers, the highest affirmation must always be in excess of any particular affirmation itself, and must therefore become, in Eriugena's words, the "dark intelligible abyss."

Negative theology articulates one facet of the ontology of life after Aristotle: life defined in terms of its temporality, its generosity, its superlative nature. But in so doing, it is led to what appears to be the opposite: life as "nothing." And much of this is predicated on the interplay of light and darkness, as analogues of the logic of affirmation and negation. Here let us pose a question: would it be possible to preserve this notion of life-as-nothing, while at the same time bypassing the dichotomous thinking of light-darkness? That is, is it possible to refuse the dichotomy of light-darkness while not attempting to resolve the contradiction of life-as-nothing?

Let us consider something other than light or darkness—perhaps something like glowing, or duskiness, or luminescence. Medieval Arabic philosophy provides us with a number of examples. One is the tradition of "illuminationist" (*ishrāq*) mysticism, associated with thinkers such as Shihāb al-Din al-Suhrawardī. Like the tradition of negative theology, Suhrawardī's works display both the influence of Aristotelianism—filtered through thinkers such as Avicenna—as well as a marked influence of Platonic and Neoplatonic thinking (not to mention the array of Greek Gnostic, Hermetic, and Persian Zoroastrian elements that are also part of Suhrawardī's works). Though he made contributions in metaphysics, cosmology, mystical poetry, and logic, Suhrawardī—who was accused of heresy concerning his views on the access to mystical knowledge—also developed a complex ontology of illumination. This is presented in texts such as the late-twelfth-century *Philosophy of Illumination*, though, as scholars such as Henry Corbin have suggested, it is a motif already present in early works such as *Temples of Light*.

Suhrawardī's primary interest lies in a conception of the divine, and the world as divine, in terms of light—everything is understood in terms of luminosity and illumination, lightening and darkening, dependent and autonomous lights ("light in its own reality"), "accidental" lights ("light that is a state of something else"), and the "Light of Lights." In one sense, Suhrawardī's ontology of light follows a broadly Neoplatonic pattern, in which a divine source radiates outward into the world. But this ontology of light must also take account of darkness. Although the *Philosophy of Illumination*'s primary concern is light, it is often darkness, darkening, and luminosity that prove more difficult to conceptualize. These are, on the one hand, simply a lessened instance of pure or non-accidental light: "Darkness is simply an expression for the lack of light, nothing more."[132] This absolute differentiation means that light can no more cause darkness than something can be created out of nothing. Here Suhrawardī distinguishes between light in its effected or accidental state, and Light as a causal radiating source.

But then where does darkness come from, or can one even say that it is produced at all—or that it "is" at all? Suhrawardī appears to divide darkness into an incorporeal and corporeal instantiation (the "dusky substance" and "dusky body," respectively). If the latter are understood to be concrete, physical entities, then the former are "barriers," through which light is cut off. At the same time that the Light of all Lights is carried above and beyond darkness, the question of the light of darkness persists: "Thus, that which gives all dusky substances their lights must be something other than their gloomy quiddities and dark states."[133] While the dark light or the dark body may not directly partake of the Light of Lights, its very existence presumes a minimal luminosity—"that which gives them their lights must be something other than the barriers and dusky substances."[134] This effectively leads Suhrawardī to conceptualize a light—or better, a superlative radiation—that is neither the Light of Lights, nor the mere privation of all light. "You will learn that dark states are caused by light, even though the light itself may also be accidental."[135]

Ultimately, Suhrawardī's ontology of light opens onto an affirmation of the divine as superlative. But, considering how the concept of superlative life always turns on its negation, we might speculate about the role of darkness in Suhrawardī and its relation to Eriugena's concept of *nihil*. The "dusky" or the luminous is, for Suhrawardī, neither pure light nor darkness, but the continuum or the spectrum of lighting or darkening; it is luminescence, iridescence, and glow.[136] Illumination is Suhrawardī's first principle, but it is both immaterial and unfixed; it is not quite the Aristotelian distinction of form and matter, but neither is it quite the Neoplatonic stratification of divine source and its strict hierarchies. This emphasis on a spectrum as a first principle implies that every assertion of transcendence must also assert, equally, an assertion of immanence. When Suhrawardī notes that all illumination exists by virtue of a Light of Lights, this must be countered by the continuum of this Light of Lights in all entities that it constitutes. If we were to take a strong reading of Suhrawardī, we would say that every assertion of a first principle, a Light of Lights, must also be an assertion of the diffusion that is light itself.

The insight of luminosity and duskiness in Suhrawardī's works is that it is a variant on the idea of participation: everything participates *in* and *of* illumination. Illumination is, on the one hand, the animating principle of each individuated being—it is at once *ousia* and *psukhē*—and it is, on the other hand, that which conditions the interrelation of all things. Suhrawardī's ontology of illumination therefore takes light as both a source and diffusion, as both origin and continuum. For Suhrawardī, a key generative characteristic of light is that of intensity; intensity of illumination determines the ontological status of any being. This is less a Neoplatonic, aggregative notion, in which the further away one is from a source, the less reality one has. Instead, there can be degrees of intensity at all levels. This is never directly stated by Suhrawardī; it remains an unexplored notion, and tends to glossed over by an assertion of a hierarchical paradigm of illumination (the Light of Lights emanates a Second Light, a Third Light, and so on). But its implication is that light is always illumination, and illumination is always intensity or a fluctuation, and intensity brings one more into the domain of luminosity, the dusky, and the glowing; illumination is more like luminescence or flickering. If this is the case, then the Aristotelian framework of Life and the living, as the Dionysian-Eriugenan framework of superlative life—this would then become dissolved into a sort of pulsing field of glowing substances, dark accidents, flickering formal causes, and a luminous void that functions as the animating principle of the world.

Suhrawardī's ontology of luminosity does something as powerful as it is simple: by structuring an ontology around the spectrum of light and darkness, Suhrawardī renders irrelevant the Aristotelian distinction between substance and accident. This has implications for the distinction between Life and the living. While Life is distinct from the living, it is also, for Aristotle, inseparable from it; Life is not another instance of the living, and there is no Life in itself. But whereas Aristotelianism can only assert the non-distinction between Life and the living by first positing that distinction, Suhrawardī's illuminationism asserts a continuum between Life and the living by asserting the ontological priority of that continuum over the Life-living distinction. Insofar as light or illumination stands in for Aristotle's life-principle (*psukhē*), the question posed by Suhrawardī is whether one can conceive of illumination without a source, diffusion without a cause, radiation without a center—be that an absent or a negated center. If an ontology of life demands, as one of its aspects, a way of thinking of life in terms of its generosity, its generativity, and its superlative nature, then the illuminationist question is whether this superlative nature can be thought of as something like a "luminous void."[137]

Univocal Creatures

For this whole world is called new because it is not eternal and therefore is nothing.
—Eriugena

3.1 ON SPIRITUAL CREATURES

In the first part of this book, we considered the concept of life defined
in terms of time and temporality. There we found that the ontology of
"life" relied upon a notion of Life that was in pure excess of the living—
both as its source and as its ontological ground. Life was thus defined in
terms of its generosity, its flowing-forth, and its being "superlative life."
But we also saw that, within this framework, there was another anti-
tradition in which Life was defined not in terms of its affirmation but in
terms of negation. Life is in this case not that which is subservient to the
divine, but that which describes the absolute negation of the divine, its
limit to all thought, its not constituting a discrete object of thought, but
the limit of thought itself. At this limit, we arrive at a notion of Life that
is superlative precisely because its immanence implies that it is, literally,
nothing (*nihil*).

This contradiction—Life that is superlative because it is nothing—
leads us to ask how this concept of superlative life is, in a way, bound
to a concept of the living. If Life is related to the living as an ontological
ground to that which it grounds, and if Life is superlative in the sense that
we've discussed, then what does this say about the concept of the living itself? We have considered the ontology of life as structured around a certain
pulling-apart between Life and the living. Here we can approach things
from a different direction: how does the idea of superlative life condition

a certain binding-together between the Life and the living? That relation has several dimensions to it. It is, first, a relation between an ontological ground and that which it grounds; Life as that concept which is necessary in order to think the living. But it is also a causal relation, a relation in which a principle of causality structures that which can possibly exist. Life is not simply that which grounds the possibility of thinking the living as the living, but Life is also that which encompasses the production of the living. Put simply, Life is that which conditions the creation of the living. Thus, when we speak of the relation between Life and the living, we are also speaking about a process of creation that defines this relation. In Scholastic philosophy, the terms Creator, creation, and creature delineate the contours this discourse.

The term "creature" in English has several modern connotations, one of which is nearly synonymous with "animal" or even "monster." Indeed, creatures seem to be positioned somewhere between animals and monsters, the normal and the pathological, the well-formed and the de-formed. This connotation has become part of our popular vernacular: in the early twentieth century, for instance, Hollywood studios produced "creature-feature" films that featured the icons of genre horror—Dracula, Franken-stein's monster, the Wolf Man, the Creature from the Black Lagoon, and so on. The creature is, in these instances, not quite the animal, for the animal can be named, assigned a species, and analyzed as a living organism. The creature is animal-like, but also not quite an animal—perhaps something like Schopenhauer's "metaphysical animal." It is either less than an animal (e.g., the plant-creatures of *The Thing From Another World*), some hybrid of animal and human (e.g., the morphologies of *The Wolf Man* or *Cat People*), or, in some cases, the creature that actually transcends the animal (e.g., the telepathic "thought creatures" of *Fiend Without a Face*).

Such examples are worth taking seriously, for they suggest that the creature, as that which is not-quite-animal, is also that which is not-quite-spiritual. The modern avatars of these "spiritual creatures" demonstrate the ways in which horror and theology are always intimately connected with each other. Similarly, in the Scholastic era, a central concern is that of the ontological status of intermediary beings between the earthly and the divine, including angels, demons, and the more anonymous "primordial causes" of Neoplatonism. Aquinas' comments on the subject summarize many of the main questions, which, to modern eyes, appear fantastical, almost absurd: Do intermediary beings like angels have bodies, and if so, are they then subject to the effects of growth and decay? If intermediary beings do have bodies, are they transcendent bodies, above

and beyond the earthly bodies of humans and animals? Insofar as intermediary beings do have bodies, is there a distinction between angels and demons, with the latter often defined by their incarnations in and as beasts?
Do angels get hungry, eat, and defecate?

The problematic of the creature is more than a category problem, however, for it touches upon a central philosophical-theological problem for
Scholastic thinkers: once one posits the absolute distinction between the
divine and the earthly, the supernatural and the natural, Life and the living, then how does one account for the relation between them, given that
the human is, doctrinally speaking, partially divine? That is, if the human
is more-than-animal, then it is also less-than-spiritual. Hence the problem
of the *creatura* is also a problem of mediation. And some form of mediation is required to account for the fuzzy ontological status of the living
being, especially the living being that is the human being.

The concept of creation comes to play this mediating role. Its function is outlined quite early by the Church Fathers. Augustine, in a commentary on Psalm 73, states the question—"How do I know that thou art
alive, whose soul I see not?"—and immediately provides the answer—"By
the operations of the body I know thee to be living, canst thou not by
the works of creation know the Creator?"[1] This is, generally speaking, the
logic of theophany. The divine Life in itself is not knowable except by its
manifestations in the earthly incarnations of the living. It is formalized
in the many treatises on the creature in Scholasticism by Aquinas, Bonaventure, William of Auvergne, and others. From this natural philosophy
would derive the notion of the Book of Nature, and, as Bonaventure would
note, the very status of the creature would be understood as a trace (*ves-
tigium*) or "footprint" of the divine on earth.

The triad of Creator, creation, and creature has had a decisive impact
on Western philosophical and theological reflections on nature. Nested
within them is a concept of Life and the living whose relation is structured
through causality. But the central problematic is in articulating what type
of causality this is—in particular, whether the creature is created from-
without or from-within. During the highpoint of Scholasticism, this view
was far from being the only view on the topic; the debates that ensued often revolved around whether or not one could think the creature in terms
that were more immanent than transcendent, more auto-morphic than hylomorphic, more a "univocal" creature than a creature defined in terms
of analogy and representation. Before considering these debates, however,
we can spend a bit of time reviewing the role of form and causality as it
pertains to the Life-living relationship.

3.2 LIFE AS FORM IN ARISTOTLE

When the concept of life is thought of in terms of Creator, creation, and creature, life appears in a twofold guise: the life-that-is-formed and the life-that-forms. In the former sense, life is that which is formed in the various forms of life that can give us the stratifications of plant, animal, and human life.[2] In a more important sense, life is the very principle by which such forms of life take form. Here life is neither the individuated living being, nor even the larger categories (such as species) within which such beings are situated. Life in this second sense is more like the life-that-forms, the life which itself produces the various life-forms.

What is apparent, then, is that the issue of causality is at the center of the relation between Life and the living; every life-form necessitates some principle by which this particular life is formed. Note that while this principle itself is necessitated, the question of whether this principle is internal or external to the life-form is not determined. Even if the life-form is regarded as having its causality internal to itself—and thus self-causing—the necessity of a casual principle is still preserved, though modified. In short, the life-form necessitates the forming of life, and thus a mode of causality specific to life. Aristotle refers to this necessary cause as *psukhē*, or the life-principle. The life-principle is simply that by which life is formed, a life-forming principle, or, to refer to our earlier, more cumbersome phrase: as a principle of causality, *psukhē* is that-by-which-the-living-is-living. This distinction between life-forms and the life-that-forms, between the living and Life, is crucial for the way the concept of life itself is formed in the ontology of Aristotle. And, it is Aristotle who, perhaps more than any classical thinker, provides us with a systematic way of thinking about life in terms of form, causality, and a life-principle.

The *De Anima* is dedicated to explicating the concept of *psukhē* as it is manifested in various types of life, which Aristotle generally divides up in an ascending order of complexity: a nutritive *psukhē* (plants), a sensate and motile *psukhē* (animals), and a rational *psukhē* (humans). This stratification is not only hierarchical for Aristotle, but cumulative as well—the nutritive is contained within the sensate-motile, while both of these are contained in the rational. The *De Anima* thus conceptualizes a life that is at once abstract and real, a life-forming principle that is at once inseparable from the types of life-forms in which it is manifest, while not being reducible to them.

But here we must note that the concept of life appears to be threefold, for while *psukhē* is not the actual animal, it is still internally divided between *psukhē* as the life-principle in itself, and *psukhē* as manifested in different forms (plant, animal, and human types of *psukhē*). It appears that there are different types of *psukhē* that correspond to different types of life-forms, and yet Aristotle goes to great measures to ensure the coherence of a single *psukhē* in general that unites all of these. Thus we have three aspects to this relation between life and form: *psukhē* as a principle, *psukhē* as types, and the actual living creature.

Another conclusion to be drawn from Aristotle is that the first *psukhē*, *psukhē* as the life-forming principle, this *psukhē* in itself does not, strictly speaking, exist. The life-principle or *psukhē* has being only to the extent that it is qualified by bearing some formal relation to the essence of what it is to be a plant, animal, or human. Even then, the question of whether such universals as "plant" or "animal" really exist cannot be taken for granted. All we are left with, then, is the direct observation of individual entities (which we may subsequently name plants, animals, humans, or the Old Ones). What Aristotle conceptualizes as the very essence of life, *psukhē*, is itself unavailable to any sensory or empirical verification. This is, furthermore, a necessary part of the concept of *psukhē*. If it were something in itself like an object, or something available to our senses like light, then it would cease to be a life-principle or life-that-forms, and would become a life-form, and the problem of thinking life in itself would thus remain. Again, the conceptual requirement that Aristotle has set himself is that one move from *that* the living is living to *how* the living is living. On a philosophical level, any such requirement makes a contradictory demand: that one think the living by thinking beyond the living.

What, then, enables Aristotle to claim that there is something such as a life-principle or *psukhē* at all? Aristotle must make a wager (and the *De Anima* can, in a sense, be read as an extended conceptual wager on the question of life itself). This wager is the following: that there is a concept of life in which life is not reducible to the living. On the surface this may seem quite ordinary, but it has several components to it: first, it posits the key ontological distinction between Life and the living. The conceptual requirements of causality necessitate this distinction, and its necessity remains, as we've noted, even if the idea of self-causality is entertained. In addition, Aristotle makes the wager that this notion of life can be adequately thought—in other words, that life is available to thought, that life is intelligible "for us." That life can be thought is no small claim. It means that the concept of life is a concept that is specific to philosophy and not, for instance, mysticism or science. The implicit wager in the *De Anima* is that there is a logic to life such that the thought of life would become commensurate with life itself, all the while refusing mysticism or science. This is the real challenge of any ontology of life, and Aristotle is arguably the first to formulate it: how to think a concept of life that is, on the one hand, irreducible to the living, and, on the other hand, which does not immediately evoke the mystical or is compromised by the scientific? It is not difficult to see how this challenge structures much of the philosophical thinking that follows: vitalism vs. mechanism, organicism vs. materialism, nature-as-poem vs. nature-as-matheme.

But such a wager raises the problem of method—how should one go about thinking the concept of life, given that this challenge is also about thought itself? Aristotle's solution is to adopt different methods—philosophical exegesis in the *De Anima*, and classification and description in works such as the *Historia Animalium*. Here the distinction between Life and the living requires two separate methods, metaphysical speculation for the life-that-forms and empirical description for the life-forms. Aristotle says relatively little about the connection between them, though the domain of animal life-forms predominates in both kinds of works.[3]

So while Aristotle adopts different methods based on the distinction between Life and the living, or between the life-that-forms and the life-form, this separation of method leaves open the question of the relation between Life and the living, the life-that-forms and life-forms. Hence one of the central, enigmatic questions of Aristotle's ontology of life: Is the life-principle itself living? Is the life-that-forms also a life-form?

On the one hand this is precisely what Aristotelian philosophy cannot affirm, for if the life-principle is itself living, then this would necessitate a further principle by which the life-principle was living, and so on. The question of the vitality of the life-principle itself follows Aristotle's arguments for a first cause—one that is "first" not merely sequentially, but ontologically. On the other hand the treatment of *psukhē* as the life-forming principle is perplexing because it seems to sidestep the traditional Aristotelian metaphysical scenario. In the *De Anima* the life-principle *psukhē* is variously described as a primary substance, a hylomorphic process (form as active, matter as passive), as an essence particular to life, and as the very boundary between the living and nonliving. Let us suppose that the life-principle *psukhē* is not itself living. We would then have an instance in which life would be caused by non-life; life would be caused by that which is its own negation, or better, which bears no relation to it at all. But the life-principle cannot not have any relation to the living whatsoever, for the very act of causality implies some relation, and therefore something fundamentally in common. If we take the other position and

assume that the life-principle *psukhē* is identical to the living, we have no
way of distinguishing the fact *that* something is alive from *how* it is alive,
and have removed the need for a concept of life at all. At this point one
would, presumably, simply live, and not think at all . . .

  Psukhē is a strange, hybrid concept, positioned between a physics of
life-forms (the *phusis* of plant, animal, human) and a metaphysics of first
causes. Part of this confusion derives from a distinction (between Life
and the living) that methodologically becomes a division (between a life-
essence and particular animals). It is precisely this problem that comes to
occupy a central place in Scholastic thinking about the relation between
a life-principle and the various instances of the living. But, as we will see,
the methods are different. Some, such as Aquinas, prefer a more top-down
approach, by which one begins with the divine and descends to the creaturely. Others, such as Ockham, assert that there can only be a bottom-up
approach, beginning from what we know for certain to exist, which are
discrete individuals. Still others, such as Duns Scotus, employ both approaches, but in order to reach a commonality between the life-that-forms
and the life-form. Whatever their methods, Scholastic thought takes up
the wager and the challenge offered by Aristotle: the wager that there is a
distinction between Life and the living, and the challenge of how to think
a concept of life that is neither reducible to the living (let us say "biology") nor identical to mysticism and the ineffable (let us say "theology").
In modern terms, the concept of life as a philosophical concept becomes,
in Scholastic thought, poised between biology and theology . . .

  There are a few lessons that Scholasticism draws from Aristotle. The
first, recall, is that Aristotle's concept of *psukhē* or the life-principle is
itself bifurcated between *psukhē*-in-itself and *psukhē*-as-types, and both
of these are further distinguished from the actual instances of living creatures described in Aristotle's natural philosophy. We therefore have something called "life" that, while retaining its unity, is also existent in at
least three forms: in itself, in various types, and in individuals.

  Another lesson is that of these instances of life each does not exist in
the same way. For example, as an entity in itself, *psukhē* is never present
as such, but only in the various types or in individuals. Furthermore, if
psukhē is present in the various types, this would require a theory of universals to account for the types of plant, animal, and human as really, and
not ideally, existing. This leaves us with the discrete individuals, and the
question of whether such individuals, as really existing, can be thought
without recourse to either *psukhē*-in-itself or *psukhē*-as-types—the for-

mer of which does not exist, and the latter of which presumes universal existence.

The innovation of Scholastic thinking on this issue is to have brought these two lessons from Aristotle together into a single challenge: *how to think life as a relation between the life-that-forms and life-forms*, or, using our own terms, as a relation between Life and the living. Both the Aristotelian, tripartite aspect of *psukhē* (as in itself, as types, and as individuals), as well as the idea that *psukhē* in itself cannot be thought except via its manifestation—both of these notions dovetail into what will become the central concern of Scholastic thinking: the relation between Creator and creature, divine and earthly, the life-that-forms and its attendant life-forms. This is one way of understanding the emergence of the concept of the creature (*creatura*) in Scholastic philosophy—that it serves as a condensation point for thinking about the relation between the life-that-forms and life-forms.

For Scholasticism, this challenge also involves a new problem—if being for Scholastic thinkers is the proper provenance of philosophy, and if the divine is the proper provenance of theology, then this third question—that of life—opens onto a set of discourses that sit somewhere between them: natural theology, natural philosophy, theodicy, theophany. Simplifying a great deal, we can suggest that one of the central problems of Scholasticism is that Life as a concept is not necessarily different from the problem of God or Being—though it is not identical to them either.

In context, such problems did not arise without a great deal of debate and controversy. They seem rather trivial and "scholastic" by contemporary standards, but in thirteenth-century Paris or Oxford they could carry the weight of condemnation or heresy. The translation of Aristotle's works in natural philosophy in the thirteenth century opened up new ways of thinking, but they were also situated at the center of a series of philosophical, theological, and political controversies. Endless debates ensued over whether Aristotle proposed the eternity of the universe as opposed to divine creation, or whether Aristotle's *De Anima* really did deny personal immortality in his notion of the "Active Intellect." At its pinnacle such debates resulted in a series of censures by the Church. The most famous of these occurred in 1277, issued by Bishop Étienne Tempier, at the request of the pope. These condemnations of some two hundred specific articles forbade the Faculty of Arts at the University of Paris from teaching certain portions of Aristotle's works (principally the works in natural philosophy), as well as the teachings of Aristotle's Arabic commentators such as Averroës, and contemporary Christian thinkers working in the

Aristotelian tradition (including, at first, parts of Aquinas' teachings, as well as radical Latin Averroists such as Siger of Brabant). Prominent thinkers at the University of Paris, such as Henry of Ghent, served on the committee that drafted up the condemnations—and it was, in part, precisely against the position of Henry that later philosophers such as Duns Scotus outlined their positions. Later historians of philosophy would dub such positions as "pantheist," though the more dreaded label at the time would have been that of heresy.[4] And yet, as Gilles Deleuze would later note, these so-called heretical philosophies are also some of the most radical approaches to thinking the major challenge put forth in the *De Anima*: the irreducibility of the relation between Life and the living.

3.3 THE CONCEPT OF THE CREATURE

In Medieval philosophy, the concept of creation is shaped by several authoritative sources, including Platonism as filtered through early Christian thinkers such as Augustine, Boethius, and Porphyry, as well as the authority from scripture in its interpretation by the Church Fathers. As the tale is commonly told, attempts were made early on to synthesize these sources into a system of thought that would adapt Platonic philosophy to the requirements of Christian theology.[5] The Neoplatonic tradition, as developed by Philo, Proclus, and Plotinus, would set out the basic terms of creation—Creator, creation, and creature. Moreover, Neoplatonism would also stress that the concept of creation has to do with the relation between these three terms—a primary or preeminent cause, a process of divine emanation, and a series of primary effects.

The elaboration of these three terms—Creator, creation, and creature— may seem unremarkable, but the distinction of a cause, an action, and an effect is noteworthy for what it implies. First, it implies that a Creator need not be identical with the act of creation; a causal agent is not necessarily identical with a causal act. The Creator creates in an analogous way that a subject causes an effect in an object. If a Creator were simply identical with creation, there would still remain the problem of accounting for the genesis of creation itself (that is, not the act of creation but its conditions). By contrast, the Creator cannot be totally separate from the act of creation, since the Creator is in part defined by this act of creation being central to it. This distinction between Creator and creation (or causal agent and causal act) led to a number of dilemmas, apparent in the work of the Pseudo-Dionysius, and in Eriugena's *De Praedestinatione*. Does all creation necessitate a source or point of origin? If not, does creation go on for eternity, or does it stop, either by "running out" or through an act of divine will?

The distinction of Creator-creation-creature also implies that creation itself—as a process implying temporality—is not necessarily identical with creatures. The term "creation" can certainly be used as both verb and noun, denoting the (divine) act of creating creatures, as well as the product of creation ("all of creation"). But early Medieval thinkers such as Eriugena are careful to distinguish different levels of creation, and more often than not the term "creation" is used to refer to the supernatural, divine act of creation, rather than the production or making of things by creatures themselves. Eriugena, for example, distinguishes between "that which creates and is not created," which is the Creator, and "that which creates and is created," which, in a Neoplatonic vein, are the Intelligences, the intermediary spheres that create actual creatures from the first emanations of the Creator. In short, the Platonic-Patristic doctrine of form is synthesized with the Christian doctrine of divine creation. This synthesis culminates in what later Scholastic thinkers would call exemplarity: just as Platonic forms are arranged in an ascending order of perfection from the perfect Idea to the imperfect thing, so does the created world radiate from the unity of a perfect, infinite Creator to the multiplicity of dependent, finite creatures.

Creation is, however, not simply a theological affair. Even in its formulation in Patristic and early Medieval thought, creation is always held in a tension-filled zone between Creator and creature. In fact, it is this term *creatura* that often proves the most frustrating for philosopher-theologians. Thinking the Creator is, in many ways, a simple affair—either one adopts the positive way and proceeds to enumerate the attributes of the divine (e.g., God as eternal, infinite, etc.) or one adopts the negative path and then proceeds to evoke the divine through a poetics of evasion (e.g., God as that which is beyond all thought, etc.). What is often called Augustinian abstraction adopts elements of these methods through the simple method of subtraction.[6]

But thinking the creature is beset by several difficulties, one of which is its twofold nature, at once partaking of the earthly and the divine, the material and the spiritual, the natural and supernatural. One question concerns causality and the transmission of attributes between cause and effect. If the Creator is taken to be infinite, then to what degree can the creature—that which is defined by its finitude—also be said to be infinite? Does it make sense to say that the creature is quasi-infinite, or somewhat perfect, or "kind of" One? Assuming that every creature, having been created by the Creator, obtains in some measure the attributes of the Creator (that is, that each effect obtains within it some aspect of its cause), then to what degree can the creature—that which is earthly—be said to participate in or partake of the divine? Finally, if one does admit that the creature is in some sense related to the divine or to the supernatural, then what is the character of this divine-supernatural element in the living creature? Is the divine or supernatural simply a component within a part of the creature? But then this would disqualify the divine or supernatural as such, rendering them as finite, as a part in a greater whole. Or is there some third characteristic—and perhaps this is what the divine or the supernatural is—that is commonly expressed to both Creator and creature, forming a continuity between them? But then this would require a higher principle "above" both Creator and creature and thereby connecting them.

There is, then, an indeterminacy that is central to the concept of the creature in Medieval philosophy. In this "creaturely indeterminacy," the twofold nature of the creature situates it between seemingly incommensurate attributes (infinite-finite, simple-complex, unity-multiplicity). While the creature is not simply identical to the divine or supernatural, neither is it simply one thing among others (for then a rock or river or the climate would be a creature—a point to which we will return later . . .). Furthermore, there are distinctions between creatures, not only as individual entities, but within the greater schema of the natural world. What, then, makes the creature unique, being neither divine nor elemental? On one level it is the fact that the creature is created that qualifies it as a creature. But many things are created other than creatures, since creation itself only defines an action and the relation of cause and effect. The creature is unique because, while it may be argued that its essence is of supernatural origin, its existence takes place within the domain of nature. And this existence can only be described as "living."

The creature is thus not only a theological entity—a testimony to the fundamental relation between creature and Creator, and the passage between the natural and supernatural—but the creature is also, let us say, a biological entity, having its sole existence within nature and the Aristotelian temporality of growth, decay, and finitude. Already this twofold aspect is seen in Aristotle's works, between the *De Anima* and the works in natural philosophy. This twofold aspect is also seen in the numerous compendium books of the natural world.[7] Though there are examples from antiquity (e.g., Pliny's natural history books), the Medieval bestiary constitutes one of the central genres in which the theological aspects of the

Life/living distinction is demonstrated—entries in the twelfth-century Aberdeen Bestiary, for instance, range from familiar species of animals to mythological creatures such as unicorns and griffins.[8] Despite the prevalence of bestiaries and other creaturely compendiums, however, the concept of the creature is rarely raised as an explicitly ontological problem until the period of Scholastic thinking.[9]

If we consider these and other historical influences—the proliferation of books that classified creatures (bestiaries and the like), the establishment and growth of the universities, and the influx of new translations of Aristotle into those universities, it is possible to regard the twelfth and thirteenth centuries as a time ripe for thinking and rethinking the concept of life within a philosophical context. But more than this, what the debate over the creature in Scholasticism does is to take up the distinction set out by Aristotle—the life-that-forms and life-forms, Life and the living—and place it within an explicitly theological context, whereby a correlation between two terms (Life and the living) is ramified into a tripartite, or should we say, trinity of terms (Creator, creation, creature). In so doing, the Aristotelian separation between Life and the living is reframed as a relation—or, the articulation of this relation now becomes the central problematic for conceptualizing the different meanings of life.

Let us suggest, then, that what the life-forming principle (*psukhē*) is to Aristotle, the relation of creation is to Scholasticism. To the question "What is the relation between Life and the living?" Aristotle proposes a concept rooted in the principle of form—*psukhē*. But Aristotle says little about how *psukhē* is itself formed, or by what means it is able to express itself as a life-forming principle. The exhaustive cataloging of descriptions, behaviors, and habitats only serves to exacerbate the question. What is the form of form, the creation of creation—the Life of the living?

3.4 UNIVOCITY I: DUNS SCOTUS VS. AQUINAS

It is in response to this Aristotelian problematic that Scholasticism offers the intermediary concept of creation, poised between a transcendent Creator and a field of manifest creatures. The terms still betray their Aristotelian origins, but they are now connected via a continuum that presumes an existing relation, of whatever type, between Creator and creature, the life-that-forms and the life-form, Life and the living. However, as we will see, this trinity of concepts opens onto still other difficulties, the most pressing of which surrounds the concept of univocity. The question posed by Aristotle, "What is the relation between the life-that-forms and life-forms?" is now reformulated as "If something is held in common, is that something commonly held?"

The dilemma posed by the relationship between Creator and creature is best summarized by Aquinas, who provides an account in his *Summa Contra Gentiles* as well as the massive *Summa Theologica*. Let us briefly look at Aquinas' argument from the latter work, for it will set up an instructive contrast with a counterargument from Duns Scotus.

3.4.1 UNIVOCITY IN AQUINAS' *SUMMA THEOLOGICA*

In a group of questions commonly referred to as the "Treatise on the Divine Nature" (roughly, the first thirteen questions from the *Prima Pars* of the *Summa*), Aquinas considers the relation between Creator and creatures, first in terms of knowledge (question 12) and then in terms of naming (question 13).[10] The former question deals with whether we as creatures can have any natural knowledge of the Creator, apart from divine revelation. Aquinas is here picking up a long-standing debate in the so-called divine names tradition: seeing how creatures are defined by their finitude and the Creator by its infinitude, how can any adequate statement concerning the latter be made by the former, without implying their identity? That is, to what extent does a natural knowledge of the Creator or the supernatural render it as creaturely or natural? As we saw in the previous chapter, the mystical tradition inherited from the Pseudo-Dionysius takes the negative path, asserting that we as creatures can only make negative claims about the Creator. Inasmuch as there is a positive path, all knowledge of the Creator or the supernatural is made possible by super-sensible, divine revelation. Thus, it appears that, while the creature is of the Creator, it cannot know the Creator; the effect cannot adequately reflect back upon the cause, even though it is of the cause.

Aquinas' reply is a compromise, one that proceeds in stages.[11] Here he makes use of a distinction previously made by Avicenna—that between essence and existence, or the distinction between "what" some thing is and "that" some thing is. Inasmuch as our natural knowledge begins from the senses, we as creatures can obtain a knowledge of the divine in "that" it exists. One primary way in which this is done is through a bottom-up approach, beginning from creatures and working towards the Creator. One can begin from the attributes of creatures—as finite, as temporal, and so on, and then, regarding these as imperfections of more perfect attributes, proceed to thinking a higher being that would condition these attributes of creatures, a being that would be infinite, eternal, and so on. If the creature is X-minus-something, then the Creator would simply be X. Still, any wholly positive, natural knowledge of the divine essence in itself is not possible, or is possible only to a privative degree, as a knowledge of something in excess of the knower.[12] What kind of a knowledge, then, is this knowledge of the divine existence, excluding as it does any knowledge of the essence of the divine?

Aquinas' answer comes by way of a focus on the name. In both a theological and philosophical sense, to name is to know. Hence we can rephrase the question: if naming implies knowledge, what kind of knowledge is obtained for the creature in the naming of the Creator? Let us suppose that the names of the Creator, or the act of naming the divine or supernatural, is not a simple affair: there is some distance and difference between names and things; that any name does not necessarily capture the essence of the thing named; that names are often not literal but metaphorical or allegorical; and that the divine, as naturally unknowable, may have more than one name.[13] This brings Aquinas to the question posed in the fifth article: "Whether what is said of God and of Creatures is univocally predicated of them." Following the pattern of much of the *Summa*, Aquinas offers three objections, a general answer, and then three replies to the objections.

To begin with, Aquinas notes that there seem to be two basic positions on the relation between Creator and creatures—univocity and equivocity. A univocal relation between any two terms would presuppose something in common to both terms, while an equivocal relation between any two terms would posit an absolute difference between those terms. Sometimes terms are used equivocally—as when "cat" is used to denote a meowing cat and a catfish. Here the term is used in two unrelated senses (e.g., the knowledge of a meowing cat will not help one domesticate a fish). One term is, in a way, just as significant as the other; their absolute non-relation implies their autonomous equivalence. In other instances a term may be used univocally, as when "cat" refers to all animals of a particular species—each of them, in spite of individual differences of coloration, amount of hair left on furniture, or air of superiority, contains something in common that enables them to be classified as cats. Any two terms related in this way imply an essential continuity between them, and therefore, an essential identity. Let us say that univocal terms posit a continuity of relation between terms—they posit *all relation*. By contrast, let us say that equivocal terms posit a discontinuity between terms—they posit *no relation*.

But here we already run into difficulties. The problem with equivocal terms that bear no relation to each other ("cat" and "catfish") is that one could argue that their very *unrelatedness* constitutes a minimal relation—that is, they are being unrelated within a particular context, be it in another, third term (the category "animals") or even a topic of discussion (an essay on equivocity). Thus "all equivocal terms resolve into univocal terms." But the problem with univocity for Aquinas is that it does not distinguish between different types of likeness. For example, there can be a likeness of identity, in which one thing is exactly like another; or likeness by degree, in which one thing is more or less of a certain quality of another; or generic likeness, in which two members of a set vary in the particulars of their characteristics. All of these, Aquinas notes, are different from the likeness that follows from a causal relationship:

> It is impossible that anything be predicated of God and creatures univocally. For every effect that does not match the power of the agent cause receives from the agent a likeness that is not of the same nature; rather, it receives it in a lesser way, with the result that what exists in the cause simply and in the same way exists in the effects in a divided and multiple way.[14]

This is what Aquinas will refer to as analogy. The analogical relation between Creator and creature is predicated on their causal relationship as the foundation for their likeness. This is clearly not a likeness of equal terms, but a likeness of cause and effect. What, then, is the form of this analogical likeness? Aquinas shifts his view on this question. His early writings describe analogy in terms of what he calls "proportionality." The analogy of proportionality has the form of "what *A* is to *B*, *C* is to *D*." Thus what finitude is to creatures, the infinite is to God, and so on. However, when Aquinas writes the *Summa*, he seems to prefer another type of analogy, the analogy of "proportion." This is any term *A* which has different meanings depending on its uses *A′*, *A″*, and so on. Aquinas provides an example from medicine, which itself has two aspects to it:

> It therefore must be said that names of this kind are said of God and creatures according to analogy, that is, according to proportion. This can happen with names in two different ways: either when many have a proportion to one, as health is said of medicine and urine insofar as they both have an order and proportion to the health of the animal, one being the sign of health and the other being its cause; or when one has a proportion to another, as health is said of medicine and an animal insofar as medicine is the cause of health in the animal. It is in this

latter way that something is said of God and creature analogically, and not by pure equivocation or univocally.[15]

Causality—especially Aristotelian efficient and final causality—is central to the doctrine of analogy, be it of proportion or proportionality. For Aquinas, both the positions of univocity and equivocity go too far, one implying an absolute identity between Creator and creature, the other implying an absolute difference between them. The doctrine of analogy attempts to preserve certain elements of both univocity and equivocity, while avoiding the implications each of the other positions entails. Equivocity is, at a basic level, untenable. There must be some relation between Creator and creature, or else no natural knowledge would be possible at all. But that relation, as necessary as it is, cannot be univocal, because such a position is unable to account for the causal hierarchy between Creator and creature (that is, between the life-that-forms and life-forms, an ontologically first cause and all secondary causes). Analogy works in between univocity and equivocity, positing a partial relation, a differential likeness. Perhaps we can abbreviate, and suggest that between the position of "no relation" (equivocity) and "all relation" (univocity), Aquinas puts forth the position of *some relation* (analogy).

In this way, the doctrine of analogy serves as a solution to a particular problem: the relation between Creator and creature. A relation must necessarily be posited, which must contain within itself a fundamental separation or non-relation, if that relation is to be thought at all. Now, this is, to some extent, a feature of relation itself, since the relation of any two terms A and B presupposes their non-identity (even if A is formally related to itself as A' and A'', or as two attributes of a single substance). But Aquinas, like other Scholastics, is not concerned with the relation of any two entities; the issue is the relation that in some way constitutes life itself. What is specific to the concept of the creature is, as we've noted, its twofold nature, at once earthly and divine, material and spiritual, and so on. And what is specific to the concept of the Creator in relation to the creature is the process whereby the creature is created, the "soul" (*psukhē*) is ensouled, and Life is made living. This not only raises the question as to whether the Creator-creature relation is itself living, but it also opens onto the potentially hazardous terrain of suggesting that Life is living, or that the Creator is creaturely—that God is a beast.

Aquinas, following the tradition of the Pseudo-Dionysius, suggests that if God is living, it would have to be in a wholly different sense from the life of creation or creatures themselves. Following the doctrine of analogy, we can at most say that "life" describes the Creator and the creature in an analogical sense—in the same way that "health" is ascribed both to the practice of medicine and the digestion of an animal (in Aquinas' example), so would "life" be ascribed to Creator and creature. The Creator, as a kind of super-life or superlative life, would be a negatively determined life—life without temporal or spatial finitude, without the necessities of growth and decay, and so on.

There are, however, a few complications. The principle of causality plays a central role in Thomistic analogy, and this is due as much to the Aristotelian framework that he appropriates as it is to the doctrinal requirements that condition this synthesis of Aristotle and Christian theology. Not all relations are equal, and in the doctrine of analogy there is greater emphasis placed on the role of causality in the relation between Life and the living, Creator and creature.[16] This emphasis on relation in turn leads to reflection on the relation of the relation, the life of the Life-living relation itself, as it were. The challenge becomes how to demonstrate a continuity of relation between Creator and creature while not implying either their real or formal identity.

For many Scholastic thinkers, the position of analogy was the common, and even dominant, mode of addressing the relation between Creator and creature. Its general contours had already been suggested by William of Auvergne, Albert the Great, and Bonaventure, before Aquinas had formalized it in the *Summa*. As a compromise, the doctrine of analogy attempts to resolve the potential gulf that could exist between Creator and creature if one accepted either of the positions of equivocity ("no relation") or univocity ("all relation"). At one end of the spectrum, one would have to accept absolute agnosticism and forgo any adequate knowledge of either the natural or supernatural; at the other end, one would have to accept pure pantheism, and conceive of divine and earthly, supernatural and natural, as effectively flattened into a single form that would disallow any differentiation between Creator and creature. As Aquinas notes, analogy is situated at the midpoint between equivocity and univocity, and it is from this vantage point that both Creator and creature can be said to be "living" in a related but fundamentally different way.

As Aquinas himself notes in the "objections" to his reply, this approach itself runs into several problems. In the attempt to simultaneously bring together and keep separate, Aquinas' common analogical term must itself become diversified. This requires that the concept of analogy—which must at once bring together and hold apart—be rendered as internally split. As Aquinas notes, there are two kinds of relation, that between one creature and another, and that between Creator and creature. While we may use terms univocally between one creature and another (e.g., to talk about two animals being "living" or two Shoggoths being "living"), such terms cannot be used univocally when thinking about the relation between Creator and creature (e.g., to suggest that both a person and God are "living" in the same way). We can reframe the question again: there is the relation between the living (between one living creature and another) and then there is the relation between Life and the living (between the principle-of-life and the life-forms that flow from it). Aquinas is not the first to make this distinction, but he does assert its centrality in the argument for analogical thinking.

Therefore, a single term X can be used relationally between two terms A and B, insofar as both are presumed to already exist univocally (e.g., an animal and plant both related univocally as "living"). This single term X can also be used, not just between two terms A and B, but in two qualitatively different kinds of relations α and β (where α is the relation between Creator and creature, and β is the relation between creature and creature). There can be no confusion, according to Aquinas, between these two kinds of relations—one is based on a horizontal comparison between like entities, while the other is based on a vertical, causal relationship. Hence, one problem that arises in Thomistic analogy is, if it is necessary to distinguish types of relations (the relation between A and B and the relation between α and β), what is to keep us from simply using two different terms or referring to two different natures? For if we persist in using a common term, even if used analogically ("in some ways the same, in some ways not"), then, given that there are different kinds of relations, we are led to consider *the relations between relations* as themselves being either equivocal, univocal, or analogical. This process can go on forever, with Aquinas' game of compromise jumping ahead at each step. In sum, Aquinas utilizes analogy—and in particular, the analogy of proportion—as a way of smoothing over what would seem to be the progressive unraveling of a common term or common nature into disparate natures.

3.4.2 UNIVOCITY IN DUNS SCOTUS' *OPUS OXONIENSE*

We can state the problematic of Thomistic analogy in a different way: given that there are relations and relations of relations, what is it that prevents the total separation of terms related, even when, in the case of the Creator/creature relation, they are deemed to be fundamentally different from each other? This is the question posed by Duns Scotus. While he does not frequently target Aquinas by name, it is against the dominant Thomistic position of analogy that his concepts are directed. Aquinas' argument is that univocity stops short because it provides no way of differentiating between entities or between types of relations. Duns Scotus, by contrast, argues that univocity "never stops" and that the real philosophical challenge is in accounting for the persistence of univocity, despite the most radical assertions of differentiation.

Scotus provided a number of arguments for univocity, and it appears to be one of the most consistent concepts in his thinking.[17] Scotus' arguments for univocity are all the more remarkable given their historical context. His entry into the University at Oxford is dated in the late 1280s or early 1290s—following upon the Condemnations of 1277, which were to have a decisive impact at both Oxford and Paris. One of the burning issues raised by the Condemnations had to do with Aristotelian natural philosophy and its implication for a concept of a univocal, divine being. Several articles attributed to Aquinas were, for a time, included in the Condemnations, before being withdrawn and absorbed into an acceptable Church doctrine. Other thinkers, such as Siger of Brabant, were immediately accused of heresy, and a cluster of such thinkers were even pejoratively tagged as Latin Averroists. Scotus, however, remained a troubling figure within this intellectual climate, for his positions seem to rail against nearly all the existing schools of thought, from Neoplatonic Augustinianism to mystical theology to the high Scholasticism of Aquinas and the new Aristotelians. And yet Scotus always stops just short of a fully-fledged pantheism or a fully immanent materialism.

By the time Scotus began to prepare his lectures at Oxford in or around 1300, the Aristotelianism of Aquinas had slowly come to gain ground over the less "scientific" approaches of the neo-Augustinianism that followed on the coattails of the 1277 censures. The split between reason and revelation, philosophy and theology, could itself come under cautious questioning. No longer was reason confined to gaining knowledge about nature, with revelation the proper domain of supernature. One could inquire as to whether any natural knowledge of the supernatural was possible, as did a number of Scholastic thinkers from across the theological spectrum— Aquinas, who incorporated the newly available natural philosophy of Aristotle; Henry of Ghent, who served on the council that condemned Aquinas' teachings; and Duns Scotus, who directly attacked Henry of Ghent, and indirectly attacked Aquinas. We will have more to say about this intriguing triangle of relations later; for the moment we can consider one of

Scotus' major arguments for univocity against the argument for analogy provided by Aquinas.

The lectures Scotus gave at Oxford were framed as commentaries on what was the major textbook of the period, Peter Lombard's *Sententiae* (*Sentences*). The *Sentences* formed a model for philosophical and theological discourse, posing key questions, providing summaries of existing arguments, and offering counterarguments and resolutions. Because they were given while he was at Oxford, Scotus' lectures have come to be known as the *Opus Oxoniense* (the "Oxford work"), or alternately, as the *Ordinatio* (denoting lecture notes later reedited by the author).[18] The *Ordinatio* is, like many such texts, a massive and comprehensive work that spans theology, philosophy, ethics, Church doctrine, and the study of nature. For our purposes, we can select one particular question that deals with the issue of the creature, and which serves as an instructive counterpoint to the argument of Aquinas given previously. It comes as the third question, in the second distinction, in the first book of the *Ordinatio*. As per the tradition of the time, it follows a systematic approach whereby a question is posed, existing positions "pro" and "contra" given, before Scotus provides his own argument, which is then followed by replies to the positions given at the opening.

Scotus' opening question has to do with the simplicity of God: ". . . whether there is but one God." In order to grasp this as a philosophical question, we can understand Scotus' concept of God, as with many Scholastics, as a decisively non-anthropomorphic concept, pertaining less to a personal God granting salvation or doling out punishment than to the question of the divine nature or the supernatural in itself. With some caution, let us rephrase Scotus' question: is the Creator (as opposed to the creature), or Life (as opposed to the living) itself "One" or "many," unity or plurality, simple or complex? In the context of Scotus' *Ordinatio*, this question follows upon the question of proofs for the existence of God, but it also comes before consideration of the nature of creatures in themselves. Scotus gives the arguments for there being many gods, making use of both biblical and early Medieval sources. In the process, it becomes apparent that Scotus' original question is itself actually several questions. There is, first, the question of number—is there one God or many gods? Then there is the question of essence—supposing there is just one God, is the nature of God itself unified or plural? Finally, there is the question concerning God as known by and through creatures (and here Scotus makes many references to Aristotle)—supposing a single, unified essence for God, does this unified essence imply God's univocity with respect to creatures?

These form the three major questions that Scotus addresses in the posing of the opening question.[19]

The main body of the question proceeds speculatively. Let us suppose that the divine is in every way simple (there is but one God, with a unified essence, bearing some essential relationship to creatures). Given this, can this divine simplicity, this supernatural Oneness, be shown naturally, or is such a demonstration dependent on revelation through faith? This is Aquinas' question, rephrased—given the simplicity of the divine, is there a natural knowledge of this simplicity? Scotus' strategy in his arguments is the following: he begins from the position he *does not* hold—which is that the divine is not simple but complex, not One but many. He then shows how such a thought must in turn be correlated to the traditional concept of the divine as superlative in every way. When this shores up its own limitations, Scotus then shows how every thought of the divine requires a univocal concept in order that the divine can be thought at all (that is, "naturally").

This concept of univocity is central to Scotus' metaphysics and his natural theology. In the *Ordinatio*, Scotus provides a definition of what he means by univocity: "I designate that concept univocal which possesses sufficient unity in itself, so that to affirm and deny it of one and the same thing would be a contradiction. It also has sufficient unity to serve as the middle term of a syllogism."[20] We will return to this definition below, when we consider Scotus' debate with Henry of Ghent. For the time being, we can note that Scotus uses the term "univocity" in a specific way contra Aquinas. Whereas Aquinas stresses the way that univocity effaces all distinctions, Scotus will emphasize the way that univocity allows for a formal continuity between terms without simply effacing them altogether. In the third question of the *Ordinatio* that we are considering, Scotus attempts to show, as an implicit reply to Aquinas, how this univocal concept does not simply homogenize all creation, but that an internal differentiation is a central component of the concept of univocity. Scotus thus provides a means of articulating difference in conjunction with univocity, through a concept known as the "formal objective distinction."

Let us briefly consider Scotus' proofs for the univocity of the divine. In the main body of his reply, he provides seven proofs against the notion that the univocity of the divine can be known only through divine revelation, and not through natural knowledge. The first proof is from the "infinite intellect," and is roughly as follows: suppose there were two divine beings, or two infinitely perfect beings A and B. Being infinitely perfect, each would have an infinitely perfect thought of the other; that is, A's knowledge and intuition of B would not be incomplete or partial, and vice-versa. But already, the very presupposition of there being two separate, infinitely perfect beings implies a minimal, irrevocable difference between them, and thus A can never perfectly think B, simply because B is not A. Here Scotus proposes a possible solution, though one that is almost immediately brushed aside:

> But suppose we say that A through its own essence knows B because of the great similarity between the two, so that A knows B through some nature common [*in ratione speciei communis*] to A and B. To the contrary: This answer saves neither of these two points: viz. (1) that A knows B most perfectly, and therefore, (2) that A is God. For any such knowledge that is merely general and in virtue of some likeness is neither perfect nor intuitive. Consequently, A would not know B intuitively or most perfectly, which is what we set out to prove.[21]

On the surface, Scotus' argument is that there cannot be more than one God, if God is defined in superlative terms as infinite, most perfect, and so on. The very existence of two such divinities would be a logical impossibility, since their very difference with respect to each other would negate their attributes of being infinite, most perfect, and so on. This is even the case, Scotus points out, if we say that these two divinities are related through analogy, likeness, or similitude, for this only ramifies the problem. The relation itself—call this X—would have to be conceived of as higher than or preeminent in relation to either A or B. A and B can't simultaneously be divine (infinite, perfect, etc.) and yet subordinate to, and dependent upon, a higher principle, which is their relation X. Thus it would not be possible to say that either A or B were infinite, perfect, and so on.

The only conclusion, Scotus implies, is that A and B are in fact identical and univocal. Or, to be more particular, the only philosophically viable conclusion is that A and B obtain their relation by way of a nature that is common to both of them; their relation is in this way univocal. Scotus' reasoning here is tricky, for, while he dispenses with the idea of there being more than one God, his argument does not necessarily dispense with the idea behind the argument itself. That idea is of a third term X common to both terms in the relation between A and B. Let us call this, following Scotist terminology, the *common nature*.

3.4.3 THE COMMON NATURE OF THE CREATURE

The common nature is utilized by Scotus in nearly all of the other six proofs that follow from the first. The second and third proofs, from "infinite will" and "infinite goodness," respectively, replicate the same argument in terms of a hypothetical relation between two infinitely perfect entities A and B. In the first proof ("infinite intellect") the relation was predicated on the knowledge of B by A and vice-versa. In the second proof the relation is based on divine love, and in the third, on divine goodness. Both involve a relation based on the diffusion of A into or out towards B, and vice-versa. Without a univocal concept, each term, as infinite and perfect, ends up canceling out the other term (diffusing out as infinite love or seeking out as infinite goodness). In all cases, the relation requires something common between the two terms without which they cannot coexist in a non-contradictory manner.

Univocity is also argued by Scotus in the fourth proof (from "infinite power"), where it is linked to the concept of causality. Here Scotus argues against there being two "total causes" of a single effect. As divine entities, both A and B cannot simultaneously be First Causes without leading to the contradictory conclusion of an effect that is both existent and nonexistent (existent with respect to A and non-existent with respect to B, but caused by both). The idea of a total cause bears upon the relation between Creator and creature; it suggests that a single, univocal Creator or principle-of-Life courses through the multiple instances of creatures or the living.

In the almost aphoristic fifth proof, Scotus makes an argument for univocity based on the idea of absolute infinity, or "that which cannot be excelled." Here he positions himself diametrically against the Augustinian tradition, which had been gaining some momentum following the Condemnations of the 1270s. Citing Augustine's work on the Trinity, where a perfection is deemed "more perfect" if it is present in several, numerically distinct things, Scotus argues for "absolute perfection," which exists outside of number: "what is absolutely infinite cannot be found in several numerically different things."[22] Scotus is taking up the concept of infinity as it was understood by the Scholastics: first, in a theological sense (as boundless, endless, super-eminent), but also in a logico-mathematical sense (as fully actual, as more than the numerical or the countable). God, as first being, is often taken to be infinite in a theological sense, but this is also qualified by a logical sense, for if "infinite" means that which is incomplete or sequentially infinite in time, then God cannot be infinite.

Scotus nuances his comment on absolute infinity later on in the reply, distinguishing between two uses of number—number as numerical and number as ontological. The former involves countable, individuated, created beings—"four creatures." The latter use, however, is less countable and more a number that grounds thought, the number as a kind of ontological grounding, as in "God is One" (or "I am Legion"). Scotus' proposal here is that if we are to think the divine as infinite, then the divine must be thought of as "one"; but this is not a countable "one" but a oneness that Scotus elsewhere describes as "less-than numerical"—the oneness involved in univocity. Univocity then, is not countable, but, for Scotus, still thinkable as "one."

Up until this point, Scotus' proofs for univocity have dealt mostly with stressing the continuity implied in univocal being—that is, the way in which univocity emphasizes the oneness of the divine in the earthly, or the Creator in relation to creation. The first five proofs highlight the continuity of the divine univocity through the concept of infinity, such that its various forms—intellect/knowledge, will/love, goodness/generosity, and power/causality—culminate in the notion of the infinite in itself, or absolute infinity (a "less than numerical" unity). In the final two proofs (from "necessary being" and from "omnipotence"), Scotus shifts emphasis from the continuity of univocity to its discontinuity, or its intrinsic differentiation. It is hard not to read these proofs as direct replies to Aquinas, in which the relation between Creator and creation is above all an analogical relation. As we saw, Aquinas proposed analogy as the middle ground, or compromise, between the poles of univocity ("all relation") and equivocity ("no relation"). The principal problem outlined by Aquinas was that the approach of univocity left little room for differentiating between the strata of creation, and the transcendent hierarchy between Creator and creature. Scotus does not explicitly deny the causal relation between Creator and creature, and neither does he deny the relation of transcendence between divine and earthly. He does, however, take up the position of univocity as the only viable philosophical position if the relations between Creator and creature, Life and the living, are to be thought at all.

How does Scotus balance the position of univocity against the Thomist critique that it allows no room for internal differentiation? The sixth proof provides an argument for a principle of internal differentiation that is famously known as the "formal distinction." Scotus presents it in two guises. The first is by way of an argument for a distinction in any thing between its common nature (that which makes it a certain type of thing it is) and its individuating principle (that which makes it this particular thing). Scotus suggests that, while the univocity of the common nature cuts across individual instances of that nature, it is not determined with respect to those individuated instances:

> One thing of a given kind is not related to others of its kind in such a way that it is limited to just this plurality or to a certain number of such things. There is nothing in the nature itself which requires that there be just so many individuals, nor in a cause that says there must be only so many things caused . . . Therefore, deity as such is not determined to any certain number of individuals nor can it be so determined by anything other than itself, for this would be repugnant to what is truly first. Therefore, deity exists in an infinite number of individuals.[23]

Put simply, in the concept of univocity, the common nature that cuts across individual things is not itself determined by any one individual thing. The common nature is not totally separate from the creature, for it is the very relationality that defines the creature as finite, incomplete, and capable of being related; the common nature is, in a sense, the connective tissue of creaturely life. But at the same time the common nature is neither reducible to nor determined by the individual, created creature. As a principle of generosity and generativity, it is not exhausted in the creation of so many or a certain number of creatures. The common nature is "in" each individual creature, but it is also not identical with it, since its nature is to relate, to point outwards, to render the interior exterior. Scotus caps off his statement concerning the common nature with a striking turn of phrase: "This argument, as we see, is based upon the notion that primacy of itself is indetermined (*primitas est de se indeterminata*)." The creature, then, harbors both a real, numerical existence (it is an individuated, countable thing) as well as a less-than-numerical, formal existence (it is related to other creatures, to the world, and to the Creator through a principle of univocity that produces such relations). We might say that, for Scotus, the univocity inherent in the creature means that the creature obtains a *creaturely indeterminacy*.

This indetermination is further formalized in the second variant of the argument Scotus gives. Let us suppose that there are several entities whose existence is necessary—that is, there is some component of each that, if taken away, would annul not only the existence but the very essence of that entity. Let us call those necessary components *A* and *B* and so forth. And, for the sake of simplicity, let us take these as akin to the abstract attributes of classificatory schemes, so that *A* and *B* etc. are like species characteristics. We can refer to this as α. But, as we know, any two entities can be put in relation to each other based on something held in common that is not itself in the species characteristics A and B of each entity. We can refer to this as β. Note that in both cases of α and β, individuated entities are set in relation to each other, but in different ways: in α by way of similarities or differences in species characteristics, and in β by a context, event, or situation that involves them in some way. Now, one of the questions Scotus poses is whether any entity is ultimately defined by both α and β, or indeed if β must always follow the primacy of α in determining the nature of the entity in question.

Scotus argues that an entity's nature cannot be determined by both α and β, because this would mean that, for example, α could be removed and the entity would still exist by virtue of β, and vice-versa. The entity's nature would be divided and contradictory; an entity would rely for its necessity on something that could be removed, and thus unnecessary:

> If several necessary beings existed, they would be distinguished from one another by some real perfections. Let us call these A and B. Then I argue, either these two necessary beings which differ by A and B are necessary formally in virtue of A and B, or they are not . . . If, however, these two beings are formally necessary in virtue of A and B, in addition to being necessary by reason of what they have in common, then each being contains two reasons why it is formally necessary. This, however, is impossible for neither of these two reasons includes the other, and hence if either of the two were absent, the being would still exist necessarily in virtue of what remains. In such an impossible situation, something would owe its formal necessity to what could be removed and still leave the being a necessary being.[24]

Scotus' logic may seem excessively . . . scholastic, but it is important to keep his overarching concern in mind: the question of whether the fundamental relationship between creatures is a univocal or analogical one. The only solution, for Scotus, is that there must be a single univocal way in which an entity is related to its principle, a creature to a Creator, and the living to Life. This univocity cannot be so constrained that it pertains only to certain entities, for then one would still have to account for the very ability to think entities and their relations at all. But univocity also cannot itself be an entity among other entities, since for Scotus it is less that which is related and the capacity for relation itself. Univocity must be at once integral to the existence of the creature and yet not reducible to it;

it must form a fundamental part of the creature and yet run through it, cut across it. Scotus thus qualifies his terms by saying "formally necessary" (*formaliter necesse*) or "formal reason" (*ratio formalis*) as a way of simultaneously designating the way in which univocity is an integral part of the creature and yet not a thing in itself.

We can pause for a moment and outline Scotus' logic in the fifth proof, taking a few liberties with the form of the argument, and our choice of examples:

- Cthulhu and Shoggoths are both supernatural creatures that really exist. (They are thus both "weird.")
- Cthulhu and Shoggoths, as supernatural or weird creatures, are distinguished from each other in several ways:
  - *A*: Cthulhu is many-tentacled, while Shoggoths are without tentacles.
  - *B*: Cthulhu has binocular vision, while Shoggoths are many-eyed.
- Either Cthulhu and Shoggoths are formally necessary by virtue of *A* and *B* or they are not.
  - If they are not, then *A* is not a formal reason for the necessary existence of Cthulhu and Shoggoths, and the same follows for *B*.
    - Thus, whatever contains *A* and *B* is not necessary by virtue of the presence of *A* and *B*, because *A* and *B* are not the essence of Cthulhu and Shoggoths, and neither are they an essence in themselves.
  - If they are, then Cthulhu and Shoggoths are formally necessary creatures for two reasons: (i) by virtue of *A* and *B*, and (ii) by virtue of their common nature.
    - *A* and *B*, insofar as they are principles of distinction that presuppose a relation between Cthulhu and Shoggoths, are not identical to the common nature.
    - The common nature between Cthulhu and Shoggoths would not be an additive commonality (*A* plus *B*), but something like "supernatural creatures" or "weird creatures," within which *A* and *B* can become operative as distinctions.
- However there cannot be two separate reasons for the necessary being of Cthulhu and Shoggoths, since the necessary being is, by definition, the being that is dependent for its existence on a single reason or principle.

- Insofar as Cthulhu and Shoggoths have a common nature, this is a principle-of-life. Cthulhu and Shoggoths are distinguished from each other by A and B. The common nature says nothing about A and B as necessarily existing, and A and B as abstract properties say nothing about the common nature in itself.
- If Cthulhu and Shoggoths were necessary beings by virtue of both the common nature and A and B, then one of these could be removed and they would still necessarily exist by virtue of what remains (e.g., the common nature could be removed and Cthulhu and Shoggoths would still exist by virtue of A and B, and vice-versa if A and B are removed). Thus, in either case, Cthulhu and Shoggoths would necessarily exist by what could be removed from it as unnecessary. Hence the contradiction.
- For there to be creaturely life, and for this creaturely life to be thought as such, its being must necessarily be univocal. Even in the extreme case, in which the common nature is "many" or "multiple," the common must resort to the univocal.

Scotus' notion of univocity is here presented as actually having three layers to it. There is, at the level of the creature, the individuating principle or "thisness" (*haecceitas*) of the creature. Then there is the common nature, which enables any two creatures to be related as similar or as different. But here the common nature must itself be distinguished, between the common nature as a species, category, or set (the common nature "animal" enables two creatures to be related or differentiated), and the common nature as the univocity of all common natures. For even at the level of categories, one must still rise up a level, at which point one common nature is related to another (the common nature "plant" related to "animal" not as individuals but as categories). At some point one will either have to accept that there are many common natures, or that there is some principle that makes common natures possible, but that is not simply one of them. This is what univocity is for Scotus—the nature of all common natures. And this is why Scotus opts for the basic distinction between the common nature and the individuating thisness in a creature. Univocity is what enables them to irreducibly coexist and yet remain distinct.

The question is not whether one can really separate or render autonomous the common nature in itself, and neither is it simply that "all is one." Presaging later debates between empiricism and idealism, Scotus argues for a formal distinction of entities that is neither simply "in your

head" nor really "out there" in the world.[25] The formal distinction articulates something that really exists, but that is not unproblematically accessible via the senses. In other words, within the creature, the common
nature (that which cuts across, that which is held in common) is related to
its individuating thisness (that which makes it this particular instance of
some nature) in a univocal manner. The common nature and the individuating thisness are *formally distinct and yet really identical.*

At its core, many of Scotus' arguments for univocity are based on the necessity of a third term. The argument is that any relation between any two
terms A and B presupposes a third term, X, that enables the relation to
exist at all. That is, any two terms must have something in common—a
common nature—that enables the relation to take place. The existence of
a common nature raises a number of questions. The most obvious one is
whether the common nature has a real existence, or whether it is simply
the result of a cognitive selection (it is not difficult to see how the question
of univocity overlaps with that of natural philosophy and the classification
of nature). But further questions arise. Is the common nature something
in itself, with an independent existence, or does it exist latently within
each of the entities A and B that it relates? Supposing that it is something
in itself, does it preexist the relation of A and B, or is it in effect produced
by that relation?

But this argument deals exclusively with the supernatural domain,
and only concerns the relationship between two hypothetically existing
divinities. That is, it pertains to the question of whether there can be two
Creators or two forms of Life. What is its relation to creatures and the living? In one sense, the argument doesn't really hold when applied to the
natural domain of the creature. For any two creatures a and b can and
are often related via a higher third term x, be it in terms of the classifi-
cations of species or the hierarchies of the Great Chain of Being. What
makes this possible is the finitude, incompleteness, and indeterminacy of
the creature—in other words, its very propensity for being related. The insight of Scotus' arguments for univocity is that the finitude of the creature
is fundamentally connected to its capacity for generating relations. And it
is this concept of relation that is itself unrelated—that is, while the relation x between creatures a and b can itself be related to another relation
y between creatures d and e, we must also recognize that, strangely, the
relation itself bears no relation. The fundamental propensity for relation
in creatures ultimately leads to a concept of relation itself under the guise

of the "common nature." Such a concept, Scotus argues, cannot but be a univocal concept.

In a sense the question Scotus poses is whether the concept of univocity—of one "voice" (*voce*) immanent to all creation—can be thought at all . . . and, if it can, to what degree this thought *is* univocity itself. This latter is not a question posed by Scotus, at least not directly. But it is, in a way, the question that runs throughout Scholastic discourse on the creature, in the clash of cultures between Aristotelian natural philosophy, Arabic commentaries, and the varying Scholastic factions, from neo-Augustinians to Latin Averroists, all of whom debated the status of the *creatura*.

By way of summary, we can highlight three main attributes from Scotus' arguments for univocity. The first is the idea of the "common nature," the third term that enables a relation between any two terms to take place. As we saw, the nature of the common nature itself opened onto other questions, such as whether the common nature was a thing in itself or reliant on the terms of the relation. Univocity implies a common nature simply by virtue of the propensity for relation that exists in and between creatures, a key aspect of Scotus' natural philosophy. But the sort of unity that is univocity is not simply a numerical one (and arguably, not simply a "monotheistic" one); univocity requires a kind of numerical unity that is logical but not simply countable, a "less than numerical" unity by which the univocity of the Creator or of Life is commensurate with creatures and the living. This less-than-numerical notion of number is the second attribute of Scotus' concept of univocity. But even this less-than-numerical attribute, this near non-distinction between Creator and creature, Life and the living, must address the main question posed earlier by Aquinas: if the relation between Creator and creatures is indeed univocal, then what guarantees their differentiation? This is where Scotus offers the "formal distinction," the third attribute of univocity. The formal distinction suggests that there may exist a distinction between aspects of an entity that are in reality unified. For instance, in a creature, the common nature may be univocal, but also distinguished from the principle of individuation, the "thisness" (*haecceitas*) of the individual creature that makes it *this* creature.

3.5 UNIVOCITY II: DUNS SCOTUS VS. HENRY OF GHENT

Scotus' proofs are certainly not without their own weaknesses, but his assertion of univocity has a decisive impact on the Scholastic debate on the creature.[26] If the Creator-creature relation is univocal, then the divine is distributed in a radical way that is inseparable—but distinct—from the earthly. This alone would prove that it can be thought, since thought itself would be in some sense caused or expressed by this univocity. But the very act of thinking the divine also presupposes a certain distance from it, so that it can become an object of knowledge and a subject for thought. Scotus is working in a pre-Cartesian universe, to be sure, but the Scholastic logic of propositions requires a minimal distance between thought and that which is thought. The thing that guarantees that univocity can be thought—the relation of univocity, even if a partial one, between Creator and creature—this must be forgone in order to think univocity as a concept. Given this tension of continuity and discontinuity, it is not hard to see why earlier Medieval thinkers such as Anselm took this to mean that the thought of the divine was impossible, leading to an impasse that itself signaled the existence of the divine.

The question of whether there can be natural knowledge of the univocity of the divine is, on one level, a question about the knowledge of the divine in itself, whether this is possible, or whether reason and revelation must forever remain separated. But on another level, Scotus is not just asking whether there can be a thought of the divine, but he is also saying something about the nature of the relationship between the divine and the earthly, the supernatural and the natural, Creator and creature. Beyond the Scholastic dispute over whether there is a (reasoned, natural) thought of the divine, Scotus poses a further question—supposing that the divine is not analogical or irrevocably transcendent, but univocal and even irreducibly immanent—what would be required of thought in order to accommodate this notion of univocity?

3.5.1 UNIVOCITY IN HENRY OF GHENT

The question carries theological weight, for it asks the extent to which there can be any knowledge of the divine or supernatural at all, and, as a correlative to this, whether such knowledge, if it exists, is by revelation or by reason. An earlier Medieval tradition, whose most famous exemplar is Anselm, denies that any such knowledge is possible. The divine or supernatural can be posited only as a limit for thought ("that beyond which nothing greater can be thought"). Other traditions, extending from Augustine onwards, make room for a particular kind of knowledge of the divine, but a knowledge that is made possible by, and ultimately points to, beatitude. A tradition of a different sort is found in the work or Henry of Ghent, and the differences between his comments on the creature and those of Duns Scotus.[27]

Henry of Ghent is in many ways Scotus' nemesis. Arguably, Scotus' concept of univocity can only be adequately understood in relation to Henry, and Henry's position does indeed form the backdrop for the proofs of God's existence and the proofs for univocity in Scotus' *Ordinatio*. As we know, Henry was deeply involved in the Condemnations of 1277. He was a secular master of theology at the University of Paris, and between the mid-1270s and the 1290s he acted as the chair of theology (a position previously held by Aquinas). He was among the most prominent theologians of the thirteenth century who worked from an Augustinian (or neo-Augustinian) basis, and, when in 1277 the bishop at Paris took on the task of reporting on possible heretical teachings at Paris and Oxford, Henry was included as a member of the committee that helped to identify the 219 condemned articles.

In the *Ordinatio* Scotus provides a summary of Henry's argument, which implies a kind of equivocity between creature and Creator. In the tradition of Scholastic discourse, Scotus is here ventriloquizing Henry's position:

> The *most* general knowledge we have of God comprises three stages. To know any being as "this being" is already to conceive God in a very indistinct way; for "being" is included, as it were, as part of the concept. This is the first step. The second step consists in removing the "this" and conceiving simply "being." For "being," in so far as it is a concept and not simply a part of a concept, is already conceived as analogically common to God and creature. We are in the third stage, if the concept of "Being" which pertains to God is distinguished from the concept of "being" which pertains analogically to creatures, if, for instance, God is conceived as a being that is *negatively* undetermined, that is, incapable of being determined, while a creature is conceived as a being that is *privatively* undetermined. In the first instance, "undetermined" is conceived abstractly as something self-subsistent and incapable of being participated in, like a form that lacks all matter. In the second, "undetermined" is a universal abstracted from particulars and not actually shared by them.[28]

Scotus' summary generally follows the presentation given in Henry's *Summa of Ordinary Questions* (*Summa Quaestionum Ordinarium*), this latter text written in the late thirteenth century during Henry's tenure at

the University of Paris. Here, in a series of questions that deal with the
existence of God, Henry asks "whether God has being in common with
creatures."[29] Henry does not necessarily deny that there can be natural
knowledge of the divine or supernatural. On this question he and Scotus
appear to agree. However, Henry sharply distinguishes different types of
knowledge of the divine or supernatural. There is the most mediate kind
of knowledge, which begins from the creaturely world, the kind of knowledge produced by natural theology, for instance. This knowledge is based
on individuated, concrete instances of creaturely life—this life, this animal, and so on.

Above this is an abstract knowledge of that part of creaturely life that
is not reducible to or dependent upon its individuated, concrete instantiation. Here Henry adopts the Augustinian mode, and simply subtracts the
qualifiers "this" from "this life," leaving us with the abstract idea of life
in itself, irrespective of any particular instance of life. Scotus also allows
that such a thought is possible, though, as we've seen, he arrives at this
point by different means than Augustinian abstraction. Here Henry and
Scotus part ways, for in this second mode of knowledge, Henry stresses
that in abstracting "life" from "this life," the relation between knowledge
of "this life" of the creature and the "life" in itself of the Creator must
form an analogical relation:

> Hence, because the creator and a creature agree in any one real fac-
> tor much less than two creatures, namely, substance and accident—in
> fact, the creator's manner of being differs from a creature's manner
> of being much more than one creature's manner of being differs from
> another's—in no way can being be something real and common to
> God and to a creature . . . Hence, if being or to be is predicated of God
> and creatures, this is by a commonality of name only, not by any real
> commonality. And so, it is not predicated univocally in accord with
> the definition of univocal terms, not purely equivocally (by chance)
> in accord with the definition of equivocal terms, but in a middle way,
> namely, analogically.[30]

Henry stresses that there are two qualitatively different kinds of creaturely
relations—relations between Creator and creature, and relations between
any two creatures. This distinction is much less emphasized in Scotus,
though he does not deny it altogether. In Henry's argument, the analogy
would be of the type, "what contingent being is to the creature, necessary
being is to the Creator," or, "what corporeal life is to the creature, spiri-

tual life is to the Creator." Henry thus allows for a commonality of terms, but he also follows the Thomistic path in arguing for analogy.

What kind of analogy is this? Following his distinction between the two types of creaturely relations, Henry provides another distinction between two types of analogical relation based on analogy as a *formal* relation:

> [I]t must be noted that the agreement of one thing with another is seen especially in form, and this in two ways, in so far as there are two ways of having some form in common. One way is in terms of the same intelligibility. This is called an agreement of likeness and is found in those things that participate in one form in terms of its reality, as two white things participate in whiteness and two human beings in humanity. These are produced by a univocal agreement of the sort that, as we said, God and a creature do not have in being. The second is an agreement of form in terms of different intelligibilities. This is called an agreement of imitation and is universally found in makers and their products, in causes and their effects.[31]

The distinction between the two types of creaturely relations—between Creator-creature and between creature-creature—is here correlated to two kinds of formal analogical relations—the agreement of imitation and the agreement of likeness. What the Creator-creature relationship is to imitation, the creature-creature relationship is to likeness. The former is defined by Henry in terms of causality (in particular, its efficient and final causality), while the latter is defined in terms of generic similarities. The agreement of imitation is similar to the idea of exemplarism, and the notion that any effect bears some relation of similitude to its cause, by virtue of being caused. By contrast, the agreement of likeness is based on identifiable formal comparisons between any two individuals of a species. An important ontological consequence here is that, by defining univocity exclusively in terms of creature-creature relationships (and not between Creator-creature), Henry implies that univocity can only ever be something that exists "in name only," and not in reality. What we call univocal is simply a name given to a set of identical attributes between two members of a species. It is secondary to the more primary analogical relationship between Creator and creature, and the essential action of causality defined within it. Thus, for Henry, univocity is always reducible to a nominalism of likeness, while analogy is the only way to understand the real, causal relationships that exist in the creature.

3.5.2 Negative vs. Privative Indetermination

These are, thus far, the two kinds of knowledge of the divine or supernatural given by Henry: a first kind that begins from creatures ("this life"), and a second kind that abstracts its term ("life" in itself) and is based upon a fundamental analogical relation between Creator and creature. But there is still a third kind of knowledge for Henry, and it is in the third type of knowledge that Henry provides the striking distinction between the possibility of the knowledge of creatures, and the ultimate impossibility of knowledge about the Creator.

The terms Henry utilizes to describe this limit to knowledge is *indeterminatio* ("indetermination" or better, "undetermination"). Let us look at his introduction of this term:

> But that something common seems to be conceived by the term "being" is due to the fact that, whether there is conceived something that is the divine reality or that is a creature, when being, nonetheless, is conceived without determinately and distinctly conceiving the being of God or of a creature, it is conceived only indeterminately, that is, without determining the concept to the being of God or of a creature . . . It must, nonetheless, be understood that this indetermination with respect to the being of God is other than it is with respect to the being of creatures, because indetermination is twofold: one that is negative, but the other by way of privation. For there is a negative indetermination when what is indeterminate is by nature not able to be determined, as God is said to be infinite because he is by nature not able to be limited. There is, however, privative indetermination when what is indeterminate is by nature able to be determined, as a point is said to be infinite, when it is not determined by lines by which it is naturally able to be determined.[32]

Here the term originally attributed of creatures in the first type of knowledge ("this life"), moves from its abstraction in the second type ("life" in itself), and is now raised to such a degree of perfection that it exceeds all creaturely thought. To be privatively indeterminate is, in a sense, to be not-yet determined, or at least to be always in the state of being potentially determined. This is the domain of creaturely life, inscribed as it is by finitude and temporality. By contrast, to be negatively indeterminate is to be essentially and fundamentally indeterminate—to be by definition indeterminate, in total, for all time. Again, Henry and Scotus part ways here, and, in a sense Henry even parts ways with the theological tradition he is referencing: one question that Henry's distinction raises is whether negatively indeterminate being also forecloses the possibility of revelation or beatitude, or whether it simply marks the horizon beyond which natural knowledge cannot go. To articulate this horizon, Henry resorts to the language of negative theology. Here the super-eminent or superlative notion of being or life so far surpasses creaturely thought that it can only be negatively articulated (as that which surpasses all creaturely thought). Here, "indeterminate being belongs to God by negation and to the creature by privation."[33] The highest point, then, is also the point of the greatest negation.

The major insight of Henry's position is that what is predicated univocally between creatures can be predicated only analogically between creature and Creator. That is, between one creature and another there can be univocity, but between creature and Creator, where a different order of being is the case, there cannot be a univocal relation. Henry utilizes the equivocity of the creature in relation to the Creator to bifurcate the kinds of relationships that can be known: univocal relations between creatures (horizontally) and analogical relations between Creator and creature (vertically). For Henry, claims about univocity of the type that Scotus will make are simply confused, a symptom of the limits of creaturely thought.

3.5.3 ABSOLUTE INDETERMINATION

As we've seen, Scotus positions his concept of univocity against Aquinas, who argues for analogy. But Scotus is even more explicit in his disagreements with Henry of Ghent, whom he explicitly names in the *Ordinatio*, where Scotus provides a definition of univocity. We have already mentioned Scotus' definition in his debate with Aquinas. Let us cite here the definition in its totality:

> I say that God is conceived not only in a concept analogous to the concept of a creature, that is, one which is wholly other than that which is predicated on creatures, but even in some concept univocal to Himself and to a creature.
>
> And lest there be a dispute about the name "univocation," I designate that concept univocal which possesses sufficient unity in itself, so that to affirm and deny it of one and the same thing would be a contradiction. It also has sufficient unity to serve as the middle term of a syllogism, so that wherever two extremes are united by a middle

term that is one in this way, we may conclude to the union of the two extremes among themselves.[34]

The question being considered is precisely that which gave rise to the controversies of the late thirteenth century. As Scotus poses it: "Whether the intellect of man in this life is able to know God naturally." In short, is there a natural knowledge of the supernatural?

Scotus' definition of univocity is actually given in two variations. The first is more general, in which a univocal concept is that "which possesses sufficient unity in itself, so that to affirm and deny it of one and the same thing would be a contradiction." This seems commonsensical, almost not worth mentioning. However, a statement of affirmation or negation can proceed by affirming or negating a subject as well as a predicate. For example, the statement "the cat is purring" and the statement "the cat is not purring" affirm and deny something about the same thing in question. This would be, in Scotus' definition, a contradiction—unless the subject "cat" was being used not univocally but equivocally. Thus if the cat in the first statement is a feline mammal, and the cat in the second statement is a catfish, then there would be no contradiction (but also no univocal term).

The same follows for statements in which the predicate is taken univocally or equivocally. For example, the statement "Shoggoths exist" and "Shoggoths do not exist" would be contradictory, unless the predicate of existing be taken equivocally and not univocally. If taken equivocally, in the first statement "exists" would mean "having a reality in the literary imagination," while in the second statement "exists" would mean "not having an extra-mental reality in the world."

Thus Scotus' first variation on univocity has the simple form of a disjunction between two sentences of the type "A is X" and "A is not X." These two statements, taken simultaneously, would be contradictory insofar as A or X is a univocal term. From this, Scotus can argue for the univocity of existence between Creator and creature, Life and the living: the statement "the Creator exists" and the statement "creatures exist" can be understood as univocal terms, insofar as existence means "opposed to nothing." In this example, existence is common to both Creator and creature, not simply by virtue of their causal relationship (as with Aquinas), and not by the participation of creatures in the Creator (as with Henry), but by the immanence of existence to both Creator and creature. Aquinas will tend to bypass this distinction, arguing that any statement concerning the univocity of Creator and creatures necessarily denies the hierarchy and transcendence of the former in relation to the latter. In a different vein, Henry argues against univocity because there can be no common term between Creator and creature. For Henry, the Creator and the domain of the supernatural are "negatively indeterminate," forever beyond the domain of thought and qualitatively different from the indetermination of creatures.

Scotus also gives another variation on univocity that follows his first. A univocal concept "has sufficient unity to serve as the middle term of a syllogism," so that any two terms having this middle term in common are univocally related. This is a more formal variation than the first, making use of Aristotelian logic. It also has a simple form of the type "All *A* are *B*, and all *B* are *C*, therefore all *A* are *C*." Thus, all creatures are living, and all living things are finite, therefore all creatures are finite. This is all fine as far as elementary logic is concerned, but things get messy when syllogisms of a radically Scotist type are used, such as "all creatures have life, all life is divine, therefore all creatures are divine" and so on. But even in its more conservative guise, the Scotist syllogism stresses the role of the middle term, as that which even those things that are equivocal have in common. The sticking point is to what degree this common nature presupposes identity between terms; for Aquinas and Henry it tends to, and thus one must either choose a compromise (analogy) or assert a non-relation (equivocity).

These are some facets, then, of Scotus' definition of univocity; at this point in the *Ordinatio* he has not yet gone on to argue for its real existence. After summarizing Henry's positions concerning the Creator as negatively indeterminate and creatures as privatively indeterminate, Scotus offers five counterstatements to Henry's position. It is in the second statement that Scotus explicitly states that the relation between Creator and creature is univocal, and then gives the above definition. This is immediately followed by five arguments for univocity. Briefly, these are as follows:

- First argument: "Every intellect that is certain about one concept, but dubious about others has, in addition to the concepts about which it is in doubt, another concept of which it is certain."[35] One may debate whether the creature is natural or supernatural, finite or infinite, but common to either position pro or contra is some concept of "nature" or "finitude" that is being debated. This is not always the case, of course, since many disagreements amount to equivocal uses of terms. But, Scotus argues, any debate presupposes

something in common, and this common term is what Scotus repeatedly stresses as central to a univocal concept of the Creator-
creature relation.

• Second argument: "No object will produce a simple and proper concept of itself and a simple and proper concept of another object, unless it contains this second object essentially or virtually."[36] In this
Aristotelian argument, Scotus argues for a fundamental continuity between a correlated subject, object, and the natural knowledge
of the latter by the former, even if this knowledge is established
"essentially or virtually." Either analogical or equivocal relations
between intellect and world lead to an essentially inaccessible object of knowledge. "With the co-operation of the active and possible
intellect, any object revealed in the sense image or existing as an
intelligible species at the very most can produce in the intellect as
its adequate effect (a) a proper concept of itself and (b) a concept of
all that is essentially or virtually included in it."[37]

• Third argument: "The proper concept of any subject provides sufficient ground for concluding to everything conceivable which necessarily inheres in that subject."[38] This follows from the previous
argument, but it is also a radicalized variant of Augustinian abstraction (in which the creaturely qualifier "this" is removed from
any attribute; repeated in the fourth argument as well). Any mediate relation between two terms can be followed via the middle term
to an immediate relation. It is possible to work from the bottom up,
from creatures to Creator: "In the concept of a creature, however,
no notion or species will be found to represent something proper to
God which is wholly different in nature from anything pertaining
to a creature."[39]

• Fourth argument: "Either some pure perfection has a common
meaning as applied to God and creatures (which is our contention),
or not. If not, it is either because its meaning does not apply formally to God at all (which is inadmissible), or else it has a meaning
that is wholly proper to God, in which case nothing need be attributed to God because it is a pure perfection."[40] As Scotus points
out, this contradicts the position of Anselm, for whom a barrier exists in the creaturely knowledge of the Creator. Without a univocal
concept, Scotus argues, either no knowledge beyond the creature is
possible, since all concepts would be equivocal. As Scotus notes,
"We would have no more reason to conclude that God is formally

wise from the notion of wisdom derived from creatures than we would have reason to conclude that God is formally a stone."[41]

This fourth argument is also, in many ways, the most radical of Scotus' claims, for it encompasses the three previous ones by stressing relations of continuity. Unlike Aquinas or Henry, he comes very close to positing univocal being as something "beyond" both creature and Creator. Insofar as the Anselmian or Augustinian modes of abstraction proceed by privative means, they end up attributing perfection to God. What Scotus does is to begin and end with the common nature, the middle term, as the fundamental component of any natural knowledge. As a univocal term, it is less something attributed to greater or lesser degree to Creator or creature, and more that which conditions their relation altogether.

Between Scotus, Henry, and Aquinas we have three positions on the nature of the Creator-creature relationship. For Aquinas, that relationship must be analogical if it is to preserve the relation of transcendence, eminence, and causality between Creator and creature. For Henry, the fundamental separation between Creator and creature implies a kind of equivocity, by which one term of the relation remains absolutely inaccessible to the other term. Finally, for Scotus, the relation between Creator and creatures is univocal, though they are not by necessity reduced to this univocity.

3.6 UNIVOCITY III: DELEUZE'S SCHOLASTICISM—THREE VARIATIONS

The horizon of any thought about the Creator-creation relationship is pantheism. This kind of pantheism not only entails the negation of the divine, but it also entails a radical distribution of the divine, such that it cannot be separated from the earthly, or even the material (thus the horizon of pantheism is materialism). The challenge is how to think the univocity between Creator and creature, or between supernatural and natural, to the point of thinking their non-separation, their identity. Whether this identity is a formal or real identity is left partially open by Scotus—a formal identity (the "formal distinction") enables differentiations to exist that are coextensive with univocity, but a real identity is only a step or two away from this position, positing an absolute immanence between the common nature and the individuating "thisness" (*haecceitas*). In this sense Scotus participates in a more subterranean tradition of Medieval pantheism that stretches from Eriugena, to Nicholas of Cusa, to Spinoza. The thought that is opened up by this tradition is the thought of a fully univocal relation between Creator and creature, Life and the living that, at the same time, does not simply efface or render subordinate the differentiations between them.

This is one of the many ways that the work of Gilles Deleuze intersects in an important way with Scholastic thinking.[42] But, as we will see, Deleuze's own engagement with Scholasticism raises many of the same problems, though cast in a more contemporary vernacular. On a literal level, Deleuze's works both early and late often make reference to Medieval philosophers, from the Pseudo-Dionysius to Duns Scotus to Nicholas of Cusa. On another, more methodological level, in works such as *Expressionism in Philosophy* there is a sense in which Deleuze incorporates elements of Scholastic discourse—e.g., in the method of articulating finer and finer distinctions in the tradition of the *Summa*. However, Deleuze not only makes literal or methodological reference to Scholasticism, but, more importantly, his long-term commitment to the issues of the One and the Many, of univocity and multiplicity, and of a " pure immanence," all serve to draw his thought back to Scholastic problems. As Deleuze provocatively states in *Difference and Repetition*, "There has only ever been one ontological proposition: Being is univocal. There has only ever been one ontology, that of Duns Scotus, which gave being a single voice."[43] In the same way that Deleuze intentionally reads philosophy against itself (as in his famous notion of the history of philosophy as a form of sodomy), so does Deleuze also recast Scholasticism in terms of the then-heretical questions of univocity and immanence (but a strange univocity that is at once materialist and spiritualist). Insofar as Deleuze engages with Scholasticism, then, his Scholasticism is of this "heretical" type, concerned principally with shoring up the limitations of analogical and representational thinking.

As a way of drawing out this intersection between Deleuze and Scholasticism, we can consider three examples. Each can be considered a variation on a theme. That theme is the univocity of the relation between Creator and creature. In each variation, Deleuze seeks to radicalize the Scotist tradition of univocity, and he will do so via what is essentially a Scholastic reading of Spinoza's ontology. The first variation is the most specific. In his study *Spinoza et le Problème de l'Expression* (*Expressionism in Philosophy: Spinoza*), Deleuze rethinks univocity through the Spinozist notion of the attributes, at once restating and extending the Scotist common nature. A second variation is more general, and involves the question of univocity in itself, most clearly presented by Deleuze in *Difference and*

Repetition. Deleuze engages with a dilemma that confronted Scotus: how to posit a univocity of being without flattening all distinctions within being. Finally, in a third variation, Deleuze provides a recasting of the debate on the creature in terms of analogical or representational thinking. In a fascinating lecture given during one of his courses at Vincennes, Deleuze will not only connect the Scholastic debate on the creature to the work of Spinoza (in effect delineating a "Scholastic" Spinoza), but he will also connect this to a contemporary interest in the concept of power and affect more broadly.

3.6.1 VARIATION I: *SPINOZA ET LE PROBLÈME DE L'EXPRESSION*

Let us begin with Deleuze's explicit rethinking of the Scholastic concept of univocity. Deleuze's book *Expressionism in Philosophy*, published in 1968, is ostensibly a study of Spinoza. In contrast to Descartes or Leibniz, Spinoza asserts a "substance monism"—the idea that there is a single principle of being for all beings, and that this single principle exists not above and beyond the world, but is fully immanent in and through it. Simplifying to the extreme, there is a single, unified, immanent principle—Spinoza's "substance"—that connects everything, that is, all instances of that principle—the "modes." Spinoza also offers a radicalized version of the relation between Creator (substance) and creatures (modes), one that proposes to collapse the distinction altogether, in favor of a Creator fully immanent to all creatures. As we saw, the central problem in the Scholastic debate on this issue was how to articulate both a distinction and connection between these terms (Creator-creature, substance-mode). One could posit equivocity ("no relation"), but then an irremediable gulf would exist between Creator and creature; one could posit univocity ("all relation"), but then there would be no way to account for either causal relations or differences among individuated creatures. In a sense, Spinoza picks up where Scotus leaves off, for, between substance and modes, Spinoza offers an important mediate concept—the "attributes." Thus the Spinozist framework: a single substance, two attributes existing in parallel (thought and extension), and a multiplicity of modes, defined first by their relation to other modes, and only secondarily by their intrinsic properties. Spinoza will argue for a single substance for all attributes, one that is immanently expressed in each mode. "Expression" here implies causality, and thus creation, but it is a creation in which the Creator is fully immanent, a concept that only implies a horizontal distribution of causality, but one that also begins from the notion of self-causality or auto-creation.

Substance, attribute, and mode—this is Spinoza's conceptual triad that recasts the Scholastic debate on the Creator-creature relation.[44]

Now, Spinoza uses the term "attributes" in an unorthodox way. Usually attributes are either properties or vehicles: for example, one attributes certain properties or characteristics to an entity (an animal with certain physiological characteristics, etc.), or one characterizes an entity in terms of possible actions that are attributable to them (an animal does this or acts in this way, etc.). But for Spinoza the attributes are more than just intermediaries. They are not simply Neoplatonic Intelligences that serve to mediate between a transcendent Creator and its eminent relation to creatures. This is primarily because, for Spinoza, the Creator does not lie outside of the creatures that are created, but is fully immanent to them, and also because the Creator does not relate to the creature via a nested series of hierarchical "spheres" that would order creation in a linear way. Spinoza's notion of substance is related to modes via attributes that are neither causes nor effects. What then, are they? Deleuze provides one answer:

> It amounts to giving us a knowledge of the divine attributes which begin from that of "creatures" [*les attributs de Dieu à partir des "creatures"*]. But its way is not through abstraction or analogy. Attributes are not abstracted from particular things, still less transferred to God analogically. *Attributes are reached directly as forms of being common to creatures and to God* [*des formes d'être communes aux creatures et à Dieu*], *common to modes and to substance.*[45]

Attributes are less mediators or vehicles of divine causality, and more like the very viscosity of relation itself. In Spinoza's ontology, the incessantly distributed nature of causality or creation means that one must prioritize relations over things: "Attributes are thus forms common to God, whose essence they constitute, and to modes or creatures which imply them essentially."[46] We are not far from the Scotist notion of "common natures," except here, with Spinoza, the attributes (or common natures) imply an inherent, distributed form of causality, both between substance and mode, and between one mode and another. Scotus is hesitant to actually grant the common nature a causal power, for this would imply that the common nature somehow causes the individuating thisness or *haecceitas*, and his primary intention is to demonstrate their formal, but not causal distinction. In Deleuze's reading, Spinoza has no such hesitation. But what this requires is that Spinoza rethink causality less in terms of a first cause or first principle, and more in terms of a self-causality or auto-creation—that is, in thinking of attributes as a distributive causality, Spinoza must recast causality as a fundamentally immanent principle, in diametric opposition to orthodox Scholasticism, as well as to Descartes.

Thinking about attributes in this way, as Scotist "common natures," involves a subtle but important shift in the debate on the creature. Earlier, we saw how Scotus' notion of the "formal distinction" attempted to find a way of thinking univocity without effacing or subordinating individuating difference. This is part of what led Scotus to posit the coexistence of a common notion, as well as an individuating thisness. The challenge posed by Scotus' formal distinction is a remarkably modern one: how to think a distinction that, on the one hand, is not simply in the world, and, on the other, is also not simply an idea with no relation to the world? In the Scholastic context, the creature was an exemplary instance of this problem, for, while creatures really existed in the world, they also bore a relation to some principle or set of principles that themselves did not exist in the world. Each creature implied some relation to a direct, second cause (the generation of the creature), but also a relation to an indirect, primary cause (that by which the creature was generated as a creature). For every creature, a relation to some non-apparent condition of creation; for every life form, a relation to a life-that-forms.

In Scholasticism there are several types of distinction, and it is here that Deleuze leverages Spinoza's radicalization of Scotus. Traditionally, there are real distinctions—for instance, between any two creatures, or any two books on a desk, any two cats, and so on. Part of what makes them real distinctions is that they can exist independent of each other (if Cthulhu dies, the Shoggoths still live, etc.). Then there are rational distinctions, which may not pertain to anything really existing in the world—for instance, when one posits the difference between Cthulhu and a griffin based on their physiology or general temperament, even though they remain purely imaginary creatures. There is also a numerical distinction, which can inhere in real distinctions—for instance, when independently existing entities can be counted, added, subtracted, etc.—but which can also inhere in ideal distinctions—for instance, one can enumerate imaginary characteristics for equally imaginary creatures.

For Scotus, the formal distinction could operate at different levels: between a group and an individual member, between the universal and the particular, or between two general characteristics inherent in a single being. Thus, in the Aristotelian example of the human being as a "rational animal," one could posit a common nature (of being a living thing; of having the capacity for reason) without sacrificing the thisness that made any given human being "this" human being. Between any two human beings there is a *real distinction*. But, within any of those human beings, there is a *formal distinction* between, for instance, its capacity for sensation and its capacity for thought. Thus the formal distinction was less than a real distinction, but more than an ideal distinction. In the parlance of the later generation of Descartes and Spinoza, we might say that the formal distinction was less than empirical but more than ideal, less than real but more than rational.

For Deleuze, the innovation of Scotus-Spinoza was to conceive of the formal distinction as ontologically prior to real or ideal distinctions. This involves several steps. In the first step, one takes real distinction as implying numerical distinction—two things A and B having extra-mental reality can be counted as two things. One would then move from the numerical distinction between A and B to that which they have in common, X—that is, to that which enables their distinction to take place at all. This commonality would not only serve to distinguish A and B, but it would, at the same time, serve to set them in a relation, but a relation of difference. In Scotus' terms, the common nature between A and B always points to a "less than numerical" unity between them. In Spinoza's terms, one can begin from the numerical distinction between modes, but this inquiry will eventually require the positing of some common term, which will in turn imply a certain numerical *indistinction* between any two modes. This kind of indistinction is not simply the lack of distinction, but the peculiar relationality of univocity itself—at once relating and separating. As Deleuze notes, "[T]here are numerical distinctions that are at the same time real or substantial."[47]

At this point, however, a concept is required that is adequate to this "less-than-numerical" distinction, this *real indistinction*. Here formal and real distinction become one: "Formal distinction is definitely a real distinction, expressing as it does the different layers of reality that form or constitute a being . . . Real and yet not numerical, such is the status of the formal distinction."[48] The formal distinction, as less than real but more than ideal, serves to express something that is neither. But it is also true that real and numerical distinctions are not identical:

> On the one hand, one deduces from the nature of numerical distinction that it is inapplicable to substance; on the other, one deduces from the nature of substance its infinity, and thus the impossibility of applying it to numerical distinctions. In either case, numerical distinction can

never distinguish substances, but only modes that involve the same attribute.[49]

In short, while all numerical distinctions are real, not all real distinctions are numerical.[50] What is "real" in the formal distinction is precisely the univocity of relations—between Creator and creature, substance and mode, etc. Univocity is, in this case, neither a thing in itself, nor is it a mental representation. Scotus calls this a formal distinction, in contrast to either a real or ideal distinction. Spinoza will utilize the concept of the attribute to express this formal distinction, as one between substance and modes.

3.6.2 Variation II: *Différence et Répétition*

In many ways, Deleuze's Spinoza is as much informed by Scholastic thinking as it is by the modernity of Descartes. In fact, in *Expressionism in Philosophy*, Deleuze goes so far as to say that "it takes nothing away from Spinoza's originality to place him in a perspective that may already be found in Duns Scotus."[51] Central to this sentiment is the importance of the concept of univocity, not just for the heretical strand that Scotus represents, but for a whole lineage that Deleuze—not without some dispute—extends to Spinoza, Nietzsche, and Bergson.

In *Difference and Repetition*, Deleuze takes up the concept of univocity in a way that places it at the center of his ontology of difference. For Deleuze, traditional ontology is predicated on the concept of identity (vs. difference), of the One (vs. the Many), of Being (vs. becoming), and so on. That-which-differs can be regarded only as in some way falling away from, or dependent upon, that which does not differ, or that which is whole, Ideal, One. As Deleuze states at the outset, his aim is to think the concept of difference not as secondary or derivative, but in some way as primary to our thinking about that-which-differs as well as to the processes of differentiating and creating differences. Hence Deleuze's much-quoted project of "inverting Platonism." In particular, the concept of difference is, for Deleuze, poised against the fourfold aspect of identity ("identity of the concept"), analogy ("analogy of judgment"), opposition ("opposition of predicates"), and resemblance ("resemblance of the perceived").

The Scholastic concept of univocity comes to function as one of the many ways by which Deleuze attempts to think against the ontological tradition of identity, analogy, opposition, and resemblance. On the surface, this seems contradictory, for, if one wanted to counteract the dominant Platonic ontology of identity, wouldn't one want to instead propose a concept of difference or the multiple, or of non-identity or anti-identity? This is, to an extent, what Deleuze does, but he does so through a reworking of the concept of univocity, a concept that, for the Scholastics, denoted not difference but identity, not discontinuity but continuity. We saw how, for Aquinas, the assertion of a univocal relation between Creator and creatures could only imply their identity and continuity, threatening to efface the hierarchy between them. This was also the challenge that confronted Duns Scotus, who, though he posited the univocity of Creator and creature, struggled to find a way to simultaneously accommodate individuating differences without flattening them altogether. For the tradition of analogy represented by Aquinas, as well as the tradition of univocity represented by Scotus, the problem is difference. In Aquinas' context, the priority was how to preserve the difference (in particular, the causal hierarchy) between Creator and creature, while for Scotus, the challenge was how to allow for a distinction (a formal distinction) that would not collapse beneath the demands of univocal thinking.

Deleuze's proposition is that only by thinking difference in terms of univocity can Scotus' challenge be overcome. This basically requires thinking a certain non-difference of difference, a univocity of difference:

> In effect, the essential in univocity is not that Being is said in a single and same sense, but that it is said, in a single and same sense, of all its individuating differences or intrinsic modalities. Being is the same for all these modalities, but these modalities are not the same. It is "equal" for all, but they themselves are not equal. It is said of all in a single sense, but they themselves do not have the same sense . . . Being is said in a single and same sense of everything of which it is said, but that of which it is said differs: it is said of difference itself.[52]

If univocity is the univocity of difference, then how is it to be distinguished from the Platonic assertions of identity in the Idea or the Parmenidean One? Deleuze offers two axes through which univocity (as the univocity of difference) can be distinguished from the tradition of identity-analogy-opposition-resemblance. One axis concerns a phenomenon of distribution. Distribution is one of the perennial questions of ontology: what is the passage from a unified concept of Being and the multiplicity of individuated beings? The Neoplatonic response was to separate God and creatures as the One and the many, and between them posit divine Ideas or Intelligences whose function was to serve as causal intermediaries between Creator and creatures. The process proceeded downwards and outwards; it was thus both hierarchical and emanative. This is a "distribution which implies a dividing up of that which is distributed . . . It is here that the rules of judgment and analogy are all-powerful."[53] This is the distribution of Neoplatonism, but it also applies as much to the earthly or geological domain (e.g., distribution of land or resources) as it does to the divine. But there is also another type of distribution, one that attempts to extract distribution from its being nested inside hierarchy. "Here, there is no longer a division of that which is distributed but rather a division among those who distribute *themselves* in an open space."[54] What would distribution be if it was extracted from the Neoplatonic order of emanation? It would be something like a distribution without any real distinction in relation to that which was distributed: "To fill a space, to be distributed within it, is very different from distributing the space."[55] Deleuze, using terminology that would become more prominent in his later works, calls this a "nomadic distribution" (he also refers to this type of distribution as "demonic," in that it operates at the interstices, intervals, and cracks). In contrast to the Neoplatonic distribution, which is fixed and relies upon a pyramidal, cascading distribution from the One to the many, from a source to its recipients, this univocal distribution involves the distribution of distribution itself. When distribution is thought of in terms of univocity, what results is a kind of auto-distribution.

In addition to the axis of distribution, there is also the axis of hierarchy, and this too has two forms, according to Deleuze. There is "a hierarchy which measures beings according to their limits, and according to their degree of proximity or distance from a principle."[56] Deleuze's target here is obviously Plato, but it is also Aristotle, for it inculcates the priority of category, especially in terms of how Aristotelian logic was read by early and late Scholasticism. By contrast, there is also "a hierarchy which considers things and beings from the point of view of power."[57] "Power" here should be understood in the tradition of French anti-humanist philosophy—a Nietzschean field of thresholds and intensities. A hierarchy of principles is predicated on a set of essential properties that are taken to inhere in and preexist any creature in which they are manifest. By contrast, a hierarchy of power, or what Deleuze refers to as "crowned anarchy," holds together the twofold aspect of the formal distinction: a common nature in which "everything is equal," as well as individuating differences through which "everything is connected." In contrast to the *dividing-up* of Neoplatonism, then, the *spreading-out* of univocal or nomadic distributions. In contrast to the hierarchy of *principle* inherited from Aristotle, the hierarchy of *power* or the relations of difference, intensity, and thresholds.

The concept of univocity, then, must be thought of not only as a univocity of difference, but this difference or differentiation must itself be distinguished in its distribution (spreading-out vs. dividing-up) and its hierarchy (power vs. principle). Where in the history of philosophy do we find such concepts of univocity? Deleuze identifies three key moments: Duns Scotus, Spinoza, and Nietzsche. Each takes up and extends the thought of the former. Scotus, for Deleuze, takes the first step, which is to assert, the univocity of Creator and creature. Scotus' greatest insight, according to Deleuze, is to realize the fundamental *neutrality* or *indifference* of univocal being. In the philosophy of Scotus, "being is understood as univocal, but univocal being is understood as neutral, *neuter*, indifferent to the distinction between the finite and the infinite, the singular and the universal, the created and the uncreated."[58] While Scotus was able to articulate a common nature, on the one hand, and an individuating "thisness" on the other, he was left with no way to think their relationship to each other.

This is where Spinoza, and then Nietzsche, pick up the concept of univocity and radicalize it beyond its Scotist definition. In the case of Spinoza, the debate with Descartes is similar to the debate between Scotus and Aquinas. Against Aquinas' notion of analogy between Creator and creature, we have Scotus' notion of the univocity that runs through them; against the Cartesian notion of separate substances of thought and extension, we have the Spinozist assertion of a single substance for all attributes. But Deleuze also states that what Spinoza adds to the Scotist notion of univocity is an emphasis on the generativity of univocal being. That is, the Scotist notion of univocity as *neutral being* is transformed by Spinoza into a notion of univocity as *affirmative becoming*. This move is, it is important to note, absolutely central to Deleuze's ontology—and he has been taken to task for it.[59] In short, it amounts to an ontological assertion of being as fundamentally generous—being always flows, is always productive and proliferative, is always in excess.

Now, there are clear limitations to such a stance—it is, in a sense, a radical Neoplatonism without a center (a "subtractive" Neoplatonism); but it remained a position that Deleuze would hold throughout his life, and, arguably, it has its roots in Duns Scotus and the concept of univocity. While Scotus articulates the relation between Creator and creature as univocal, he says relatively little about how this univocity transforms the generative process of creation itself. Presumably, univocity would entail a mode of creation different from either the Neoplatonic example of emanative Intelligences or the Aristotelian-Thomistic example of hylomorphism. But it is with Spinoza's substance monism (one substance for all attributes; "God or Nature") that Deleuze discovers a concept of *univocity* that is also a concept of *creation*—superfluous, generous, affirmative being. In short, *the "life" of univocity*, as it were. "With Spinoza, univocal being ceases to be neutralized and becomes expressive; it becomes a truly expressive and affirmative proposition."[60] From the Scotist notion of univocity as neutral, we have moved to the Spinozist notion of univocity as affirmative.

There is a final step, and it is provided, for Deleuze, by Nietzsche and his concept of the eternal return. Like Scotus and Spinoza, Nietzsche seeks a concept of univocity, but one that would remain resolutely against the theological prescriptions of transcendence and the romanticism of the great beyond. Nietzsche's solution to this problem is to suggest that a common notion of being is not necessarily a cumulative notion of being—univocity can remain neutral (as it is in Scotus), and it can remain affirmative (as it is in Spinoza), but, in order to think though its consequences, one would have to deny it any teleology. It doesn't stop, and it's not going anywhere (at least anywhere predetermined from outside). What is left, then, is not a cumulative being heading towards some ideal end, but a univocity becoming, a becoming that doesn't become any thing in particular: "Returning is being, but only the being of becoming. The eternal return does not bring back 'the same' but returning constitutes only the Same of that which becomes. Returning is the becoming-identical of becoming itself."[61]

Beginning with Duns Scotus, Deleuze builds up a concept of univocity that is at once Medieval and contemporary. Univocity is indifferent or neutral, in that it cuts across (Scotus); univocity is also affirmative and generative (Spinoza); finally, what univocity affirms is difference itself, a univocity of difference (Nietzsche). What is univocal is difference in itself. In Scholastic terms, this would mean that the two orders identified by Aquinas and Henry of Ghent—the relation between Creator and creature, and the relation between one creature and another—would have something in common, and this common nature would be difference, the relation of difference, or differentiation itself. This would also mean that the principle of causality that structures analogical thinking—that is, that between Creator and creature there is a primary causality, that then determines the secondary causality between one creature and another—this analogical structuring of causality is really a univocal causality that pertains to both of the relations (Creator-creature, creature-creature). And this in turn means that both of the relations (Creator-creature, creature-creature) have in common a modality of differentiation. What they have in common is the priority of relationality (of relations over the terms of the relation), this relationality being constituted through differentiation. For Deleuze it is difference, then, that cuts across the relation of Creator-creature, just as it cuts across the relations of relations (Creator-creature, creature-creature).

3.6.3 Variation III: Cours de Vincennes

In a lecture given at Vincennes in 1974, Deleuze, passing by a "terminological detour," evokes the three terms at the center of the Scholastic debate on the creature—equivocity, univocity, and analogy. Deleuze notes that, even though philosophers have abandoned such terms, the issues they raise are absolutely contemporary, as they pertain to, for instance, the concepts of community, difference, or power. Deleuze outlines each of the three positions in simple terms. Equivocity means that "being is said in several senses of which it is said [*l'être se dit en plusieurs sens de ce dont il se dit*]."[62] The rock, the chair, the animal, the human being, and God all exist, but each in an absolutely different sense. This is the assertion of absolute difference; this is "being without common measure." Univocity, by contrast, means that "being has only one sense and is said in one and the same sense of everything of which it is said [*l'être n'a qu'un sens et se dit en un seul et meme sens de tout ce dont il se dit*]."[63] The rock, the chair, the animal, the human being, and God exist in the same sense throughout. Whereas equivocity is the position of absolute difference, univocity is the position of absolute identity. Whereas equivocity implies total autonomy, univocity implies total interconnectedness.

The problem, Deleuze notes, is that the positions of equivocity and univocity both edge towards heresy; they demand too much, theologically speaking. It is better to say "God is not" than to say that God exists equivocally, for, if all beings exist in a different way, then they also exist equally and without measure. The problem is that this implies that the being of the rock is equal to the being of God. Thus it is better to deny being to God, thereby positing God as superior to and outside of being, than to say that God is no more or less a being than the rock. The heretical aspect of univocity is similar to equivocity, for both flatten the necessary hierarchy between Creator and creature. With equivocity, God exists and the rock exists, and there is no correlation between them. With univocity,

God and the rock exists along the same plane or continuum. The rock is God. God is the rock.

We have seen how this dilemma played out in Aquinas—one needs to posit some relation between the orders of being, but without flattening them altogether. Mediating between them is the position of analogy, which for Deleuze means "being is said in several senses . . . only these senses are not without common measure; these senses are governed by relations of analogy [*l'être se dit en plusieurs sens . . . seulement ces sens ne sont pas sans commune mesure: ces sens sont régis par des rapports d'analogie*]."[64] Aquinas provides several modes of analogy, including the analogy of proportion (e.g., God is good and the creature is good, but God is formally good, while the creature, being created, is secondarily good), and the analogy of proportionality (what finite good is to creatures, infinite goodness is to God). Deleuze's central point concerning analogy is that it is indelibly linked to category. Both of the major traditions inherited by the Scholastics—early Medieval Neoplatonism and late Medieval Aristotelianism—are predicated on thought as proceeding via category, either in exemplary Ideas or a hierarchy of species.

What is "category" in this context, Deleuze asks? "One calls categories the concepts which are said of every possible experience."[65] For Aristotle, these might be form and matter, for Avicenna, these might be essence and existence, and, for Aquinas, these might be substance and accident, and so on. Deleuze does not, of course, assert that thought can take place totally independent of category, but he does point to the centrality of category to analogical thinking. Category presumes intuited objects of experience, experience presumes relations of causality, and, in the Aristotelian-Thomistic mindset, causality presumes a fundamental separation of cause and effect, primary and secondary causes, a cause exterior to its effect, and so on. Thus, one impact of the dominant Thomistic-analogical viewpoint in the Scholastic period was to have articulated an essential link between category, analogy, and causality: "Therefore there's no question of a thought proceeding by categories if it does not have, as background, the idea that being is analogical, which is to say that being is said of what is in an analogical manner."[66]

This is where Deleuze will present Duns Scotus as a key thinker working against the analogical-representational tradition of Aquinas. For Deleuze, it was Scotus who takes up the position of univocity and follows it to its conclusions. But Deleuze also notes that Scotus tempers his position of univocity between an assertion of being as "univocal metaphysically," and yet "analogical physically."

[I]f someone happened by speaking of univocity of being, he was quickly spotted, he could pack his bags; that meant, yet again, that a chair, an animal, a man and God are in one and the same sense. Then what: you treat God as matter? Are a dog and a man in the same sense? Quite tricky, that. And nevertheless there is a man, the greatest thinker of the Middle Ages, who says yes, being is univocal, that is Duns Scotus. This story of Duns Scotus' univocal being turns out rather badly—but happily he took precautions, he said yes but be careful: being is univocal insofar as it is being. That is to say that it's metaphysically univocal. He said: sure it's analogical, which is to say that it's said in several senses physically. This is what interests me: he was at the border of heresy, had he not specified metaphysically univocal and physically analogical, he would have been done for.[67]

We can read this in terms of Scotus' concepts of the univocal "common nature" and the individuating "thisness" or *haecceitas*. Here univocity is tempered such that any individualized instance of thisness can be distinguished from the common nature. But again we are confronted with the question of the relation between them, in effect replicating the Creator-creature dichotomy. If the ontological principle between Creator and creature is that of univocity, then how does one adequately account for the multiplicity of differences in and between things in the world? Should we say that the multiplicity of beings are merely illusions or Platonic simulacra? If one refuses to adopt the framework of category-analogy-causality, then how can individuating difference be articulated in relation to univocity?

For Deleuze, this problem is the link between the concept of univocity in Scotus and the concept of substance in Spinoza. In Deleuze's reading, Spinoza's triad of substance, attribute, and mode takes up the Scotist notion of univocity and extends it further. In Spinoza's famous formulation "God or Nature" (*Deus sive natura*), a single substance is posited for all attributes (thought and extension), which are then expressed in differentiated, individuated modes (bodies and their relations). And what Spinoza offers, according to Deleuze, is a way of replying to the challenge Scotus found himself faced with—how to think univocity without resorting to category and analogy.

In particular, Spinoza offers two axes by which univocity can be thought of alternatively. First, that beings are constituted by a special kind of difference, a "univocal difference" that distinguishes them not according to preestablished categories or species or genus, but according to their "degrees of power" (*puissance*). This notion of univocity as expressed according to degrees of power corresponds to another axis, by which beings are distinguished by affect—the capacity to affect and the capacity to be affected. Here Deleuze employs the term "affect" in its Spinozist sense, in which affect is opposed to "emotion" or "feeling" (which would take us back to the analogical, and, arguably, phenomenological framework). Affect, in Deleuze's usage, itself has several aspects to it: (i) affects are external, in the sense that affects are not "inner feelings" or something held interior to subjects, but that which is always tending outside them; (ii) it follows from this that affects manifest the primary of relations over the things related, both in an ontological and epistemological sense; (iii) as the nexus or tissue of being, affects are, finally, "impersonal" and "anonymous," to use terms favored by Deleuze—affects do not so much express the interiority of subjects as they are themselves anonymous expressions of a univocal being, a common substance for all attributes.

Thus, for Deleuze what Scotus starts, Spinoza finishes. Both work from the premise that the relation between Creator and creatures is a univocal relation, and even that this univocity ontologically conditions the very distinction of the terms of the relation. Deleuze summarizes, citing an example that would make its way into *A Thousand Plateaus*:

> We have this group of notions: being is said in one and the same sense of everything of which it's said; hence beings are not distinguished by their form, their genus, their species, they're distinguished by degrees of power. These degrees of power refer to powers of being affected, the affects being precisely the intensities of which a being is capable . . . In a sense it's a thought so very far from the ordinary notions of species and genus that, once again, between two members of the same species there can be more differences, more differences in the degree of power than between two beings of different species. Between a racehorse and a draft horse, which belong to the same species, the difference can perhaps be thought as greater than the difference between a draft horse and an ox.[68]

In a sense, what Deleuze does in his reading of Scotus is to translate the Scholastic debate over the relation between Creator and creature into a modern question about the relation between idealism and realism. For Deleuze, the most radical thought is the one that thinks the relation between

the supernatural and natural, or Creator and creature, as a univocal relation. For a Scholastic thinker like Scotus, this thought involved the challenge of asserting univocity while also accounting for multiplicity. As
we've seen, Scotus, in his debates with Aquinas and Henry of Ghent, proposes the distinction between, on the one hand, a common nature that
exists univocally across individual instances, and a *haecceitas* that forms
the individuating differences of this particular creature. Between the common nature and the thisness, Scotus posits a "formal distinction" but not
an actual separation. Thus the common nature and thisness are "formally
distinct, but really identical." Yet, Scotus' formal distinction, while it accounts for the difference between the common nature and the individuating thisness, says little about their connection or their coexistence. Although Scotus does make the move of positing the univocity of being, this
univocity still remains tethered to the Thomistic framework of category,
analogy, and causality. One can view things analogically, from the point
of view of creatures, Scotus admits, but the key thing is to move from the
creaturely view to the view of the relation between creature and Creator,
and to see this relation as essentially continuous, and hence, univocal.

This ontological commitment also has the effect of problematizing
Deleuze's Scholasticism. The appeal to univocity in terms of a continuum
would seem to push Deleuze's philosophy into either an immanentist
mysticism (in which the thought of univocity would become isomorphic
with univocity, losing all "definition") or into a sophistic hyperbole, an
exploration of the twists and turns of aporia and contradiction. Medieval
and Scholastic philosophy often finds itself in a similar position, poised
between mystical theology and the logical rigor of the *Summa*.

It would not be difficult to argue that Deleuze's major works attempt
to do both, continually generating concepts while also undertaking "finer
and finer distinctions." This is where, for Deleuze, Spinoza's ontology enters the scene. Spinoza reframes Scotus' pairing between the common nature and individuating thisness into a triad of terms: a single substance,
for all attributes, that express individuated modes. In so doing, Spinoza
also does what Scotus does not do, which is to place the idea of univocity
within a framework that is not that of analogy. What replaces the framework of category is relation, and in particular the twofold axis of relationships of power and the circulation of affects. Thus the means by which
creatures are comprehended as univocal is less along the lines of species
and genus, and more along the lines of power (relations of intensity, relations of relations) and affect (the capacity to affect and to be affected).

3.7 UNIVOCAL CREATURES

Inasmuch as the concepts of Creator and creature are about their relation, we can suggest that univocity implies all relation, while equivocity implies no relation. A univocal relation between Creator and creature would imply, in Aquinas' view, a continuity of being between Creator and creature, and this continuity would, in turn, imply an equality of being, effectively flattening the relation of causal transcendence between Creator and creature. By contrast, an equivocal relation between Creator and creature would imply the inverse, a radical discontinuity between Creator and creature, in which both would exist in an absolutely unrelated and different sense. A creature is a being and a Creator is a being, without any relationship between one and the other whatsoever. Reducing to the extreme, we can say that univocity (all relation) points to the view that "all is one," while equivocity (no relation) points to a view that is something like the phrase "to each their own." Univocity is compromised by the fact that, while it flattens the Creator-creature distinction, it must still account for causal relationships in the creation of the creature by the Creator. Likewise, equivocity is compromised by its assertion of absolute non-relation, which itself becomes a relation.

Both positions, for Aquinas, pose significant problems for thinking about the creature, especially if we bear in mind the way that the Scholastic pair of Creator-creature extends the Aristotelian pair Life-living. Aquinas' primary interest is in adequately articulating their relation. While he does not deny the difficulty in thinking the concept of univocity, Scotus takes up the concept in a way that is almost opposite to that of Aquinas. His primary interest is in adequately articulating the creature between the two axes of Creator-creature and creature-creature. For Aquinas, what has to be accounted for is the relation between Creator and creature in a way that would preserve the causal hierarchy between them. What cannot be allowed in Aquinas' argument is any fundamental indistinction between Creator and creature, the supernatural and the natural, Life and the living, Primary and Secondary cause—whether this indistinction be real, numerical, or formal. The same can be said of Henry's arguments, though, as we've seen, Henry also argues against Aquinas. For Henry what cannot be allowed is any fundamental indistinction—thus his statement that what appears to natural knowledge to be a single thing is really a confused perception of two kinds of things (one as "negatively indeterminate" and the other as "privatively indeterminate").

For Scotus, what has to be accounted for is not so much the relation between the two entities Creator and creature, but the entities situated between two or more relations. Let us read Scotus as a contemporary. Scotus, at once taking up the thread of univocity, and pushing it forward to Spinoza, comes very close at times to implying the ontological priority of relation to the terms related. Even the relation between Creator and creature presupposes some common term, some common nature, through which they are at once linked and distinguished from each other. At its furthest reaches, Scotus' philosophy returns to this common term, this univocity, but without ever forgoing the creaturely manifestations from which it can never be totally separated. This dual commitment is worth pausing on. It implies a thought of univocity ("all relation"; Life, that-which-forms) that is inseparable from the concept of the creature (as living, as life-forms, as temporality, as finitude). The arguments for univocity developed by Scotus lead to the paradoxical notion of a *univocal creature*. A univocal creature would be a creature that, by its very contingency as living, as a life-form, as "creaturely indeterminacy," would equally express univocity. That which is, by definition, contingently living, is also necessarily Life. A univocal creature is not simply any given creature that exists in a univocal relation with another creature; rather, it is the concept of the creature as a kind of nexus in which relation is already actualized as prior to its terms.[69]

Within the concept of the univocal creature lies a contradiction—the living that is constrained on all sides by Life. The univocal creature, as a sort of living contradiction, opens onto a series of similar concepts. Let us extend this a bit further. In Scotus' proofs for univocity, there is a brief comment about the way in which a creature is unable to have any adequate knowledge of that which is "uncreated":

No object will produce a simple and proper concept of itself and a simple and proper concept of another object, unless it contains this second object essentially or virtually. No created object, however, contains the Uncreated [*increatum*] essentially or virtually—at least in the way that the two are actually related, namely as what is by nature secondary is related to what is by nature prior."[70]

On the surface, this simply means that a creature can have no adequate knowledge of anything that does not imply its being created, and thus "essentially" or "virtually" related to the Creator. But it is difficult not to ask the question—what would a creaturely knowledge of the uncreated be like? Would such an "uncreaturely" knowledge still be univocal? That is, would there exist a univocal relation between the creature (that which is created) that the "uncreature" (that which exists as uncreated)? Would the creature then obtain an immanent and univocal relation to that which is its negation, resulting in a kind of *uncreated univocity*?

In the Scholastic tradition, the creature is not only that which is created, but also that which is related. As created, the creature is defined by its finitude, by its being incomplete, indeterminate. As such, this finitude, incompleteness, and indetermination of the creature means that it has a certain openness. The creature is neither total nor absolute, and it is by virtue of this that it exists relationally. Thus the creature is finite and open, indeterminate and relational. Now, while the analogical approach makes of these characteristics part of a whole creature (so that the finite part is the animal life and the open part is the soul), the approaches of univocity and equivocity assert the identity of the twofold attributes of the finite and the open, the indeterminate and the relational. But then, one would have to entertain the idea of a creature that is at once individuated and actualized, and yet fully exteriorized and fully distributed—one can only think of a kind of inverted creature, or a kind of exploding creature, or better, a kind of "cosmic animal" that would not be separate from either nature or supernature. A univocal creature would be a creature that maximizes this tension between its finitude and openness, its indeterminacy and its propensity for relations—not as quantized parts of a theological whole, but as coextensive attributes that resist both pure spirit and pure matter.

The same follows for the inverse concept—the equivocal creature— except here the tension is maximized in a way that forecloses any common term at all, a kind of absolute negation between any two entities, a relation of non-relation (or a relation of the void). Recall that the key question of this debate is whether the relation between Creator and creature, or between Life and the living, was one of univocity (all relation), equivocity (no relation), or analogy (some relation). For Deleuze, it is the position of univocity that is the most radical. Why is this? Because with univocity one must think of Creator and creature not in terms of transcendence, and not even in terms of eminence or emanation, but in terms of immanence. Creator and creature, the divine and earthly, the supernatural and natural, Life and the living—each term is fully immanent in relation to the other. This is a difficult thought indeed, for it requires thinking that which is "above" the human as equal to that which is "below" the human. The angel and the insect both exist immanently. As Deleuze notes, "God is a tick" (or, perhaps, God is a swarm . . .).

So, when we think about the creature in this sense, what we have to think about is neither the individuated creature *nor* the universal Creator, but that it is the relation that constitutes the living as that-which-is-living, and Life as that-by-which-the-living-is-living. There is a "univocal creature," not because an individual animal is living, and not because a universal principle of Life guarantees the living. Instead, the creature is univocal because, in a sense, the relationship between Life and the living is actually a non-relation, compressed into a single, continuous "voice"— *une voce.* The life "after life" is another way of saying that the relation between Life and the living is a univocal relation—*and thus not really a relation at all.* "No relation"—is this not the opposite position, that of equivocity? On the surface of things, it seems that we have passed from univocity to equivocity.

This is the other alternative that Deleuze's Vincennes lectures furtively point to, for while Deleuze never explicitly took up the position of equivocity, implicitly all the talk of univocity and immanence moves towards this horizon. Equivocity has its own tradition, just as univocity does. The position of equivocity can be traced back to the "divine names" tradition in mystical theology, of which the Pseudo-Dionysius is the most common reference. The divine is, by this definition, absolutely inaccessible to human understanding. Anselm would later formalize this inaccessibility in the so-called ontological proof for God's existence. Arabic philosophy would also explore equivocity, in a mystical vein in Suhrawardī, and in a more analytical vein in Avicenna.

Equivocity posits no common terms between Creator and creature, Life and the living. Equivocity is blank thought, the thought of the neutral. Being is said in several senses, each in its own way, indifferent to each other instance. Perhaps equivocity is even more enigmatic than univocity. Where univocity posited the breakdown of all category, equivocity posits a God, a Being, a Life, that cannot be posited. This strange Being that does not exist, this Life that is not living, is at once necessary for thought itself to continue, but remains the absolute void that cannot be thought. Not existing in itself, but also not not existing. At once foundational and yet, in itself, nothing. Life as anonymous, indifferent, a void . . . the thought of the relation between Life and the living as equivocal opens onto the notion of an *equivocal inexistence,* in which the creature is absolutely differentiated from Creator.[71]

In fact, it is, perhaps, in their point of intersection that the dichotomy between Life and the living can be broken down. This is, arguably, the central point in Deleuze's reading of Scholasticism, and also what makes it contemporary: the point at which univocity becomes isomorphic with equivocity, *the point at which "all relation" becomes isomorphic with "no relation."* This is precisely the moment in which the question of life becomes evocative for Scholasticism. In the dichotomized space between the supernatural and natural, the divine and earthly, either there is an absolute gulf in which that which exists only exists equivocally, or there is an absolute continuum in which all is one:

> Prefiguring the relations between man and the infinite, the natural relation unites the living being with life. Life, in the first instance, seems to exist only through and within the living being, within the individual organism that puts it in action . . . That is to say that universality, the community of life, denies itself, gives itself to each living being as a simple outside, an exteriority that remains foreign to it, an Other.[72]

Again, inasmuch as the question of life was, for the Scholastics, less a question about what we would call biological or animal life, it increasingly becomes a question of some principle that is able to mediate between the purely material and the purely spiritual. In Scholasticism, Life is more than Being but less than God. But this is too general a statement. We should really say that insofar as the questions of the nature of Being and the nature of God were a primary question for Medieval philosophy, the debate surrounding the Creator-creation relationship became a key point of mediation between them. That this debate is significantly shaped by the Scholastic reception of Aristotelian natural philosophy means that the concept of life comes to be much more than classification and description of the natural world. As we've seen, life becomes primarily an issue of form, and the nature of the relationship between that which forms (or, the life-that-forms) and that which is formed (or, life-forms). For the Scholastics, the concept of life becomes a concept that seeks an ontological grounding in Being, and a theological grounding in God, but which retains something in excess of either of these terms.

But what is this "something more" or "something other"? Is it some further attribute that would distinguish Life from Being or God? Or must it remain shrouded in mysticism, amounting to a negative definition (e.g., "Life is that which is in excess of, but irreducible to, Being or God")? This is where the debate on univocity-equivocity-analogy becomes relevant, for each position says something about what this "something other" than Being or God is. It is not difficult to see how the position of analogy, for-

malized here by Aquinas, offers a way out of the apparent nihilism of
univocity/equivocity. Thomistic analogy is thus a kind of apology for the
creature. Against the notion of an equivocal inexistence (the creature in
and as the void, as it were), the doctrine of analogy asserts an essential
relation between Creator and creature, Life and the living. And, against
the notion of a univocal creature, the position of analogy preserves the relationship of causal priority and hierarchy between Creator and creature.
Only analogy offers a sufficiently adequate human view of the relation
between the supernatural and natural, divine and earthly. It does this by
asserting that the relation between Creator and creature exists solely by
virtue of causality. Here causality is taken in its Aristotelian guise, stressing efficient and final causality, but it is also mixed with Neoplatonic and
Avicennian notions of an emanating causality. That causality of this sort
is the sole arbiter between the Creator and the creature means that causality is in turn predicated on relations of exteriority: each cause external to
its effect, all the way up to the First Cause, which itself is uncaused.

The concept of life seems to forever come up against boundaries beyond which it simply becomes a matter of either classification or revelation. Perhaps this is why so few Scholastic philosophers went all the
way in support of univocity, and why nearly none throw in their support
for equivocity. We should also remind ourselves of the inherent non-
anthropomorphic tendencies of Scholastic heretical thinking in this regard. The question of the creature is not a metonym for any humanist
crisis or the question of the human being's place in the world. The finitude of the creature is not defined by any anguish or privileging of the
human. Neither is its openness a sign of the innate sociability of the creature. Quite the opposite—the question of the creature bears upon the relation between Life and the living in a way that arcs across the scale of
the human being. The positions of univocity and equivocity are difficult
thoughts precisely because they ask us to think about the Creator-creature
relation, or the Life-living relation, in a way that is both above and below
the scale of the human.

3.8 ELLIPSES: DŌGEN AND UNCREATED UNIVOCITY

While the Thomistic synthesis of Aristotle and theology would not go
without its own controversies, the emphasis on the relation of analogy between Creator and creature would gradually become the dominant position in post-Aristotelian Scholasticism. The Thomistic position of analogy
constructs a framework of theological (or really, theologico-political) tran-

scendence that is enabled by Aristotelian hylomorphism. One conserves the hierarchy of relations implicit in the process of creation and production, while also allowing for a more logically rigorous means by which this hierarchy of relations is conserved. Rarely if ever does one encounter an assertion of either full univocity or full equivocity, in spite of the modern readings that have been offered here of Duns Scotus. To the extent that there was really a debate, it comes to look more like a series of untenable hypotheses that are passed over in favor of the edifice of high Scholasticism, as displayed in the *Summa Theologica.*

But even the positions of univocity and equivocity are still subsumed within the larger topic of form, causality, and production. Hence a question: what would it mean to think life in terms of the limit-concepts of univocity and equivocity, but without the overarching framework of production (Creator, creating, creature)? This would be tantamount to inquiring into the points where univocity overlaps with, and becomes identical with, equivocity, the "everywhere" overlapping with the "nowhere."

Perhaps the various traditions in Buddhist thinking provide one way of doing this. Dōgen Zenji, the thirteenth-century Japanese teacher and philosopher, is commonly known as the founder of the school of Sōtō Zen. He is also known for his emphasis on a technique of seated meditation that has come to be closely identified with Zen Buddhism. Both Dōgen's meditation manuals, as well as his most well-known work, the *Shōbōgenzō*, emphasize the role of the Buddhist concept of "emptiness," not only in an epistemological sense (in terms of enlightenment), but, as a property of the world in itself.

Emptiness has several meanings for Dōgen. It applies to the subject, which is neither fixed nor static, and least of all defined by any innate or essential characteristics; the subject is an effect, not a cause. Emptiness also applies to the noumenal world of things-in-themselves. One of Dōgen's preferred phrases is "the nature of things," a phrase that includes the natural and spiritual worlds together: "All living beings, for infinite eons, have never left absorption in the nature of things."[73] Here the "nature of things" is that any discrete thing is in itself indefinable, in that it is preceded by a cluster of relations—and here the emptiness of the subject coincides with the emptiness of the world, both ultimately dissolved by this priority of relation. Finally, emptiness also inheres in the relation between self and world, the self always positing something about a world that, by definition, must remain in part inaccessible to the self. Together, these facets of emptiness reveal themselves in what Dōgen calls "absorption in the nature of things."[74] What emptiness is, is also the process of

emptying—emptying the self, the world, the self-world relation. This is
an enigmatic kind of totality, at once omnipresent and yet omni-evasive.
"This *totality of phenomena* and the *nature of things* are far beyond any
question of sameness or difference, beyond talk of distinction or identity . . .
is not past, present, or future, not annihilation or eternity . . ."[75]

To these Dōgen will add a final type of emptiness, which is that of
emptiness in itself (that is, the dissolution of the "in itself" of emptiness,
without any positive content). This emptiness, which seems to be at once
univocal to all things, and yet equivocal to any one of them, has no content in and of itself. It does not itself become a relation, a thing in the
world, or a self: "In the *nature of things* there are no heretics or demons—
it is only *eating breakfast, eating lunch, having a snack.*"[76] But then this
is like saying that the relation between Creator and creature is at once
fully continuous, and yet fully discontinuous. There can be no Creator,
since there is only a single, univocal continuum of creation and creativity;
likewise, there is also no creature, since the creature is simply an effect of
this continuum. Life is far from natural and organismic life, but becomes
nearly indissociable from a concept of being. As Dōgen notes, "*[A]ll living
beings do not leave living beings.*"[77] But neither should we rest at the point
of there being pure creation or creativity, since such terms presuppose basic relations of causality that require, in some shape or form, a Creator and
creature. What, then, persists? Perhaps it is Dōgen's fourth type of "emptiness" that persists, and that is univocal-equivocal. Here we would have
to think the concepts of univocity and equivocity as subtracted from the
conceptual framework of form, causality, and production. This would be
akin to thinking something like an *uncreated univocity*, or, alternately,
an *equivocal emptiness*.

In the concept of emptiness, Dōgen poses the question that is the greatest threat to philosophy—or at least the question that always threatens
to undermine thought as specifically philosophical. That is the question
of absolute relation—to assert the priority of relation (over self, over the
world, over relations themselves) is also to assert a fundamental emptiness that *is* this relation. The question that Dōgen raises is to what extent
"emptiness" in all its connotations is also the univocity of emptiness. Can
an ontology of life account for this fourth type of emptiness? "If you call
living beings living beings, it is *if you speak of it as something, you miss
it*. Speak quickly, speak quickly!"[78]

Dark Pantheism

Why do human beings expect an end of the world at all? And if this is
conceded to them, why must it be a terrible end?
—Kant

4.1 EVERYTHING AND NOTHING

Our inquiry into the concept of life began from a deceptively simple
question—the degree to which "life" can be an object of philosophical
inquiry. This led us, in our introductory comments, to the distinction between that-which-is-living and that-by-which-the-living-is-living, or, more
simply, the living and Life. The latter term denotes a general principle that
grounds or conditions the specific instances of the former, while remaining itself inaccessible. In the second chapter, we saw how this delineated
a structure of thought equivalent to negative theology. But we have also
seen that these two terms exist in relation to each other. Hence, in the
third chapter, we were led to the problem of how to think the distinction
between Life and the living while at the same time thinking their relation
and co-relation. This problem is that of the relation between Creator and
creature found in Scholastic discourse of the twelfth and thirteenth centuries (analogy, equivocity, and univocity). In the second chapter, the concept of life was split between Life and the living, with the former placed
forever beyond thought in a domain that was essentially that of the divine itself. In the third chapter, the concept of life was caught somewhere
within the relation between Creator and creature, with the concept of life
denoting both the concrete manifestations of living beings, as well as the
abstract principle by which living beings are living.

We are now in a position to take another step, and consider not just the

distinction of Life and the living, and not just their relation, but the continuum that runs through each and every instance of the living, as well as
between the Life-living relation—in other words, the *immanence* that not
only "runs through" but that constitutes Life and the living. We have seen
how the mystical theology tradition denies that any such a concept is possible, since by definition the divine is that which is beyond all conception.
Later, the Scholastics would temper this position and give it a more rigorous formal language. Scholasticism would suggest that, while the divine is
unknowable in itself, it can be indirectly known via its manifestations—
thus the Creator can be known via creatures.

In this chapter we can consider another approach, one that argues for
a positive conception of the divine in itself, but which does so through
the negation of its relation to anything outside of it. This approach we
can broadly refer to as that of "pantheism." But we should use the word
pantheism with some caution, for, while the term itself was not in use in
the Middle Ages, it has since come to describe a wide range of positions
that, in one way or another, deny the absolute transcendence of the divine, in effect equating the divine with the earthly, the supernatural with
the natural—or, as Spinoza infamously put it, "God or Nature."[1] Thus, in
considering the concept of life ontologically, we have moved from a basic distinction (Life-living), to a fundamental relation (Creator-creature),
to our concern here, which will be concerned with a type of continuity
(transcendence-immanence).[2]

Life can be thought of in terms of that which changes, becomes, or
flows outward in its generosity. Life can also be thought of in terms of that
which causes, which forms and shapes, or which creates and produces. To
these two definitions of life—as time and as form—we can add a third.
This is life as that which organizes and self-organizes, which disperses
and is itself pervasive—life as organizational and topological, at once omnipresent and yet immaterial; this concept of life we can refer to in terms
of spirit.

What is the concept of life when defined in terms of spirit? We can
begin with the following: life in terms of spirit is the life beyond all instances of the living, while remaining inseparable from them. We have,
on the one hand, a consideration of life in itself ("Life"), but this Life is
also understood to be inseparable from the multiple instances of the living. Thus when the concept of life is thought of in terms of spirit, this
implies several meanings of the term: Life-in-itself (that is, as opposed to
any relation to the living), but also the notion of the life-beyond-all-living
(which presupposes a relation via negation). The concept of Life is at once

that which is thought in itself, transcendent to the particular manifestations in the living, but also that which courses through them, that cuts across them, that *is* them—the "common" that is also all individuations. Life, in terms of spirit, is at once omnipresent and yet in itself, unmanifested, "inexistent." Its relation is through negation; that which is thought via a negative relation between Life and the living. When considered through the ontological (or onto-theological) lens of spirit, Life is at once transcendent—distinguishing itself from that which is manifested—and also immanent—accessible to thought only when conceived of as inseparable from its manifestations or "expressions."

4.2 LIFE AS SPIRIT IN AQUINAS

In Scholastic thinking, this dialectic between transcendence and immanence creates hybrids of nature and supernature, the earthly and the divine. The concept of "life" is, in this context, a theological concept before it is a biological or naturalistic concept. *That* life is, is given testimony by the many treatises on natural history, not to mention bestiaries and the like. Aristotle's *Historia Animalium* provides us with the blueprint for this type of thinking. But the question that persists is *what* life is—what gives testimony to this question? A work of metaphysics? A work of theology? A work of mysticism?

In addition to the "that" there is the "what": this is the life-of-all-life, the "super-Life"—which in many instances tends to be equivalent to the divine itself. Though they differ in their approaches, both Augustine and the Pseudo-Dionysius impute a superior, transcendent Life to the divine. This superlative Life not only makes possible all instances of the living, but its absolute transcendence is such that it comes to be identified with the divine itself. Between these two extremes, one above the scale of the human being, the other below the human being, there are all the manifold instances and types of life that continue to inform modern thinking: the life of the cognizing, reasoning being, the life of the community, the spiritual life of religious ritual, the political life of the body politic, and so on. Here we come back to a recurring problem: once the concept of "life" is decoupled from its naturalistic basis, it seems to all-too-quickly encompass nearly every sphere of human existence—in many cases encompassing the nonhuman spheres of nature and the elements as well. How, then, should we understand this bifurcation of the concept of life—at once above and below the scale of the human?

Aquinas provides us with one example, which we can take as the hegemonic statement on the topic. In the *Summa Theologica* Aquinas not only sets out the terms for thinking about life in terms of spirit, but he also articulates the specificity of this "life" of the divine nature. Indeed, one of the surprises that comes out of the first part of the *Summa* is question 18 (hereafter q18), simply titled "The Life of God." Covering a short four articles, it forms part of a longer series of meditations on the nature of the divine that take up most of the first part of the *Summa*. The q18 is noteworthy because, if only briefly, it raises the question of an ontology of life that had been previously posed by Aristotle. In terms of its organization, q18 is situated in an interesting way. It comes between the initial ontology of divine Being and the later questions (q44–47) on creation and the relation between Creator and creatures. If the first thirteen questions deal with the Being of the divine, and if the later questions deal with creatures and creation, then q18 stands squarely in between them, considering the divine both in itself and in relation to creaturely life.

Before confronting the issue of the divine life, Aquinas asks how natural life is attributed—what he takes as the founding distinction between the living and the nonliving. Quoting both Aristotle and the Pseudo-Dionysius, Aquinas notes that it would seem to be the case that life is attributed only of those things existing in nature, since, according to Aristotle, movement is a key attribute of all natural things, and since all natural things participate in movement of some kind. Following Aristotle, Aquinas notes that movement can either be movement from an external source, or movement from an internal source. Self-movement and other-movement become the basic conceptual poles around which Aquinas (via Aristotle) defines life.

Aquinas' strategy is to expand the notion of life beyond the natural domain. He does this first by defining life in a way that attempts to go beyond mere tautology, specifically in terms of the capacity for self-movement and self-causation:

> Whereby it is clear that those things are properly called living that move themselves by some kind of movement, whether it be a movement properly so called, as the act of an imperfect thing, i.e., of a thing in potentiality, is called movement; or movement in a more general sense, as when said of an act of a perfect thing, as understanding and feeling are called movement.[3]

Then, referencing Aristotle, Aquinas frames this question of self-movement within a kind of celestial or cosmic hierarchy:

These words of the Philosopher may be understood either of the first movement, namely, that of the celestial bodies, or of the movement in its general sense. In either way is movement called the life, as it where, of natural bodies, speaking by a similitude, and not attributing it to them as their property. The movement of the heavens is in the universe of corporeal natures as the movement of the heart, whereby life is preserved, is in animals.[4]

Note the ambiguity of this last passage—throughout q18, it remains unclear whether both Creator and creatures are alive in varying degrees of perfection, or whether Creator and creatures are both living, but in incomparable, equivocal ways. The phrase "speaking by similitude," as well as the image of the "celestial heart" both suggest that Aquinas makes use of analogical predication here, the kind that he had previously explicated in the questions on the divine names and analogy.

As if unsatisfied with this analogical image of the "cosmic organ" (what the heart is to the organism, all natural bodies are to the heavens), Aquinas then goes on to make an even more striking analogy:

> Similarly also every natural movement in respect to natural things has a certain similitude to the operations of life. Hence, if the whole corporeal universe were one animal, so that its movement came from an *intrinsic moving force*, as some in fact have held, in that case movement would really be the life of all natural bodies.[5]

The resulting implication of this passage is that if life is not only movement, but specifically self-movement, and if this self-movement occurs in the celestial as well as earthly domains, then there is at least the possibility of thinking "life" in relation to the divine—though what exactly this relation is is left somewhat open.

Life is, for Aquinas, defined as being more than the factical existence of natural, biological organisms; it is, following Aristotle, the capacity for self-movement. It would seem, Aquinas notes, that life is a process and not a product, an act and not a thing. Yet Aquinas counters this notion. His support is a single and enigmatic phrase from the *De Anima*: "It seems that life is an operation . . . On the contrary, the Philosopher says, *In living things to live is to be*."[6] Aquinas has previously suggested that life be defined in relation to movement, so much so that he was willing to postulate a kind of "cosmic animal." This opened the door to thinking about the divine in terms of life, and life in terms of movement. But just at the moment when he would have to admit that life is movement (and life is the divine), he pulls back and, quoting Aristotle, asserts a relation between "life" and "being." There appears to be a tension here, between life as dynamic becoming and life as static being, life as the coming-to-be and passing-away of nature and life as the omnipresence of the divine.

At this point Aquinas' Aristotelianism confronts his Neoplatonism. The reason, he explains, why life is not identical to movement, process, or change has to do with the distinction between essence and existence. Just as we gain knowledge of the world from our senses, and just as this knowledge ultimately points to something beyond what we sense, so does the notion of life-as-movement ultimately point beyond the manifestation of movement to . . . what? To an essence of life? To a divine cause? To a divine life? Aquinas refuses to take up any of these possibilities. What he does assert is that names (in the divine names tradition) refer to something beyond the sensible and material, and this is the case with life as well. The name "life" refers to the sensed materiality of movement, but more profoundly it gives us an essence of life—or, we can say, that by which life is movement:

> The name ["life"] is given from a certain external appearance, namely, self-movement, yet not precisely to signify this, but rather a substance to which self-movement and the application of itself to any kind of operation, belong naturally. To live, accordingly, is nothing else than to exist in this or that nature.[7]

That by which life is movement is at once something other than life (something other than the particular type of life-that-is-movement—vegetative, sensitive, etc.), but it is at the same time "life itself," the life that encompasses the four types of life given by Aristotle.

Aquinas' move here is complicated. It involves two gestures. One is to attempt to explain an incongruity derived from Aristotle. In the *De Anima*, life is both a life-principle (*psukhē*) as well as a list of the different manifestations of that life-principle (vegetative, sensory, rational). Aristotle never makes clear the relation between, on the one hand, the principle, and on the other, the types. Aquinas finds himself caught in this lacuna. He attempts to smooth it over using his analogy of proportion, in which a single term is predicated of many things, but in different ways. Recall his privileged example of the analogy of proportion, drawn from medicine: "healthy" is predicated in one sense of a kidney, in another sense of urine produced by the kidney, in another sense of the whole organism, and still in another sense of the practice of medicine. So, here "life" can be predicated of a natural thing that moves, and also of that by which a natural thing moves. "Life" can be an actual living thing, such as an animal, or it can be an essence that conditions that animal (as well as other living things): "The Philosopher here takes *to live* to mean an operation of life. Or it would be better to say that sensation and intelligence, and the like, are sometimes taken for the operations, sometimes for the existence itself of the operator."[8]

This may seem to be a rather shaky cover-up for "the Philosopher," but an important distinction comes out of it: the distinction between life-as-essence and life-as-existence. In Thomist terminology, that by which life is movement is Life or an essence, whereas the particular manifestation of life-as-movement is the living or an existence. The former is necessary, and without it life cannot be thought as such; the latter is contingent, and may or may not exist, irrespective of the essence.

Aquinas has articulated a division, one that remained implicit in Aristotle. But even if we accept this division between Life and the living, there still remains the question of the relation between them, and to what extent they are both called "life." This is addressed in the third article for q18, "Whether Life Is Properly Attributed to God." It would seem that life cannot be attributed to the divine, for God is eternal, whereas life stops and starts, lives and dies. God does not have movement as an attribute or as an effect, even in the sense of self-movement, for otherwise God and the beast would be identical. Furthermore—Aquinas again pulls from the *De Anima*—all living things are said to have an essence, or a principle of life. But God does not have an essence, God is essence, or, more specifically, the meeting point of essence and existence. If God has a principle of life, then there would need to be something else, something higher by which God can be said to be living.

This last point is crucial. To say that there is an essence of life in God, that God has a life-principle, is tantamount to suggesting that there is a being above God, or at least, that there is something else by which God can be said to exist. Bizarrely, this is precisely what Aquinas appears to state: "*I answer that, Life is in the highest degree properly in God.*"[9] The key qualifier here is the phrase "in the highest degree." Aquinas does not say that life is univocally predicated of Creator and creature, God and human being. What he does is conceive of life in terms of degrees of perfection. Aquinas again makes use of analogy (rather than posit univocity or equivocity), but it is a different type of analogy than in the previous article. There the analogy of proportion is used, where a single term is predicated in a different sense of different things: "[S]ince a thing is said to live insofar as it operates of itself and not as moved by another, the more perfectly this power is found in anything, the more perfect is the life of that thing."[10] Aquinas then goes on to enumerate the stages in the degrees of perfection of life. Each is distinguished from the others, from lowest to highest, by the proximity of their existence (as actually living) to their essence (as the form-of-Life): the life that moves itself through the simple execution of its nature (plants), life that moves itself through the execution of its form (animals), life that moves itself through an understanding of its form (humans), and life that is itself understanding, form, and movement in one (God). Note that Aquinas follows Aristotle's division—up until we reach supernature or the divine, which is, as it were, the *supernatural life*: "Wherefore that being whose act of understanding is its very nature, and which, in what it naturally possesses, is not determined by another, must have life in the most perfect degree. Such is God; and hence in Him principally is life."[11]

At this point Aquinas appears ready to again equate the divine with life. Elsewhere in the *Summa* (in his proofs for God's existence) Aquinas describes God as that being in which essence and existence are the same. Here, in q18, God is that being in which Life and the living are the same, the absolute coincidence of that-which-is-living and that-by-which-the-living-is-living. Everything else—all creatures, from humans to plants—are imperfect manifestations of this supernatural life, since in them the distinction between Life and the living is more evident.

A final problem still remains. Aquinas has given us a definition of life in line with Scholastic theology, a definition according to the essence-existence distinction (which becomes isomorphic with the Life-living distinction). He has also articulated a relation between life and the divine, and he has described the relation between them (according to analogy). And he has qualified in what sense life can be predicated of God (using another type of analogy). But if God is living in the most perfect sense, and if the difference between creature and Creator is simply one of degree, then what is to prevent any creature, for instance, from climbing further up the ladder and attaining divinity? Conversely, what is to prevent God from descending, as it were, into the realm of the all-too-human, the bestial, or even the botanical? In short, an onto-theological problem remains, and that is the problem of creation, and it is a problem because Aquinas has described a cause that appears to be both transcendent (in that the cause remains apart from its effects) and immanent (in that there is a gradient of attributes from cause to effect).

The fourth and last article of q18 takes up this problem. Aquinas asks, are all living things living "in" God? This is, more than any of the others, a rhetorical question, and it serves as an instance of Aquinas having his (philosophical) cake and (theologically) eating it too. In short, Aquinas notes that all things that are living are in God, simply because God is the cause of all things. But this belies a duplicity at the heart of Aquinas' notion of life. On the one hand the divine being is transcendent, a cause of life, a principle of life, a that-by-which-the-living-is-living. Yet, on the other hand, the divine being is also immanent, a gradient of life that is diffused or emanated.

While Aquinas' overarching project is as much theological as philosophical, his articulation of the Life/living distinction—here within the method of analogy—is nevertheless foundational. It not only has the effect of recuperating the ontology of life into onto-theology, but in so doing it produces a strange, "weird" concept of supernatural life as its core. Aquinas' text not only highlights what would otherwise be a lacuna in Aristotle's thought, but, by linking this distinction of Life/living to a question of the divine nature, he also sets up a provocative debate concerning the concept of immanence. This debate, which would include thinkers such as Duns Scotus and Nicholas of Cusa, would shape the discourse of pantheism in the late-Medieval period.

4.3 THE CONCEPT OF THE DIVINE NATURE

The original articulation of the concept of life as a concept—that of the split between Life and the living provided by Aristotle—is formalized in Scholasticism in terms of the discourse on the divine nature. The concept of the divine nature is a concept that deals with spirit, the omnipresent and yet unmanifested *esse* that is the divine. This, in turn, requires a dialectic of transcendence and immanence—the divine or supernatural as that which is beyond precisely because it is pervasive and everywhere.

We can understand the phrase "divine nature" here in several basic senses—first, as the nature or essence of a thing, but also, in a more modern sense, as the natural world.[12] And this is the sticking point for many of the positions dubbed heretical during the late Middle Ages—for so-called pantheists such as Amaury of Bene or David of Dinant, the divine nature was at once an essence but also "natural." In Eriugena's *Periphyseon*, the divine nature, or simply *natura*, is given an expanded definition: "Nature, then, is the general name, as we said, for all things, for those that are and those that are not."[13] As we will see, there are echoes of Eriugena's concept in Duns Scotus and Nicholas of Cusa, before it goes on to obtain a stronger assertion in Spinoza's notion of a single substance for all attributes. In short, the discourse on the divine nature puts at stake the relation between the "divine" and "nature," be it in terms of their transcendence (as in Aquinas) or their pure immanence (as in the variants of Medieval pantheism).

In Medieval thought, the terms of the discourse on the divine nature are split between transcendence and immanence. And yet, in the myriad mixtures that produce Scholastic discourse—from Patristic theology to Aristotelian natural philosophy—these two terms are not opposed to each other. It is important to note that, contrary to contemporary "theory," there is no conflict of interest between transcendence and immanence; more often than not, immanence is granted a subordinate role within the larger ambit of transcendence. Not only is there more than one kind of transcendence or immanence, but the two concepts are shaped within a political-theological context, one in which the maxim of philosophy playing handmaiden to theology was not infrequently contested.

There are two major philosophical concerns here: one has to do with causality. The investigation into causes not only underpins Scholastic metaphysics, but causality and its attendant terms—production and creation—deal more explicitly with the political and theological implications of sovereignty and community. The other philosophical concern is that of order. Nearly every proof for the existence of God among the Scholastics contains some form of an argument from the implicit order in the natural world—and by extension, among the hierarchy of creatures in that world. Order is often tied to hierarchy, which verticalizes order and intimately ties it to the concerns of causality. But the metaphysical gulf between Creator and creature, the divine nature and earthly nature, also necessitates the recognition of a more horizontal order, one that is more distributive. In thinking the concept of "life" through the divine nature, the primarily challenge for Scholastic thinkers is how and in what way to correlate these two issues of causality and order.

This, however, does not mean that there is a single chorus of philosophical consensus among the Scholastics; indeed, the fine and subtle distinctions in Scholastic texts often reveal major philosophical differences. For example, through a cursory look at Medieval thought up to the late twelfth and early thirteenth centuries—that is, the period of the introduction of Aristotle's natural philosophy into the Latin West—one can outline several variations on the divine nature, understood as a dialectic between transcendence and immanence: (i) there is the long tradition of

Neoplatonic thinking, which has its source in Plotinus and the notion of divine emanation, and which also finds expression in the systematicity of Arabic thinkers such as Avicenna; (ii) there is also a rich tradition of mysticism that emphasizes the motif of light and radiation, found in the Greek and Latin Fathers, but also, later, in the Arabic-Islamic tradition of "illuminationist" thinking; (iii) and there is the thin and fragmented thread of Medieval pantheism, which finds its most explicit formulation in the controversies surrounding the reading, interpretation, and teaching of Aristotle's natural philosophy in the thirteenth century. Each of these tendencies grapples in some way with the role of immanence in the divine nature—each also stops just short of a full-blown immanentism, either by recourse to a first cause, or by a canalization of immanence in a single, outpouring source.

The through-line that we will follow will deal with the relation between the concepts of life and immanence. We will consider three forms of life-as-immanence: that of Eriugena, whose work *Periphyseon* (*The Division of Nature*) has often been read as asserting the equivalence of the divine and nature; that of Duns Scotus, whose arguments for the existence of God reveal another dimension of his concept of univocity; and finally that of the mystical thinker Nicholas of Cusa, whose major work *De Docta Ignorantia* (*On Learned Ignorance*) develops a more complicated notion of life-as-immanence. These three figures of life-as-immanence will then enable us to consider a more contemporary example in Gilles Deleuze, in his Scholastic-influenced reading of Spinoza and the concept of "expression."

If, broadly speaking, pantheism refers to any system of thought in which the divine and nature are indissociable, then there is a sense in which one can make a claim for Eriugena, Duns Scotus, and Cusa as thinkers that engage with the problem of pantheism. This is not to say that they fully espouse or unproblematically assert a pantheist doctrine. It is to suggest that, insofar as pantheism deals with the relation between the divine and earthly, supernatural and natural, it must also deal with the concept of immanence, and the role of immanence in a philosophical and theological context. Each of these thinkers deals with two central questions concerning the concept of immanence, questions that will guide us in our readings below.

The first question is whether the concept of immanence must always be thought of in terms of transcendence. Does every concept of immanence imply the transcendence of that-which-is-immanent? Further, must any concept of immanence be thought of secondarily or in a derivative way, from transcendence? How do Scholastic thinkers deal with the ten-

sions between transcendence and immanence? To what degree is it possible, or even desirable, to think of immanence as not subordinate to transcendence, as what Deleuze calls "pure immanence"? This question deals
with what we can refer to as the "insubordination of immanence."

A second question follows from this: what is the relationship between
immanence and nature? Is what we call pantheism simply the equivalence of immanence and nature? Does every concept of *natura* in the general sense imply some notion of immanence? Conversely, to what degree
does any concept of immanence imply a notion of *natura*, either in terms
of creation and causality, or in terms of its manifestation or theophany
(what Deleuze, borrowing from Nicholas of Cusa, calls "complication"
and "explication")? Is there a concept of immanence that is neither reducible to *natura* in the narrow sense, nor absolutely above and beyond
natura? This question deals with what we can generally call "supernatural
immanence."

4.4 IMMANENCE I: ERIUGENA'S *PERIPHYSEON*

The *Periphyseon* is often discussed as an important nexus between philosophy and theology as it developed in early Medieval Christianity. Working during the ninth-century Carolingian renaissance, Eriugena's writings
incorporate a number of influences that would be central to the shaping
of later Medieval intellectual currents. In addition to the textbooks of the
Trivium and *Quadrivium*, there is also the influence of Neoplatonism:
early on, Eriugena wrote a commentary on a fifth-century text by Mar-
tianus Capella, the *Wedding of Philology and Mercury*, that appears to
be one of his main Neoplatonic sources. Eriugena also synthesized influences from both "eastern" and "western" theological traditions: his work
displays a familiarity with Greek Fathers such as Gregory of Nyssa (whom
he translated), as well as a familiarity with Latin Fathers such as Augustine and Ambrose. But the single most important influence on Eriugena's thinking is the Pseudo-Dionysius. Eriugena completed a translation
of the Pseudo-Dionysius' *Mystical Theology*, which became something of
a textbook for thirteenth-century Scholastic thinkers. The influence of
the Pseudo-Dionysius can be seen in Eriugena's *Periphyseon*— book 1, for
instance, devotes considerable space to the discussion of affirmative and
negative theology, and the idea of the divine as that which is essentially
inaccessible to thought, and therefore "nothing" (*nihil*). With this background in mind, let us take a closer look at the role that *natura* plays in
Eriugena's work.

4.4.1 *NATURA* AND THE UNTHOUGHT

If Eriugena formalized and rationalized the mystical theology of the Pseudo-Dionysius, he also added a great deal, in particular a concept of "nature" (*natura*) that was neither the "nature" of natural philosophy nor the "nature" of theological essence.[14] What then is *natura* for Eriugena? In the *Periphyseon*, Eriugena has his interlocutors—a teacher (Nutritor) and a student (Alumnus)—discuss the concept of *natura*. The Nutritor opens book 1 with a definition:

> As I frequently ponder and, so far as my talents allow, ever more care-fully investigate the fact that the first and fundamental division of all things which either can be grasped by the mind or lie beyond its grasp is into those that are and those that are not, there comes to mind as a general term for them all what in Greek is called φυσις and in Latin *Natura*.[15]

Here Eriugena provides two axes along which the concept of *natura* can be thought. One axis deals with all that is and all that is not (we have al-ready encountered this in an expanded form in chapter two, in Eriugena's five modes of being and nonbeing). This is Eriugena's primary definition of *natura*, an all-encompassing term, which the Nutritor defines again: "Na-ture, then, is the general name, as we said, for all things, for those that are and those that are not."[16] Another axis deals with that which can be thought and that which cannot be thought. This follows the same dialec-tic of the first axis, but here the emphasis is on the ideation of *natura*. The Alumnus, responding to the Nutritor, puts it this way: "For nothing at all can come into our thought that would not fall under this term [*natura*]."[17] These two axes both have the dialectical structure of affirmation and ne-gation (that which is vs. that which is not; that which can be thought vs. that which cannot be thought). But the affirmation and negation in each sense is not simply an opposition, for "that which is not" is still affirma-tively considered to be a part of *natura*. Similarly, the negation of "that which cannot be thought" is not simply a privative negation, or a poten-tiality (e.g., "that which may possibly be thought in the future"), but a paradoxical affirmation of the limit of thought—"that which by defini-tion is inaccessible to thought," or simply, that which is *unthought*. This dialectic between affirmation and negation produces a kind of oscillation between terms. The various syntheses of affirmation and negation actu-ally set things in motion; they "vertically" govern the modes of being and

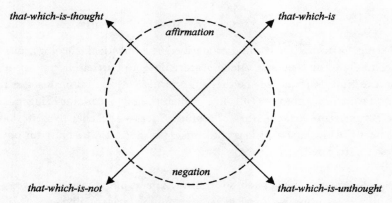

Figure 2. The two axes of *natura* in Eriugena's *Periphyseon*.

nonbeing, thought and unthought, but they also distribute *natura* horizontally throughout all its manifestations. In one instance we have an affirmation of a negation, in which "that which is not" is affirmed as such;
in another instance we have a negation of an affirmation, in which the affirmative inclusion of "that which is not" in *natura* is itself negated, since
"that which is not" is nothing (*nihil*).

Thus, there are really three elements to Eriugena's concept of *natura*:
an empirical axis of being and nonbeing, an ideational axis of thought
and unthought, and a dialectical valence of affirmative negation and negative affirmation—we can call this third element the "valence of dispersion." They form a basic diagram (figure 2) that structures the overarching ontology of the *Periphyseon*. Already a number of questions arise from
this diagram of *natura*.[18] For instance, is every instance of "that which
is not" also an instance of "that which cannot be thought"? That is, can
nonbeing be thought, without turning into being? It would seem that in
Eriugena's distinction between the negation of being and the negation of
thought is an implication that "that which is not" can also be "that which
can be thought." Likewise, does every instance of "that which cannot be
thought" presume a parallel instance of "that which is not"? That is, does
every unthought imply an inexistent? Numerous other conundrums can
be derived from Eriugena's apparently straightforward definition. But what
is arguably the most important element in the above diagram is not the
two axes of being or thought, but the dynamics of affirmation and negation that give coherence to the two axes. Thus, there are also questions
concerning the role that affirmation and negation play in producing a dy-

namic set of relationships between being and nonbeing, thought and unthought, being and unthought, nonbeing and thought, and so on.

This is the crux of Eriugena's concept of *natura*—that it is not a static
diagram but one that contains trajectories, vectors, and dispersions. Dispersion in this case is not simply a random scattering of some attribute or
property; in the concept of *natura* it sets *natura* into motion through affirmations and negations, and the variable syntheses between them. Affirmations and negations are always coupled in *natura*, and, in many cases,
synthesized in paradoxical formulations—e.g., the divine as both pure affirmation and pure negation, the notion of the divine as the "darkness of
super-essential light," and so on. Arguably, Eriugena's notion of *natura* is an
indelibly dispersional notion, asserting at once the transcendence of the divine nature, while also implying its immanence along the two axes, themselves conditioned by the processual nature of affirmation and negation.

Eriugena enframes this entire diagram (of being/nonbeing, of thought/
unthought, of affirmation/negation) within the concept of *natura*. This is,
as the Nutritor notes, at once a classical, even presocratic notion of "nature" (as *phusis*), but also a theological notion, synthesizing as it does
the notion of essence with a monistic view of "the One." If everything—
including that which is not—is encompassed within *natura*, then how can
one account for the different senses of "nature," from the narrow notion
of natural philosophy, to natural theology, to the mystical notion of divine
nature? There appears to be a gulf, then, between the overarching principle of *natura*, and the manifold affirmations and negations that constitute
"nature" in the other senses, and which are contained within the single,
monistic *natura*. This is, certainly, a problem of the One and the Many—
but more importantly, it is a problem of the relations, dynamics, and above
all the dispersions between the One and the Many, between *natura* and
"nature" in the narrow sense.

It is in order to address this question that Eriugena turns to what is
perhaps his most well-known doctrine, the four basic divisions of *natura*.
Just following his definition, the Nutritor provides a brief outline of the
divisions of *natura*:

> It is my opinion that the division of Nature by means of four differ-
> ences results in four species, (being divided) first into that which cre-
> ates and is not created, secondly into that which is created and also
> creates, thirdly into that which is created and does not create, while
> the fourth neither creates nor is created.[19]

For the sake of clarity, we can simply list the four divisions as follows:

- That which creates & is not created (God/Universal Nature)
- That which creates & is created (Intellect/Ideas)
- That which does not create & is created (nature, creatures)
- That which does not create & is not created (God/Universal Nature)

As the Nutritor goes on to explain, the four divisions of *natura* form a single, unified system, with each division related to the other through the "dispersive" dynamics of affirmation and negation, creation and un-creation. The first division—that which creates and is not created—is the divine nature in itself. Only God is that which is the uncreated Creator. The second division—that which creates and is created—is what are vari-ously called the Intelligences, Ideas, or Primordial Causes. Here Eriugena's Neoplatonic influence shows most clearly, for the Ideas are neither the di-vine in itself, nor the multiple instances of creatures in the world; they are precisely the mediators between Creator and creatures, existing in a perfected state. They are, in a sense, the models of creatures. The third division—that which is created and does not create—is the world of crea-tures and "nature" in the narrow sense. Eriugena, following a common theological trend, makes a distinction between "creation" and mere "mak-ing" or "production," the latter the activity of certain creatures such as human beings. Finally, there is the fourth division—that which does not create and is not created—which is also, like the first division, the divine nature in itself. Thus the four divisions form a circle, the final returning to the first, all affirmation culminating in a negation, which itself circles back to a superlative affirmation.

As we've noted, Eriugena's concept of *natura* deals not only with cre-ation and the relation between Creator and creature, but with the dis-persions of *natura* through a dialectics of affirmation-negation. The four divisions of *natura* are interrelated in this way. As the Nutritor notes, "[W]ithin these four [divisions] there are two pairs of opposites. For the third is the opposite of the first, the fourth of the second; but the fourth is classed among the impossibles, for it is of its essence that it cannot be."[20] Let us keep with our wobbly diagram and present the four divisions of *natura* as in figure 3. Following the Nutritor, we can see that the first and third are inversely paired according to the dialectic in creating and being created. The same can be said for the second and fourth divisions. From another perspective, the first and second divisions can be paired together

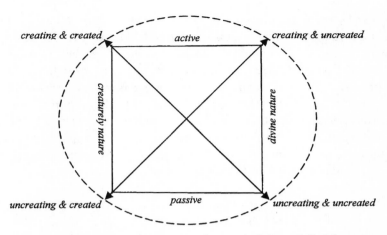

creating & created — active — creating & uncreated

creaturely nature

divine nature

uncreating & created — passive — uncreating & uncreated

Figure 3. The creation and uncreation of *natura* in Eriugena's *Periphyseon.*

as active principles, while the third and fourth can be paired together as passive principles. Finally, the first and fourth divisions are identical, in that they both define the divine nature in itself, while the second and third divisions are identical, in that they both describe the domain of creation. Everything, however, returns to the single principle of *natura*, wherein Creator and creature become indistinct: "So the universe, comprising God and creature, which was first divided as it were into four forms, is reduced again to an indivisible One, being Principle as well as Cause and End."[21] In a rather tidy fashion, the four divisions of *natura* are in this way unified: four becomes two (God and creation), and two becomes one (*natura*).

The concept of *natura* in Eriugena is clearly more than "nature" in the narrow sense of natural philosophy. But it is also not simply the divine "nature" in an absolutely transcendent sense. The concept of *natura* is not a stand-alone concept, but one that, as the *Periphyseon* states, must be thought of in terms of its divisions and dispersions. This dialectic of splitting-apart and re-unifying has the effect of bifurcating the concept of *natura* into that which is manifested (the second and third divisions) and that which is not (the first and last divisions). *Natura* is both that which has a concrete, manifested, and created reality (the creation of the Ideas and the world), but also that which has an abstract, unmanifested, and uncreated reality (the divine as alpha and omega, as "universal nature"). Paradoxically, *natura* is at once something (creatures, the natural world) and nothing (the divine as a negation that is not a privative negation, but a superlative one).

And it is here that the question of life comes into focus. As we've noted

previously, there are several notions of life at work in Medieval ontotheology: the life of the natural world (the biologistic sense), the life of
the divine nature (the theological sense), and the life of their relation (the
ontological sense). Eriugena does, certainly, account for the first sense of
naturalistic "life," but much of the *Periphyseon* is are concerned with the
latter two types of life—the superlative life of the divine nature in itself,
and the relational, dynamic life of Creator and creature. These latter two
notions of life—the first defined in terms of immaterial spirit, the second
in terms of an equally immaterial relation—come together in Eriugena's
dispersional notion of the "life" of the divine:

> For the whole river first flows forth from its source, and through its
> channel the water which first wells up in the source continues to flow
> always without any break to whatever distance it extends. So the Di-
> vine Goodness and Essence . . . first flow down into the primordial
> causes . . . flowing forth continuously through the higher to the lower;
> and return back again to their source.[22]

In Neoplatonic fashion, Eriugena borrows the notions of emanation, outpouring, and flux not as the divine in itself, and not as the manifold creatures that flow out from the divine source, but as the continuum or dispersion that runs through them, the life to come that is at once temporally
placed in the afterlife as well as spatially distributed throughout all of *natura*.[23] This continuum stretches between the creaturely life and the divine
life, but it is not simply "life" in terms of the dynamics of sovereign creation. Eriugena does assimilate the Neoplatonic notion of a divine source
and emanation, but he also situates it within what is a unique framework
of affirmation and negation, division and unicity, *esse* and *nihil*. Neither is
this life that of creatures or creation. Eriugena devotes considerable time
to the life of creatures and creation—in book 3 he articulates an ascending
order of creation, from natural bodies such as rocks (subsistence), to plants
(subsistence and life), to animals (with senses), to rational animals, and
the primordial causes (located in the spiritual creatures).[24] However, what
is of primary philosophical interest is the way in which he articulates a
universal life that runs through them, establishing a continuity within
natura while also establishing differentiations.[25] Thus, in each instance
in which Eriugena asserts either the creaturely life or the divine life in itself, he also asserts the interrelational continuum or dispersion that runs
through them.

4.4.2 UNIVERSAL LIFE

This tension is best demonstrated by a brief discussion in book 3 around the concept of universal life. Here the Nutritor engages in a bit of thinking aloud. The Nutritor asks why, amid all the scriptural talk of creation and *natura*, there is no mention of "life": "Throughout the four days of the creation of natures that have already been discussed we read of no mention of the soul (*animae*) either simply or absolutely or with the qualification 'living' (*uiuentis*), and it is not inappropriate to ask why."[26] The Nutritor offers one, provisional response. Since neither life nor ensoulment is mentioned in the Hexameron, the natural world, which was created during this time, is therefore neither alive nor ensouled.

> For there are those who say that the elements of this world, I mean the heaven with its stars, and the ether with its planets, the air with its clouds and breaths of wind and lightnings and other disturbances, the water also and its flowing motion, likewise the earth with all its plants and trees, are not only without soul (*anima*) but also without any kind of life (*uitae*) at all.[27]

But this is too literal a response, for, as the Nutritor notes, reflection on life is a central part of classical thought: "Plato, the greatest of the philosophers, and his sectaries not only affirm a general life of the world (*generalem mundi uitam*), but also declare that there is no form attached to bodies nor any body that is deprived of life; and that life, whether general or special, they confidently dare to call soul (*animam*)." As the Nutritor notes, scripture agrees with this, "affirming that plants and trees and all things that grow out of the earth are alive." Thus, in contrast to the first, literal response (that "life" is not mentioned in the Hexameron), the Nutritor offers a second, alternative response by way of a Platonic-Neoplatonic "soul."

But even this just touches the surface for the Nutritor, who then goes on to offer a third response, again by way of classical thought—this time by way of a Neoplatonic filtering of Aristotle:

> Nor does the nature of things permit it to be otherwise. For if there is no matter which without form produces body, and no form subsists without its proper substance, and no substance can be without the vital motion (*uitali motu*) which contains it and causes its subsistence—for

everything which is naturally moved receives the source of its motion from some life—, it necessarily follows that every creature is either Life-through-itself (*se ipsam uita*) or participates in life and is somehow alive, whether the vital motion is clearly apparent in it or is not apparent but the sensible species itself shows that it is hiddenly governed [through] life.[28]

Thus for the Nutritor, this is confirmed by the concepts of (Neoplatonic-Aristotelian) metaphysics. There is no body without matter and form, no form without substance, and no substance without the vital motion of ensoulment. All creation is either self-ensouled or ensouled through another source than itself.

Given this framework, the Nutritor is led into some interesting territory. If the fundamental principle of life is not limited to the individual organism or to the species of living being to which the organism belongs, then it would seem that a meta-level concept of life would be necessary, a concept of life beyond either organism or species. It is here that the Nutritor posits the existence of a *universal life*:

> For as there is no body which is not contained within its proper species, so there is no species which is not controlled by the power of some life (*uitae*). Therefore, if all bodies which are naturally constituted are governed by some species of life (*specie uitae*), and every species seeks its own genus while every genus takes its origin from universal substance, it must be that every species of life which contains the numerousness of the various bodies returns to a universal life (*generalissimam quandam uitam*), by participation in which it is a species.[29]

The Aristotelian outlook leads to a hierarchy of life forms, in terms of body-species-life, with the middle term, species, serving as an abstract, mediating set-concept. But this then requires that one conceive of a higher life-concept beyond the individuated organism or body, and beyond the set or category concept of species—but without simply relinquishing the concept of life so that it is equivalent to God or Being.

Interestingly, Eriugena has the Nutritor pursue a line of thought concerning life in such a way that the concept resists being sublimated into a discussion of metaphysics or the divine nature. It is for this reason that the Nutritor comes up with the striking phrase "universal life." This universal life is not itself a type or instance or life—it is something like meta-life, a life-beyond-life, which ontologically structures both the life of species and organisms. But this then leads to the question of how this universal life—which the Nutritor links to the Neoplatonic soul—is different from the divine nature itself.

> Now, this universal life (*generalissima uita*) is called by the natural philosophers the Universal Soul (*uniuersalissima anima*) which through its species controls the totality which is contained within the orbit of the heavenly sphere, while those who contemplate the Divine Sophia call it the common life (*commumem uitam*), which, while it participates in that one Life which is substantial in itself and is the fountain and creator of all life, by its division into things visible and invisible distributes lives in accordance with the Divine Ordinance, as this Sun which is known to the senses pours forth its rays on all around.[30]

It is easy to see the corner into which the Nutritor has painted himself. On the one hand the existence of *natura* in the sense of the created, natural world is testimony to the existence of a life-beyond-life, a life not limited to individual organisms or species categories. But then, theologically speaking, one would also have to distinguish this "universal life" from the divine nature itself, otherwise there would remain little to separate the supernatural from the natural, the divine from the bestial. Philosophically speaking, the challenge is to explain how a metaphysical principle concerning life is to be distinguished from the structure of natural theology. Either one preserves the distinction—and thus the transcendental hierarchy—or else one admits the equivalence, in a generalized pantheism—and thus the absence of any conceptual grounding at all. How can life be thought as such without resorting to a structure of thought that is basically theophanic?

The Nutritor attempts to nuance this through a series of conceptual modifications. The first is a modification from the Neoplatonic figure of the sun (radiation, emanation, from a divine source) that is adapted to the quasi-Aristotelian figure of nature and animism. As the Nutritor notes, "[T]he way in which life reaches all things is not the same as that in which the rays of the Sun do; for these do not penetrate all things . . . But no creature, whether sensible or intelligible, can be without life (*uitae*)."[31] So, at some level, the ontological concept of life must be distinguished from the Neoplatonic, emanative "soul."

The second modification is a shift from life as the source of growth, development, and generosity to life as a continuum that is also involved in decay, decomposition, and negation. Here the exemplar is not the living organism but the corpse, which is, for the Nutritor, not devoid of life but still filled with it—that is, living though a generosity or givenness of decay and decomposition. This process returns the discrete to the continuous, and thus to an immanence or Life. This is what the Nutritor provocatively calls the "unrelinquished corpse":

> For even the bodies which appear to our senses as dead are not entirely abandoned by life (*uita relinquuntur*). For just as their composition and formation were accomplished by the administration of their proper life, so also is their dissolution (*solutio*) and unforming (*informitas*) and return (*reditus*) into the things from which they originated subject to the obedience of the same.[32]

The third modification the Nutritor makes is to move from life as a principle above and beyond the living to life as a process within the living (e.g., life as "in" the decaying body). Here he makes use of a figure well-known within Pauline discourse—the botanical figure of the seed as emblematic of growth and development. But the Nutritor is keen to link this figure of growth with the "necrological" processes of decay and decomposition alluded to earlier:

> Seeds which are committed to the earth will not put on life again unless they first die; and their death is the separation of matter and form; and that life which quickens the seminal force and through the seminal force does not abandon them until they are resolved into dissolution, but ever cleaves to them, is indeed that life which dissolves them . . . For where would that life be at the time of the body's dissolution but in the body that is undergoing dissolution?[33]

In these modifications the Nutritor attempts to at once assert the immanence between the divine and *natura*, while at the same time preserving their metaphysical hierarchy. Life is not simply identical with Neoplatonic theophany or emanation from a divine Source, for there is not simply a life of the individuated organism and a life of the species, but a "universal life" that ontologically grounds the other two. Life is also defined in terms of dynamical processes, processes that include growth and decay, development and decomposition. Both of these imply a continuum: a vertical continuum of life along organism-species-universal life, and a horizontal continuum along which life operates as biological as well as necrological.

Granted, we are using modern terms to describe the Nutritor's ruminations on what is still an onto-theological concept of life. But in rearticulating life as a continuum, the Nutritor raises the possibility that it is precisely this continuum that both relates and separates the divine and *natura*, the supernatural and natural. At its limit, we might ask whether Eriugena's concept of *nihil* comes to describe this continuum of universal life. Is *nihil* precisely that which provides the principle of immanence between God and Nature?

4.4.3 Four Statements on Pantheism

Answering this question requires that we revisit the theme of pantheism. In his discussion of the divine nature, Eriugena synthesizes the poetics of mystical theology with the logic of classical and Neoplatonic thought, and it is here that the works of the Pseudo-Dionysius become important. It is this concept of *natura* that Eriugena sets side by side with the Dionysian concept of nothing (*nihil*). We have seen how the question of life in Eriugena's *Periphyseon* is stratified along three lines: the life of nature in the narrow sense of creatures and the natural world, the life of the divine nature considered in itself, and finally the life of the divisions, relations, and dispersions between the first and second kinds of life. This third kind of life is what we have referred to as the "dispersional nature." It is at once subordinate to the first two, insofar as it constitutes the relations between primary entities; but in a way it is also superlative to them, since Eriugena's notion of *natura* as *nihil*—as "divine negation" or the "super-essential nothing"—raises this property of dispersion to the level of an ontological principle. The question, then, is whether the *Periphyseon* does indeed foreground this dispersional nature, or whether it remains secondary and subservient to the divisions within *natura*. If the *Periphyseon* can be read— albeit in a radicalized way—as ontologically foregrounding this third type of life or dispersional nature, then we are led to consider the concept of life in relation to Eriugena's two central terms: *natura* and *nihil*. The implications in Eriugena's *Periphyseon* are, one must admit, intriguing: if the divine is essentially "nothing" in an absolute and superlative sense, and if "nature" broadly speaking derives from the divine, then to what extent should one think of *natura* as *nihil*? In other words, to what extent does the continuum between the divine-as-nothing and nature-as-nothing reveal a concept of immanence that is common to them both?

However, an inquiry into the immanence-in-itself of *natura* is possible, for Eriugena, only through the negative or apophatic way. Immanence cannot be a thing since it would then cease to be immanence; but neither can it be everything since the term would lose all meaning. In this way, immanence must be thought in relation to transcendence—be it immanence as subordinate to transcendence, or immanence-in-itself. Eriugena's approach in the *Periphyseon*, particularly in books 1 and 2, is to offer a number of variations on a theme, with the Nutritor often repeating and revising arguments at different moments in the dialogue. While there is no single, formalized proof for the divisions of *natura* in the *Periphyseon*, the arguments can be segmented into four stages.

First statement of the transcendental circle. God is the beginning, middle, and end of all things: that from which all things originate, that in which all things participate, and that to which all things return. God is self-organizing, at once uncreated and yet, in the act of creating, creating God's self.[34] "And while it is eternal it does not cease to be made, and made it does not cease to be eternal, and out of itself it makes itself, for it does not require some other matter which is not itself in which to make itself."[35] Thus creation is at once divine and eternal (since God is created in its creation), and yet earthly and temporal (since creation is created by God):

> There is no one of those who devoutly believe and understand the truth
> who would not persistently and without any hesitation declare that
> the creative Cause of the whole universe is beyond nature and beyond
> being and beyond life and wisdom and power and beyond all things
> which are said and understood and perceived by any sense.[36]

Second statement of dispersional immanence. Despite the necessity of the transcendental circle, God and creatures form "an indivisible One, being Principle as well as Cause and End."[37] God is unity, "since all things are from Him and through Him and in Him and for Him."[38] However, for Eriugena it is unclear if *natura* is also a unity in the same way. Since God is unity, nothing can be coeternal or coexistent with God. Thus all that is not-God must be in some sense related to God. Thus all that is creation (not-God in the absolute sense) is actually God (in the contingent, theophanic sense):

> And do not be surprised if you find something said in this book about
> the return of the creatures to their Beginning and End. For the pro-
> cession of the creatures and the return of the same are so intimately
> associated in the reason which considers them that they appear to be

inseparable the one from the other, and it is impossible for anyone to give any worthy and valid account of either by itself without introducing the other, that is to say, of the procession without the return and collection and vice versa.[39]

Third statement of antinomial syntheses. God is at once within *natura* and yet remains above it, at once immanent in God's creations and yet remaining transcendentally above creation.[40] "But if the creature [is] from God, God will be the cause, but the creature the effect. But if an effect is nothing else but a made cause, it follows that God the Cause is made in His effects."[41] God is therefore unity in diversity, the One in the many:

> It follows that we ought not to understand God and the creature as two things distinct from one another, but as one and the same. For both the creature, by subsisting is in God; and God, by manifesting Himself, in a marvelous and ineffable manner creates Himself in the creature, the invisible making Himself visible and the incomprehensible comprehensible and the hidden revealed and the unknown known.[42]

Fourth statement of the problematic of pantheism. It is from the third to this fourth statement that the question of pantheism arises. "For the procession of the creatures and the return of the same are so intimately associated in the reason which considers them that they appear to be inseparable the one from the other."[43] "So when we hear that God makes all things we ought to understand nothing else than that God is in all things, and He alone is everything which in the things that are is truly said to be."[44] And here we arrive at a series of questions that, while not directly posed by Eriugena, are at least evoked by a number of central passages in the *Periphyseon.* Q_1: Is God subsumed within Nature? Is Nature subsumed within God? Q_2: Is God-in-itself identical with God-in-others? That is, is the divine nature identical with manifestation or theophany? Q_3: Is God-as-absolute (that is, as *nihil*) identical with God-as-manifestation (as theophany)? And finally, Q_4: Are God and Nature identical?

> God is the Maker of all things and is made in all things; and when He is looked for above all things He is found in no essence—for as yet there is no essence—but when He is understood in all things nothing in them subsists but Himself alone; and 'neither is He this,' as he says, 'but not that,' but He is all.[45]

"Life" never means one thing for Eriugena; as with many concepts in the *Periphyseon*, one must pay attention to the dialectics of affirmation and negation. It is for this reason that contemporary Eriugena scholars have suggested that the *Periphyseon* be understood not just as a negative theology in the Dionysian sense, but also as a negative ontology. If a negative theology stops at the point of super-essential negation—God is inaccessible and thus all knowledge can only be of a negative type—a negative ontology would follow this thought to its antinomial conclusion. The implication is that the concept of life as dispersional nature is ultimately thought in terms of antinomy—and that this conjunction of "life" and antinomy describes the particular form of pantheism often attributed to Eriugena's philosophy.

4.5 IMMANENCE II: DUNS SCOTUS' *REPORTATIO* IA

The tension between transcendence and immanence in Eriugena's *Periphyseon* is extended further when we consider the work of Duns Scotus. In the previous chapter, we saw how Scotus' central concept of univocity positioned him against both the position of analogy and the position of equivocity. For Scotus, the concept of univocity is a relational concept; that is, it deals primarily with the relationship between Creator and creature. To argue that the relationship between Creator and creature is univocal would be to argue for an ontological continuity between them—in spite of, or perhaps because of—the relation of cause and effect between them.

The problem encountered by Scholastic thinkers was how to balance the identity and difference between Creator and creature. On the one hand, the relation of causality between Creator and creature (the latter defined precisely as that which is created) would seem to imply a fundamental, essential difference between them—the Creator not only creates the creature, but in so doing remains outside the creature. On the other hand, a central aspect of the concept of causality, as it was understood by the Scholastics, was the continuity between Creator and creature, the former in some way subsisting in the latter through the act of creation itself. There were, of course, variations on how this occurs, such as in the Neoplatonic notion of intermediary Intelligences, but the basic idea of the Creator "in" the creature remains. Hence the dilemma—how can one entity *A* cause another entity *B* while at the same time remaining inseparable and even coextensive with it?

4.5.1 Univocal Immanence

In the context of Medieval philosophy, either of the options of univocity or equivocity points to a dilemma. To claim absolute equivocity would be tantamount to either agnosticism, or the most radical form of "darkness mysticism." To claim absolute univocity would effectively flatten Creator and creature into a single continuum, in which God and Nature are identical. Historically, no such positions were held, for even though contemporary thinkers such as Deleuze choose to radicalize this pantheistic component in Scotus, Scotus' writings themselves often tend towards a more balanced, tempered univocity. But the suggestion is still there, and it remains relevant for the kinds of questions it raises concerning the concepts of Life and the living. In the reading of Scotus adopted here, we will intentionally push the positions of univocity and equivocity to their extremes, in order to foreground the aporias inherent in the Scholastic discussion on the divine nature.

We should also note a terminological dilemma as well. If one posits a univocal relation between Creator and creature, and if this proposition means that there is something "common" to them both, something that runs through them, then is this not an argument for a relation of immanence as well? What, then, is the difference between the concept of univocity and that of immanence? While Scotus does favor the term univocity (*univocum, univocationis*), he rarely mentions the term immanence, or speaks of the divine in terms of immanence. Certainly, part of the reason for this is historical, as the terminology of the twelfth- and thirteenth-century Scholastics centered around the triad of univocity-equivocity-analogy. At the same time, however, Aquinas will often speak of the divine in terms of transcendence, and numerous Neoplatonic thinkers employ the language of immanence to describe the diffusion of the divine into its theophanies.

So, one question is whether Scotus' concept of univocity—which describes a relation between Creator and creature—also evokes a concept of immanence. The concept of univocity can be mapped onto the concept of immanence, of course, but only partially so. For example, the position of analogy would argue for a fundamental difference between Creator and creature, such that one would say that what good acts or the state of being alive is to the creature, the Good itself or Life itself is to the Creator. This presupposes a limit to the natural knowledge of the divine, a limit that is, for Aquinas, negotiated through analogy (not *A* in itself but *a*, which is "like-*A*"). The divine remains not just inaccessible, but also transcendent, both in terms of natural knowledge and in terms of causality.

It is interesting to note that the position of equivocity implies something similar. Equivocity also implies a basic inaccessibility with regard to the divine, but it pushes this further, making this inaccessibility the ground for the relation between Creator and creature itself. The problem, of course, with equivocity is that it cannot account for the relation between Creator and creature, other than to posit that it exists. The positions of analogy and equivocity are inversely related on the issue of transcendence: with analogy, one can account for the relation between Creator and creature, but not the Creator in itself, while with equivocity, one can account for the Creator in itself (if only to assert its absolute difference), but not the relation between Creator and creature. With analogy, one can state *that* God is, but not *what* God is, while for equivocity, one can state *what* God is (even if God is that which is absolutely other), but not *that* God is (since God is absolutely inaccessible).

One could argue that the positions of analogy and equivocity prioritize the divine attribute of transcendence—the Creator remains absolutely separate from the creature (its absolute difference in terms of essence), and the Creator remains causally prior to the creature (its absolute difference in terms of existence). Immanence comes into play only insofar as some account must be made of the relationality between Creator and creature, of the relation that itself constitutes the process of creation. Immanence would then derive from an ontologically prior transcendental relation: first you have the transcendental relation between Creator and creature, based on causality, then you have the dispersion of the former—in the form of spirit—throughout the latter, while never being totally confused with it such that they would be identical. This is, more or less, the position found in Aquinas.

If this can be accepted, then it would seem that the position of Scotist univocity, privileging as it does the continuity between Creator and creature, would be paired with immanence. Not only that, but Scotist univocity would invert the hierarchy (or flatten it), instead arguing for the primacy of immanence in itself. In this radicalized position, immanence would not be derived from transcendence, but the inverse: the ontological priority of immanence would result only secondarily in the coalescence of discrete hierarchies surrounding causation. But then the question is whether the immanence in this "univocal immanence" is the same as the derivative, secondary immanence in the former case (an "analogical immanence" and an "equivocal immanence"). Contemporary readers of Scotus such as Deleuze tend to emphasize the uniqueness of univocal immanence as diametrically opposed to analogical or equivocal immanence:

Because I say: being is univocal, this means: there is no categorical difference between the assumed senses of the word "being" and being is said in one and the same sense of everything which is. In a certain manner this means that the tick is God; there is no difference of category, there is no difference of substance, there is no difference of form. It becomes a mad thought.[46]

Again, one can read Scotus in this radicalized way, and there is a great deal of reason to do so, especially if one places him in relation to other, "immanentist" thinkers such as Eriugena before him, and Spinoza after him. But the difficulty in pinning a single position to a thinker like Scotus is that, in his writings, further and further distinctions are always made, distinctions that nearly always have the effect of complexifying his statements and his concepts. While Scotus will assert quite strongly the univocity of Creator and creature, as well as the possibility of a natural knowledge of the divine, he will also make the distinction between that which is *metaphysically* univocal and yet *physically* analogical.[47] Thus, that which is in-itself may be univocal, but in-another, or in relation to others, it may be analogical (or, for that matter, equivocal).

There are, then, several kinds of immanence possible with regard to Scotus' philosophy. One kind of immanence would pertain to the relation between Creator and creature. This is based, in part, on a relation of causality, and the distinction between secondary and tertiary causes (of abstract Intelligences or of creatures), and primary or first causes (of the Creator). But there are also two other kinds of immanence to consider: the immanence that pertains to the Creator-in-itself (or the divine-in-itself, or Life-in-itself), and the kind of immanence that would pertain to the relation between one creature and another creature. The first—the Creator-in-itself, the divine nature—is defined as that which is absolutely "above"—above nature, above natural knowledge, and so on. The second—the creature-creature relation—is conversely defined as that which is "below"—below the divine, below revelation, and so on. But what if the first (supernature) is coextensive with the second (nature)? As we saw in the last chapter, this is a distinction that both Aquinas and Henry of Ghent make—but they do so in order to conserve the hierarchy between Creator and creature, supernature and nature. Let us pose a question: what if there is a concept of immanence that presumes the distinction between the divine nature and nature, *but only in order to assert the continuity between them*?

Perhaps this describes Scotus' position regarding "univocal imma-

nence." Not only is immanence the derivative form of the relation between
Creator and creature, but it may also deal with these two other instances:
the Creator-in-itself (the divine nature), and the relationality between any
two creatures (and is this not one description of what natural philosophy
is for the Scholastics?). In order for Scotus to make an argument for the
primacy of immanence, or for a univocal immanence, it seems that two
propositions would have to be made: first, Scotus would have to suggest
that the divine nature is in itself immanent (while also transcendent in
relation to non-divine nature), and, second, that the relation between any
two creatures is an immanent relation. But do Scotus' writings bear this
out, and can one read him—or creatively misread him—as making such
claims?

4.5.2 ACTUAL INFINITY

To answer this question, we should remind ourselves that Scotus' major
writings are not solely concerned with the debate on the creature. More
well-known are his proofs for the existence of God, which are found, with
a degree of consistency, throughout Scotus' early lectures at the University
of Oxford and his later lectures at the University of Paris. Scotus provided
several versions of this proof, and there is some confusion as to the exact
relation of each version to the others, which came first, and which was
deemed authoritative by Scotus himself.[48] For instance, scholars estimate
that there are at least four variations of Scotus' proofs for the existence of
God: the original lectures (*lectura*) given at Oxford, an initial collection of
the Oxford lectures (*ordinatio*), the collection of the lectures at Paris, written down by someone other than Scotus (*reportatio*), and a possible final
collection of the Oxford lectures (a second *ordinatio*). Matters are made
more confusing by the fact that there does not exist a definitive edition of
the Oxford works.[49] Thus, while the problem of the transcendence and the
immanence of the divine nature remained a central concern for Scotus,
the themes and variations on the topic seem to imply that Scotus may
have never been totally satisfied with a single, definitive statement on the
subject. For our purposes here, we want to focus on the way in which Scotus develops a concept of "univocal immanence"—and how he structures
the pantheistic implications of this univocal immanence with the theological and philosophical demands of divine transcendence and ontological prioritization.

The structure of Scotus' argument for the existence of God repeats
with a great deal of consistency between the Oxford *Ordinatio* and the

Parisian *Reportata*. In particular, we can look at this argument as it is presented in the first question in the *Ordinatio* (I, dist. II, q. i), and in the first book of the *Reportata* (known as *Reportatio* IA). This hybrid approach will enable us to extract the basic argument from both the "early" and "late" Scotus, and from this we can then draw out a central tension in the Scotist concept of univocal immanence, a tension that is, we will see, at the heart of the question of the concept of Life.

Scotus' proof for the existence of God is of a particular type. Scotus does not simply set out to prove *that* God is, but also, in a sense, *what* God is. This is how Scotus puts it in the *Reportatio*: "Regarding the existence of God, I propose three questions. First, in the world of beings, is there some being that is first in an unqualified sense? Second, could several different sorts of being possess such primacy? Third, is some being actually infinite in an unqualified sense?"[50] The first two questions have to do with causality, and the necessity of positing a first cause or prime mover for all creation. Scotus' statement of these questions would seem to imply that these questions were not to be taken for granted. But the third question is different, and it is this question that appears in a nearly identical form in the *Ordinatio*. Here we have not a string of questions dealing with causality, but a single one dealing with infinity: "First I inquire about those things which pertain to the unicity of God, and I ask first whether in the realm of beings something exists which is actually infinite?"[51]

The phrase "actually infinite" is important, for it not only implies an ontology of the divine—that the divine "is"—but it also stipulates the specific criteria for the being of the divine—that of its actuality as opposed to its potentiality, and that of its existence as opposed to its essence. Scotus is not just setting out to prove that the divine exists, but the emphasis on actual infinity means that Scotus is also seeking to prove what the divine is, and even how it exists. These latter points immediately evoke modal questions, questions about becoming, change, and dynamics. But that which the modal describes (as actually or potentially existing) is something as abstract as the infinite, understood in the Scholastic and theological sense as "being without category." Thus something that is actually infinite, as opposed to potentially infinite, would be infinite in an immediate and absolute sense—everything, everywhere, for all time. This is, it would seem, a radically horizontal concept of the divine. Although Scotus never makes any claim for a pantheistic notion of the divine-as-infinite, this notion of "actual infinity" places as much emphasis on the immanent relations of divine manifestation as it does on the transcendental relations of causality between Creator and creature.

There is, certainly, a rich discourse on the infinite in modern mathematics and philosophy.[52] But prior to this modern mathematization, the concept of the infinite opens onto the general notion of the boundless (in space) and the limitless (in time). That which is infinite is that which cannot be bound in space or limited in time—and, therefore, that which cannot be categorized by thought. This is, at least, the "naïve" view of infinity. In the Scholastic theological tradition, the divine is conceived as that which is neither a genus nor a species (that is, God is not a creature among other creatures, but that by which the creation of creatures as genus and species is possible). To encircle the divine within such a categorical framework would be to negate the very concept of the divine—as not only being above category of thought, but as the very principle through which category is possible.

Scotus can thus define the infinite as follows: "The infinite is that which exceeds the finite, not exactly by reason of any finite measure, but in excess of any measure that could be assigned."[53] The definition is repeated almost exactly in the *Reportata*. Keeping in mind our "naïve" perspective, there are two basic types of infinity in Scotus' definition: a numerable infinity that is infinite because it extends forever (in space) or goes on forever (in time), and a nonnumerable infinity that is infinite because it is simply beyond or above all things. The first type of numerable infinity he refers to as "relative" infinity, while the second, nonnumerable infinity he refers to as "absolute" infinity. Relative infinity deals primarily with the divine-as-infinite in relation to that which is not-divine. In other words, relative infinity deals with the relation between Creator and creatures. By contrast, absolute infinity deals with the divine-as-infinite in itself.

Here Scotus runs into a methodological problem. The divine, insofar as it is defined as that which is absolutely beyond all natural knowledge and human comprehension, cannot really be understood as the divine-as-infinite in itself. The concept of absolute infinity forbids its own conceptualization. Therefore, one must get to the concept of absolute infinity (the divine-as-absolute) through the back door—that is, through the naturally knowable manifestations of the divine in the relation between Creator and creature. This is a common strategy in Scholastic thinking that can be traced back to the Church Fathers. One cannot know the divine in itself, but only secondarily, as it were, through the effects of the divine in nature. But Scotus will add a twist. While never disavowing the relation of analogy between Creator and creature, Scotus also makes strong claims for the univocity of the relation between Creator and creature. This we saw in the previous chapter, where Scotus positions himself vis-à-vis both Aquinas and Henry of Ghent. But, as we've seen, this concept of univocity leads to a notion of the divine nature that places as much emphasis on its immanence ("within") as its transcendence ("above").

How then, to achieve this dual emphasis on immanence as well as transcendence? The problem is not simply that transcendence is "bad"— a claim of "theory" that is quite foreign even to Medieval pantheism. Rather, the problem for Scotus can be stated as follows: how to correlate two conceptions of the divine into a single concept: the concept of transcendence—which implies that there is a reality that actually exists, but which is not apparent to the senses or to thought—and the concept of immanence—which implies that that which is transcendent is literally nowhere in particular, precisely because it is everywhere in general.

4.5.3 THE PATHOLOGY OF THE TRIPLE PRIMACY

Scotus' approach to the question of the divine nature is not simply to prove its existence as such, but to imply that the question of what it is and how it is be taken simultaneously with the question that it is. In so doing, Scotus will emphasize a notion of the divine in terms of "actual infinity"—that it is at once transcendently infinite, in that it is above and beyond all things, but also that it is immanently infinite, in that its infinity is actual (everything, everywhere, all the time). The questions through which Scotus addresses the problem of the divine nature are twofold: First, is it possible to develop a concept of the divine nature in itself that would be accessible to natural knowledge (that is, without relying on faith or revelation)? From this there follows a second question: Is it possible to develop a concept of the divine nature in itself that would place a dual emphasis on its immanence as well as its transcendence (that is, without becoming ensnared in pure antinomy)?

This is, to be sure, an ambitious endeavor. The first question concerning natural knowledge of the divine in itself is one that preoccupies Scholastic thinking in general, with thinkers positioning themselves all along a spectrum, from mystical theology to nominalist logic. The second question is more specific to Scotus—indeed, it is the second question that folds back onto the first question, and which enables Scotus, via the emphasis on univocity, the "common nature," and immanence, to assert that the *divine* nature is also a divine *nature*.

Scotus' approach in his proofs for the existence of God has roughly the same structure in both the Oxford and Paris lectures. His question

concerning the "actual infinity" of the divine is, in both texts, divided
into two parts—one approach, which deals with the divine nature in itself
("the absolute properties of God"), and another approach, which deals with
the divine nature relationally ("the relative properties of God").[54] As we've
seen, while Scotus aims to address the former question, the paradox inherent in the "in itself" of the divine nature means that Scotus must gain
access to the divine through the backdoor—that is, through the manifestation of the divine in the earthly, of the supernature in nature.

This latter approach concerning the relative properties of the divine nature is in turn made up of three components: a first component concerning
the primacy of the divine nature, a second component concerning the interrelation of these primacies, and a third component concerning the overall unity of the divine nature itself (in the Scholastic obsession for neatness
and numerology, each of these components in turn has three conclusions).
Taken together, these arguments lead Scotus into interesting territory
regarding the relation between the immanence and transcendence of the
divine nature, especially regarding the possibility of there being a "univocal immanence." In the first article of *Ordinatio* I.II.i, Scotus lays out his
strategy in summary form:

> Wherefore I shall show that in the realm of beings something indeed
> exists which is simply first according to efficiency, and also that some-
> thing exists which is simply first in the order of ends, and that some-
> thing exists which is simply first by reason of pre-eminence (*eminen-
> tiam*). Secondly, I shall show that what is first in virtue of one kind of
> primacy is also first in virtue of the others. And thirdly, I shall show
> that this triple primacy (*triplex primitas*) pertains to but one nature,
> so as not to be found in several specifically or essentially different
> natures.[55]

This approach, emphasizing as it does the divine nature as relational ("relative properties of God") implies both the essential inaccessibility of the
divine in itself, while also maintaining the pervasiveness of the divine in
a way that is not separate from its manifestation.

We can begin with the first component: the primacy of the divine nature. Here Scotus utilizes an argument concerning the "triple primacy" of
the divine: that the divine obtains its primacy or transcendence, not via
its absolute separation or division from the earthly, but from its relative,
relational, and even processual aspects. His focus is not just on causality,
but also on the ontological grounding that makes causality possible (the

absolute preeminence of the divine nature). The first two primacies deal with Aristotelian causality, and in particular on efficient and final causality as it is manifested in the divine nature.

The argument concerning efficient causality and final causality follow similar lines of argument, and they are arguments that are common in Scholastic discourse, though it is possible to read Scotus as departing from these mainstream arguments. Generally, the argument concerning causality is that, in order for the concept of causality to hold, one must presuppose both a first cause as well as a final end. But Scotus does not simply mean "first" and "final" in a chronological sense. A first efficient cause is not the first efficient cause at time = 0, but rather that by which causality in itself is caused, or the potentiality of cause.[56] Similarly, the final cause is not a chronological end time towards which all things tend, but the determinate organization or patterning of causal relationships that allow us to analyze and conceptualize causal relations to begin with.[57] Thus, the primacy of efficient causality is like the cause of causality, while the primacy of final causality is the organization inherent in causality. Both, Scotus notes, are "actually existing," and not simply potential or possible existences. That is, their actual existence is required as ontological principles that ensure that causality is continually in effect (efficient causality) and determinately patterned (final causality). Scotus, while arguing for the transcendent primacy of efficient and final causality, also sets causality within a domain of continual relation. Things seem to be already in motion and in patterning . . .

There is also a third primacy in addition to that of efficient and final causality, which Scotus calls the primacy of "preeminence" (eminentiae). In the same way that the primacy of the first efficient cause is not literally first, and in the same way that the final cause is not literally last, so is the preeminence of the divine nature not simply the most perfect in a spectrum of perfection, the most complete in a spectrum of the less-complete.[58] Scotus' notion of preeminence at times comes close to asserting a kind of idealism. After stating that "some eminent nature is simply first in perfection," Scotus comments that "[t]his is evident because an essential order exists among essences, for as Aristotle puts it, forms are like numbers." So the divine nature obtains a primacy of preeminence because it is not simply a higher perfection among lesser perfections, but is itself an essential, abstract, even mathematical perfection. But then, in the very next sentence, Scotus appears to materialize this abstract preeminence in terms of creation: "And in such an order an ultimate nature is to be found."[59] The language here is a mixture of Aristotelian formalism and Neoplatonic exemplarism, both assuming a basic distinction between abstract forms and their concrete manifestations.

The point of tension in the triple primacy is the caveat that appears for each of them: that the efficient, final, and preeminent primacy of the divine nature be an *actual* primacy, and not simply potential, or possible, or, for that matter, even "virtual." Part of the reason for this stress on the actuality of the divine nature is the way in which the problem is logically posed: there is the necessity of a first cause, one that is "first" ontologically and not just chronologically or serially. Such a first cause cannot, by definition, itself be caused, or else the series of causes would continue back forever, undermining the concept of causality itself. This is, at least, the common form of the argument in much Scholastic discourse, influenced as it was by Aristotle. This idea is explained by Scotus in the *Reportatio*:

> Rather, the whole collection of what is caused depends upon some other prior cause that is not a part of that collection, for then something would be a cause of itself. Since the whole collection of dependents depends, it does so not upon something that is part of that collection, because everything there is dependent. Consequently it depends upon something that is not part of that totality. And this I call the first efficient. Hence, even if there is an infinity of causes, they still depend upon something that is not a part of that infinity.[60]

The cause remains outside of its effects—we can accept this, if only provisionally. But to this Scotus adds something, a variation, in effect, but one that places less emphasis on the sovereignty of the cause vis-à-vis its effects, and much more emphasis on the immanence or univocity between cause and effect:

> But no succession can continue indefinitely except by virtue of something permanent that is coextensive with the succession as a whole. For no change in form is perpetuated save by virtue of something uniform that is not a part of the succession itself, since no part can persist throughout the entire succession and still be only just a part of it.[61]

What Scotus seeks is a concept of the divine nature in terms of causality, such that it is an "uncaused cause"—a bit like the notion of an "uncreated Creator." This is something like the condition for causality, or, perhaps, the setting-into-motion of the very possibility of causal relations themselves. As we noted, this strange *uncausality* cannot itself be caused.

How then, can one account for its existence at all? It cannot be thought
of in terms over which it governs—causality, relationality, process—for
this only necessitates a higher-level principle of necessity. It must, therefore, be both uncaused and yet not nonexistent. It must be both immateri-
ally pervasive, as an ontological ground, and yet manifestly existent in the
nexus of causal relations that it occasions. In other words, the causality of
the divine nature must be both a transcendental ground and an immanent
manifestation.

The triple primacy is but one of three components of the divine nature. The other two components—the interrelation of the three primacies, and the unity of the divine nature—are meant to address the tensions
that develop out of the first component of the triple primacy. The second
component—the interrelation of the three primacies—sets each of the primacies in relation to each other. For instance, Scotus argues that the first
cause is also a final cause, since the first efficient cause is seen to act in
terms of itself and from itself—a kind of primary self-causation or self-
organization.[62] Similarly, Scotus also argues that the first cause is also the
preeminence of the divine nature, since the first cause is not a genus or
species, or one among the other causes, but that which conditions causality itself—"the supreme nature" (primum eminens).[63]

The interrelation of the efficient, final, and preeminent primacies
then leads Scotus to argue for their fundamental unity, for not only are
the three primacies inseparable from each other, but the self-causing and
interrelational aspect of the divine nature implies its univocity.[64] Scotus'
proof for the unity of the divine nature is similar to that given in other
places in his works. It argues that any two entities A and B must have both
a differentiating factor, or "thisness" (haecceitas), as well as a univocal
"common nature" that allows A and B to be set in relation at all. These
two elements—the "thisness" and the "common nature"—are not at once
distinct and yet inseparable. They constitute a "formal objective distinction" whereby their distinction and unity are neither simply in the mind
of the perceiver nor simply in the objective world. In the Ordinatio, where
this argument appears, Scotus offers another variant that is as dense as it
is intriguing:

> The efficient cause which is first by this triple primacy is of itself neces-
> sarily existent. Proof: It is completely incapable of being caused, for it is
> contradictory that it should have anything prior to it in the order of effi-
> ciency or finality . . . From this I argue, nothing can be non-existent un-
> less something either positively or privatively incompatible with it can

exist. Now nothing can be positively or privatively incompatible with a being which exists of itself and is totally uncaused; therefore, etc.[65]

Here Scotus seems to be making the same argument for univocity, but this time through a framework of ontological negation. Negation or nonexistence requires opposition, but of two types: a positive or additive opposition, in which A is opposed by the addition of B (where $B = A^{-1}$), and a privative or subtractive opposition, in which A' is subtracted from A (where $A' = A$ itself or some essence of A). A divine nature that is defined by its primacy—that is, by being uncaused or self-caused—has no opposing term, and without this, it cannot be nonexistent. Therefore it must exist. But it cannot exist in the sense of caused existents, for this would recuperate the divine nature back into the sphere of causality and oppositions (it would be a thing among things, a cause among causes). It seems that the divine nature's unity is such that it is both existent (in that it has no opposing term) and nonexistent (in that it does not exist in terms of caused existents). Only a notion of the divine nature that is literally no-thing, precisely because it is every-thing, can fulfill these criteria. The divine nature's primacy would have to be predicated on a strong notion of immanence (or "univocal immanence") rather than one in which immanence is situated secondarily with respect to an external, transcendent causality.

This is noteworthy because many of Scotus' other arguments for univocity and the divine immanence take place via an additive or superlative gesture—one begins with discrete entities A and B, and then posits something x that courses through them or that conditions their very possibility of relation. The discrete individuations or "thisness" point to a One, but this One derives its unity via a horizontal relationality, One becomes All. But in the above passage the conditions are the opposite: univocity is necessary because the One is All, and this One-All is also, in a way, "nothing" (in Scotus' phrasing, *nihil potest non esse*).

From one perspective, Scotus' proofs for the existence of God are really about the concept of immanence, and its secondary relation to transcendence. When Scotus asks, "is there a being that is actually infinite?" we can read him as asking "is there a concept of immanence that is not subordinate to transcendence?" And the way in which Scotus frames this inquiry is through an emphasis on the processual or dynamic aspects of the divine nature: the first component of the triple primacy, the second component of their fundamental interrelation, and the third component of their essential unity.

The main challenge facing Scotus is that there must be some ontological ground that is at once transcendentally beyond particular manifestations and immanently coursing through them. For the primacy of efficient causality, this is the cause of causality itself, the ontological grounding of *relation* that governs cause and effect. For the primacy of final causality, this is the determinate organization of different cause-effect chains, the grounding of *patterning* that enables causal relation to be thought. And for the primacy of preeminence, we have the exemplary idea of perfection or completion itself, the grounding of the *abstract* or the ideal. For Scotus, the triple primacy of the divine nature—if it is not simply that which is first, final, or most perfect in the gradation of things—is laced with contradictions: it is the cause of all causes that is itself not caused (in efficient causality); it is the end of all ends that itself is not directed towards any end (in final causality); and it is the perfection of all imperfections that is not simply one among other beings (in preeminence).

Scotus' conception of the divine nature is structured around a number of internal tensions, tensions that are at once Aristotelian and Neoplatonic: a tension between cause and effect, a tension between the ideal and material, a tension between the actual and the potential, and so on. In a sense, these tensions arise from what can be seen to be Scotus' overall project: *to think a concept of univocal immanence as indissociable from the divine nature*. On the one hand, Scotus' arguments for the primacy of the divine nature imply transcendental attributes (the cause of causality, the end of finality, the form of perfection). On the other hand, Scotus' central criterion for this transcendence of the divine nature—and indeed for his proofs of the existence of the divine in itself—is that their modality be actually existent. This means that it is without reserve, but also that it is without incompletion. This is inherent to the notion of primacy or preeminence itself, if taken to mean "completion" or "fullness." But this static view of the fully actual is again put into tension by the emphasis on the dynamic causal relations of the efficient, the final, and the completed. Hence Scotus' arguments from causality open onto notions of relation and interrelation, of the divine in terms of *dunamis* or flow. And this is the real lesson from Scotus' discourse on the divine nature—not that it is a full-blown pantheism, but that it reveals the contradictions between the divine-as-*plenum* and the divine-as-flow—or, put another way, Scotus' proofs on the divine nature reveal a relationship between two notions of immanence—*an immanence of fullness and an immanence of flow.*

4.6 IMMANENCE III: NICHOLAS OF
CUSA'S *DE DOCTA IGNORANTIA*

As we've seen in the example of Eriugena and Duns Scotus, the concept of immanence or univocity is central to any ontology of life, insofar as "life" does not remain exclusive to the natural domain. This last point is central, for it not only raises the question of the equivalence of the supernatural and natural, "God or nature," but it also raises the possibility of a concept of life that runs through the supernatural and natural, when perceived as a continuum.

The tradition of speculative mysticism is worth considering in this regard. The problem of how far to push the concept of immanence in the divine nature was a central concern of late Scholastic and early modern thinking. It is there, in a conflicted way, in Descartes' bifurcation of thought and extension, in Leibniz's monad, and in Spinoza's substance monism. One also sees the problem of immanence addressed by thinkers such as Nicholas of Cusa, whose *De Docta Ignorantia* (*On Learned Ignorance*) remains emblematic of the limits and tensions in the concept of immanence.

Cusa is also known as the author of a treatise that promoted, during a time of tension between Church and empire, a system of resolution based on the balance of hierarchy and consent through councils. This treatise, *De Concordantia Catholica* (*The Catholic Concordance*), would have an influence on the growing "conciliar" movement, though schisms of all types between pope and king continued throughout the fourteenth and fifteenth centuries. In the latter part of his life Cusa was named cardinal and then bishop, serving as papal legate until his death. In his politics—not unlike his philosophy—Cusa reflects an amalgam of tendencies, at once encouraging the preservation of politico-religious hierarchy, and yet also promoting a more progressive lateralization of deliberation through councils.[66]

Cusa's *De Docta Ignorantia* was written around 1440, and belongs to a set of Cusan philosophical-mystical works that also includes *De Quaerendo Deum* (*On Seeking God*), *Dialogus de Deo Abscondito* (*Dialogue on the Hidden God*), and *De Visione Dei* (*On the Vision of God*).[67] The *De Docta Ignorantia* is composed of three books, each with subdivided chapters. The first book deals with the divine nature in itself, the second book with nature or the created world, and the third with their combination in the figure of Christ, the god-man. As the title indicates, the premise of Cusa's philosophical and mystical outlook is that human, natural understanding of the divine or supernatural is always determined by a horizon of thought, and this thought itself is a kind of dark illumination, a "learned ignorance." This idea—that the divine is precisely the thought of the unthought—is also found in earlier mystical writings, such as those by Augustine, the Pseudo-Dionysius, and Eckhart, and their influence is reflected in Cusa's own references. What remains of interest in Cusa's speculative mysticism, however, is his evocations of an unknown divinity—as per his many suggestions of an *unknown nature*, a nature so thoroughly conceptualized in terms of immanence that, as Cusa would note, "God is in all things and all things are in God."

4.6.1 THE COINCIDENCE OF OPPOSITES

A central component of Cusa's thought is a sort of non-synthetic monism. That is, Cusa's concept of the divine is an ontological monism that preserves oppositions and contradictories, rather than simply effacing or elevating them. Nevertheless, Cusa's thought is monist, and it is monist in the sense that all things reduce to a single entity, which Cusa refers to as the "maximum." This maximum is absolute, in that it is nonnumerical, without measure, and encompasses everything. The maximum is, in Cusa's words, "that beyond which there can be nothing greater."[68] To describe this absolute maximum (*maximum absolutum*), Cusa frequently evokes a mystical trope from geometry: the circle whose center is everywhere, and circumference nowhere.

For Cusa, the divine is this absolute maximum, and a key feature of the absolute maximum is what Cusa calls the *coincidentia oppositorum*, the "coincidence of opposites." In the created, natural world, things appear distinct and separate from each other. The existence of oppositions of all types—the supernatural vs. the natural, the living vs. the dead, the present vs. the past/future, matter vs. form, etc.—all these imply a finite world in which such oppositions are possible. Using the opposition of large and small, Cusa argues that the very conditions of opposition point to a larger, fundamentally incomprehensible unity:

> Maximum quantity is maximally large, while minimum quantity is maximally small. Therefore, if you free maximum and minimum from quantity by intellectually removing "large" and "small," you will clearly see that maximum and minimum coincide. For both maximum and minimum are superlatives. Therefore, absolute quantity is not maximum quantity more than it is minimum quantity, because in it the minimum is the maximum in a coincident way.[69]

Borrowing a technique from mystical theology, Cusa removes the qualifiers of "large" and "small," and what remains is a single continuum of degrees. He begins from oppositions in the world (large vs. small), and then,
subtracting the qualifying terms, arrives at something that is not opposition but instead "coincidence." The infinitely large and the infinitely
small become one and the same, the maximum the minimum, culminating in a single ontological principle that underlies all reality: "the maximum is such that in it the minimum is maximum, so that the maximum
infinitely and completely transcends all opposition."[70]

It is easy to see the appeal of this move from a mystical-theological
standpoint, since it provides a way of thinking about theophany. All things
in the natural world can be viewed as unified by a single, divine source
that is both its cause and its foundation. The problem, ontologically speaking, is that this tends to reify the world in two ways: first, it frames the
world in terms of an anthropomorphized Creator-creature, with all comprehension of the latter relying on an impossible comprehension of the former; second, it places the essence or foundation of the world in something
outside of it, as opposed to something internal to it or inherent in it. Now,
Cusa was both a philosopher and a mystic, and as such, he certainly does
not deny the absolute transcendence of the divine or its ontological foundation. But in other ways, he actively avoids both the anthropomorphic,
personal Creator-God, as well as the transcendence of the Neoplatonic
One. How does he do this?

In his discussion of the concept of the maximum, Cusa is careful to
point out that the *coincidentia oppositorum* does not simply imply the
synthesis of all oppositions. While the absolute maximum "infinitely and
completely transcends all opposition," this does not mean that it transcends all contradiction. Likewise, the coincidence of opposites is not simply the synthesis of opposites. In the divine all distinct and separate things
are regarded as one—*as they are, in their contradictory facticity.* But such
a thought would mean that, if there is an ontological monism, it would
have to be one that is not synthetic, but a kind of disjunctive unity—a *disjunctive monism.* How is it possible to think an ontological monism that
remains disjunctive in this sense? One solution that Cusa offers is that
one would have to think any principle of monism as fully immanent to
all that through which it is, a principle that spans across rather than rises
above: "But it [the absolute maximum] is a 'this' in such a way that it is all
things, and it is all things in such a way that it is none of them, and it is a
'this' maximally in such a way that it is also a 'this' minimally."[71]

It is in response to this problematic—how to think an ontological monism that is also disjunctive, or non-synthetic—that we see the language of pantheism recur throughout Cusa's writings. While the term is not used by Cusa, the idea of the maximum as "in" all things, and all things as "in" the maximum, is a touchstone in the *De Docta Ignorantia*. Pantheism in Cusa's work is more than the presence of the divine in the natural world; it is a way of conceptually flattening the "vertical" relation between the supernatural and natural, while maintaining the "lateral" internal differentiations that inhere in the world.

4.6.2 THE FOLDS OF LIFE

Cusa develops his own particular brand of pantheism through several concepts, which we can examine here—the twin concepts of *complicatio* (enfolding) and *explicatio* (unfolding), and the concept of *contractio* (contraction). The concepts of enfolding (*complicatio*) and unfolding (*explicatio*) are used by Cusa to account for the relation between God and the world, the supernatural and the natural. Cusa borrows the terms from a passage by Hermes Trismegistus, in which the divine is described as all-encompassing, as folding all things within itself. The root of the terms themselves, *pli*, evokes the process of folding or wrapping (perhaps as one would fold sheets of paper into a folio). We might say that with enfolding, the terms *a'* and *a"* are enveloped in *a*, and that with unfolding, the terms *a'* and *a"* are developed out of *a*. "God, therefore, is the enfolding of all in the sense that all are in God, and God is the unfolding of all in the sense that God is in all."[72] This runs like a leitmotif throughout the *De Docta Ignorantia*. All things in the world are enveloped or enfolded in God, while God is manifest only as developed or unfolded in all the things in the world. Cusa uses these terms in different ways, however. In some cases they are used to imply a full immanence between God and nature, while in other instances they serve to reinforce the irrevocable separation and hierarchy between them.

Consider the first process, that of enfolding. Enfolding describes the way that something exists within its principle, as that principle. Something is actual or potential, possible or impossible, coming-to-be or passing-away, by virtue of being enfolded in something else, which is its principle or essence. Thus, when Cusa says that "all things are enfolded in God," this does not mean that all things are sublimated into the divine unity as so many parts to a whole, but rather that all things inhere in the divine in their differentiations and their individuations. This implies that the unity of all things does not lie above and beyond them, but is rather consonant with them. When Cusa inverts his previous statement and says that "God is in all things," this likewise does not mean that the divine is parsed out among things, but that the divine courses through all individuations and differentiations: "Therefore there is one enfolding of all times—which is the present, and the present, indeed, is unity. In the same way, identity is the enfolding of difference, equality the enfolding of inequality, and simplicity the enfolding of divisions or distinctions."[73]

Statements such as these reveal the tensions within Cusa's pantheism. On the one hand, there is a decisive separation between terms, as well as a prioritizing between them (identity-difference, where the former is more fundamental than the latter, etc.). But, on the other hand, such separations serve to reinforce the connection between them, resulting in the coincidence of oppositions. "In this way the infinite providence of God enfolds both the things that will happen and also those that will not but can happen, and it enfolds contraries, as a genus enfolds contrary differentiae."[74]

Something similar can be said for the process of unfolding. For Cusa, unfolding is not exactly the mirror image of enfolding. While the enfolding of all things in God obtains a certain perfection, the unfolding of all things from God is seen to move further away from that perfection. If we understand unfolding as a process of manifestation or theophany, then any instance of unfolding will imply the prior existence of enfolding; what is unfolded was always already enfolded. As Cusa notes, "[T]o posit enfolding is not to posit the thing that was enfolded, but to posit unfolding is also to posit enfolding."[75] In a sense, we might also say, what is natural was always already supernatural. This asymmetry between enfolding and unfolding is most evident in Cusa's evocations of pantheism:

> There is, consequently, one enfolding of all things; there is not one enfolding of substance, another of quality or of quantity, and so on, for there is only one maximum, with which the minimum coincides and in which enfolded difference is not opposed to enfolding identity . . . God, therefore, is the enfolding of all in the sense that all are in God, and God is the unfolding of all in the sense that God is in all.[76]

Cusa's pantheism is of a particular type; it operates more via negations than positive assertions. The refrain that Cusa employs—that God is in all things and all things are in God—has to be understood negatively. It is not a mereology of parts and wholes, for the divine cannot be understood by additively or cumulatively piling up all that exists. Neither is it a topology of the One and the Many, since the divine is not a One that is composed of Many, even infinite, parts. It is not a participation of the Many in the One, or of the material in the ideal, since the divine is not separate from its participations. Finally, it is not an exemplarism of Idea and its instantiation, or a theophany of source and product, for the divine is not simply the perfection of each thing, but rather inheres in its existence as actual or potential, as possible or impossible.

Enfolding and unfolding are thus ways of accounting for the natural world in three ways: (i) they describe the way something exists as individuated from and apart from its principle of individuation; (ii) they describe the way something exists as differentiated from other things; (iii) they require that the principle of a thing and its instantiation be thought together in a single thought. This last point is important, for it takes Cusa beyond Peripatetic natural philosophy into a consideration of a pantheism of pure immanence between the supernatural and natural, God and world.

However, given Cusa's tendency to both separate and unite God and world, how does he account for the relations between the processes of enfolding and unfolding themselves? It is here that another of Cusa's central concepts—that of *contractio* or contraction—enters the picture:

> In the First Book it was shown that God is in all things in such a way that all things are in God, and now it is evident that God is in all things, as if, by mediation of the universe. It follows, then, that all are in all and each is in each . . . In each creature, the universe is the creature, and each receives all things in such a way that in each thing all are contractedly this thing. Since each thing cannot be actually all things, for it is contracted, it contracts all things, so that they are it.[77]

The processes of enfolding and unfolding are themselves related by contraction. On a general level, contraction for Cusa is the restriction of the divine, as absolute maximum, into the world, or what Cusa calls the "contracted maximum." What the absolute maximum is to God, the contracted maximum is to the world; what the absolute is to the supernatural, the contracted is to the natural. For Cusa, contraction is the means by which God is in all things, the means by which the absolute maximum (God) becomes the contracted maximum (world). But contraction also works in the opposite direction, via a delimitation or dedifferentiation of the world in God:

> For just as God, because God is boundless, is neither in the sun nor in the moon, although in them God is absolutely that which they are, so

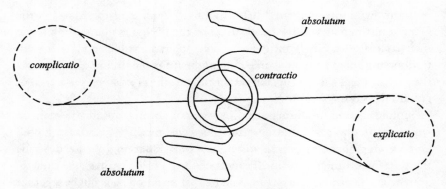

Figure 4. Enfolding and unfolding in Cusa's *De docta ignorantia*.

the universe is neither in the sun nor in the moon but in them is con-
tractedly that which they are. The absolute quiddity of the sun is not
other than the absolute quiddity of the moon . . . But the contracted
quiddity of the sun is other than the contracted quiddity of the moon,
for whereas the absolute quiddity of a thing is not the thing, the contracted quiddity is not other than the thing . . . But God is not in the
sun "sun" and in the moon "moon"; rather God is that which is sun
and moon without plurality and difference.[78]

Thus, to God, which is nature without differentiations, is paired nature,
which is the unity of all differentiations. The process of contraction—as
the relation between enfolding and unfolding—is thus counterposed to
the non-process of the absolute, which both encompasses everything and
is, in Cusa's language of mysticism, without circumference (see figure 4).

   We thus have two sets of terms that Cusa utilizes in his pantheistic
philosophy: enfolding and unfolding (*complicatio* and *explicatio*), and the
absolute and the contracted (*absolutum* and *contractum*). Enfolding and
unfolding work through contraction to give us the world, which Cusa describes as a "contracted maximum." Likewise, enfolding and unfolding
work through the absolute to point to the horizon of the divine, which
Cusa refers to as the "absolute maximum."

4.6.3 ABSOLUTE VS. CONTRACTED PANTHEISM

Cusa's pantheism is as much about the concept of immanence as it is
about the concept of nature. Insofar as Cusa's pantheism supports relations of immanence, it actually involves two types of immanence that are,

nevertheless, closely related. There is, first, an encompassing, enveloping, overarching process of enfolding, in which all that is and is not is onto-logically contained in the divine or supernatural. To this is paired a move-ment of unfolding that cuts across, flows through, and is pervasive among all things in the world. The first is a vertical immanence, an immanence between God and world, supernatural and natural. This vertical imma-nence is the immanence of theology, the immanence of God in the world. What results from this is an *absolute pantheism* in which God and nature are identical, or, alternately, in which God and the world are reciprocally and asymmetrically folded in each other. The second type of immanence is a lateral immanence, an immanence that operates between each indi-viduation, in which "each thing is in each thing." This lateral immanence is the immanence of natural philosophy, the immanence of each thing in each thing. This gives us a *contracted pantheism*, one in which nature is in fact self-emergent and coextensive with itself. Together, these two kinds of immanence form the two aspects of Cusa's pantheism—the im-manence of the supernatural in the natural, and the immanence of the natural in itself.

A brief recap of Cusa's pantheism is in order. There is, first, the coin-cidence of opposites (*coincidenta oppositorum*) that underlies all reality, a principle of ontological monism (or disjunctive monism) that Cusa re-fers to as the maximum (or absolute maximum). Here Cusa makes a sub-distinction between opposition (greater vs. lesser) and coincidence (greater and lesser). This coincidence of opposites is achieved through the twin processes of enfolding (*complicatio*) and unfolding (*explicatio*), in which nature is enfolded in God, and God is unfolded in nature. As a subset, this gives us two types of immanence—a vertical immanence between God and nature, and a lateral immanence of nature with itself. The means by which enfolding and unfolding occur—that is, the relation between en-folding and unfolding itself—is that of contraction, or the delimitation of God in relation to nature. This also gives us a subset, in which we have an absolute pantheism (God in nature) and a contracted pantheism (nature in itself).

In a sense, Cusa's pantheism is caught between a fully immanent pantheism—a pure immanence of supernatural and natural, God and world—and a tempered, transcendental pantheism (or, perhaps, a panen-theism) in which God, as absolute maximum, transcends the world by its very encompassing of the world, and the coincidence of all its opposites. Yet, even in this transcendental mode, the way in which Cusa places the divine, as absolute maximum, beyond the pale of the world, invites further

questions. The divine is not transcendental simply because it causes, creates, or governs the world (as it is in Aquinas, for example). For Cusa, the
divine is transcendental because, as the absolute maximum, as the point
where maximum and minimum are identical, at this point, the divine remains forever outside the reach of human thought and comprehension.
The divine is transcendental, for Cusa, because it is absolutely equivocal.

This is, certainly, part of the impulse behind Cusa's approach of speculative mysticism, and it can be witnessed in his other writings, such as
the *De Visione Dei*. What is noteworthy is that Cusa will often describe
this condition less in terms of mystical poetry and more in terms of philosophical logic. Consider, for instance, the following passage, where Cusa,
after having set out the distinction between God and nature and Creator
and creation, proceeds to deconstruct such distinctions:

> Who, therefore, can understand the being of the creation by uniting in
> it both the absolute necessity from which it exists and the contingency
> without which it does not exist? It seems that the creation, which is
> neither God nor nothing, is, as it were, subsequent to God and prior to
> nothing and between God and nothing . . . And yet the creation can-
> not be composed of being and not-being. It seems, therefore, neither to
> be, since it descends from being, nor not to be, since it is before noth-
> ing, nor a composite of both. Indeed, our intellect, which cannot leap
> beyond contradictories, does not reach the being of creation either by
> division or by composition . . . Derived being, therefore, is not under-
> standable, since the being from which it exists is not understandable.[79]

Passages like this are not uncommon in the *De Docta Ignorantia*; indeed,
from Cusa's vantage point, they point to the horizon of our ability to think
the divine at all. Put another way, the thought of the divine is not simply,
in the Anselmian manner, the limit of thought; it is, more specifically, the
thought of contradiction itself. In this sense, "pantheism" is not simply
the omnipresence of the divine in nature, but the full immanence of the
divine, as unknowable contradiction, throughout nature:

> But the absolutely maximum transcends all our understanding, which
> is unable by the path of reason to combine contradictories in their
> source, for we proceed by means of the things made evident to us by
> nature, and reason, falling far short of this infinite power, cannot join
> together contradictories, which are infinitely distant.[80]

The Cusan notion of "learned ignorance" is closely related to the form of pantheism put forth in the *De Docta Ignorantia*, and it is important to understand Cusa's evocations of the limits of thought within this framework.

In this regard, Cusa sets up for himself a particular problem. The central concepts of enfolding (*complicatio*) and unfolding (*explicatio*) dynamically produce a continuum in which, as Cusa notes, the maximum becomes minimum, and vice-versa. Enfolding and unfolding together restructure the ideas of the supernatural and natural, in effect flattening the relation between God and nature, Creator and creature. This has a number of effects: first, it lateralizes the vertical, governmental hierarchy between God and nature, the one implicated in the other, and each implicated in each. Second, it removes the ontological need for intermediaries, be it in the Neoplatonic guise of primordial causes or in the Peripatetic guise of hylomorphic causation. Third, it displaces thinking from the strictures of either dogmatic theology or a theological metaphysics, both of which require a principle of transcendence as a condition of any principle of immanence.

The logical conclusion of these effects of *complicatio* and *explicatio* is the Cusan refrain, "God is in all things in such a way that all things are in God."[81] If this is indeed a pantheism, then it is one that has a number of key requirements to it: (i) that the co-implication of the supernatural and the natural be predicated on a principle of pure immanence, and (ii) that this immanence of the supernatural and the natural be inseparable from a dynamic, processual life of *complicatio* and *explicatio*. What is immanent, in this Cusan pantheism, are the vitalist processes of folding (*plicare*) themselves. Pantheism, in this sense, means neither that the divine is natural, nor that the natural is divine, but that the co-implication of the supernatural and natural takes place through a conjunction of immanence and vitalism.

But this means that Cusa is then faced with the absolute indistinction between supernatural and natural, God and nature. What is to prevent this type of pantheism from becoming all-encompassing, such that there is nothing that is not within the ambit of this "absolute maximum"? Cusa does not outright dispense with the relations of mediation, hierarchy, or causality in his evocations of pantheism. As we've noted, the immanence of enfolding and unfolding is always doubled by Cusa's reaffirmation of the asymmetry of this immanence (that is, unfolding is a descent or derivation from a divine source, whereas enfolding always obtains a higher unity).

Cusa's pantheism—as a conjunction of immanence and vitalism—stands in an ambivalent relation to his reaffirmations of the sovereign transcendence of the divine as absolute maximum. The processes of enfolding and unfolding are no more caused by God than is nature; the question of will, so indicative of a doctrinal, anthropomorphized God, is conspicuously absent in Cusa's *De Docta Ignorantia*.

Added to this ambivalence is another. The conjunction of immanence and vitalism is really a tension, almost a contradiction. Pure immanence, in traditional theological terms, denotes a spatialized *plenum*, a fullness and actuality of the divine in all that is. By contrast, the movements of enfolding and unfolding are dynamic processes, which, though they are not about creation in the divine, *Genesis*-sense, they are about the immanent, ongoing creation of the continuum God-nature (God in all things, all things in God). At the heart of Cusa's pantheism is a tension, then, between an immanence of the divine that is a *plenum*, and the processes of enfolding/unfolding that is a *dunamis*; an immanence that is placid, expansive, and silent, and a vitalism that is always folding, creating, and producing; something that is everywhere, all at once, and fully actual, and something that is nowhere, continually differentiating, and fully virtual. In short, the tension within the Cusan notion of pantheism is really about the contraction between immanence and life.

In the *De Docta Ignorantia* Cusa offers what may be regarded as somewhat disappointing, conciliatory solutions to these problems. He does this throughout the text by repeatedly insisting on the asymmetrical distinction between God and nature—for instance, in the distinction between the absolute and the contracted maximum, the former the divine in itself, and the latter the unfolded nature. This is, in turn, predicated on a basic correlation between God and nature that, despite the frequent evocations of pantheism, still serves to inform Cusa's overall system. Finally, in the third book Cusa offers a doctrinal compromise by way of a figure of mediation—Christ, as the god-man, embodying in himself both the absolute and contracted maximum, both God and nature. Even here, however, in these all-too-human resolutions, Cusa's language enters a zone of poetic obscurity, suggesting that the absolute is never quite absolute, just as the contracted is never quite contracted.[82]

In highlighting the role of pantheism and its attendant tensions, we are, obviously, choosing to read Cusa's *De Docta Ignorantia* in a very particular way. Nevertheless, there are one basic argument and one basic question to come out of this exegesis. The argument: for a concept of pantheism in Cusa that is a conjunction of immanence and life. And the question: whether such a pantheism can be thought without itself becoming defined by contradiction.

4.6.4 SPECULATIVE PANTHEISM (DELEUZE'S INTERLOCUTORS)

These are precisely the points that Gilles Deleuze highlights in his own, Spinozist-inflected reading of Cusa. Or, we might do better to say that Deleuze's understanding of Spinoza, and of Spinoza's own pantheism, is uniquely indebted to the "post-Scholastic" pantheism of Cusa. As Deleuze notes, "The traditional couple of *explicatio* and *complicatio* historically reflects a vitalism never far from pantheism [*un vitalisme toujours proche du panthéisme*]."[83] And, in this vein, what Spinoza accomplishes is to "restore a Philosophy of Nature" to a place beyond the terms set out by Descartes. However, Deleuze is also careful to distance the pantheism of Cusa and Spinoza from "vitalism" in its biologistic vein. If the processes of *complicatio* and *explicatio* are vitalist, this is because they have to do with the constant creation and innovation of forms, not because they teleologically lead to the animal, the organism, or the species. This is an important move, and it characterizes nearly all Deleuze's writing on Spinoza. This gesture—pulling vitalism away from biology and reconnecting it to pantheism—is also found in a more subtle way in Maurice de Gandillac's writing on Cusa.[84] Gandillac, who was Deleuze's advisor for *Difference and Repetition*, also points to the inherently dynamic, processual qualities of *complicatio* and *explicatio*. Significantly, he also warns against an understanding of such processes that would reduce them to biology: "*Explicatio* could not, therefore, be the simple unrolling of a film of all eternity already wound up, like the 'preformed' leaves (*feuilles*) of a bud, or the miniature animal in germinal form as imagined by the adversaries of 'epigenesis.'"[85] If the Cusan terms *complicatio* and *explicatio* are to be understood in a vitalist way, this is not because they produce already-existent forms of life; it is, instead, because they are temporalized processes that are defined by a superlative generosity (an excess that is always creating, inventing, and so on).

If Deleuze's understanding of Spinoza is structurally indebted to his understanding of Cusa, it is in the Spinozist philosophy of nature that one finds the Cusan terms taken to their extreme. However, the way in which Spinoza accomplishes this is also quite different from that of Cusa. Whereas Cusa, not unlike Eckhart or Bruno, will utilize the method of speculative mysticism, in the *Ethics* Spinoza opts for a more rigorous, "axiomatic" approach to understanding the relation between God and Nature.

This point is made by Ferdinand Alquié in his 1958–59 lectures on Spinoza. Alquié, who served as Deleuze's advisor for *Expressionism in Philosophy*, will likewise warn against the biologistic reading of pantheism—in this case, in regard to Spinoza's naturalism:

> In effect, this idea of a self-sufficient Nature, of a substantial Nature, of a divine Nature, of a Nature that is co-existent with God, is not Spinozist, but a product of the Renaissance . . . What, then, constitutes the profound originality of Spinoza? What will finally permit this naturalism of the Renaissance to depart from the mystical confusion in which it remains? . . . What will permit Spinoza to give to spiritual processes a rational and precise sense, what will permit him to think Nature apart from all the shadows of finality, will be the mathematical method, and that alone.[86]

This nonreductive pantheism is not a form of idealism; it is not the case that Spinoza simply abstracts the biological or natural into a Platonic domain. For Alquié, the key to this lies in Spinoza's refusal to see mathematical truths and biological-naturalistic truths as mutually exclusive. As Alquié notes, "[B]y way of considering the mathematical theory in relation to the biological theory, which was that of Aristotle, we are witness to an important transformation in the definition of truth."[87] That transformation entails not only a naturalism but an ontology, not only a philosophy of nature (a pantheism), but also an ontology of immanence.

The Cusan "coincidence of opposites," where the maximum is the minimum and vice-versa, is streamlined in Spinoza into a single, univocal substance—one substance for all attributes. This univocal substance is, in Spinoza's celebrated phrase, "God or nature," one and the same. This univocal substance may be expressed through the attributes (for Spinoza, the attributes of thought or extension). Hence Cusa's twofold, vitalist processes of enfolding and unfolding are, in Spinoza, an array of attributes whose dynamic is that of "expression." These attributes in turn express the multiplicity of modes (for example, modes of speed or slowness, affecting or being affected). The Cusan process of contraction into nature is, in Spinoza, the expression of modes of movement and affect.

However, for Deleuze, Spinoza does more than simply extend the basic tenets of Cusan pantheism. Deleuze outlines two significant modifications that Spinoza effects to Cusan pantheism. The first is to note that the important thing about types of folding in Cusa (*complicatio* and *explicatio*) is not what they produce, or what is unfolded, but rather the process of creation itself. Thus, Deleuze proposes that what Cusa calls *explicatio* is actually two, coupled processes: *involvere* (infolding, involving, implicating) and *explicare* (unfolding, evolving, explicating). These two processes are not in opposition to each other, but are like two sides of the same page. Deleuze's distinction between *involvere* and *explicare* further points to their synthesis in a third term: "Precisely because the two concepts are not opposed to one another, they imply a principle of synthesis: *complicatio*."[88]

In his reading of Cusa-Spinoza, Deleuze suggests that there are actually three terms in play: *involvere* (to implicate), *explicare* (to explicate), and *complicare* (to complicate). These are all "terms inherited from a long philosophical tradition, always subject to the charge of pantheism."[89] What unites them, what is common to each process, though inflected in different ways, is what Deleuze calls "expression":

> To explicate is to evolve, to involve is to implicate. Yet the two terms are not opposites: they simply mark two aspects of expression. Expression is on the one hand an explication, an unfolding of what expresses itself, the One manifesting itself in the Many (substance manifesting itself in its attributes, and these attributes manifesting themselves in their modes). Its multiple expression, on the other hand, involves Unity. The One remains involved in what expresses it, imprinted in what unfolds it, immanent in whatever manifests it.[90]

The concept of expression frames Deleuze's entire book on Spinoza. Though the term is not frequently used by Spinoza himself, Deleuze expands it to talk about the concept of creation itself. Rather than take creation as a term framed by the relationship of God-nature or Creator-creation, where the former term would express the latter term as some thing, expression in its Spinozist guise is about the enfolding and unfolding between two terms (in this case, "God or nature"). "Expression in general involves and implicates what it expresses, while also explicating and evolving it."[91] Expression is the dynamic that does not express any thing, except itself; in this sense expression is the demonstration of the univocity or immanence between God and nature, the supernatural and natural.

This is, in a sense, an inversion of the approach of speculative mysticism, which, in its more dogmatic vein, always rises up through successive abstractions to a horizon beyond which thought cannot go. Traditional mysticism always draws together and raises up—this is evidenced in book 3 of Cusa's *De Docta Ignorantia*, where the problematic of pantheism elicits a conservative response. By reading Cusa through Spinoza's more rigorous version of pantheism, Deleuze suggests not a speculative mysticism, but a speculative pantheism, one that always descends and spreads out—either in terms of the delimitations of *complicatio*, or in the proliferations of *explicatio*. In Deleuze, the Cusan terms of *complicatio* and *explicatio* are transformed by Spinoza into a philosophical pantheism in which the supernatural and natural, the material and spiritual, are continually folded into each other:

> In Spinoza, Nature at once comprises and contains everything, while being explicated and implicated in each thing. Attributes involve and explicate substance, which in turn comprises all attributes. Modes involve and explicate the attribute on which they depend, while the attribute in turn contains the essences of all modes.[92]

With Cusa, we saw how the injunction of pantheism led to a central tension, a tension between the immanence of the divine nature and the vitalist processes of *complicatio* and *explicatio*. At the core of Cusan pantheism is a contradiction between immanence and life. The Spinozist concept of expression suggests not a contradiction, but, true to Cusa's thought, a coincidence of immanence and life, a spatialized fullness and a temporalized creativity.

The pantheism in Spinoza is, then, different from the pantheism in Cusa. Nevertheless, the conjunction of immanence and life is central to any ontology of pantheism. But what is a point of tension, or even contradiction, in Cusa, itself becomes the principle of immanence in Spinoza— this is Deleuze's argument, at least. This means that to the pantheism of Cusa and Spinoza, we must also bear in the mind the pantheism of Deleuze, in his particular readings of the former two thinkers. Let us, then, move from a consideration of Deleuze's reading of Cusan pantheism more directly to his reading of Spinozist pantheism.

4.7 PANTHEISM AND PURE IMMANENCE

In *Expressionism in Philosophy*, Deleuze explicitly frames Spinoza's concepts in terms of pantheism:

> Spinoza accepts the truly philosophical "danger" of immanence and pantheism implicit in the notion of expression. Indeed he throws in his

lot with that danger. In Spinoza the whole theory of expression supports univocity; and its whole import is to free univocal Being from
a state of indifference or neutrality, to make it the object of a pure affirmation, which is actually realized in an expressive pantheism or
immanence.[93]

Statements such as these can be read as applying equally to Deleuze's philosophy itself as to that of Spinoza. Deleuze's long-standing engagement
with the concepts of univocity and immanence bears testament to this
Spinozist commitment. This is why, for Deleuze, concepts of life or vitalism, nature or pantheism, enter the stage. For Deleuze, Spinoza's pantheism is not a philosophy of nature, much less a natural philosophy: "It is
in short a philosophical concept of immanence, which insinuates itself
among the transcendent concepts of emanative or creationist theology."
As Deleuze notes, such a position brings with it a "philosophical danger":
"pantheism or immanence—the immanence of its expression in what expresses itself, and of what is expressed in its expression."[94]

The "danger" of which Deleuze speaks is not just a political sort,
though, in the historical context of Spinoza, it is certainly that too. Rather,
the danger is also philosophical, in the sense that the idea of a pure, expressive immanence—of each thing in each thing, of all in all—brings
with it a number of fundamental problems. One of these has to do with
the problem of production, creation, and invention. If immanence is pure
immanence, immanent to nothing but itself, then how can immanence
also be a ceaseless creation and invention of the new? How can creativity
emerge out of what is already fully actual? We have seen this problematic arise before, with Cusa's notions of *complicatio* and *explicatio*, and
with Duns Scotus' proofs for the univocal relation between Creator and
creature.

This problem turns onto another one, which deals more with the peculiar logic of pantheism. As we've seen, sometimes the thought of pure
immanence will elicit a reactionary response that reaffirms the transcendence of the divine. Eriugena does this in his quandary over the tension
between the divine will and necessity (the divine must, ontologically
speaking, flow forth, but must also be undetermined and without limit),
and Duns Scotus does this in his repeated qualifications for the concept
of univocity (e.g., that univocity presupposes a basic hierarchy between
Creator and creature). Certainly, from a modern vantage point, such
a pulling-back can be regarded as symptomatic of the religious climate

within which such thinkers were working. But what is equally important is that such reactions may also be indicative of the strictures of logic that underpin philosophical discourse. As we've seen, Eriugena's own brand of pantheism arises from the thought of something that is nowhere in particular and everywhere in general, a dispersive concept of the divine that, at certain points, becomes coextensive with *natura* itself. Similarly, in Duns Scotus the "triple primacy" of Creator in relation to creature gives way to a foregrounding of the interrelation of the triple primary, and, ultimately, its unity. Finally, with Cusa, the supernatural and natural, divided though they are (as absolute and contracted), are still, at certain points, rendered as a fully immanent continuum of enfolding (*complicatio*) and unfolding (*explicatio*).

Each of these reactionary moments has, as its double, the thought of immanence-in-itself, immanence taken to its logical conclusion. In Eriugena this is a fully dispersive notion of immanence, in which *natura* and *nihil* become one and the same—fully creative, efflusive, outpouring, and yet "nothing." In Duns Scotus this is the primacy of univocal relations—a radical equality of all things, and yet differentiated along the lines of Creator and created. And in Cusa this is the thought of a "coincidence of opposites"—a continuum of supernatural and natural, and yet an asymmetry between enfolding and unfolding. Hence, in all these cases, the gesture of pulling-back masks the thought of pure immanence, an immanence that is at once a fully actual field and yet continually generating, creating, and inventing. At its limit, the thought of pure immanence becomes tantamount to the thought of contradiction itself. If, as Deleuze provocatively suggests, pantheism is a philosophical danger, it is because pantheism—as the conjunction of immanence and life—opens onto the thought of contradiction itself.

This takes a particular form in Deleuze's reading of Spinoza. While Spinoza does not offer any easy solution to the problems raised by the idea of pure immanence, in Deleuze's reading he does perform a number of important operations on the concept of immanence. In Deleuze's *Expressionism in Philosophy*, we can identify three main Spinozist operations: a critique of the subordination of immanence in onto-theological discourse; the idea of the common ("common nature," "common notions") as supplying an ontological framework for immanence; and a leveraging of the notion of expression to question the priority of being over life. Together, these three operations reveal concepts that are central to Spinoza's own pantheism—immanence, the common, and expression. We can briefly consider these in turn.

4.7.1 The Insubordination of Immanence in Deleuze

The concept of immanence has a conflicted history in onto-theological discourse. For Deleuze, it is not simply that the concept of immanence is always opposed to transcendence, but that immanence is consistently subordinated in a way that allows it to perform limited functions. However, a notion of "pure immanence" would not only imply an absolutely superlative concept of immanence, but it would also imply a renewed concept of life that would itself be fully isomorphic with the concept of immanence. Immanence would not simply be static, spatialized, full being, and life would not simply be that which is defined by the temporality of growth, decay, development, and change—the conjunction of immanence and life would also require a synthesis, whereby immanence is temporalized as expressive, inventive, and creative, and life is laterally dispersed across the traditional boundaries of species and set.

But this requires a lot, for such a pantheism tends to exclude nothing and encompass everything. It is, in short, the philosophical danger of which Deleuze speaks in regard to Spinoza, and this is reflected in Deleuze's three overarching ontological principles in *Expressionism in Philosophy*: (i) Being is affirmation (principle of generosity); (ii) everything is everywhere (principle of relation); and (iii) all is One (principle of univocity). In Spinoza's pantheism, Deleuze finds concepts that threaten to efface (or relativize, depending on one's viewpoint) basic ontological categories: if Being is pure affirmation, then it is also pure excess, and the concept of negation loses its meaning; if everything is everywhere, then the distinction between object and relation, actor and act, is likewise meaningless; and if all is One, then the interplay between the One, the Many, and even the multiple ceases to be relevant. Deleuze does not, we should note, go this far—the Scholastic rigor of Spinoza and his predecessors prevents pure relativism. Nevertheless, for Deleuze, this thought of the absolute coincidence of immanence and life is the very "vertigo of philosophy."

How, then, has immanence been subordinated in the history of philosophy? How has the concept of immanence historically been separated from the concept of expressive, inventive life? Deleuze suggests that there are three phases to this history. The first is in terms of the concept of participation. This is a classical mode, whose exemplar is Plato and Platonism. In Plato, immanence is conceived of in terms of participation, and this can have three meanings: it can mean "to take part in," which implies a basic distinction between the participator and the participated. Thus, a part is immanent in relation to a whole of which it is a part; it is the whole, part of the whole, and an individual part all at once. Participation can also mean "to imitate" in a conventional Platonic sense, as when a chair produced by an artisan participates in the abstract idea of a chair. This, however, necessitates an external concept of imitator or artisan (who is, in the case of nature, God-as-Creator), so that all instantiations of an idea are only partially or imperfectly immanent in the idea. Finally, participation can also have a demonic meaning, in the Greek sense of *daimon*, in which one is a recipient of the influences of a spiritual entity. This necessitates a theory of mediation or representation, whereby the immanence outside the subject is mediately immanent within the subject. Thus "[p]articipation was understood, according to these schemes, either materially, or imitatively, or demonically."[95]

All of these notions of immanence-as-participation are, Deleuze argues, on the side of the participant, rather than the participated. Immanence is only ever a derivative, secondary manifestation of something equivocal and inaccessible, something transcendent. A shift occurs, for Deleuze, with Neoplatonism. "Neoplatonists no longer start from the characteristics of what participates . . . They try rather to discover the internal principle and movement that grounds participation in the participated as such."[96] The emphasis is not on the derivative, secondary instantiation of immanence, but on the processes by which such instantiations are produced from a transcendent source. This necessitates a concept of production that at once accounts for the immanence of the source in its products, while preserving the hierarchy of relations between source and product. Some thing—a divine source—must be conceived as being everywhere—in its productions—while also remaining a source. It must not be absolutely transcendent, since there must be some connection between source and product, but it also must not be absolutely immanent, since it is the very hierarchy between source and product that grounds the ontology. In short, "[p]articipation is neither material, nor imitative, nor demonic; it is emanative."[97]

In this second phase, immanence is understood in not in terms of *participation*, but in terms of *emanation*. Here Neoplatonism is the exemplar, with Proclus and Plotinus as Deleuze's reference points. Emanation entails a logic of generosity and gift. "Emanation has in general a triadic form: giver, given, and recipient. To participate is always to participate through what is given."[98] Whereas in the first phase—immanence as participation— the emphasis was on the participant as derivative, here, with immanence as emanation, the emphasis is on the side of the participated. Neoplatonic emanation inadvertently points to the possibility of a pure immanence, in that it focuses on the processes rather than the products (e.g., articulations of the stratified spheres of emanation in Plotinus' cosmology). But emanation is still a subordinated immanence, since it must preserve a notion of the participated that is above or beyond all things. This emanative source itself remains non-immanent: "Everything emanates from this principle, its gives forth everything. But it is not itself participated, for participation occurs only through what it gives, and in what it gives . . . only occurs through a principle that is itself imparticipable."[99]

These first two phases—immanence-as-participation, immanence-as-emanation—have something in common, however, and that is that they remain in themselves in their production. The Idea or the Source always remains in itself, either because it is abstractly beyond all things of which it is the perfected form, or because it is processually above all things it emanatively produces. "Their common characteristic is that neither leaves itself: they produce *while remaining in themselves.*"[100] There are a number of important differences, then, between this partial immanence-as-emanation and a notion of immanence taken in itself. "While an emanative cause remains in itself, the effect it produces is not in it, and does not remain in it."[101] "A cause is immanent, on the other hand, when its effect is 'immanante' in the cause, rather than emanating from it."[102] The cause of emanation is outside of what it gives or produces; whereas with immanence the effect is immanent in the cause. In this way Deleuze articulates one of his central points: that the key to thinking immanence in itself lies not in opposing it to transcendence, but in its subordination to "emanence" or emanation.

This leads to a third phase Deleuze considers, one in which immanence is no longer subordinate to either participation or emanation. And this is, in Deleuze's eyes, what Spinoza's philosophy provides—a concept of insubordinate immanence whose real opposition is not between transcendence and immanence, but between immanence and emanence. How does Spinoza's philosophy do this? How can immanence be thought in itself, without resorting to either the necessity of an external Source (as in Neoplatonic emanation) or to the necessity of an abstract Idea (as in Platonic exemplarism)? As Deleuze suggests, one has to understand Spinoza's Scholasticism, and the way that Spinoza takes up and transforms Scholastic onto-theological concepts. It is here that Deleuze turns to the Cusan terms of complication (*complicatio*) and explication (*explicatio*):

> Such is the origin of a pair of notions that take on greater and greater importance in the philosophies of the Middle Ages and Renaissance:

complicare and *explicare*. All things are present to God, who compli-
cates them. God is present to all things, which explicate and implicate
him . . . Immanence corresponds to the unity of complication and explication, of inherence and implication.[103]

As we saw with Cusa, the processes of complication and explication are
"folded" onto the same, singular, divine nature; but they are also asymmetrical, for while this is a two-way street, the direction of complication
clearly bears the more authentic stamp of the divine than the explication
into the things of the world. Deleuze suggests that Spinoza, in his substance monism, takes up these Cusan terms and radicalizes them. In the
Spinozist framework, if one is to think immanence in itself, one has to see
the processes of complication and explication are absolutely equivalent:
"A co-presence of two correlative movements comes to be substituted for
a series of successive subordinate emanations . . . An equality of being
is substituted for a hierarchy of hypostases; for things are present to the
same Being, which is itself present in things."[104] One of the requirements
of thinking immanence in itself is, then, thinking the processes of *complicatio* and *explicatio* in terms of an absolute immanence.

   This is the first move Deleuze makes in relation to Spinoza's
philosophy—linking the dynamic processes of complication and explication to immanence. The second move Deleuze makes is to then link immanence to an inventive, creative, and vitalist concept of expression:

> Participation no longer has its principle in an emanation whose source
> lies in a more or less distant One, but rather in the immediate and
> adequate expression of an absolute Being that comprises in it all be-
> ings, and is explicated in the essence of each. Expression comprehends
> all these aspects: complication, explication, inherence, implication.
> And these aspects of expression are also the categories of immanence.
> Immanence is revealed as expressive, and expression as immanent,
> in a system of logical relations within which the two notions are
> correlative.[105]

Expression, insofar as it is a principle of inventive, creative life, is here
indelibly tied to the concept of immanence in itself—"immanence is revealed as expressive, and expression as immanent." Expression, though
it implies a basic temporal, causal dichotomy of expressor and expressed,
Creator and creature, producer and produced—expression must take this
dichotomy and flatten it out in terms of immanence, such that the expres-

sor is not just "in" the expressed but coincident with it as well. Likewise, immanence, though it implies a static, fully actualized distribution, must take this *plenum* and render it dynamic and processual, such that immanence is precisely that which constantly invents and creates nothing other than immanence itself.

For Deleuze, this conjunction of immanence and expression—or really, *of immanence and life*—has three fundamental principles, principles that push the limits of the concept itself. First, the *principle of equality*: "pure immanence requires as a principle the equality of being, or the positing of equal Being: not only is being equal in itself, but it is seen to be equally present in all beings."[106] Immanence is not only the immanence between Creator and creature (a vertical immanence), but the immanence between creature and creature (a horizontal immanence)—what Cusa calls "each thing in each thing." There is also the *principle of univocity*: "pure immanence requires a Being that is univocal and constitutes a Nature, and that consists of positive forms, common to producer and product, to cause and effect."[107] Immanence, which here becomes synonymous with pantheism, is at the same time dispersive and inventive, distributive and creative, supernatural and natural. Finally, there is the *principle of affirmation*: "[i]mmanence is opposed to any eminence of the cause, any negative theology, any method of analogy, any hierarchical conception of the world. With immanence all is affirmation."[108] If there is to be a specifically Spinozist pantheism, Deleuze articulates it along these three lines: a purely immanent equality, in which the supernatural is fully immanent to the natural, and vice-versa; a univocity of all things that implies a fully immanent and vitalistic continuum between one thing and another; and an ontological affirmation that supports a notion of being as purely superlative, affirmative, and creative. Together, these three principles of equality, univocity, and affirmation constitute the pantheism unique to Spinoza's philosophy, where "pantheism" implies the conjunction of immanence and life.

These are difficult concepts, to be sure, for in actuality they stretch the limits of the concept itself. As Deleuze notes, "Immanence is the very vertigo of philosophy, and is inseparable from the concept of expression."[109] But they also have a tactical function, which is to critically question the concept of immanence in itself. For Deleuze, this notion of pantheism, this conjunction of immanence and life, this has always been historically opposed to transcendence, and, more importantly, subordinated to emanence or emanation. There immanence continues to function, but in a tempered, conciliatory way, either in the Idea or the emanative Source. In this way

the "expressive immanence of Being was grafted onto a transcendent emanation of the One."[110] While Neoplatonic emanation does open the door
to the explication of the world from God, it is still required to preserve
the hierarchy of the divine Source. While Medieval Scholasticism would
push this to its limits—either in the "inexpressible" of negative theology,
or the univocity of Creator and creature—it is still required to preserve
the asymmetry between divination and creation, complication and explication. The option left, the one Deleuze opts for, is to push the concept of
immanence to such a degree that it effectively becomes "nothing":

> The idea of expression is repressed as soon as it surfaces. For the themes
> of creation or emanation cannot do without a minimal transcendence,
> which bars 'expressionism' from proceeding all the way to the imma-
> nence it implies . . . The significance of Spinozism seems to me this:
> it asserts immanence as a principle and frees expression from any sub-
> ordination to emanative or exemplary causality. *Expression itself no
> longer emanates, no longer resembles anything.*[111]

In these pantheistic philosophies, predicated as they are on the fullness of
(dynamic) flow and (static) being, an inversion occurs, in which the endpoint of immanence is its own dissipation. For Deleuze, it is with Spinoza,
drawing as he does from his Scholastic predecessors, that we first encounter two thoughts central to an ontology of life: the thought of immanence-
in-itself, and the conjunction of this immanence-in-itself and expressive
life, that becomes the hallmark of a renewed pantheism, an "expressive
pantheism or immanence."

4.7.2 SCHOLIA I: THE ISOMORPHISM OF UNIVOCITY AND IMMANENCE

Is there a significant difference between the concepts of univocity and
immanence in Deleuze? One possible answer is diachronic, which would
involve comparing Deleuze's early and later readings of Spinoza. For example, earlier works such as *Difference and Repetition* favor univocity, as
in Deleuze's celebrated assertion: "There has only ever been one ontological proposition: Being is univocal."[112] By contrast, late pieces, such as "Immanence: A Life" favor the term immanence. But this contrast does not
bear itself out, for, even in a single work Deleuze will use both terms—
sometimes differently, and sometimes interchangeably. In *Expressionism
in Philosophy*, Deleuze will comment that in Spinoza, "the whole theory

of expression supports univocity." But he also points out that expression has to do with "a specifically philosophical concept of immanence."

The term "univocity" is, as Deleuze notes, derived from Scholastic discourse, and in Deleuze's particular sense, from Duns Scotus. As we've seen in the previous chapter, the question of whether the relation between God and Nature was analogical, equivocal, or univocal was a central point of debate in the twelfth and thirteenth centuries, and Deleuze's reading of Duns Scotus pushes the concept of univocity to a point where Duns Scotus himself arguably would not, or could not, go.

In Deleuze's Scholasticism, the relation between Creator and creature is a univocal relation. Being is said the same everywhere that it is said. But the essence of the divine is immanent with relation to the earthly. Both concepts presuppose a basic relation, one that is asymmetrical (Creator-creature, divine-earthly, supernatural-natural, etc.). But the relation itself, emphasizing as it does a "flat" or horizontal relation, collapses this relation into a single plane.

Immanence, by contrast, is far less common in Scholastic discourse. When one does find it, it is used in a Neoplatonic and derivative way—immanence is always, as Deleuze notes, subordinated to the theologico-political dictates of transcendence. But even in these instances, immanence seems to imply a more general state; it tends towards the static. But even if it is taken to be about the divine nature in itself, this still presupposes a minimal relation (transcendent with respect to . . . , eminent with respect to . . .). Immanence, in its *stasis* or *plenum*, always harbors within it a minimal relation that implies a *dunamis*.

Should we then say that, in Deleuze's Scholasticism, univocity foregrounds temporality, and immanence spatiality? Or should we say that univocity is a special case of immanence? Another possibility is that, for Deleuze, immanence is "expressed" as univocity. But then this would transform immanence into a state of being that is then expressed, and univocity becomes adverbial, the way in which immanence is expressed (which then opens up the question of whether immanence can be expressed equivocally or analogically . . .).

Hence, to say that univocity correlates to temporality, and immanence to spatiality, doesn't quite work out either, for immanence and univocity each have spatial *and* temporal aspects to them. They are spatially a spreading-out, a diffusion, a topology of everything-is-everywhere. But then this opens onto the Kantian (and very un-Deleuzian) question of whether there is a space—the being of space—that itself serves as the support for immanence/univocity. Does immanence, for instance, need a con-

tainer within which to be immanent? Is immanence always immanent to
some space?

Likewise, immanence/univocity are temporally a denial of external
causes (the causality of transcendence or emanence). Immanence is self-
caused, or, as we might say today, self-organized. Immanent being produces itself, in itself, through itself. There is no external causal agency.
But then this opens onto the question of whether there can be said to be
causation at all, for does not the very notion of cause presuppose a minimal
distinction between subject and object, a correlation of self and world?

Another possibility: should we modify our terms, and say that, in Deleuze's Scholasticism, univocity emphasizes relationality, while immanence emphasizes continuity? We would be led to consider to concepts
that are essentially two sides of the same page. But this only exacerbates
the problem, for it requires a third term. Is this the function that "expression" plays in Deleuze's reading of Scholasticism? When we have expressive univocity, we have the emphasis of the ontological priority of dynamic
relation and interrelation—but relations and interrelations that open onto
a flat continuum. When we have expressive immanence, we have the emphasis on the ontological priority of dispersive, pervasive being—but a dis-
persiveness and a pervasiveness that open onto a network of relations.

It is debatable whether or not expression actually plays this role in Deleuze's Scholasticism, without assigning expression the role of a mediator
or an act, and the paired terms univocity/immanence as things. This is
why Deleuze's main adversary in *Expressionism in Philosophy* is Plotinus
and not Plato. The Plotinean system attempts to have it both ways—to
posit a divine Source that is equivocally transcendent, and to posit an
equally divine emanation that is univocally present in all created things.
What remains relevant in Deleuze's usage of the terms univocity and immanence is his concerted attempt to think a dynamic, relational concept
of immanence, as well as a fully distributive, pervasive concept of univocity. Perhaps, then, Deleuze's philosophy does not amount to an attempt to
"invert Platonism," but rather an attempt to "subvert Neoplatonism"—
that is, *to think a concept of emanation without a center*.

4.7.3 SCHOLIA II: THE VITALIST LOGIC OF COMMON NOTIONS

In the *Opus Oxoniense* Duns Scotus briefly raises the possibility that
the univocal relation between God and Nature could be made possible by
something common to them both: "[S]uppose we say that *A* through its

own essence knows *B* because of the great similarity between the two, so that *A* knows *B* through some nature common (*speciei communis*) to *A* and *B*."[113] The question that Duns Scotus puts forth is whether, supposing that God and Nature are univocal, a "natural" knowledge of this univocity could be possible. To the reply that answers in the negative—that the univocity of God and Nature can be known only via faith—Duns Scotus argues that univocity can be thought, and that, furthermore, "natural reason" can provide the proofs for such a univocal relation. Hence the proof above concerning the "common nature." This, however, does not prove that *A* knows *B* perfectly—that is, univocally— nor that because of this *A* is God, in the sense of being absolutely equivocal. It only establishes a likeness, but does not say if this likeness is univocal. The idea of the common nature fades away as quickly as it is evoked by Duns Scotus.

The idea of the common nature is not only that which is common or held univocally, but that which is held univocally in a non-divine way, insofar as the divine is separate from nature. The idea is picked up later by Spinoza, but in terms of "common notions" rather than a common nature. What are common notions? Deleuze provides a number of definitions. In a formal sense, "[a] common notion is always an idea of similarity of composition in existing modes."[114] The relation between any two bodies (that is, between any two relations) reveals, at a more general level, a whole of which they are a part. This is their "common property," their "similarity or community of composition." Amid this whole is Nature, a "common notion." "As all relations are combined in Nature as a whole, Nature presents a similarity of composition that may be seen in all bodies from the most general viewpoint."[115] The implication is that only the relations change in Nature as a whole, not the constituent parts. Nature is thus both fully actual (in that the parts do not change) but also inherently virtual (in that the relations combine infinitely). From the point of view of Spinozist modes, there are less universal common notions, but there are also more universal common notions that are common to all things (e.g., extension).

Deleuze distinguishes common notions as particular kinds of terms. Common notions are not transcendental terms (the being of a thing, Being-in-itself); they are not universal terms (genera, species); and they are not abstract ideas (insofar as the latter retains only sensible differences or are based on accidental and arbitrary criteria). Common notions have to do with what Deleuze calls "structures" rather than sensible forms or functions. And it is here that Deleuze puts forth one of his many criticisms of "life" in the Aristotelian sense:

In all this Spinoza is clearly attacking, not just the procedures of common sense, but the Aristotelian tradition also. The attempt to define
genera and species through differences first appears in Aristotelian biology . . . Against this tradition Spinoza proposes a grand principle: to
consider structures, rather than sensible forms or functions. But what
is the meaning of 'structure'? It is a system of relations between the
parts of a body . . . By inquiring how these relations vary from one body
to another, we have a way of directly determining the resemblances
between two bodies, however disparate they may be . . . In the limit
Nature as a whole is a single Animal [un même Animal] in which only
the relations between the parts vary.[116]

In other works, Deleuze will use the philosophy of biology to make a similar point—whereas Cuvier will propose a comparative anatomy based on
sensible similarities and functions, Geoffroy Saint-Hilaire will propose a
single manifold plane along which each animal is isomorphic with every
other animal.[117] What Spinoza puts forth is an even wider view of living
Nature, within which a single substance courses through and yet is inseparable from the modes that constitute the world. If Spinoza is a pantheist
thinker, this is not because the divine is everywhere "in" nature; it is because the immanence of nature in and through itself necessitates an ontological framework that departs from Aristotelian natural philosophy: "For
the examination of sensible differences is substituted an examination of
intelligible similarities, which allow us to understand resemblances and
differences between bodies 'from the inside.'"[118]

It is for this reason that Deleuze, in a suggestive turn of phrase, notes
that common notions are really "biological ideas" or really, an *ideational
biology*: "Spinoza's common notions are biological, rather than physical or
mathematical, ideas. They really do play the part of Ideas in a philosophy
of Nature from which all finality has been excluded."[119] Common notions
are biological ideas in the sense that they do not presuppose the separation
of organism and environment; they are based on an idea of Nature without
teleology or finality; and they posit a notion of life that is nonorganic, in
which the organism is an effect and not a cause.

Deleuze is careful to note, however, that the common notions are "biological" not in the sense of the philosophy of biology—which, as a modern phenomenon, necessarily begins from an assumption about the ontology of life. Rather, common notions are biological in the sense of Idealist
philosophy—or better, in the sense in which all philosophies of nature are
"idealist." They are not idealist in the vulgar sense of being imaginary

or the products of purely mental operations. Rather they are idealist in the sense of German *Lebensphilosophie*, in which everything, including thought, is understood to be exterior to the subject. There is no question of nature being imaginary or perfectly malleable to intentional thought, for all thought is already given in a manner that is relational, exterior, and pervasive to individuated bodies and minds. Spinoza's pantheism is thus not only anti-Aristotelian, but anti-Cartesian as well. What metaphysically grounds any philosophy of nature is the anti-metaphysical sense of that which is common to all things, not in spite of but because of their manifold differentiations and interrelations. What grounds Spinoza's pantheism is neither Aristotelian finality or entelechism, nor the Neoplatonic emanating Source, but the relations immanent to each other that constitute "God or Nature." In Deleuze's reading of Spinoza, any philosophy of nature necessarily entails a pantheism, but a pantheism that is commensurate with "idealism."

4.7.4 SCHOLIA III: THE LIFE OF SUBSTANCE

One of Deleuze's strongest claims concerning the ontology of life comes in the chapter of *Expressionism in Philosophy* on attributes and the absolute. There, in a somewhat anomalous turn of phrase, Deleuze stridently makes a claim for "the life of substance itself": "Life, that is, expressivity, is carried into the absolute. There is a unity of the divine in substance, and an actual diversity of the One in the attributes . . . it amounts to the life of substance itself, the necessity of its apriori constitution."[120]

What exactly is the "life of substance"? It is not just that such-and-such a phenomenon is alive, in the sense of "nonorganic life," but rather that substance itself is alive. Why then, does Deleuze feel the need to make a claim beyond substance itself, to say that not only is substance absolutely infinite, but that it is alive as well?

Spinoza, in the *Ethics*, never makes reference to "life" and only occasionally to nature in its modern, biologistic sense. One might guess that, given Spinoza's metaphysical framework, life would be somewhere between an attribute (inasmuch as life is a combination of thought and extension) and a mode (actual living creatures as opposed to a principle of life). The phrase "the life of substance" asks us to consider an anachronism—a biological Spinozism. Is "the life of substance" something other than substance itself? Is it something external to substance? Is it a meta-substance, a super-substance? Is there a nonliving substance, or is the greater contradiction to suppose that substance is living?

Deleuze seems to take it for granted that Spinoza is a pantheist. But there are, of course, variants of pantheism, each responding to a particular set of philosophical and theological problems. There is the Neoplatonic version (often described as panentheism), in which nature participates "in" the divine. Here all that which changes (nature) is coupled with that which does not change (the divine) by the former being included within the latter (the latter transcendentally including the immanence of the former). A slight modification of this is found in Eriugena's *Periphyseon*, which at some points affirms the transcendental aspect (e.g., God as that which creates and is not created), and at other points seems to affirm a more immanent aspect (e.g., that which neither creates nor is created as God and nature).

The Spinozist version—as Deleuze reads it—goes further and pushes for absolute immanence. In this type of pantheism, nature equals the divine and vice-versa. *Deus sive Natura*, in Spinoza's celebrated phrase. So the phrase "the life of substance" refers to this equivalence between Nature and God, life and the divine. This Spinozist pantheism implies not only an immanence of the divine (one substance for all attributes), but also an immanence of life: if God is Nature, and Nature is all living beings, then God is all living beings.

Again, Deleuze's phraseology is very particular—he does not make life a character of substance (e.g., "substance is alive"), but implies that there is something beyond substance of which substance is the expressed; it almost implies that life courses through substance, makes it alive, perhaps even "ensouls" it. It would then appear that Deleuze grants life a kind of supereminence—if it is not simply another metaphysical category, neither is it reducible to regional philosophies, such as natural philosophy or the philosophy of biology. It is not that life is a category of being (as Heidegger would have it), but rather that being, or the being of being, is a subset of a higher form of life. This life is not simply the life of the organism, but neither is it the energetic life of vitalism, or the divine life of pantheism.

Nevertheless, there is something about modality—about change, process, becoming, and so on—that persists through Deleuze's many variants of this theme of the "life of substance." This is a modality of affirmation that one finds in so many of Deleuze's works. Only by assuming a notion of being as generosity can Deleuze grant being a higher form-of-life. Being is alive because there is always an exterior (though not an outside), because there is always the virtual (though not the potential), because *life, for Deleuze, is always in excess of being*—including its own being.

Now, philosophers such as Badiou have taken Deleuze to task for this vitalism, for, in such readings, it simply masks a theological position, or at the very least a romanticized notion of Nature.[121] Instead of the affirmative, additive approach of Deleuze, Badiou, for instance, will opt for a negative, "subtractive" ontology based on mathematics. Here the ground of being is not a superlative principle of generosity, but a subtractive gesture; not the overflowing flux, but the empty set, the void. But Deleuze's reworking of the concept of life—and with it, the concepts that ground biology and the philosophy of nature—entails, as we've seen, a critique of the Aristotelian framework of the "biological set" (genera, species, types; natural history and comparative anatomy). Hence Deleuze's frequent associations between an ontology of pure immanence and an ontology of life—the life of substance:

> It [the concept of immanence in Spinoza] gives back to Nature its own specific depth and renders man capable of penetrating into this depth. It makes man commensurate with God, and puts him in possession of a new logic: makes him a spiritual automaton [automate spirituel] equal to a combinatorial world. Born of the traditions of emanation and creation it makes of these two enemies, questioning the transcendence of a One above Being along with the transcendence of a Being above his Creation.[122]

The "spiritual automaton" is not, of course, mechanism elevated to the Platonic level of thought; it is, for Deleuze, that point at which "life" and "thought" coincide in a sort of vitalist logic of proliferation and combinatorics. Such a notion requires the presupposition of an ontology of life in which life exceeds being. The question, then, is whether this ontology of life as the One-All bears any relation whatsoever to the Aristotelian ontology from which Deleuze's philosophy distances itself. One way in which Deleuze does this is to focus on a principle of generosity and superlative excess as the ontological principle coursing through life. Purely affirmative, always changing, always transforming, totally immanent to itself— this is Deleuze's own pantheism, inflected as it is through the Scholasticism of Spinoza.

More questions emerge. Does this require that there be something that is "not-life"? If so, would this not-life also serve as the ground of the "life of substance"? And what would this ground be, but itself the pure immanence of which Deleuze speaks? We can ask another question, one that recapitulates a theme running through many of the thinkers we've encountered thus far: if Deleuze's ontology of life has little or nothing to do with its Aristotelian version, is it possible that what life is for Deleuze is precisely void, nothing, and *nihil*? In other words, is it precisely the void that is the immanent ground for "the life of substance"?

4.8 DARK PANTHEISM

A number of the thinkers we've been dealing with have put forth ideas that have been called pantheist, either at the time of their writing or posthumously. Generally, the idea that the supernatural and the natural, or God and Nature, are one and the same, tends to flatten and disperse any conceptual framework of transcendence or centralization. In its radical variant, pantheism even does away with the conciliatory, decentralized position of emanence or emanation. Such an idea brings with it obvious politico-theological dangers—any pantheist outlook essentially does away with all of Aquinas' five proofs for the existence of God, and by extension, the necessity of the power relationships internal to religious governance. Pantheism is thus heretical in the theological sense that it does away with the necessity of all mediation, be it in the form of Neoplatonic exemplarism, Patristic interpretations of the Trinity, or Thomist analogy. It is also heretical in the political sense in that, by conceiving of hierarchical mediation as unnecessary, pantheism implicitly questions the doctrinally inflected stratifications inherent within institutional structures such as University.

But, as Deleuze notes, pantheism also brings with it another type of danger, one of a philosophical type. For in doing away with the stratifications of the supernatural and natural, pantheism also does away with the stratifications between human, animal, and divine. In modern parlance, pantheism raises the question of life as a fundamentally *unhuman* phenomenon. Pantheism in Deleuze's sense points to a horizon in which both "life" and "thought" can be understood in non-anthropomorphic ways. It is not that each individual person is divine; rather, the divine is understood to be indissociable from nature, and because of this, radically unhuman, anonymous, and neutral. This pantheism is certainly far from the pantheon of Greek divinities, where human drama is displayed at a meta-level, as it were. But heretical pantheism is also markedly different from the notion of the divine in Medieval Christendom, where the divine is figured as an anthropomorphized, sovereign deity who is by turns punitive and merciful, generous and silent to all prayers. It would be tempting to suggest that the difference between pantheism and the anthropomorphized deity correlates to the difference between philosophy and theology, the latter always compromised by the dictates of religious doctrine. But this would be inaccurate, for despite the modern, radical readings of Spinoza by authors such as Alexandre Matheron, Antonio Negri, Étienne Balibar, Warren Montag, and Deleuze, Spinoza's texts themselves show an immediate awareness of the difficulty of separating philosophy and theology. This ambiguity is also reflected in Scholastic thinkers such as Duns Scotus, as well as the speculative mystics such as Cusa.

If the boundary between theology and philosophy is a moving target, then in pantheism so is the boundary between first philosophy and the philosophy of nature. In heretical pantheism, the divine is not human in the sense that the human is both derived from and a derivative form of the divine; rather, the human is unhumanized precisely because it is divine, in the sense that the divine is separable from nature, nature conceived of as a pure immanence. Heretical pantheism not only threatens to do away with the separation between the human and the divine, but it also threatens to do away with the separation between the supernatural and the natural. Hence Deleuze's striking formulation of the divine nature as "a single Animal." The "heretical" pantheism promoted by Deleuze asks us to think of a concept of pure immanence and a concept of dynamic, inventive life in one and the same thought. Something that is everywhere and at all times, but always differently. But this also implies a "something" that, since it is everywhere at all times differently, is also not-something, a "nothing." And yet this nothing-that-is-everywhere is constantly differentiating, a nothing that is also a superlative excess and affirmation.

Perhaps we can say that the pantheism of which we are speaking is a particular kind of pantheism, one opposed to the theological pantheism (or really, panentheism), for which an anthropomorphic God still serves as sovereign Creator and Source. There the transcendent God still sneaks in through the side door. But the pantheism we've been discussing is also opposed to a more modern, affectivist, "hippie" pantheism, for which the world still exists for the human, in a kind of benevolent flux and flow. In this sense, the limit to the thought of nature in the pantheist sense is the thought of extinction, the disaster, the limit-thought of life "after life." That is, pantheism in this sense thinks both life and negation in the same thought; it is poised against the presumptions of life-as-generosity, as gift, as givenness. If pantheism does involve the thought of pure immanence, then this thought will be equally misanthropic as well as simply non-anthropomorphic. For this reason, the pantheism which we've been referring to as heretical might better be called *dark pantheism*. Dark pantheism puts forth *the challenge of thinking, under the sign of the negative, the conjunction of pure immanence and inventive life*—with the caveat that this thought itself is thought as fundamentally exterior to all anthropomorphism. We would be tempted to call this "misanthropology"—and in this sense, pantheism as the conjunction of immanence and life is also the horizon of thought itself.[123]

The question of dark pantheism is, then, a question about "life," insofar as it is irreducible to any biologistic substrate, is also a question about thought. The thought of life—or rather, the limit of the thought of life—is a central preoccupation of this kind of dark pantheism. It is latent in early mystical works such as those by the Pseudo-Dionysius. It also surfaces, in a more Neoplatonic-Aristotelian manner, in Eriugena's *Periphyseon*, in Duns Scotus' comments on univocity in the Oxford and Paris works, and in Cusa's speculative mysticism. Thus when Spinoza, in the *Ethics*, puts forth his substance monism and states, almost matter-of-factly, "God or Nature," we should see an entire genealogy of dark pantheism behind such propositions.

And neither should Spinoza's pantheism be regarded as the end of this genealogy, for, after Spinoza, it is not by any means sublimated into the nascent scientific fields that would become natural history and biology. In fact, one could arguably extend this genealogy of dark pantheism into the biological era, including the complex interactions between idealism and a philosophy of life in German philosophy (Schelling's *Naturphilosophie*, Novalis, the early Hegel, the *Lebensphilosophie* tradition), as well as the nineteenth-century diversions from Darwinism (Schopenhauer's "eastern" concept of *nihil*, Nietzsche's "divine sickness" . . .).

The assertion of pantheism, even of this type of dark pantheism, brings with it a number of fundamental philosophical dilemmas. Insofar as pantheism implies a conjunction of immanence and life, it is also an attempt to ontologize life beyond its physico-biological reduction. But this antireductionism brings with it the problem of how to then articulate the nonreductive, without subsuming it within another, possibly more reductive concept. Traditionally, this issue has plagued philosophies of life, be they vitalist, animist, or pantheist in flavor. Historically, the many debates in the eighteenth and nineteenth centuries surrounding vitalism (pitting vitalists against mechanists, epigeneticists against preformationists, and so on) revolved around the issue of reductionism: could the life processes in the organism be reduced to their material and/or deterministic properties? If not, would one then be required to posit a nonempirical, immaterial, even spiritual life-force that grounds the properties specific to living versus nonliving nature?

However, such debates are often overdetermined—the issue becomes a zero-sum game in which a challenge is put forth, to explicate such-and-such a natural phenomenon. The question such a game puts forth is, *"can this or that phenomenon of life be reduced to the laws of mechanism, or the properties of chemistry?"* But reductionism works in two directions; in the other direction it is sometimes called "abstraction." This reverse question is rarely posed—or if it is, it is posed within the context of theology. The reverse question would be something like, *"is it possible to abstract this or that phenomenon of life without life-in-the-abstract simply becoming a question of God?"*

In the genealogy of dark pantheism that we've been tracing—from Eriugena, to Duns Scotus, to Cusa, and to Spinoza—there is another problematic aside from that of reductionism, and it is that of abstraction. The challenge, then, is not in giving an account of the level of temporality (becoming, change, process), or of the level of causality (morphology, nonlinearity), but in giving an account of that which is nonreductive. The challenge for dark pantheism is in giving an account of the transcendental in its relation to the purely immanent. This is encapsulated by Alain Badiou in his reading of Deleuze's "vitalist" notion of the event:

> [I]n restraining the thought of change to the vitalist simplicity of the One, though by taking the (classical) precaution of thinking the One as the power of differenciation—all like the Stoics, Spinoza, Nietzsche or Bergson before him—Deleuze cannot really succeed at accounting for the *transcendental* change of worlds. It remains impossible to submit such a type of change to the sign of Life, whether one renames it Power, *Élan*, or Immanence. It is necessary to think discontinuity *as it is*, without being reabsorbed in any creative univocity, however indistinct or chaotic this concept be.[124]

For Badiou, the ontologizing of Life in terms of time, temporality, and the event only begs the question of how to then ontologize that which transcends any single or singular event. This was precisely the question that Duns Scotus grappled with in his notion of the univocity of the divine, and it is on this point that Cusa struggles to find a common ground between the contracted and absolute Maximum.

What this means is that any ontology of life has to confront not just the challenge of reductionism, but it must also deal with the difficulty of articulating the transcendent—especially when, in dark pantheism, the ontology of life is indelibly wrapped up with a notion of pure immanence.

On the one hand, any ontology of life must avoid the objectification of life, life as thing, life as property, life as—in the modern, biological sense—a set of descriptors that are possessed by things that, in possessing them, are said to be living. But on the other hand, an ontology of life must also avoid the relativism of a purely ideational abstraction of life, such that life becomes equivalent to the subjective experience of being alive—a position that not only forecloses any real understanding of the relationality of self and world, but which also defines life in terms of the human-subjective categories of experience. There are actually two axes of contradiction in this regard: an axis of *dynamic-static*; that is, a vitalist principle of change, becoming, proliferation, and excess, and a principle of distribution, pervasiveness, spreading-out, and fullness. There is also an axis of *affirmation-negation*; that is, that which is living immanence precisely because it is a superlative negation, a kind of vitalist subtraction, the noumenal assertion of that which is *nihil*. These are the two axes along which dark pantheism attempts to think the conjunction of immanence and life. Life is not immanent because of its pure fecundity or generosity, its boundless creation or invention; rather, life is equivalent to immanence because it is, in itself, a nonbeing that pervades its own axes of contradiction.

Dark pantheism, as we've seen here in the work of Eriugena, Duns Scotus, and Cusa, involves two main transitions in its thinking. There is a first transition, from the coincidence of opposites (Cusa) to the coexistence of contradiction (Spinoza). Life and immanence shift from having separate and contradictory coexistence, mediated by the processes of complication and explication, to the real coexistence of life and immanence in a single contradiction (continually inventive and fully actual, fundamentally dynamic and a priori fully distributed). We move further away from the imperatives of synthesis here, either in the form of a mystical sublimation (Cusa's Absolute Maximum) or in the form of a modal oscillation (*complicatio* and *explicatio*, expression in attributes and modes). This coexistence of contradiction works against the higher synthesis of opposites, but it also works against the Augustinian notion of the infinite divine (the divine as positively arrived at by removing the qualifiers of "this"). The coexistence of contradiction—which is only hinted at in Cusa and formally developed in Spinoza—is not about resolution or even tension. It is, instead, about how the thought of life entails a thought of contradiction—and, further, how this thought possibly requires an affirmation of contradiction in itself.

There is also a second transition in dark pantheism, one that moves from the encompassing of all things (the One as All), to the immanence of all things and nothing (the All as *nihil*). Once one thinks the coexistence of contradiction, one also has to entertain the affirmation of that contradiction in itself. This entails a shift in pantheist, or indeed, monist thinking. Traditional monist ontologies identify a One that is immanently equal to the All ("one substance for all attributes," a single "Life" that cuts through all material-energetic orders), but in so doing they also fracture immanence from within by separating a principle of immanence from that within which it is immanent. This is, as we've seen, Deleuze's critique of the conciliatory immanence of Neoplatonism—though the argument can just as easily be applied to Deleuze's own ontology of immanence as well. A shift from the One-All dyad to an All-Nothing introconversion (where All ↔ Nothing) is also a shift from a One that is everywhere "in" the All, to an already immanent All whose immanence implies that it is also Nothing. Spinoza's pantheism does not imply the bountifulness of the divine, but rather that God/Nature are at once All and Nothing; insofar as this is a monism, it is, perhaps, a subtractive monism. What enables the plentitude is precisely the void.

By way of closing, let us enumerate several propositions concerning dark pantheism. These propositions are less resolutions of the problems outlined earlier, and more questions concerning the extent to which any ontology of life also implies a concept of its absolute, though superlative, negation, where life becomes *nihil*. These propositions can also be read as notes on method, ways of reading texts that have, in many ways, become irrevocably distant from our present condition:

- There is God/Being *in itself*, and this God/Being is, in itself, inaccessible. This follows from our propositions in the chapter on "superlative life." The divine nature is, in itself, inaccessible to human understanding (cf. the Pseudo-Dionysius, Eriugena, and Cusa). Thus God/Being is therefore equivocal, or an "equivocal inexistence," and God/Being is therefore inaccessible, or the "divine inaccessible."
- There is also God/Being *for itself*. God/Being is not only in itself, but also in others. The divine nature is also its own negation (cf. Eriugena, Duns Scotus). Thus God/Being is univocal, or the "univocal creature," and God/Being is also immanence, or a kind of pure or pathological immanence.
- "Life" is the point at which equivocity is introconvertible with univocity (cf. Duns Scotus, Spinoza). Hence univocity ("all rela-

tion") is isomorphic with equivocity ("no relation"). This is the "introconversion of relation." This introconversion is poised against Thomist analogy, which puts forth a kind of vitalist correlation.

- This leads to a question: What happens when the *equivocal* notion of the *divine* is layered onto the *univocal* notion of *nature*? One the one hand, there is a subordinate or conciliatory immanence (emanence, eminence, panentheism). Here the divine is accessible, as expressed in nature, but remains separate from it. The Creator remains beyond the creature while persisting within it. On the other hand, there is also a pure immanence (immanence in itself and not in another). Here the divine is fully expressed in nature and is not separate from it; Creator, creature, and creation exist univocally along a continuum. However, even this pure immanence is still based on a notion of life-as-generosity, and it is this premise that, for instance, informs the early-twentieth-century vitalist ontologies of Bergson, Whitehead, and even Chardin.

- If this is the case, one would then have to consider a number of conjunctions, such as equivocal inexistence + the univocal creature, or the divine inaccessible + dark immanence. One of the upshots of this is that Life, as ontologized in terms of God/Being, is the immanence of nothing. If God/Being/Life is inaccessible, equivocal, inexistence, and if the relation between Creator/creature, Life/living is univocal or immanent, then God/Being/Life is the immanence of *nihil*, a pantheism of the void, a plane of the neutral. Insofar as Life is ontologized in terms of generosity, the generosity of Life is *nihil*.

- Dark pantheism would be, taken broadly, the thought of the conjunction of immanence and life, under the sign of the negative. And the question this poses would be, quite simply: does life = generosity = *nihil*?

4.9 ELLIPSES: WANG YANGMING
AND IDEALIST NATURALISM

In the broad context of post-Aristotelian Scholasticism, the relation between Life and the living put forth in the *De Anima* is taken up in a variety of ways. While mystical philosophy and negative theology address the relation between Life and the living in terms of generosity and the superlative, the period of high Scholasticism addresses the Life-living relation in terms of causality, creation, and production. In this section we've seen a third facet of the Aristotelian ontology of Life and the living, and that is the discourse on the divine nature itself, as it stretches from Eriugena to Cusa and finally Spinoza. However, the real tension is not simply that between life-as-transcendence and life-as-immanence, but a tension between two topologies: that of emanence or emanation, and that of immanence or immanation. To assert the latter is, in the context of Scholasticism, to assert pantheism. But if one is to attempt to think life in terms of immanence, then is this akin to thinking about emanation without a center?

The problem is that once one considers something like life-in-itself, whether this is a life-principle (as in Aristotle's *psukhē*) or as an inaccessible first principle (as in Eriugena's *natura*), one must also effectively dissociate Life from the living. This is a problem because, even though Aristotle's framework leads to contradiction, the contradiction is clear: Life is that which renders intelligible the living, but which in itself cannot be thought, has no existence, is not itself living. In a way, the discourse on the divine nature and pantheism is an extended thought experiment: how to think Life without the mediation of the living. Later philosophers such as Kant would recast this dilemma in terms of an antinomy: every assertion about life as inherently ordered, organized, or purposeful, is always undermined by the assertion itself and its irrevocable object of thought. Already in the Scholastic discourse of pantheism one detects the Kantian antinomy, and the question of whether every naturalist philosophy is really an idealist philosophy.

Chinese philosophy—taken in the broadest sense—offers a rich reservoir of thinking about these problems of nature and life. Though commonly discussed in terms of its moral and ethical philosophy, it is equally a reflection on "the nature of things" and the self-world relation. In fact, for many of the canonical thinkers, such as Zhuangzi (Chuang Tzu), ethical philosophy cannot be separated from natural philosophy. Of particular interest are two thinkers, Zhuxi (Chu Hsi) and Wang Yangming (Wang Shou-Jen), the former active during the twelfth century, the latter during the late fifteenth century. Both thinkers are often referred to as emblematic of the type of Neo-Confucian thinking that combined ethical maxims with reflections on nature and cosmology. However, they are also two very different, and even opposing, thinkers, and part of their philosophical differences lies on this question of naturalism vs. idealism.[125]

Zhuxi's philosophy is an inquiry into the "nature of things," with a strong emphasis on logical coherence and unity. The ability to articulate an ethical philosophy even rests on this ability to discern the nature of things. In this endeavor, Zhuxi takes up the concept of material-energetic force, or *qi* (*ch'i*), and contrasts this to an ideational principle, or *li*. On the surface, *li* appears to be a quasi-Platonic Idea, and *qi* appears to be a quasi-Aristotelian *psukhē*. But this division doesn't exactly work. For Zhuxi, *li* is an ontological principle, but it also an undifferentiated, unchanging unity. Nevertheless, this undifferentiated unity is also manifested in the discrete things in the world. Each thing thus expresses *li* totally, as undifferentiated and unchanging. The passage from *li* in itself to its expression in the nature of things is accomplished by *qi*. There are, then, two planes of immanence for Zhuxi—that of *li* understood in itself, and that of *li* as manifested via *qi* and expressed in and across the nature of things. This twofold notion of *li* is a cosmological principle—that is, it supersedes the theological principle of the earthly and the divine: "Fundamentally, principle [*li*] cannot be interpreted in the senses of existence or non-existence. Before heaven and earth came into being, it already was as it is."[126] Importantly, Zhuxi's entire ontological-cosmological framework is itself subsumed within the *li-qi* dynamic. Rather than taking philosophy as reflecting on or commenting about the world, thought itself is understood to be inculcated within *li*, its dual planes of immanence, and the process of *qi*. The very concepts of *li* and *qi* come exemplary of *li* and *qi* themselves. Hence, while Zhuxi does not solve the antinomy of naturalism vs. idealism, his philosophy short-circuits the antinomy in favor of a holistic ontology that has become characteristic of much classical Chinese thought.

Wang Yangming offers an instructive counterpoint to Zhuxi, who was criticized by the former for being too dualist in this thinking. An apocryphal story is told by Wang Yangming, who, as a young scholar, began to undertake a study of Zhuxi's idea of the "nature of things." If, as Zhuxi's teachings explained, the *li* was "in" every thing in the world, and if, as Zhuxi's teachings also explained, one gained knowledge of *li* through the direct investigation of things, then it followed that a philosophy of the nature of things would also be a philosophy of the investigation of things. Meditation and inquiry would go hand in hand. Supposedly, Wang Yangming undertook such a study—of a bamboo plant. He and his colleagues meditated on a bamboo plant for days (or weeks?), but their investigation produced no authentic knowledge of *li* in itself or even of the plant as a plant. Indeed, they even began to feel ill after the experiment, and promptly called the whole thing off.[127]

Some time later, Wang Yangming had a revelation about this failed experiment. Whereas at the time he had simply assumed that it meant he as a philosopher was not worthy of the practice, let alone enlightenment, Wang Yangming now began to wonder whether the whole idea of accessing *li* "in" things out there was part of the problem. Seeking *li* in the world presumes a number of things—that *li* is always something external to the thinking subject; that *li* is always counterposed to the thinking subject; and that *li* is always that which is not-thought—*li* is non-thinking. Given this, in order to gain knowledge of *li*, one would have to play and endless game of cat and mouse, forever chasing *li* as something "out there."

Wang Yangming's shift was to turn inward. The principle of *li* should not be sought in things "out there," but rather in the mind itself. But this was not simply a turn towards idealism. The very reason one would turn inward is in order to collapse the interior-exterior split. Once the mind is cleared of the confusion, clouds, and froth of the daydream, then what would be left would be *li*. This would, in effect, mean that the mind had become, strangely, a *li*-receptacle. Wang Yangming combined this insight with a theory of intuitive knowledge and action. For our purposes, we can extend his notion of *li* and suggest that it points to an "idealist naturalism," in which the mind is a thing, insofar as a thing is its *li*: "Wherever the idea is, we have a thing . . . I say that there are no principles but those of the mind, and nothing exists apart from the mind."[128]

If Zhuxi attempts to resolve the antinomy of naturalism and idealism by taking the thought of *li* as itself an instance or expression of *li* generally, Wang Yangming's approach is different. His philosophy is summarized in the phrase "mind (*xin*) is principle (*li*)"—that is, *li* is mind. The term *xin* ("mind") here is, on one level, the subject, conscious, thinking mind, but even this is ultimately a current or a flow of consciousness, something that exceeds a fixed interiority. But this then means that the assertion that mind is *li* would require a rethinking of the concept of *li* as well, as not simply being a monolithic, unchanging One, as it tends to be in Zhuxi's philosophy.

Yet such a proposition is fatal for moral and ethical philosophy, for not only must one dispense with the reliability of a discrete moral subject, but, if mind and *li* are equivalent, and if the former is always in flux while the latter is unchanging, then either the self is always ideational, or the world is nothing but flux and flow. Either option is interesting, but it requires a great deal. This is a contentious point, and one that is not fully accounted for in Wang Yangming's comments on *li*. Nevertheless, Wang Yangming's equation of *li* with mind is not an assertion of idealism, transforming Zhuxi's *li* into something purely ideational. By stating "mind is *li*" Wang Yangming does not assert that the nature of things is subsumed within thought. Instead, it means the reverse—that thought is subsumed within the nature of things. We can even extend this and suggest that

Wang Yangming's equation of mind and *li* requires *the absolute exteriority of thought*. And perhaps this is the only way out of the antinomial bind of either naturalism or idealism. One has to recast thought as something other than thought—in effect, as itself the nature of things; conversely, one has to recast the nature of things as fully continuous with thought. Life comes to be this point of transition between an idealism (in which the world is never present to thought) and a naturalism (in which the world is omnipresent to thought). Perhaps this is what the classical concept of *qi* does, at least in the form given by Neo-Confucian thinkers such as Zhuxi and Wang Yangming. *Qi* not only serves as an alternative to Aristotle's *psukhē*, but it effects a dual dissolution: that of the Life that is lived (subjective, ideational) and that of the lived that is Life (abstract principle).[129]

CHAPTER FIVE

Logic and Life (On Kantian Teratology)

... the invisible glare of life ...
—Bataille

5.1 THE WANDERING LINE FROM ARISTOTLE TO KANT

We began our inquiry with Aristotle, and we will end with Kant—specifically, Kant's notion of life's organization, teleology, and purposiveness. Between them, there is a divergent thread of concepts, debates, and dilemmas dealing with the concept of "life" generally. Saying that they are "premodern" is simply a way of noting how the concept of "life" is never simply reduced to biology (be it mechanistic or vitalist) nor sublimated into theology (be it doctrinal or heretical). In a sense, the real challenge put forth to speculative thinking in this context is not how to distinguish philosophy from theology, but a challenge of a different sort. For this discontinuous tradition, a tradition we've been referring to as post-Aristotelian Scholasticism, the challenge is how an ontology of life can be thought in a way that does not immediately install the human at its center, either via an anthropotheological move (the personal, angry, benevolent, judging God), or via an anthropobiological move (the ascending pyramid of organization, order, and development).

In this book we have traced a genealogy of this question through three main lines of thought, and a precursor. That precursor is Aristotle, whose *De Anima*, though it must be read alongside Aristotle's works in natural philosophy, is also the single work that shapes the ensuing debates on the question of life. It is the *De Anima* that poses the question of life, and poses it as an ontological question. The way in which Aristotle attempts to answer this question sets up a framework within which the concept of life can be thought. This involves establishing a principle-of-life (*psukhē*) that accounts for both the multiplicity and the continuity common to all forms of life. It also entails a necessary bifurcation, a boundary-of-articulation between Life and the living.

This distinction between Life and the living makes possible a set of relationships that allows one to address three key components of any ontology of life: its temporal aspect (the superlative generosity of Life vis-à-vis the living, as expressed in the Pseudo-Dionysius and Eriugena), its formal aspect (the role of creation or causality between Life and the living, elaborated in the debates between Duns Scotus, Aquinas, and Henry of Ghent), and its spiritual aspect (the contingency of the living vis-à-vis the intelligibility of Life, reaching its zenith in the pantheisms of Eriugena, Nicholas of Cusa, and Spinoza). In turn, these three relationships between Life and the living constitute the three major ways in which the concept of life has been thought in the West. In each instance, the ontology of life requires that one think life in terms of something other-than-life (time, form, spirit). In many cases this exigency results in an almost total eclipse of the concept of life by these other metaphysical terms.

We've also seen that any attempt to formulate an ontology of life through these three approaches arrives at a point in which the intelligibility of life must also entail its opposite. The notion of life-as-time entails a contradiction surrounding affirmation and negation: superlative life is the affirmation of life as *nihil*. Similarly, the notion of life-as-form revolves around another contradiction, that of the additive and the subtractive: the analogical relation between Life and the living must rely upon a more basic univocity that remains itself uncreated. Finally, the notion of life-as-spirit is poised around a contradiction of interiority and exteriority: the emanative principle of Life with regard to the living requires an emanation without a center, or a pure immanence. In each case, a dominant position is compromised by another, so-called heretical position. That Life is superlative, generous, and gift is pushed to the point where the inaccessibility of this superlative life renders it as nothing. That the relation between Life and the living is one of analogical creation is pushed to the point where the form of life opens onto a more fundamental formlessness. And the idea of Life as a transcendently emanating principle (dynamically radiating and yet remaining the same) is pushed to the point where Life must disperse and distribute its own emanating center, becoming at once strangely spiritual and material.

Just as the ontology of life in the *De Anima* revolves around a fundamental affirmation of contradiction, so is this further developed in the

Three ontologies of life in post-Aristotelian Scholasticism.

	Ontology of life (in terms of something other than life)		
	Life-as-Time	Life-as-Form	Life-as-Spirit
Relationship between Life and the living:	Life is superlative with respect to the living	Life creates the living via analogical relationships	Life emanates itself in the living while remaining transcendent
Mediating concept between Life and the living:	Superlative Life I: Plotinus II: Pseudo-Dionysius III: Eriugena	Univocal Creatures I: Duns Scotus v. Aquinas II: Duns Scotus v. Henry of Ghent III: Duns Scotus, Spinoza	Dark Pantheism I: Eriugena II: Duns Scotus III: Cusa
Genealogy of the problematic:	Mystical theology; the divine names tradition Positive, Negative, Superlative Theology (Physicotheology)	The debate on the creature and creation Univocity, Equivocity, Analogy (Cosmotheology)	The discourse on the divine nature Transcendence, Emanence, Immanence (Ontotheology)
The problematic pushed to its limit:	The superlative is an excess that is nothing	Analogy must presuppose a further univocity	The limit of emanation is an insubordinate immanence
Internal contradictions:	Affirmation-Negation Divine Negation Apophasis	Additive-Subtractive Equivocal Inexistence Uncreated Univocity	Interior-Exterior Heretical Empiricism Dark Pantheism

post-Aristotelian Scholasticism of the thinkers mentioned thus far. The table provides a schematic of these relationships. The concept of life—and whether such a concept is possible—places philosophy in a hovering, wavering space between an onto-theology and an onto-biology. What is at stake in this concept is something that is more than epistemological puzzles or disciplinary boundaries. In the very thought of life itself is buried a problematic, a problematic concerning life-in-itself, with this "in-itself" denoting that which must necessarily remain inaccessible to our attempts to render it intelligible. This is also a problematic concerning thought-in-itself, and to what degree there is or can be an "in-itself" of thought that is not immediately sublimated into life—the most adequate thought-of-life would, likewise, be inaccessible and manifest, like life "in itself." In short, thought would become weirdly inaccessible to thought, thought-in-itself as inaccessible, unintelligible.

This is the horizon of the human; but subtracting the human from the philosophical problematic of life is tantamount to foreclosing the possibility of thinking life at all. In a sense, the very history of Western philosophy is this ongoing dilemma concerning the very possibility of "living thought." The human seems to be the very ground of the intelligibility of life, insofar as life presupposes a temporal, formal, and spiritual dimension. Without a human subject to think the concept of life, can life be said to exist at all? This question is exhaustively formalized by Kant, but it is already apparent in Aristotle's *De Anima*, where the question of *nous* (Intellect), as a privileged instance of *psukhē*, raises the question of the life that thinks itself. Is the life that thinks itself, itself living? Or, to borrow Aristotle's categories, is Life the living reflecting on itself, as the living? In a sense, then, *what is at stake in the thought of life is the life of thought itself.*

5.2 CRITIQUE OF LIFE

In many ways, Kant's comments on life, organism, and teleology serve as the point of culmination of the Aristotelian problematic. At the center of Kant's *Critique of Judgment* lies the problem of finality: the question of order and organization as it is related to teleology and purpose in nature. While mechanistic philosophies of nature may posit an order, that order is detached from any notion of teleology or purpose. Mechanistic nature is, in its extreme versions, merely blind mechanism, a chance conjunction of causes and effects governed by natural laws. By contrast, natural philosophies derived from theology (including, to some degree, early forms of vitalism), emphasize the goal-orientedness of nature, a complex whole that is itself not evident in any one of its parts. The difficulty for mechanism is not only how to account for the apparent complexity and organization of nature, but also how to account for the existence of mechanistic natural laws to begin with. By contrast, the difficulty for vitalism is not only how to account for the means by which a complex whole is derived, but also how to conceptualize a principle of organization and teleology that is not theologically driven.

For both approaches, the living organism epitomizes this problematic, and in this way life becomes the privileged locus for the critical investigation of nature.[1] While mechanism claims to have exhaustively explained the genesis and organization of the organism, in relinquishing any claim to finality, it must necessarily forgo the distinction between the living and nonliving, the organic and inorganic, that is so central to thinking about life. It is precisely for this reason that the living organism is often fundamental for the various vitalist philosophies. The living organism is the most self-evident instance of organization that is teleological and goal-oriented. This is true in the more static model of natural history, but it is also the case in the dynamic and processual characteristics of the living organism—in its physiology, its morphology, its embryology, and so on. So while mechanism accounts for life in terms of a progressive finality (e.g., how a multiplicity of parts and relations interact to produce a whole), vitalism accounts for life in terms of a regressive or retrospective finality (e.g., how a complex whole is produced from a multiplicity of parts and their relations).

The difficulty, according to Kant, is not so much that order exists in nature, and not so much how order exists in nature, but the way in which a concept of order, organization, and purpose is situated in a relation of necessity vis-à-vis the concept of nature itself. Kant's challenge is therefore how order in nature itself can be determined, without resorting to either theology—which relies upon an order transcendentally granted from outside—or to mechanism—which relies on a posited order that disavows any teleology.

Claims of finality can be contentious, or at least uncanny, especially when they have the effect of in some way decentering the human vis-à-vis the natural world. Does human DNA have as its end the expression of a unique individual being, or is the human being simply another way for DNA to replicate itself? Do microbes subsist off more complex host organisms, or do complex organisms provide a platform for the persistence of microbial life? Do we cultivate and eat plants and animals, or do plants and animals persist through us and due to us? These games of reversal are not uncommon in popular science writing; but at their core is this Kantian question concerning finality in relation to life. Kant himself poses a string of such questions: if rivers carry soil that facilitates the growth of certain plants, and if human beings benefit by the cultivation of those plants, do we suppose that the plants, the soil, and the river have as their purpose human well-being through agriculture?[2] The same follows, Kant notes, for the relation of human beings to other life forms such as plants and animals, be they relations of breeding, eating, or domestication.

The dilemma, then, is whether a claim about finality in nature can be made without it immediately being recuperated by presumptions about usefulness, even if it is of a fortuitous kind. Beyond this, there is another dilemma, one of the recurring conceptual motifs in Kant's critical philosophy—how can any claim about finality in nature be made, when such a claim must in fact *be made* (that is, by a human subject vis-à-vis a world, however that world is conceptualized)? If one forgoes this possibility, then all of nature becomes subsumed within the human viewpoint, which results in effectively dissolving the concept of nature altogether. Given this, one has to entertain the notion that the very idea of nature is always an idea of a nature for us. One would then have to consider not just this or that particular purpose or goal of nature, but a "purposiveness" of nature in general:

> Thus if there is to be a concept or a rule which arises originally from the power of judgment, it would have to be a concept of things in *nature insofar as nature conforms to our power of judgment*, and thus a concept of a property of nature such that one cannot form any concept of it except that its arrangement conforms to our faculty for subsuming the particular given laws under more general ones even though these are not given; in other words, it would have to be the concept of a purposiveness (*Zweckmäßigkeit*) of nature in behalf of our faculty for cognizing it.[3]

Even if one allows that claims about the finality of nature cannot be dissociated from the usefulness of nature for us, there still remains the more basic problem of the conditions for which any such claim is possible at all. For such conditions, one would have to minimally presuppose some sort of reliable correlation between our cognitive framework for interacting with the world, and what amounts to a necessary, but aporetic, notion of the world in itself. The condition, for Kant, is that we must presume some sort of adequate fit between the world and our ability to make judgments about the world.

Be that as it may, the concept of "finality" or "purposiveness" (*Zweckmäßigkeit*) is not simple. Kant uses this complicated term in a variety of ways. "Purposiveness" is not simply an end (*Zweck*) or a goal (*Endzweck*);

it is something like the end of the end, a condition in which an end-of-
an-end is possible at all. Purposiveness is, generally speaking, something
like the conditions for the possibility of purpose. In the closing sections
of the *Critique of Judgment*, Kant makes a number of key distinctions
within purposiveness. Primary among these is the distinction between
"relative purposiveness" (sometimes called "external purposiveness") and
"internal purposiveness" (sometimes called "objective purposiveness").
By relative purposiveness Kant means a purposiveness in relation to a living being, be it a relation of usefulness for human beings, or a relation
of advantageousness for and between animals (which may include human
beings). By contrast, internal purposiveness is the purposiveness that is
internal to nature when considered in itself, irrespective of the relations of
usefulness or advantageousness. While Kant does not suggest that we can
completely know nature in itself, in its internal purposiveness, he does
note that the idea of an internal purposiveness shores up the lie of relative
purposiveness, especially when it masquerades *as* internal purposiveness:

> If, however, the human being, through the freedom of his causality,
> finds things in nature completely advantageous for his often foolish
> aims . . . one cannot assume here even a relative end of nature . . . For
> the human's reason knows how to bring things into correspondence
> with his own arbitrary inspirations, to which he was by no means pre-
> destined by nature. Only if one assumes that human beings have to live
> on the earth would there also have to be at least no lack of the means
> without which they could not subsist as animals and even as rational
> animals . . . but in that case those things in nature which are indispens-
> able for this purpose would also have to be regarded as natural ends.[4]

The aporia of relative purposiveness lies precisely in its relativeness—one
must either subsume all relations to a single "for us," or, barring this, one
gets caught in an infinite regress of purposes (e.g., the human is the end of
the sheep, the sheep the end of the grass, the grass the end of the soil, the
soil the end of the rain, and so on). "From this it can readily be seen that
external purposiveness (advantageousness of one thing or another) can be
regarded as an external natural end only under the condition that the existence of that for which it is advantageous, whether in a proximate or a
distant way, is in itself an end of nature."[5]

How then should one begin to think the difficult concept of an internal purposiveness? Kant effectively proposes a synthesis between a relative (human-centric) and an internal (nonhuman oriented) purposiveness,

one that is also a synthesis between his earlier dichotomy of vitalism and mechanism. In what Kant calls a "natural end" (*Naturzweck*), one encompasses a form of life that is at once driven by a purposiveness, and which at the same time is governed by a set of internal processes and relations. Kant notes, in a provisional definition, that "a thing exists as a natural end *if it is cause and effect of itself* . . . for in this there lies a causality the likes of which cannot be connected with the mere concept of nature without ascribing an end to it, but which in that case also can be conceived without contradiction but cannot be comprehended."[6] Kant's example here is botanical. The tree, as living, is at once cause and effect of itself in three ways: as a species (a tree, following the laws of nature particular to the species, continues the species itself), as an individual living being (the individual tree's growth and maintenance over time), and in terms of its parts or organs (the way that seeds, leaves, roots, and branches are used in the tree's life cycle). Kant's two criteria for a natural end are (i) that, akin to vitalism, it be oriented in a way that leads to the creation of novel forms (". . . that its parts are possible only through their relation to the whole, for the thing itself is an end"), and (ii) that, akin to mechanism, it function in a dynamic and processual way solely from its internal relations (". . . that its parts be combined into a whole by being reciprocally the cause and effect of their form").[7] These come together in the idea of the natural end:

> In such a product of nature each part is conceived as if it exists only *through* all the others, thus as if existing *for the sake of the others* and *on account of* the whole . . . it must be thought of as an organ that *produces* the other parts (consequently each produces the others reciprocally), which cannot be the case in any instrument of art, but only of nature, which provides all the matter for instruments . . . only then and on that account can such a product, as an *organized* and *self-organizing* being, be called a *natural end*.[8]

It is here that the concept of the "organized being" or the *organism* plays a central role. This concept is in part related to natural history and its classificatory project of the living—which presumes an innate order—but it is also a logical term, a favorite in Aristotle, and later, in Scholasticism. The organized being, or the organism, is unique in that, for Kant, it works against the mechanistic analogue of the clock, but also against the vitalist analogue of the divine soul. "An organized being is thus not a mere machine, for that has only a *motive* power, while the organized being possesses in itself a *formative* power . . . thus it has a self-propagating formative power, which cannot be explained through the capacity for movement alone."[9] The organism is that which is at once means and the ends, and it is this, more than any other attribute, that serves as the basis for Kant's distinctions between nature and artifice, organic and inorganic, the living and the nonliving.

The organized being, the organism, is Kant's privileged example of a natural end. But it is also the limit of our ability to effectively think life apart from the dichotomous split between reflective (subjective and experiential) and internal (objective and inaccessible) purposiveness. Specifying what this limit is proves difficult for Kant. The organism has a kind of purposiveness, but one that is not directed from without. It may be analogized to the theological model of the divine soul, or to the aesthetic model of art. Whatever the case, the type of purposiveness of the organism begins to become identical to the processes of the organism itself—"purposiveness" begins to perfectly overlap with "processiveness." What it is equals how it is. Kant struggles to find an adequate conceptual figure for describing this apparent equivalence of the "what" and the "how":

> Perhaps one comes closer to this inscrutable property if one calls it an *analogue of life*: but then one must either endow matter as mere matter with a property (hylozoism) that contradicts its essence, or else associate with it an alien principle *standing in communion* with it (a soul) . . . But *inner natural perfection*, as it is possessed by those things that are possible only as *natural ends* and hence as organized beings, is not thinkable and explicable in accordance with any analogy to any physical, i.e., natural capacity that is known to us.[10]

Just as Kant begins to offer an analogy, he retracts it, effectively transforming the organism and the idea of natural end into a limit-concept. As he repeatedly notes, just because a network of rivers promotes social relations between villages, and just because the nearby mountains serve as the source of the rivers and storehouses of snow, and just because the geography of the land as a whole allows for the rivers to flow and drain, none of this really legitimizes a claim about natural purposiveness. The problem is not simply that of subjectivism, but of the very condition of the self-world relation generally. The concept of life—as the privileged category of nature—serves to demonstrate this problematic for Kant. Life is ambivalently positioned between self and world, at once a set of entities "out there" (e.g., crops for food, livestock for breeding) and yet a continuum that connects the "out there" to the "in here" (the principle of life that connects all living beings). However, Kant is adamant that any rationale for a finality of life cannot adequately separate itself from that same life viewed in terms of advantageousness. Such a logic of means and ends merely demonstrates the impossibility of distinguishing a relative ("for us") from an objective ("in itself") purposiveness. "In things that one has no cause to regard as ends for themselves, an external relationship can be judged to be purposive only hypothetically."[11]

The conciliatory move that Kant makes is to regard the concepts of organized being and natural end as "regulatory concepts," whose function is to place limits on the use of the cognitive faculties of reason or the understanding, beyond which only poetry or mysticism can lie. But this regulatory function also opens onto another possibility, which is that the organized being or organism provides "objective reality for the concept of an *end* that is not a practical end but an end of *nature*," a task that Kant allocates to natural science and the necessity of something like life in itself. But then natural science is confronted with an antinomy, which is really an *antinomy of Life*: either the emergence of life forms is explainable solely in terms of mechanical laws, or else there is something that governs the emergence of life forms that is not manifest in the entities and relations that those mechanical laws determine. The challenge then becomes how to think a concept of life, as "internally caused" and as "reciprocally cause and effect," that is at the same time not reducible to its components and relations. As Kant notes, somewhat enigmatically, "[T]he end of the existence of nature itself must be sought beyond nature."[12]

This is not a task only for natural science or for biology, for the issue that recurs throughout the *Critique of Judgment* is how the idea of purposiveness is marked by a conceptual duplicity: it is at once that which must necessarily remain inaccessible to us, and yet that which is necessary for a concept of life or nature to be thought at all. This leads to one of the greatest insights of the "Critique of the Teleological Power of Judgment": *any ontology of life must presume an* a priori *concept of finality*, the latter defined as the conjunction of organization with teleology. Part of this is, in a way, a repetition of Aristotle's statement in the *De Anima*: "nature does nothing in vain." And Kant notes how necessary the idea of finality is to the then-burgeoning fields of natural history and biology: "It is well known that the anatomists of plants and animals . . . assume as indispensably necessary the maxim that nothing in such a creature is *in vain*."[13]

Stating it in this way is misleading, however. For Kant's a priori of life is really a question, and the a priori has a number of dimensions to it. It is, first, a statement about the necessary preconditions for the concept of life to be thought at all—that precondition being, for Kant, that of finality (order and end, organization and teleology). But this a priori is not without its own aporias, an always-receding horizon that tries to avoid both the reduction to mechanism as well as the sublimation into vitalism. In a vicious circle, one posits finality as an a priori, and then undertakes the project of discovering what one originally posited. To these two dimensions is added a third, which is the more pragmatic, "regulative" function of the a priori as a limit, one that perhaps governs where philosophy ends and theology begins (or where science ends and poetry begins . . .). Taken together, the upshot of Kant's a priori of life offers a further development of Aristotle's question: What is the relation between the thought of life and living thought, the life of thought itself?

5.3 SPECTRAL LIFE AND SPECULATIVE REALISM

Between Aristotle and Kant there is a great deal; indeed, there is too much. One jumps over the long tradition of philosophical reflection on biology, from the *Historia Animalium*, to Cartesian mechanism, to Buffon and the work of classification, let alone stopping short of eighteenth-century German biology, Lamarck, and Darwin. One also side-steps the equally important, though largely forgotten, tradition of natural theology and theophany—as well as its perverse underside, the bestiary and the teratology. For every work on the Creation there is a work such as the heteronomous *Aberdeen Bestiary*, or an Ambrose Paré, whose *On Monsters and Marvels* effectively produces a teratology on the Creation of aberration; for every treatise outlining a hierarchy of angels and "spiritual creatures" there is a *De Malo* or another work of Scholastic demonology that raises the problem of necromancy, possession, and decay as a philosophical limit.

However, from the lowliest beast to the darkest luminosity of the divine, from the "worm in the blood" to the swarming chorus of spiritual creatures, there remains this question about the intelligibility of life as something that may not be fundamentally or even incidentally rooted in the human. While the shape and contour of philosophical thinking changes drastically after Aristotle and Scholasticism, the triad of life-as-time, life-as-form, and life-as-spirit is remarkable in its persistence. Sometimes one finds them parsed out into distinct approaches, as when the question of experience (the question of the human par excellence) is couched in terms of time, temporality, and an existential proximity to death (and it is thus no surprise that, for Sartre and the early Heidegger, the question of an ontology of life is not a question at all, or is at least subordinate to the loftier question of phenomenality and self-consciousness). This emphasis on time and temporality takes on a different guise in process philosophy (Whitehead) and process theology (Chardin), where the human, all-too-human question of experience is dissolved into a background flux of prehensions and a nexus of relations. More often than not, however, this triad of time-form-spirit is found in some admixture. In the organicism of the early Hegel, temporality is tightly linked to the question of form, which is itself framed by the principle of *Geist*. Some version of life-as-spirit profoundly marks the *Lebensphilosophie* thinkers, often to such a degree that, as Schelling indicates, life can perfectly coincide with death along a continuum. Even in the well-worn dichotomy of mechanism and vitalism, we find a hidden commonality, which is a contestation over the relation between life-as-time and life-as-spirit—mechanism upholding the former while negating the latter, vitalism privileging the latter as the basis for the former. And it is perhaps because of this false dichotomy that we find an attempt at a synthesis in Bergson's *Creative Evolution* (where both mechanism and finalism are critiqued in favor of an emphasis on the superlative, inventive nature of a vital force, the *élan vital*).

Life-as-time, life-as-form, and life-as-spirit. Perhaps, given the persistence of these three approaches, we can abbreviate them even further: life is always "meat" (the thickness, the facticity of life), "soul" (the formal principle of the creation of life), or "pattern" (the intangible plane of organization running throughout life). In each case, we find an attempt to ontologize life in terms of something other than life. The question then becomes, if the condition of intelligibility of life is that life be understood in terms of something other-than-life (time, form, spirit), at what point does an ontology of life quite simply become an ontology of time, or of form, or of spirit itself? In the attempt to ontologize life, does life dissipate precisely at the moment of its greatest conceptual clarity?

It goes without saying that the major challenge that faces philosophical reflection on the concept of life is not about the most accurate or coherent definition of life. Life as a concept quite effortlessly passes between the poles of reductionism and mysticism—life can be defined down to the molecular level, at the same time that the notion of the irreducibility and mystery of life raises the concept up to existential and spiritual levels. Instead, the major challenge for any ontology of life lies in being able to think its very conditions of being thought at all.

This leads to what amounts to a methodological issue. If we presume that there is something called life that is neither simply God nor Being, and if we also presume that this life is also minimally intelligible—even to the extent that it can be thought in its unintelligibility—then what sort of an object for thought is life? In the history of philosophy, the problem of discerning the object of thought is often equivalent to thought itself. Thought always presupposes or necessitates an object of thought, even if that object of thought is thought itself. This as is evident in Parmenides' poem as it is in the *Phaedrus*, and it not only characterizes the system building of a Descartes or a Kant, but it also haunts the dismantling gestures of a Nietzsche or a Bataille.

The question of thought and its object is also a central part of logical philosophy. It is formulated quite clearly in Aristotle's *Categoreia*, it serves as the backdrop for later thinkers like Fichte or Wittgenstein, and it is now a substantial part of any textbook on philosophical logic. More recently, it has been revived by thinkers who deny the rather academic but long-standing split between continental and analytical philosophy, while also reinvigorating the classical questions of the modern Western philosophical tradition. For example, Quentin Meillassoux uses the term "correlation" to talk about the problem of the self-world relationship, a problem that is a deep preoccupation for thinkers such as Hume and Fichte: "By 'correlation' we mean the idea according to which we only ever have access to the correlation between thinking and being, and never to either term considered apart from the other."[14] Correlationism is what is produced when a philosophy wishes to avoid the poles of either naïve idealism (that the world "out there" is totally reducible to thought), or naïve realism (that there is something called a world "out there" totally independent of our thinking about that world). What results is a compromise, one in which correlationism "consists in disqualifying the claim that it is possible to consider the realms of subjectivity and objectivity independently of one another. Not only does it become necessary to insist that we never grasp an object 'in itself' . . . but it also becomes necessary to maintain that we can never grasp a subject that would not always-already be related to an object."[15]

In its simplest version, correlationism has the form "all thought of X is always the *thought* of X." While the concept of correlation derives from an ontological quandary—that of subject and object, or self and world—it also has a form that can be applied to philosophical systems generally, and which neatly encapsulates the dilemma of many modern ontologies. As Meillassoux notes, "Correlationism rests on an argument as simple as it is powerful, and which can be formulated in the following way; No X without givenness of X, and no theory about X without a positing of X."[16] Note that correlationism in this sense is not simply the science-fictional dilemma of "what is real." It encompasses both the poles of idealism ("it's

all in your head") and realism (the world "out there"). It is the very condition for thought to either disavow or engage with its object.

At the root of correlationism is the relation of thought to its object, or
the relation between self and world, on which we can briefly meditate. In
one sense, the terms of self and world are intimately tied to each other:
the self cannot be thought without relation to the world, just as the world
requires a thought-of-the-world that implies a self that is thinking this
thought. Extending this further, the self must in some sense be understood in terms of the world, if only to note that the self is "in" the world,
or, conversely, that the self removes or distances itself from the world, in
order to think it. Here an asymmetry develops, for the self requires a world
in order to think itself "in" the world, but, at the same time, the world
must remain inaccessible "in itself," else it simply becomes a part of the
self (imagined by the self, an "imaging" of the world). In this asymmetry,
the very definition of the world is that which is at once necessary for and
yet inaccessible to the thinking self. The thought of the self requires the
"unthought" of the world.

It is worth noting how the post-Aristotelian Scholastic discourses surrounding life are echoed in modern correlationism, but with a twist. Negative theology, as we've seen, effectively transforms correlationism into
aporia, but one that turns out to be necessary for thinking the superlative
character of life. The debates over *creatura* and the Creator-creature relation reframe correlationism in terms of the production of novel forms,
such that correlation is inseparable from creation. Finally, the discourse
on the divine nature, which reaches its limit in a heretical pantheism,
takes up the importance of contingency in correlationist thinking and
expands it into an absolute (effectively recasting contingency in terms of
immanence).

In a similar vein, Kantian transcendental philosophy argues that it is
not an idealism due to the a priori status of the sensibility, and the division between *noumena* and *phenomena* that follows from this. Kantian-
ism is not idealism because the subject is always positioned vis-à-vis an
object. This is the Kantian variant of correlationism. Similarly, the Hus-
serlian phenomenological tradition argues that it is not idealism because
consciousness is always consciousness of something. The notion of intentionality not only secures the place of the human subject, but it also establishes the necessity of its relation to the object-world. Paradoxically,
intentionality also makes possible the phenomenological method of abstraction, or the *epoché*. The phenomenal-existential analysis developed
by Heidegger shifts the question from consciousness to being, or rather, to

being as *Da-sein*, being-in-the-world. The thrownness of the subject is the testimony against any idealism.

In these examples, correlationism is utilized as a refutation of naïve idealism, while at the same time keeping at bay the question of the world-in-itself. For Kant this is done by the emphasis on phenomena (not the world-in-itself but our perception of the world-in-itself), for Husserl this is accomplished by the idea that consciousness is always a consciousness-of something, and for Heidegger this notion is recast in terms of *Da-sein*. But what happens when correlationism either refuses or fails to keep at bay this question of the world-in-itself? One result is what Meillassoux calls "subjectivist metaphysics," which is "any absolutization of a determinate human access to the world."[17] This mode of thought entails an absolutization of the correlation itself as reality. Some part or all of the human access to reality is expanded to such a degree that it becomes equivalent to reality itself. In this extreme position, "the subjectivist claims that some of these relations, or indeed all, are determinations not only of men, but of being itself. He projects onto the things themselves a correlation which might be perception, intellection, desire, etc., and makes it the absolute itself."[18]

As Alain Badiou notes, this sort of radical subjectivism is as true for the absolutization of the subjective access to the world as it would be for the reverse—the absolutization of the objective point of contact with the subject. This is one point where phenomenology intersects with the philosophy of vitalism. In the former case, one expands intentionality to such a degree that it effectively compasses the world, whereas in the latter case one "makes of life the active name of being."[19] In both cases, there is a reliance on some minimally positive notion of "the One," a kind of "sur-existence" that provides the backdrop from which a claim about multiplicity, process, or a creative evolution can possibly be made. To think otherwise would be, for Badiou, to think of this backdrop itself in terms of negation or being-nothing (*néantisé*): "We can thus say that the term that is common to both phenomenology and vitalism—to Husserl and to Bergson, to Sartre and to Deleuze—is death, as that which certifies finite existence, that which is the simple state of an infinite sur-existence."[20]

Presumably the various ontologies based on duration, process, or becoming are indicative of this vitalist thinking. So, while these philosophies make a claim to have overcome or surpassed the correlationist impasse, from the correlationist point of view, they have simply failed to adequately acknowledge the dual necessity of all thought (e.g., "there is no X without a positing of X"). For the correlationist, any ontology that privileges duration, process, or becoming as the primordial or "abstract" flux of the world beyond the self-world relation is simply a mode of thought that takes one part of the contingent human access to the world (e.g., the human experience of time in terms of continuity) and then renders that as an absolute property of the world in itself. In all of these cases, the reality that is posited is predicated on a basic relation—that there can be a reality only if there is some sort of subjective access to that reality.

But it is also worth reflecting on the failure of this sort of vitalist thinking, the thought that fails to uphold the correlationist impasse. What does "failure" mean in this context? In these cases, correlationism fails to conserve the two key components of its thinking: (i) the separation of thought and object, self and world, and (ii) the inseparability or the necessity of their interrelation (which presumes the first step of separation). If this is a failure, it is, perhaps, an interesting one, one that is in fact produced from a concept of life that is at its core. Let us say that a *vitalist* correlation is one that fails to conserve the correlationist dual necessity of the separation and inseparability of thought and object, self and world, and which does so based on some ontologized notion of "life." Furthermore, this vitalist correlation can be comprehended within the correlationist framework only if it is understood as the absolutization of the contingent. The point here is not that Bergsonian duration, Whiteheadian process, or Deleuzian becoming offer a more progressive ontology than the concepts of Kant, Husserl, or Heidegger. Rather, what we should highlight is the way in which this vitalist correlation relies upon a rather encrypted, hidden concept of life that enables it to traverse correlation itself.

All of this leads to a simple question, one that is at the heart of the ontology of life: *is life correlational?* In other words, are all thought of life and all ontologies that attempt to provide the basis for the intelligibility of life, are all these situated within the correlationist framework? A number of possibilities present themselves:

1st reply: Existential (the correlation of life and death)

There is, as a first possibility, the existential correlation to death. Here the correlation at the heart of the concept of life could be understood as the somewhat traditional, if overused, dichotomy between life and death. While life can be known to the extent that it is lived, death remains inaccessible and yet necessary for thinking (or living) life. This is the existentialist variant of correlational life. It holds equally even when one parses out death (as Heidegger does) into "Death" and "perishing." The problem is that the distinction that grounds the correlation (the absolutism of the mutual exclusivity of life and death) tends to wear away upon further reflection. For instance, this is not simply an oppositional relationship, for many inquires into life itself—including *Lebensphilosophie*, Merleau-Pontian phenomenology, and process metaphysics—find that, upon reflection, the boundary separating life and death becomes increasingly blurry. Hence some ontological framework of a continuum comes to replace or displace the boundary of life and death.

2nd reply: Organicist (the correlation of growth and decay)

If the existential correlation of life and death is undone by one particular concept of "life"—life as that which is lived—then there is another, second possibility, which is the organicist correlation of growth and decay. Here we move beyond absolute terms like life and death, and consider the temporal aspect of life, in which the primary relation is between growth and decay, development and decomposition, or, as Aristotle notes, between "coming-to-be" and "passing-away." This has not only biological resonance, but theological as well—what the problem of decay and putrefaction is for the history of biology, the problem of resurrection is for Medieval theology. Arguably these two problems have their cultural manifestation in the gothic (Poe, Baudelaire, and graveyard poetry . . .). However, the distinction in this correlation again tends to break down, and growth becomes decay, development becomes decomposition, the corpse becomes nutritive food for worms and soil, and so on—the negative term simply becomes a new type of generative order, decomposition becomes a new type of composition.[21]

3rd reply: Ontological (the correlation between Life and the living)

Both of these variants of the vitalist correlation—the existentialist and organicist versions—revolve around some concept of life that ultimately undoes the correlation itself, thereby enabling some sort of transversalist, immanentist thinking. But they are both based on a more fundamental relation. In addition to the correlation of life in terms of opposition (life/death) or mirroring (growth/decay), there is, as we've seen throughout this study, a more basic relation, one that is ontological. Aristotle gives us such a relation—that of the relation between Life and the living (or that-by-which-the-living-is-living and

that-which-is-living). Here one term (the living) is immediate and intuitive, while the other term (Life) is mediated and abstract. As a correlation, what results is a bit awkward: The living is lived (experience,
subjectivity, *phenomena*), while Life is the un-lived (concept, objectivity, and, strangely, *noumena*). It is a correlation in the sense that the
living cannot be understood without a more general, abstract concept
of Life, which enables the living to be thought as living, but which also
remains in itself inaccessible (there is no example of Life, only of the
living). The question remains whether the Life/living distinction—as
a correlation—is ultimately recuperated into a vitalist correlation (Life
is that which cuts across all instances of the living), or whether it tends
towards an absolute incommensurability (Life is never present in itself,
and is not a manifestation).

In a sense, none of these replies is adequate. The terms of correlationism
(critical-Kantian, phenomenological-Husserlian, and vitalist-Bergsonian)
all rely on a basic distinction between self and world, thought and object.
But life does not so easily split into, respectively, self and world, thought
and object, *phenomena* and *noumena*. Should we say that, if the living is
equivalent to *phenomena*, then Life is equivalent to *noumena*? But it is
precisely the dilemma of Life that it is intelligible only to the extent that
it is manifested in the living, all the while remaining inaccessible "in itself." Correlationism is also based on an asymmetry that is rooted in a
kind of topological game of position and perspective. What makes a correlation a correlation is the impossibility of passing from one position (self)
to the other (world), even though there is a mutual dependency between
them. But what is the perspective of life? In a way, one does not regard
life solely from the point of view of self or world; one does not regard Life
solely from the point of view of the living, and vice-versa. Correlationism
is, finally, based not just on position but on a relation of some sort between
self and world. It is thus predicated on a human-centric view that, at the
same time, shores up its own limits (the empirical defined in relation to
perception, and perception in relation to verification). But as we've tried to
show in the previous chapters, Life and the living have little to do with the
human. While an ontology of life may posit, as its pinnacle, the human
as the privileged form of life (be it in terms of *nous* or the *cogito*), such an
ontology has, as its necessary predicate, the non-exclusivity of life vis-à-
vis the human (even insofar as animal, plant, microbial, or mineral life are
subsumed within the human).
Ultimately, the point we are led to is the insufficiency of correlation-

ism vis-à-vis any ontology of life. But this is not because the vitalist correlation of duration, process, and becoming somehow escape the strictures
of correlationism. Instead, it is because *the vitalist correlation is ontologically predicated not on a concept of being, but on a concept of life—even
at the same time that the latter must ambivalently presume the former.*
This concept of life enables a third step to be added to the first two of
correlationism: first, the separation of thought and object, self and world;
second, the positing of their reciprocal interrelation; and, added to this,
a third step, which is the further positing of a contradiction that doubles
back and encompasses the correlation itself.

Life is at once an object of thought, an object of study, even, of the
living "out there," and at the same time precisely that which is lived "in
here," within a conceptual framework of intuition and immediacy. These
dual notions of life are at once mutually exclusive and reciprocally necessary to think life in one way or another (e.g., as biology or phenomenology,
natural or existential). For the vitalist correlation, then, what enables its
absolutism is a *contradiction* at the heart of *correlation*.

5.4 ONTOTHEOLOGY IN KANT, ATHEOLOGY IN BATAILLE

As a subject of philosophical reflection, life is a strange concept, at once
the most opaque and reified, and at the same time the most immediate and
intuitive. To question life in terms of its ontological status would seem
ridiculous—questioning the existence, or, shall we say, the "realism"
of life would be tantamount to questioning existence itself. However as
we've seen, there are a number of traditions in post-Aristotelian Scholastic
thinking that do exactly this. Or rather, there is an entire pre-Kantian tradition for thinking about life ontologically that opens onto both dominant
and minoritarian strands.

This invites us to think about how these premodern, pre-Kantian ontologies of life might impact a post-Kantian reflection on the topic. Such
an approach would, in Ray Brassier's words, adopt "a willingness to re-
interrogate or to open up a whole series of philosophical problems that
were taken to have been definitively settled by Kant."[22] As Brassier notes,
principle among these would be a re-interrogation of Kant's oft-referenced
Copernican revolution in philosophy:

> [T]he term "realist" in continental philosophy is usually taken to be
> some kind of insult—only someone who hasn't really understood Kant
> could ever want to rehabilitate something like metaphysical realism,

or any form of realism which does not depend upon some kind of transcendental guarantor . . . And in a way, it doesn't really matter whether
you claim to have replaced the subject and the object with some form
of communicational consensus or being-in-the-world or any variant of
the latter on these issues: The transcendental function has been vari-
ously encoded in different versions of post-Kantian continental philosophy. But the thing that seems to be assumed within this tradition . . .
is that whatever structure there is in the world has to be transcendentally imposed or generated or guaranteed.[23]

We have seen how Kant's reflections on purposiveness and teleology vis-
à-vis life eventually revolve around a fundamental contradiction. In this
way, Kantian *purposiveness* recapitulates Aristotelian *entelechy*. Both
grapple with the idea that there is some sort of innate orderliness or organization in life that serves as the fundamental guarantor that the question
of Life is different from either the question of Being or the question of
God. And both Aristotle and Kant also grapple with whether this orderliness that is innate to life, this vital order, can be said to be fully internal
to life itself, or whether it must have some sort of external source.

In a way, Kant himself offers a way of reframing this question through
his comments on theology generally. Kant's comments on theology are
readily apparent in the *Critique of Pure Reason*, where he discusses the
antinomies of pure reason, which have to do with topics such as whether
the cosmos had an absolute beginning, or whether the existence of God
can be proved, and so on. At the end of the *Critique of Judgment*, Kant
reflects again on the antinomies related to purposiveness, nature, and life.
The difficulty is that if one assigns the order, organization, or purposiveness of life to some component of life, how then can one avoid assigning
causality and thus a certain authorship to life itself? For Kant, this can be
avoided only if this assignation of purposiveness is taken to be internal to
life itself: "The expression 'an end of nature' is already enough to preclude
this confusion so that there is no mix-up between natural science and the
occasion it provides for the *teleological* judging of its objects and the consideration of God, and thus a *theological* derivation."[24]

But it is in the later lectures on what Kant calls "rational theology"
that we see the most coherent and systematic treatment of the topic. While
Kant argues against any unfounded judgment concerning a transcendent
author of life, his formulation of the problem is relevant in that it gets at
the basic problem of any investigation into life (or, in Aristotle's terms,
Life and the living), any investigation that posits an ontology concerning

the innate and inherent orderliness of that-which-is-living. Thus any "attempt of reason to infer from the *ends* of nature (which can be cognized only empirically) to the supreme cause of nature and its properties" must fail, insofar as the totality of life cannot be at once the object of an intuition.[25] Kant calls this sort of judgment "physicotheology":

> Now I say that physicotheology, no matter how far it might be pushed, can reveal to us nothing about a *final end* of creation; for it does not even reach the question about such an end . . . How one even has reason for assuming that nothing in the world is in vain, but that everything *in nature* is good for something, under the condition that certain things should exist (as ends), hence for assuming that our reason can provide the power of judgment with no other principle of the possibility of the object for its unavoidable teleological judging than the principle of subordinating the mechanism of nature to the architectonic of an intelligent world-author: the teleological view of the world answers all of this magnificently and extremely admirably. But since the data and hence the principles for *determining* that concept of an intelligent world-cause . . . are merely empirical, they do not allow us to infer any properties beyond what experience reveals to us in its effects: which, since it can never comprehend the whole of nature as a system, must often hit upon grounds of proof that (to all appearance) contradict one another.[26]

In Kant's rather wordy diatribe, the idea of an anthropomorphic cause or author to life is brought under the scrutiny of a critical philosophy, which questions any claims that are effectively divorced from the basic correlation of self and world. Beyond this, one is merely speculating, and the arguments for or against some type of higher, divine, or intelligent design will go on ad infinitum, precisely because pure reason can be brought in to support either claim.

But the further problem, the problem specific to the question of life—that is, "life" as Kant's privileged exemplar of "nature"—is that *any* claim for purposiveness in life must deal in some way with its non-totality. This is arguably as true for laws of nature (even of the "self-organizing" type) as it is for the claims of natural theology and the contemporary forms of "divine Darwinism." Life is not total in the three general ways that we've outlined in this book. It is temporally based, and thus cannot be grasped in a single observation; it is rooted in the dynamics of possible forms and forming; and its changeability raises the question of some immaterial principle that is common to each of its particular instances. In short, even a non-anthropomorphic, non-transcendent concept of purposiveness must confront the notion that, interestingly, life as a topic for ontology must necessarily be speculative.

It is perhaps for this reason that Kant's later lectures on theology deal with the question of purposiveness. Kant's interest here is not just distinguishing philosophy from theology, nor even in distinguishing theology from biology or natural philosophy. Theology, in one sense, comes to have a purely practical role, giving meaning to the world—the world "for us"—as well as to guide human action in the world. But there is another function Kant gives to theology, one that is less human-centric, and, in a way, less humanistic altogether. In a sense, theology for Kant is a perfect example of a kind of thinking that is predicated on the limits of thought itself. Theology becomes a kind of reflection on antinomy itself, especially in the form it takes in the *Critique of Judgment*—as a question about the ontology of life. We can extend the Kantian definition a bit, and suggest that theology is an inquiry into the thought of that which cannot be thought (which, in the context of Medieval philosophy, is understood to be the divine or supernatural). However Kant actually distinguishes between different varieties of theology, and it is worth elaborating his system.

For Kant, all theology is, in a sense, "ontotheology." But what is ontotheology? "It is the system of the knowledge of the highest being."[27] But, as Kant points out, this endeavor—to think the highest being (*ens summum*), to think the being-of-all-beings (*ens originarium*)—is a paradoxical one, for such a thought is by definition beyond thought itself. Kant here implies an important insight from the start, an insight that was, many centuries earlier, central to the tradition of negative theology: theology implies a philosophy of absolute limits—or, what amounts to the same thing, an ontology of contradiction.

Ontotheology is the thought of "a being which excludes every deficiency," which includes both the notion of an *ens summum* and an *ens originarium*.[28] In ontotheology, one uses reason alone, divorced from all experience, to speculate about a fundamental basis for being. In ontotheology one begins from a thinking, living self to make speculative claims about a divine source of being—claims that, of course, can never be validated beyond the use of pure reason itself. Ontotheology is, then, something like the thought of the *being-of-life*. To this is added what Kant calls "cosmotheology," the thought of a "being which contains all realities in itself."[29] Whereas ontotheology is concerned with the being-of-life, cosmotheology is concerned with the *world-of-life*, not in any particular instance or state, but the life in and of the world generally, a world-of-life governed by laws or exhibiting universal attributes. If ontotheology is concerned with a highest being or being-of-all-beings, then cosmotheology is concerned with a highest intelligence or divine order (*summa intelligentia*). If ontotheology is rooted in the notion of a divine principle, then cosmotheology is rooted in the notion of a divine author or design. One begins from the life in general and then makes claims about the laws or the design of that life-in-general.

Ontotheology and cosmotheology are united in their use of pure reason, even though one begins from a thinking self or the world-in-general. But physicotheology is, for Kant, different, in that, like the former two, it also makes untenable claims about purposiveness, but it specifically starts from the idea of *life-as-it-is*. Here phenomena do play a role, but they are quickly sublimated into the abstraction of the life-as-it-is to the world-of-life, and finally to the being-of-life. For physicotheology, the primary thought is thus the *summum bonum*, "the highest good, to which wisdom and morality belong."[30] In physicotheology, this concern for life-as-it-is makes possible the Aristotelian "good life" or qualified life; life-as-it-is thus begins from a sort of primal scene, in which all the attributes of life-as-it-is orbit around the human subject that governs those attributes from its fixed center.

In a sense, physicotheology shores up the anthropomorphism of both ontotheology and cosmotheology. In its concern with life-as-it-is, it is a concern with life-as-it-is *for us*. Hence Kant characterizes physicotheology as being rooted in a divine rule or ruler, rather than a divine author (cosmotheology) or a divine principle (ontotheology). Physicotheology is the most explicit instance of a human-centric ontology of life; but it is also predicated on the cosmotheological and ontotheological views, insofar as life-as-it-is presumes a minimal notion of life in general (world-of-life) that would occasion any particular instance of life-as-it-is, as well as requiring some minimal intelligibility of life-in-itself (being-of-life) for the concept to be thought at all.

The limit, then, of the relation between theology and philosophy is not just a regulative limit. It does not only demarcate the line beyond which well-grounded reason must give way to mysticism or poetry. Kant tends to submerge some of the most interesting questions concerning theology by reassigning to them a moral-pragmatic function. What is less evident, though equally important, is the way that theology for Kant also serves to shore up not only the limits of reason, but the limits of philosophical thinking itself, when this latter is always compromised by the persistent predicate of the "for us."

In a sense, this is precisely what Georges Bataille recovers from theology, at least in its Medieval and mystical-theological guise. For Bataille, theology does not simply demarcate the line beyond which philosophy cannot or should not go; it also negatively articulates a void at the heart of philosophical thinking itself—it is an "anti-philosophy" par excellence. In his later works, Bataille reserved the term *atheology* for this function. What Kant will not admit without risking the edifice of his critical philosophy, Bataille will embrace and transform into a paradoxical unfounded foundation. What Kant breaks down into ontotheology, cosmotheology, and physicotheology, and to which he assigns a regulatory function vis-à-vis the faculty of reason, is for Bataille the core problem of philosophical thinking. His notebooks on atheology are exemplary of this kind of speculative thinking:

> The expression of thought descends with me in the mystical, and the privileged object of the mystical regains its proper place . . .
> By contrast, I've previously talked about by refusal of all presupposition. But I'm talking of God, I think of God,
> Is not God the most basic presupposition of thought?
> I don't doubt this, but this fatal presupposition is itself given in the inexorable movement of thought, it is no less given than it is, ultimately, the *fact* of its absence. Atheology expresses the fact that human thinking is above all placed before God and then before his absence.[31]

The term atheology is not exactly the negation of or the opposition to theology. Neither is it simply an inversion of theology (that is, a demonology). It is an "a-theology," a theology that is beside or alongside, a theology that is without a center, without a "head," a headless or acephalous theology.[32]

    The term atheology also described for Bataille an ongoing and never-completed work that he reworked and revised continually: *La Somme Athéologique*. The title references the Scholastic tradition of the *Summa*, being at once a compendium of central concepts and arguments, as well as a kind of philosophical manifesto. If Aquinas' *Summa Theologica* is the pinnacle of this genre of writing, then Bataille's *La Somme Athéologique* would be at once its negation and its logical conclusion.[33]

Portions of this project were published individually during Bataille's lifetime, though the project as a whole underwent continuous reorganization. This was to be, in effect, Bataille's magnum opus, the definitive statement of his philosophy, which would encompass a cluster of themes center to Bataille's writing: expenditure, eroticism and mystical ecstasy, sacrifice, base materialism, the formless, political economy, the excremental, laughter, and the death of God. But Bataille himself also wrote aggressively against the very notion of "project," totality, and completion. Hence the *La Somme Athéologique* was doomed—or fated—from the start. However, this is more a premise than a prohibition for Bataille. What remains in the *Oeuvres Complètes* is, in a way, at once incomplete and adequate to Bataille's philosophical project—meditations, fragments, aphorisms, notes, outlines, and miscellaneous scraps of paper.

In his numerous notes and drafts for the project, Bataille occasionally offers a definition of the term atheology. Sometimes it is defined in Nietzschean terms, as "the science of the death or destruction of God."[34] At other points Bataille will expand his definition, and atheology becomes the study of negation in itself. And at still other moments, Bataille conceives of atheology as the study of contradiction that is reminiscent of the negative theology of the Pseudo-Dionysius:

> The term *atheology* can not be misunderstood. Owing to the fact that theology subordinates it to its intentions, *God is impious* . . . The *Somme Athéologique* will indicate the only possibility of approaching, of highlighting the attraction that it allows us to undergo, and the interior but communicable luminosity of life.[35]

For Bataille, "life" is neither simply the biological organism nor the ensouled or experiential subject—it is instead the negation at the core of both of them. Nearly all of Bataille's key terms—excess, expenditure, gift—assert a negativity at the heart of givenness and the superlative. In Scholastic terms, "life" becomes for Bataille the concept that erodes both God and the animal, the sovereign and the beast, Creator and creature. "Life" is a necessary concept for *La Somme Athéologique*, but only insofar as it functions negatively.

Bataille's ontology of life is also difficult to pin down. It is, at best, a dichotomous ontology in which pairs of opposites are put into play, continually undergoing inversions and perversions—the erotic and the mystical, death and ecstasy, expenditure and gift, and so on. Nevertheless, a concept of "life" is central for Bataille's larger philosophical project. On the one hand, Bataille's works appear to privilege the interiority of the subject, the inner experience that constitutes the individuated living being: "It is necessary to *live* the grand problems, by the body and by the spirit."[36] But Bataille will always extend this inquiry to its absolute, at the point where interiority becomes isomorphic with a sort of exteriority, the body and the spirit turned inside-out: "Living beings, human beings, cannot communicate—*live*—other than outside of themselves."[37] All of Bataille's emphases on inner experience entail a movement of opening, wounding, unfurling, flooding: "[T]o live signifies for you not only the flux and play of light that unifies itself in you, but the channels of heat or of light from one being to another."[38]

It would be easy to read passages like these either within the framework of a phenomenology of affect, or within the framework of a romantic philosophy of the subject. Indeed, large portions of the project essentially abandon philosophy for speculative mysticism and poetry. Nevertheless, this language, with all of its romantico-naturalistic images of flux and flow, must be read in the context of *La Somme Athéologique*. Among Bataille's references, one often reads the names of John of the Cross, the Pseudo-Dionysius, Meister Eckhart, and Angela di Foligno. This is as much a stylistic as it is a conceptual strategy. The tradition of "darkness mysticism"—from *The Dark Night of the Soul* to *The Cloud of Unknowing*—is omnipresent in Bataille's *La Somme Athéologique*. It takes up one of the central themes of the tradition of darkness mysticism: the utterance of the unutterable, which dovetails into language negating itself; and the thought of that-which-cannot-be-thought, which dovetails into thought negating itself.

For all this, however, Bataille never simply dismisses or dispenses with something tenuously called "philosophy." This naturalistic language of flux and flow is not just about superlative or divine generosity; it is also, for Bataille, the language of negation and *nihil*. What appears, on the surface, to be a variant of either phenomenological or existential reflection on the subject—that is, a Kantian elaboration of ontotheology—is really the dissolution of interiority, an interiority that grounds the human as a point of reference for thought. The subject side of the correlation is never isolated, but is "the activity that links the innumerable elements that compose you to the intensive communication of these elements among themselves."[39] Furthermore, this topology contains "contagions of energy, of movement, of heat or the transfer of elements, that constitute the interiority of your organic life."[40] In this process, "where you would like to know your eternal substance, you meet nothing but a sliding [*glissement*], nothing but a disordered game of your perishable elements."[41]

In fact, for Bataille, life is most manifest at the moment that its latent negativity comes into the foreground, to affirm it. Bataille's emphasis on the political dynamics of gift and sacrifice aim to serve as examples of this negative affirmation, as does his concept of "expenditure." For Bataille, an ontology of life cannot help but to be a negative ontology:

> And the spirit is so closely linked to the body that the latter never ceases to be haunted by the former, not even at the limit, the point where spirit is never more present than when death reduces it to the status of a thing . . . In this sense the cadaver is the most perfect affirmation of the spirit. It is even the essence of the spirit to reveal the definitive powerlessness of death, in the same way that the cry of that cadaver is the supreme affirmation of life.[42]

Against the dominant notion of life as superlative flowing-forth, life for Bataille functions through what the Pseudo-Dionysius calls the *via negativa*. It is not that Life and Death become introconvertible, as if along a kind of animistic continuum. But neither is it the case that the vital processes of growth and decay continually build upon each other (and this in spite of Bataille's eccentric appropriation of Hegelian dialectics). Rather, the "supreme affirmation of life" is revealed insofar as life was always, in itself, "nothing." The problem of a notion of life as generosity is that one must account for both a cause and a teleology that would condition that generosity. This is as true for phenomenology, as it is for process philosophy, as it is for Deleuzian biophilosophy. If life is generosity, gift, givenness, and if one refuses the onto-theological option of a life-principle, much less divine cause of life, then it would seem that only a few options remain. One of them is to question the presumption that life must somehow be identical with affirmation, generosity, and givenness. Another is to question the logical consistency that any ontology of life would presuppose— there is no cause of life except life itself; there is no finality of life except life itself, etc. If we take these two options together—life as negative (*nihil*), and life as contradictory—we have, in short, a version of Bataille's atheology: "Death reveals life in its plentitude and darkens the order of the real."[43]

At its extreme point, Bataille's ontology of life becomes nothing but this interior exteriority, a movement of "contagion" that is immanent, not because it is a *plenum* or a fullness, but because it is, in the manner of

Eriugena's *nihil*, an immanence of nothing: "Immanence does not sup-
press the void but only the transcendence of the void."[44] If Bataille does
put forward an ontology of life, it would therefore have to be *an ontology
of life that is coextensive with* nihil. At times Bataille calls this "negative
immanence."[45] In another note, this pervasiveness of *nihil* is rendered at
once theological and epidemiological, what Bataille calls *theopathy*: "In
theopathy the position of the transcendent disappears beneath its own
transcendence like a game of mirrors."[46]

It would be tempting to refer to this as *cosmic contagion*, if the phrase
did not have undue mystical connotations. Whatever the case, Bataille's
ontology of life, like his epistemology of the subject, attempts to rethink
life in terms of its own negation. Such an atheology must ultimately become the "horror" of thought: "I would like to vigorously affirm the link
between thought and horror. Far from being associated with an overpower-
ing fear or with the cries of horror, it seems to me that thought is *beside*
the world and the being that it expresses."[47]

The "horror of life" evoked here is not that of existential crises or Heideggerian *Angst*. It is, arguably, a Kantian horror: the horror of the noumenal as that which can be thought and un-thought at the same time. There
is not any of the gothic or melodramatic in Bataille's atheological horror,
despite his affinity for the poetry of mysticism. This is less a horror of
an interiority confronting nothingness than a horror that is the neutral,
anonymous nothing of interiority itself. For Bataille, what atheological
thinking does is to take the contradictions at the heart of any ontology of
life, and make of them an ontological principle. What must necessarily result is a concept predicated on the thought of its own negation: life as the
conjunction of immanence and nothing—or really, a nothing that must
necessarily follow from a principle of immanence. This ontology is also
indissociable from an antinomial logic that is implicitly posed by Kant: is
there an a priori of life?

5.5 THE NIGHT LAND

We began, in the introduction, with a brief look at the weird fiction of
H. P. Lovecraft. There we suggested that the weird creatures in Lovecraft's
stories are less "monsters" in the traditional sense—implying an epistemological framework of normal and abnormal—and more about the very
intelligibility of life as such. We will close with a brief and informal meditation on another work in the supernatural horror tradition, William Hope
Hodgson's *The Night Land*.

Lauded by the likes of Lovecraft and Clark Ashton Smith, *The Night Land* is a strange mixture of lowbrow genre writing—part dark fantasy, part science fiction, part romance. Published in 1912, *The Night Land*'s conceptual innovation is matched only by its difficulty as a read—and this is, to be sure, part of its charm. It is written in a style that evokes the romanticism of Blake's prophecies, but without the latter's economy of prose or dense symbolism. It has only a skeletal plot—concerning a quest and a journey—that itself dissolves against the backdrop of the endless descriptions of the Night Land itself (over 400 pages in two volumes in the Ballantine paperback edition).[48] It describes an imminent end—the extinction of the human, and perhaps of thought itself—which never really comes to an end, but instead simply drags on. But what it lacks in style or composition, it makes up for in conceptualization. *The Night Land* is a perfect allegory of the "horror of thought" implicitly evoked by Kant, and explicitly elaborated by Bataille.

The Night Land describes a far-future world in which the sun has long burnt out, and the remnants of humanity have enclosed themselves in the Last Redoubt: a huge metallic pyramid, some 10 miles tall and over 100 miles deep, which contains thousands of "cities" within the various levels of the pyramid. It is encircled by a force-field, itself powered by an "earth-current," which is continually being depleted. The Last Redoubt is constantly besieged by an entire panoply of creatures that remain incomprehensible to those remaining human beings within the Redoubt. Entire scholastic communities have formed—the "Monstruwacans"—dedicated to the study of these unknown and incomprehensible creatures. These life forms are not named, but only described—that is, their incomprehensibility results in the substitution of description for (taxonomic) naming: aside from the more familiar creatures of supernatural horror (giants, hounds, and mutant "Ab-humans"), there is the "Watching Thing of the South," the "Headland From Which Strange Things Peer," the "Road Where Silent Ones Walk," and the inimitable "Country Whence Comes the Great Laughter." What's more, many of the creatures in the Night Land are only liminally living—the "Watchers" appear to be huge, sentient, mountain-like geological formations with "eyes" that continually and fixedly gaze at the Last Redoubt. There are also extra-dimensional entities, such as a lurking "Heap of Black Mist," the "Doorway in the Night," and a "House of Silence."

In one sense, the architectonics of *The Night Land* is decidedly Kantian. Within the Last Redoubt is the human subject, the world of phenomena and the *pour soi*. The scholars of the Last Redoubt constantly gaze out of the multiple observation towers. But they only gaze into shadows, can only describe half-discerned shapes, and what they can discern appears to be, in turn, watching them. The scholars of the Last Redoubt are like naturalists visiting a strange land, having brought the wrong bestiary with them. Not only are they unable to analyze and classify the life of the Night Land, they are unable to distinguish the living from the nonliving. In the Night Land, everything appears to be alive, but none of it is alive in any naturalistic, let alone humanistic, sense of the term. They are effectively in Kant's position vis-à-vis the question of purposiveness and order of life—able to comprehend that there is something "out there," but unable to think that something in itself.

The Night Land encapsulates, in a kind of philosopheme, the dilemma of the ontology of life, from Aristotle's entelechy, through post-Aristotelian Scholasticism, to Kant's antinomy of Life. This is why, as we stated in the introduction, supernatural horror is one of the paradigms for the concept of "life" today—not because of the fear of death, and not because of the crises that populate life, but because of a furtive, miasmatic unintelligibility that inhabits any ontology of life: the idea of a "life" that is not simply an anthropomorphic, human-centric idea of life. But to think this is to question the nature of thought itself. And that unintelligibility is itself a concept, or rather a limit-concept, that poses a basic dilemma: to think a concept of life that is itself, in some basic way, unhuman, a life *without us.*[49]

NOTES

1. Paul Éluard, *L'Amour la poésie* (1929).

CHAPTER I

1. This motif of the "ancient alien" is certainly not unique to Lovecraft. In the nineteenth century, Flammarion and Wells dwelt on the topic, and in the latter part of the twentieth century one repeatedly finds it in TV shows such as *In Search Of . . .* and *X-Files*, as well as in a whole host of films, from *Planet of the Vampires* to *Alien*, not to mention occult art films such as *Lucifer Rising . . .*

2. H. P. Lovecraft, "The Shadow Out of Time," in *The Dreams in the Witch House and Other Weird Stories*, ed. S. T. Joshi (New York: Penguin, 2004), p. 393.

3. H. P. Lovecraft, *At the Mountains of Madness,* in *The Thing on the Doorstep and Other Weird Stories*, ed. S. T. Joshi (New York: Penguin, 2001), p. 330.

4. In fact, Jonathan Barnes suggests that one read texts such as the *De Anima* as a series of lecture notes, rather than polished literary works, as one finds in Plato's early and middle dialogues.

5. Here and elsewhere I rely on the standard accounts given by Aristotle scholars such as: J. L. Ackrill, *Aristotle the Philosopher* (Oxford: Oxford University Press, 1961), Jonathan Barnes, *Aristotle* (Oxford: Oxford University Press, 1982), G. E. R. Lloyd, *Aristotle: The Growth and Structure of His Thought* (Cambridge: Cambridge University Press, 1968).

6. There exists an English translation of the Moerbeke edition, along with Aquinas' commentary. See *Commentary on Aristotle's "De Anima,"* trans. Kenelm Foster and Silvester Humphries (Notre Dame: Dumb Ox, 1994).

7. For instance, Aquinas famously suggested that the *Liber de Causis* was based not on Aristotle but rather on Proclus; indeed, sorting out the Aristotle from Neoplatonism became one of the central preoccupations of Scholastic philosophy.

8. For an overview of commentary on the *De Anima* during these periods, see H. J. Blumenthal, *Aristotle and Neoplatonism in Late Antiquity* (Ithaca: Cornell University

Press, 1996), and Richard Sorabji, *Philosophy of the Commentators, 200–600 A.D.: A Sourcebook, vol. 1—Psychology* (Cambridge: Cambridge University Press, 2005).

9. Most of the English translations of the early and mid twentieth century maintained the Latin title *De Anima*, such as those by Hicks (1907), Smith (1956), Ross (1961), and Hamlyn (1968). An important early exception is the Hett translation (1936) in the Loeb Classical Library, which uses the title *On the Soul*. Recent translations such as the Penguin Classics edition by Lawson-Tancred (1986), retain the English term "soul." However even Lawson-Tancred notes, in the glossary to the book, that the term *psyche* would be "ideally, but impossibly, rendered 'principle of animation.'"

10. For an overview of this approach in modern Aristotle scholarship, see G. E. R. Lloyd, "Aspects of the Relationship between Aristotle's Psychology and his Zoology," in *Essays on Aristotle's "De Anima,"* ed. Martha Nussbaum and Amélie Oksenberg Rorty (Oxford: Clarendon, 1999), pp. 147–68. Also see the collection *Aristotle on Nature and Living Things*, ed. Allan Gotthelf (Pittsburgh: Mathesis, 1985).

11. One debate concerns a version of the philosophy of mind, presented with decidedly Aristotelian conclusions, by Hilary Putnam, in "Philosophy and Our Mental Life," *Mind, Language, and Reality: Philosophical Papers* (Cambridge: Cambridge University Press, 1975), pp. 291–303. This has prompted a dialogue and collaboration with Aristotle scholar Martha Nussbaum on the possibility of an Aristotelian philosophy of mind— and its ensuing criticisms. See M. F. Burnyeat's critique in the collection *Essays on Aristotle's "De Anima,"* ed. Martha Nussbaum and Amélie Oksenberg Rorty (Oxford: Clarendon, 1999), pp. 15–26.

12. Brentano's study was originally published in German in 1867, and translated into English as *The Psychology of Aristotle*, trans. Rolf George (Berkeley: University of California Press, 1977). It is worth pointing out the link between Husserl, who studied for a time with Brentano, and Heidegger, who of course studied with Husserl. That one of Heidegger's early lecture courses is dedicated to the concept of "factical life" in Aristotle is therefore noteworthy.

13. Here I am in accord with recent scholarship that attempts to raise the question of "life" in the *De Anima*, in particular: William Charlton, "Aristotle's Definition of Soul," in *Aristotle's "De Anima" in Focus*, ed. Michael Durrant (New York: Routledge, 1993), pp. 197–216, and Gareth Matthews, "*De Anima* 2.2–4 and the Meaning of *Life*," in *Essays on Aristotle's "De Anima,"* ed. Martha Nussbaum and Amélie Oksenberg Rorty (Oxford: Clarendon, 1999), pp. 185–94. However, I am departing from studies such as these in suggesting the role that contradiction plays as a necessary element in the Aristotelian concept of life. J. L. Ackrill's essay "Aristotle's Definitions of *psuchê*" (*Proceedings of the Aristotelian Society* 73 [1972–73], pp. 119–33) remains an insightful contribution in this regard, in that it systematically points out the lacunae in understanding "life" ontologically in the *De Anima*—a reading that the *De Anima* nevertheless encourages from its very first sentences.

14. Aristotle, *On the Soul / Parva Naturalia / On Breath* (Loeb Classical Library, Aristotle VIII), trans. W. S. Hett (Cambridge: Harvard University Press, 2000 [1936]), II.1.412a. Unless otherwise noted, all translations are from this edition.

15. Ibid., II.4.415b.

16. Ibid., I.1.402a.

17. Ibid., II.2.413a.

18. Interestingly, the terms *bíos* and *zoē* are more frequently utilized than *psukhē* in the opening passages of the *Politica*. In contemporary philosophy, Giorgio Agamben makes much of the distinction between *bíos* and *zoē*, as it forms the boundary around which the political relation between sovereign and the "bare life" that is caught in the state of exception. However, Agamben does not comment on how *psukhē*, as that which conditions the very distinction of *bíos* and *zoē*, also conditions the relation of politics to "life itself." Roberto Esposito's book *Bíos* does take up this question, though Esposito emphasizes a different boundary—the modern medical metaphor of immunity and immunization. See *Homo Sacer*, trans. Daniel Heller-Roazen (Stanford: Stanford University Press, 1998), pp. 1–5, 186–88; Roberto Esposito, *Bíos: Biopolitics and Philosophy*, trans. Timothy Campbell (Minneapolis: University of Minnesota Press, 2008), pp. 45ff.

19. Aristotle, *On the Soul*, II.1.412b.

20. Ibid., II.2.413a.

21. *On the Soul*, trans. J. A. Smith, in *The Complete Works of Aristotle*, ed. Jonathan Barnes (Princeton: Princeton University Press, 1984), I.1.402a.

22. Georges Canguilhem, *Knowledge of Life*, ed. Paola Marrati and Todd Meyers, trans. Stefanos Geroulanos and Daniela Ginsburg (New York: Fordham University Press, 2008), p. 62. Canguilhem's terminology in *La Connaissance de la Vie* can appear somewhat irregular. For instance, he will use the term *vie* in some instances to refer to life in general (including the experience of living), and in other instances to refer to the Aristotelian ontological concept Life. Likewise, the term *vivant* can sometimes mean the life of biological organisms in general (e.g., as species), and at other times to refer to the individual organism in its singularity. Arguably, both of these usages of *vivant* are equivalent to "the living."

23. Martin Heidegger, *The Fundamental Concepts of Metaphysics: World, Finitude, Solitude*, trans. William McNeill and Nicholas Walker (Bloomington: Indiana University Press, 1995), §9, pp. 32–33.

24. Ibid., §9, p. 33.

25. Martin Heidegger, *Being and Time*, trans. Joan Stambaugh (Buffalo: SUNY Press, 1996), §10, p. 44.

26. Ibid., §2, p. 5.

27. Ibid., §4, p. 10.

28. Heidegger, *Basic Concepts*, trans. Gary E. Aylesworth (Bloomington: Indiana University Press, 1998), §7, p. 38.

29. *Requiemæternam dona eis.* One of the ironies of classical music during the early modern period is that the development of the Requiem Mass takes place roughly concurrent with the flowering of polyphonic choral music. The Requiem—perhaps the darkest of the liturgical rites—is also among those musical forms that, at an early stage, incorporates polyphonic elements into its structure. The Mass for the Dead, which so clearly enunciates its gothic themes in the passages of the *Requiem Aeternam* ("Eternal Rest") and the *Dies Irae* ("Day of Wrath"), is in musical terms the greatest expression of life, with its multitude of interdependent and interweaving voices. The earliest Requiems—by Dufay, Ockeghem, Brumel—give expression to this inner antagonism.

CHAPTER 2

1. On the idea of extinction as a limit for thought, see Ray Brassier, *Nihil Unbound: Enlightenment and Extinction* (London: Palgrave, 2007), pp. 205ff.

2. F. W. J. von Schelling, *Ideas for a Philosophy of Nature*, trans. Errol Harris and Peter Heath (Cambridge: Cambridge University Press, 1995), p. 36.

3. On pathological anatomy, see Michel Foucault, *The Birth of the Clinic*, trans. A. M. Sheridan Smith (New York: Vintage, 1994), pp. 127ff.

4. Schelling, *First Outline of a System of Philosophy of Nature*, trans. Keith Petersen (Buffalo: SUNY Press, 2004), pp. 68–69.

5. A standard account is given in John Bussanich, "Plotinus' Metaphysics of the One," in *The Cambridge Companion to Plotinus*, ed. Lloyd P. Gerson (Cambridge: Cambridge University Press, 1996), pp. 38–65.

6. See, for example, the essays in *Neoplatonism and Nature: Studies in Plotinus' "Enneads,"* ed. Michael Wagner (Albany: SUNY Press, 2001). Also see H. J. Blumenthal, *Plotinus' Psychology: His Doctrines of the Embodied Soul* (The Hague: Martinus Nijhof, 1971). Earlier, though still useful studies are René Arnou, *Le Désir de Dieu dans la philosophie de Plotin* (Paris: F. Alcan, 1921), and A. H. Armstrong, *The Architecture of the Intelligible Universe in the Philosophy of Plotinus* (Cambridge: Cambridge University Press, 1940). Michael Wagner, *The Enigmatic Reality of Time: Aristotle, Plotinus, and Today* (Leiden: Brill, 2008), offers an interdisciplinary view.

7. H. J. Blumenthal's work has, perhaps more than that of any other scholar, explored the relationship between Aristotle and Plotinus. See his early essay "Soul, World-Soul, and Individual Soul in Plotinus," in *Le néoplatonisme* (Royaumont: Éditions Colloques internationaux du Centre national de la recherche scientifique, 1971), as well as his study *Aristotle and Neoplatonism in Late Antiquity: Interpretations of the "De Anima"* (Ithaca: Cornell University Press, 1996).

8. Plotinus, *The Enneads*, trans. Stephen MacKenna (New York: Penguin, 1991), II.4.3. All citations are from this edition unless otherwise noted.

9. Ibid., I.1.2.

10. Ibid., III.7.3.

11. Ibid.

12. Ibid.

13. Ibid., III.7.11.

14. Ibid.

15. Ibid.

16. Ibid., IV.3.1–8.

17. Ibid., III.7.11.

18. On negative theology, see Bruce Milen, "Four Theories of Negative Theology," *Heythrop Journal* 48 (2007): 187–204; Raoul Mortley, "The Fundamentals of the *Via Negativa*," *American Journal of Philology* 103.4 (1982): 429–39, as well as the first two chapters of Denys Turner, *The Darkness of God* (Cambridge: Cambridge University Press, 1995). On the relation between negative theology and contemporary philosophies of difference, see Conor Cunningham, "The Difference of Theology and Some Philosophies of Nothing," *Modern Theology* 17.3 (2001): 289–312.

19. This is, generally speaking, a motif present in nearly all of the late Derrida. See, for example, *The Gift of Death / Literature in Secret*, trans. David Wills (Chicago: University of Chicago Press, 2007), as well as the fascinating piece "How to Avoid Speaking: Denials," in *Derrida and Negative Theology*, eds. Harold Coward and Toby Foshay (Albany: State University of New York Press, 1992). One should also mention the work of Jean-Luc Marion, who more directly brings the themes of continental philosophy to bear on negative theology. See Jean-Luc Marion, *God Without Being*, trans. Thomas Carlson (Chicago: University of Chicago Press, 1995), pp. 53ff.

20. While in Athens, Paul preaches in the Areopagus: "When they heard about the resurrection of the dead, some of them sneered, but others said, 'We want to hear you again on this subject.' At that, Paul left the Council. A few men became followers of Paul and believed. Among them was Dionysius, a member of the Areopagus, also a woman named Damaris, and a number of others" (Acts 17:32–34, New International Version). Interestingly, Paul notes an idol marked "The Unknown God," a phrase that perhaps bears some relation to what the Pseudo-Dionysius calls "The Unnameable One."

21. In a report titled "Epistle of Innocent the Maronite concerning a Conference Held with the Severians," the authorship of Dionysius the Areopagite is questioned in the same breath as Dionysius' works are first named as a single body of work (the *Corpus Areopagiticum*). By the early fifteenth century, Italian Neoplatonist philosophers could show, by comparing passages of the Pseudo-Dionysius with his Neoplatonic influences, that the author of the *Corpus Areopagiticum* could not have been Dionysius the Areopagite. But just who the author is remains a mystery. Numerous arguments have been given for the identity of the Pseudo-Dionysius, though indisputable documentation is lacking. The greatest evidence seems to be that of textual comparison: the *Corpus Areopagiticum* shows the marked influence of the Neoplatonic thinker Proclus (412–485), and the first undisputed reference to the Pseudo-Dionysius' works is by the monophysite thinker Severus of Antioch (ca. 518–528), so, the reasoning goes, the Pseudo-Dionysius must have been working sometime in the late fifth to early sixth century.

22. Of the many secondary works on the Pseudo-Dionysius, the following have been instrumental in this study: Dierdre Carabine, *The Unknown God: Negative Theology in the Platonic Tradition* (Grand Rapids: Eerdmans Publishing, 1995); Jon Jones, "Sculpting God: The Logic of Dionysian Negative Theology," *Harvard Theological Review* 89.4 (1996): 355–71; Andrew Louth, *Denys the Areopagite* (London: Continuum, 2002), 99ff.; Michael Sells, *Mystical Languages of Unsaying* (Chicago: University of Chicago Press, 1994); Denys Turner, *The Darkness of God: Negativity in Christian Mysticism* (Cambridge: Cambridge University Press, 1995), 19–49. Turner's book is especially insightful concerning the role of negation in negative theology generally.

23. For an overview, see Denys Turner, "The Art of Unknowing: Negative Theology in Late Medieval Scholasticism," *Modern Theology* 14.4 (1998): 473–88.

24. Pseudo-Dionysius, *The Mystical Theology*, trans. Colm Luibheid, in *The Complete Works* (New York: Paulist Press, 1987), 3.1033B, p. 139. All citations are from this edition.

25. Ibid., 3.1033C.

26. Ibid., 3.1033A.

27. Ibid., 3.1033B.

28. Ibid., 2.1025B.

29. Ibid., 3.1033C.

30. Ibid., 1.1000A–B.

31. Pseudo-Dionysius, *The Divine Names*, trans. Colm Luibheid, in *The Complete Works* (New York: Paulist Press, 1987), I.1.585B–588A. All citations are from this edition.

32. Ibid., I.1.588A.

33. Ibid.

34. Ibid., I.1.588B.

35. Ibid., IV.3.697A.

36. Ibid., I.6.596A.

37. Ibid., VI.1.856B.

38. Ibid., I.6.596Bff.

39. Ibid., II.10.648C–D.

40. Ibid., IV.3.697A.

41. Ibid., I.3.589C.

42. Ibid., II.3.640B.

43. Ibid., II.11.649B.

44. Ibid., II.5.644A.

45. Ibid., II.11.649B.

46. Ibid.

47. In addition to Derrida's writing on the gift, see Jean-Luc Marion's perceptive study of generosity and givenness within a phenomenological framework, *Being Given: Toward a Phenomenology of Givenness*, trans. Jeffrey Kosky (Stanford: Stanford University Press, 2002). One is tempted to add—or really, to contrast—the notion of generosity, gift, and excess in the work of Georges Bataille to this phenomenological strand.

48. Pseudo-Dionysius, *The Divine Names*, II.5.644A.

49. Ibid., II.11.649B; 649C.

50. Ibid., IV.2.296Bff.

51. Ibid., VI.1.856B.

52. Ibid., VI.2.856C.

53. Ibid., VI.2.856C–D.

54. Ibid., VI.1.856B.

55. Ibid., VI.3.857B.

56. Ibid., V.5.820A.

57. Ibid., V.5.820A–C.

58. Ibid., roughly IV.18.716–34.733C.

59. Ibid., IV.21.721C. The Pseudo-Dionysius also notes: "Remove the Good entirely and there will be nothing—good, or mixed with something else, or absolutely evil. For if evil is imperfect Goodness, the complete absence of the Good will do away with complete and incomplete goodness. Evil will only be and be seen by contrast with what it opposes, for it will be distinct from them, since they are good. The fact is that things of the same kind cannot wholly contradict each other in the same respects. And so it is that evil is not a being" (IV.20.721A–B).

60. Ibid., IV.20.717C; 32.733C.

61. Ibid., IV.19.716D.

62. Or an "unemployed negativity," to use a phrase favored by Georges Bataille.

63. Pseudo-Dionysius, *Mystical Theology*, 5.1048A–B.

64. A standard general study is J. J. O'Meara, *Eriugena* (Oxford: Clarendon Press, 1988).

65. Johannes Scottus Eriugena, *Periphyseon (De Diuisione Naturae)* IV, trans. John J. O'Meara and I. P. Sheldon-Williams, ed. Édouard A. Jeauneau (Dublin: Dublin Institute for Advanced Studies, 1995), 758A.

66. Johannes Scottus Eriugena, *Periphyseon (De Diuisione Naturae)* I, ed. I. P. Sheldon-Williams with Ludwig Bieler (Dublin: Dublin Institute for Advanced Studies, 1968), 522B.

67. Even its first printing in 1681 at Oxford was later included in the 1864 *Index of Prohibited Books*—in the condemnations of 1225, Pope Honorius II went so far as to order that the work be burnt.

68. This book uses the Sheldon-Williams/O'Meara edition, published by the Dublin Institute for Advanced Studies, as it both accounts for manuscript variations and offers a facing English language translation to the Latin. All citations are from this edition: Books I (1968), II (1972), and III (1981) are edited by Sheldon-Williams and Ludwig Bieler, and Book IV (1995) is edited by Édouard Jeauneau with translation by Sheldon-Williams and John J. O'Meara.

69. Scholarship that informs this study include the following: Édouard Jeauneau, "Néant divin et théophanie: Erigene disciple de Denys," *Diotima* 23 (1995): 121–27; Bernard McGinn, "Negative Theology in John the Scot," *Studia Patristica* 13 (1975): 232–38; Dermot Moran, *The Philosophy of John Scottus Eriugena: A Study of Idealism in the Middle Ages* (Cambridge: Cambridge University Press, 1989); Dermot Moran, "Idealism in Philosophy: The Case of Johannes Scottus Eriugena," *Medieval Philosophy & Theology* 8 (1999): 53–82; Donald Duclow, "Divine Nothingness and Self-Creation in John Scottus Eriugena," *Journal of Religion* 57 (1977): 109–23; J. J. O'Meara, "The Concept of *Natura* in John Scottus Eriugena," *Vivarium* 19.2 (1981): 126–45; Willemien Otten, "In the Shadow of the Divine: Negative Theology and Negative Anthropology in Augustine, Pseudo-Dionysius, and Eriugena," *Heythrop Journal* 40.4 (1999): 438–55; René Roques, "Théophanie et nature chez John Scot Erigène—Explication de quelques passages du 'De divisione naturae,'" *Annuaire de l'Ecole pratique des Hautes Études* 74 (1966): 162–67. Of these Moran's work is especially interesting in that it achieves a nice balance between the historical onto-theological context of the *Periphyseon* and its juxtaposition to the modern philosophical debates surrounding idealism. The essays by Jeauneau, Moran, and Otten are particularly interesting in their discussion of *nihil*.

70. Eriugena, *Periphyseon*, I 441A.

71. Ibid.

72. Cf. ibid., II 527B

73. Cf. ibid., I 443A–D.

74. Cf. ibid., I 444A–C.

75. Cf. ibid., I 440D–445A.

76. Cf. ibid., I 445B–C.

77. Ibid., III 728D–729A.

78. This reading is indebted to, but also departs from, much Eriugena scholarship on *nihil*, especially Jeauneau, "Néant divin et théophanie"; Otten, "In the Shadow of the Divine"; and Moran, "Idealism in Philosophy."

79. Eriugena, *Periphyseon*, roughly III 634B–688B.

80. Ibid., III 634B.

81. Ibid., III 634C.

82. Ibid., III 634D, with hand-written additions to original Rheims 875 ms.

83. Ibid., III 636B.

84. Ibid., III 637A–B.

85. Ibid., III 638A.

86. Ibid., III 647A.

87. Ibid., III 647B–C.

88. Ibid., III 651B.

89. Ibid., III 653B-C.

90. The distinction is borrowed from Alain Badiou, "The Being of Number," *Briefings on Existence*, trans. Norman Madarasz (Albany: SUNY Press, 2006), pp. 125–32.

91. Cf. Eriugena, *Periphyseon*, III 652Bff.

92. Ibid., III 657B.

93. Cf. ibid., III 677A–C.

94. Ibid., III 641C.

95. In this reply, scriptural exegesis is used in ibid., III 641A, 641C, 659A, 660A.

96. Ibid., III 669A–B.

97. Ibid., III 639C.

98. Ibid., III 667C–D.

99. Ibid., III 638D.

100. Ibid., III 667D.

101. Ibid., III 670B.

102. Ibid., III 670C–D.

103. Ibid., Cf. III 671A–D.

104. Cf. Ibid., III 673B–674A.

105. Cf. Ibid., III 674C–675A.

106. Ibid., III 677C.

107. Ibid., III 680D–681A.

108. Ibid., III 681A.

109. Ibid., III 635B.

110. Ibid., III 646C–D.

111. Ibid., III 635C.

112. Ibid., II 549Bff.

113. Ibid., II 552A.

114. The topic of darkness mysticism tradition and its ontology of being and nonbeing has been discussed recently by Nicola Masciandaro, in his talk "The Sorrow of Being," given at New York University, 12 November 2009.

115. Cf. *A Thirteenth-Century Textbook of Mystical Theology at the University*

of Paris (Dallas Medieval Texts in Translation), ed. L. Michael Harrington (Louvain: Peeters, 2004).

116. Gottlob Frege, "Negation," trans. P. Geach, in *Translations from the Philosophical Writings of Gottlob Frege* (Oxford: Blackwell, 1975).

117. A. J. Ayer, "Negation," *Journal of Philosophy* 49.26 (1952), pp. 804–805.

118. Alain Badiou, "Destruction, Negation, Subtraction," lecture at the Art Center College of Design in Pasadena (6 February 2007), available at www.lacan.com.

119. Ibid.

120. Ibid.

121. Badiou, "On Subtraction," in *Theoretical Writings*, ed. and trans. Ray Brassier and Alberto Toscano (London: Continuum, 2004), p. 103.

122. Ibid., p. 104.

123. Ibid., p. 105.

124. Ibid., p. 107.

125. Ibid., italics removed.

126. Ibid., p. 108, italics removed.

127. Badiou, "Destruction, Negation, Subtraction."

128. Heraclitus, *Fragments*, trans. T. M. Robinson (Toronto: University of Toronto Press, 1987), fragment 49a.

129. Specifically, in Book Γ, chapter four.

130. Graham Priest, "What Is So Bad About Contradictions?" *Journal of Philosophy* 95 (1998), p. 416.

131. Ibid., p. 425.

132. Suhrawardī, *The Philosophy of Illumination* (*Hikmat al-ishrāq*), trans. John Walbridge and Hossein Ziai (Provo: Brigham Young University Press, 1999), II, first discourse, p. 77. Suhrawardī later reaffirms this, stating that "the Light as light engenders only light . . ." (second discourse, p. 90).

133. Ibid., p. 78.

134. Ibid.

135. Ibid.

136. The ontology of iridescence has been discussed by Alexander Galloway. See his "Fury, Iridescence, Hermeneutics," lecture given at the SUNY–Stony Brook Humanities Institute, 16 April 2009.

137. *et lux perpetua luceat eis.* While the Requiem Mass is in its content concerned with death, in its musical form it is concerned with life (the life of polyphony). In the arrangement of the Proper and Ordinary sections it is also concerned with narrative: one begins in darkness and ascends towards the light. Something different occurs in the *Tenebrae*, the collection of Matins and Lauds traditionally performed during Holy Week. In its traditional form, a candle is extinguished after each section until the last one, which is sung in total darkness (*in tenebris*). Like the Requiem, the *Tenebrae* theologically implies a coming transcendence, though in the former the theme is that of the afterlife, while in the latter the theme is that of resurrection. Unlike the Requiem, however, the *Tenebrae*—at least in the examples of Gesualdo or Victoria—is not so much a teleologically driven work as it is a sustained musical meditation on the themes of darkness and sorrow.

CHAPTER 3

1. Augustine, *Exposition on the Book of Psalms*, ed. Philip Schaff (Peabody: Hendrickson, 1999), section 16.

2. We can, of course, expand these forms of life to include mineralogical, noological, or cosmological life, but such an expansion of phyla still relies on this basic distinction of the life form and the life-that-forms. Thus, from a certain perspective, even "nonorganic life" must presume the Aristotelian framework—if only to annul it after the fact.

3. In the *De Anima* Aristotle merely makes the distinction between *psukhē* considered in itself and *psukhē* as particular to the plant, animal, or human strata. In the biological treatises, attempts to connect Life and the living are even more scant, though there are passages in works such as the *Historia Animalium* in which the central argument of the *De Anima* is in effect summarized.

4. While the term "pantheism" is not commonly used until the eighteenth century, the concept itself—of God being identical with Nature—remains an issue of some controversy. By the late nineteenth and early twentieth centuries, the term begins to be used with some regularity in histories of Western philosophy to describe the work of thinkers such as Spinoza. See, for example, Étienne Gilson's two-volume *La philosophie au moyen-âge* (Paris: Payot, 1922).

5. Standard accounts in the history of philosophy include: Frederick Copleston, *A History of Medieval Philosophy* (Notre Dame: University of Notre Dame Press, 1972); Étienne Gilson, *The Spirit of Mediaeval Philosophy* (Notre Dame: University of Notre Dame Press, 1991); Anthony Kenny, *Medieval Philosophy* (Oxford: Oxford University Press, 2007).

6. The process is broadly as follows: first take a creaturely attribute, such as "this life," then take away the creaturely limit term "this" (resulting in "life itself" or Life), then take the attribute in itself and maximize it ("eternal life" or "spiritual life" or superlative life), then take this term—however compromised—and render it equivalent to the divine ("God is eternal life," etc.).

7. See the wonderful collection *The Monstrous Middle Ages*, ed. Bettina Bildhauer and Robert Mills (Toronto: University of Toronto Press, 2004).

8. See *The Book of Beasts, Being a Translation from a Latin Bestiary of the Twelfth Century*, ed. T. H. White (New York: Dover, 1984).

9. Part of the reason may be historical—though Aristotle's works in logic were known to Medieval thinkers, it was only in the twelfth century that the works in natural philosophy were translated into Latin. These works were often not direct translations from Greek, but re-translations via Arabic and Syriac, or sometimes both. Furthermore, as was the tradition, Arabic scholars often commented extensively on Aristotle's texts, so much so that it is often difficult to distinguish a commentary text by, say, Averroës, from the source text of Aristotle. It is for this reason that Aristotle simply became known as "the Philosopher" to the Scholastics, while Averroës became "the Commentator."

10. Thomas Aquinas, *The Treatise on the Divine Nature*, ed. and trans. Brian Shanley (Indianapolis: Hackett, 2006). All citations and references are to this translation

unless otherwise noted. Other editions consulted include *Summa Theologiae, Vol. 3 (Ia, 12–13): Knowing and Naming God*, ed. Herbert McCabe (Cambridge: Cambridge University Press, 2008), and *Summa Theologiae, Questions on God*, ed. Brian Davies and Brian Leftow (Cambridge: Cambridge University Press, 2006). The Thomistic secondary scholarship is massive, and I cite here only those recent works that have been directly useful: W. Norris Clarke, "Analogy and the Meaningfulness of Language about God," in *Explorations in Metaphysics: Being—God—Person* (Notre Dame: University of Notre Dame Press, 1994); Anthony Kenny, *Aquinas on Being* (Oxford: Oxford University Press, 2003); Ralph McInerny, *Aquinas and Analogy* (Washington, DC: Catholic University of America Press, 1996); Gregory Rocca, *Speaking the Incomprehensible One: Thomas Aquinas on the Interplay of Positive and Negative Theology* (Washington, DC: Catholic University of America Press, 2004). The McInerny book is a standard account of Thomistic analogy, while the book by Kenny offers a useful account of Thomistic onto-theology in relation to natural theology and natural philosophy. An earlier, still useful study along these lines is Anton Pegis, *St. Thomas and the Problem of the Soul in the Thirteenth Century* (Toronto: Pontifical Institute of Medieval Studies, 1976 [1934]).

11. To summarize, Aquinas' argument can be outlined as follows:

- The question: "Whether what is said of God and of creatures is univocally predicated of them?"
- Objection 1: It seems that they are univocal because all equivocity reduces to univocity.
- Obj. 2: Since there is no likeness at all between equivocal things, and since the creature is made in the likeness of the Creator, it seems that they are univocal.
- Obj. 3: There is a relation of likeness between measure and that which is measured, cause and that which is caused. God as the first measure is like the creatures that are measured.
- On the contrary, something can be predicated of two terms but not in the same sense. One name can be given to many things, but not with the same meaning. The name of God is not God itself, since God is not a genus or species. Further, God is not related to creatures as along a spectrum, but is of a wholly different order.
- Answer: There is no univocity between God and creatures because one is the cause of the other, and each effect, though it contains some aspect of the cause, is also a lesser version of it. Each effect is similar but less than its cause. What imperfection is in the effect (creature), perfection is in the cause (Creator). There is no equivocity between God and creatures, since then nothing at all could be naturally known about God by creatures. Thus it must be said that God and creatures are analogously related.
  - There is the analogy of proportion—"health" of a body is used in relation to the terms "urine" and "medicine," but in different proportions (a symptom/sign in the former and cause in the latter).
  - There is the analogy of proportionality—what A is to B, C is to D.
- Reply obj. 1: Although all equivocity reduces to univocity, for all univocity

there must be a first non-univocal agent that precedes it, or else that continues to infinity (dialectic of univocity-equivocity). This "universal agent" is an analogical agent, in which all univocity reduces to a unity, which is being.

- Reply obj. 2: The likeness between creature and God is by definition imperfect, but this does not imply univocity.
- Reply obj. 3: God is not a measure in proportion to the thing measured since they are not in the same genus by which measurement of them would be possible.

12. Cf. Aquinas, *The Treatise on the Divine Nature*, pt. I, q. 12, a. 4; a. 7.

13. Ibid., q. 13, a. 1–4.

14. Ibid., q. 13, a. 5., reply.

15. Ibid.

16. This plays out in the actual composition of texts as well, for while Aristotle's *De Anima* is relatively separate from the works in biology, Medieval approaches integrated perspectives from classical natural philosophy, natural theology, and metaphysics into single texts that, in a strangely interdisciplinary way, eschew any neat divisions between theology, philosophy, and biology. Commentaries on Aristotle are a good case in point, as evidenced in William of Auvergne's *On the Soul* or *The Universe of Creatures*.

17. A number of secondary works have been helpful for my reading of Duns Scotus. These include: Richard Cross, *The Physics of Duns Scotus: The Scientific Context of a Theological Vision* (Oxford: Clarendon Press, 1998); Stephen Dumont et al., "The Univocity of the Concept of Being in the Fourteenth Century," *Mediaeval Studies* 49–51 (1987–89); Stephen Dumont, "Transcendental Being: Scotus and Scotists," *Topoi* 11 (1992): 135–49; Alexander Hall, *Thomas Aquinas and John Duns Scotus: Natural Theology in the High Middle Ages* (London: Continuum, 2007); Peter King, "Duns Scotus on the Common Nature and the Individual Differentia," *Philosophical Topics* 20 (1992): 51–76. The book by Hall is especially relevant to the discussion here, as it teases out the implications of Scotus' concepts for continental philosophy. In addition, earlier studies by Gilson and Wolter remain relevant: Étienne Gilson, *Jean Duns Scot: Introductions à Ses Positions Fondamentales* (Paris: Vrin, 2001 [1952]), and Allan Wolter, *Transcendentals and Their Function in the Metaphysics of Duns Scotus* (Washington, DC: Catholic University of America Press, 1946).

18. In Scholastic terminology, the original lectures, or *lectura*, could be copied down by a student or scribe, and then known as a *reportatio*. If lecture notes were later reedited, changed, or corrected by the author, the work would be known as an *ordinatio*. It is thought that Scotus' original lecture notes at Oxford were later reedited over a process of several years between 1300 and 1304, that is, between his tenure at Oxford and his move to Paris.

19. We can outline the argument for univocity given by Scotus as follows:

- Q: Can there be but one God? Is God one or many? Is God univocal?
    - Pro
        - Biblical quote on "many gods and many lords."
        - If God exists, then gods exist (singular implies plural).
        - Every single thing can be traced back to its essence.

- A greater number of good things is better than a lesser number.
- Necessity of existence (if gods exist they are necessarily existing).
- Contra
  - Quote from Bible ("There is no God besides me").
- Body of the Question: Let us suppose God is One or univocal—is there a natural knowledge of this univocity?
  - First Opinion: The univocity of God is known only by faith.
  - Scotus' Opinion: The univocity of God is known by natural reason. Proofs for this:
    - From infinite intellect. The knowledge of B by A presupposes something in "common" to both A and B.
    - From infinite will. The love of B by A presupposes a "natural will" that connects A and B.
    - From infinite goodness. The goodness of A in B presupposes a will or necessity of goodness that flows between A and B.
    - From infinite power. A (God) creates B and C by an act of "total cause," not two Gods A and B creating a single creature C.
    - From absolute infinity. God as infinity is absolute infinity, and thus "less than numerical" or "non-numerical" since number is proper to creatures.
    - From necessary being. The divine is "indeterminate" in the infinite, but it determines multiple individuals. There is a "formal necessity" or distinction between an individual and its nature.
    - From omnipotence.
  - Reply to First Opinion: On singularity, individuality, and the formal objective distinction.
- Reply to Pro Arguments
  - "Many gods" refers to idols not actually God.
  - "Number" is not applicable to the divine but to things.
  - The essence of each essence is a single essence God; "pure perfection" vs. "mixed perfection."

20. Duns Scotus, *Opus Oxoniense*, in *Philosophical Writings*, ed. and trans. Allan Wolter (Indianapolis: Hackett, 1987), I., dist. III, q. i, p. 20. All citations and references are to this edition unless otherwise noted. In addition to this volume, Scotus' Quodlibetal Questions on *creatura* were also consulted. See Duns Scotus, *God and Creatures*, trans. Felix Alluntis and Allan Wolter (Washington, DC: Catholic University of America Press, 1995).

21. Scotus, *Opus Oxoniense*, I., dist. II, q. iii., p. 85.

22. Ibid., p. 89.

23. Ibid., I, dist. II, q. iii, p. 88.

24. Ibid., p. 89.

25. It would be more accurate to say that Scotus' formal distinction is a response to the Medieval debates over universals, particularly as established by Abelard. In this way, Scotus can be seen to be positioned somewhere between the twelfth-century debates over universals and the later Ockhamist debates over nominalism.

26. Étienne Gilson's *History of Christian Philosophy in the Middle Ages* (New York: Random House, 1955) devotes entire sections to "Scotism" following the 1277 Condemnations (which he refers to as a "Second Augustinianism"). See also Hall, *Thomas Aquinas and John Duns Scotus.*

27. On the relation between Duns Scotus and Henry of Ghent, see Jerome Brown, "Duns Scotus on the Possibility of Knowing Genuine Truth: The Reply to Henry of Ghent in the 'Lectura Prima' and in the 'Ordinatio,'" *Recherches de théologie ancienne et médiévale* 51 (1984): 136–82. Also see Allan Wolter's introductory material in Duns Scotus, *Philosophical Writings.*

28. Scotus, *Opus Oxoniense* I, dist. III, q. I, p. 18.

29. Henry of Ghent, *Henry of Ghent's Summa: The Questions on God's Existence and Essence*, ed. Roland Teske, trans. Jos Decorte and Roland Teske (Leuven: Peeters, 2005), XXI, q. ii.

30. Ibid., p. 49.

31. Ibid., pp. 49, 51.

32. Ibid., p. 57.

33. Ibid., p. 59.

34. Scotus, *Opus Oxoniense* I, dist. III, q. i, arg. I, p. 20.

35. Ibid.

36. Ibid., arg. II, p. 23.

37. Ibid., arg. II, p. 22.

38. Ibid., arg. III, p. 23.

39. Ibid., arg. IV, p. 29

40. Ibid., p. 24.

41. Ibid., p. 25.

42. For instance, in his book on Spinoza, Deleuze repeatedly cites the classic French study on Duns Scotus, Gilson's *Jean Duns Scot*. On Deleuze's Scholasticism, see Peter Hallward, "'Everything Is Real': Deleuze and Creative Univocity," *New Formations* 49 (2003): 61–74, as well as Daniel Smith, "The Doctrine of Univocity: Deleuze's Ontology of Immanence," *Deleuze and Religion*, ed. Mary Bryden (New York: Routledge, 2001). Many of Smith's essays deal explicitly with Deleuze's engagement with Scholastic and onto-theological themes.

43. Gilles Deleuze, *Difference and Repetition*, trans. Paul Patton (New York: Columbia University Press, 1995), p. 35.

44. While my reading of Spinoza is intentionally inflected through Deleuze, a number of Spinozist studies in addition to Deleuze have been helpful. This includes older scholarship, such as H. A. Wolfson's *The Philosophy of Spinoza* (Cambridge: Harvard University Press, 1983 [1934]), which frames Spinoza in relation to Scholasticism, as well as more modern studies, such as Alexandre Matheron's *Individu et communauté chez Spinoza* (Paris: Éditions Minuit, 1969) and the collection *The New Spinoza*, ed. Warren Montag and Ted Stolze (Minneapolis: University of Minnesota Press, 1998).

45. Gilles Deleuze, *Expressionism in Philosophy: Spinoza*, trans. Martin Joughin (New York: Zone, 1992), p. 46 [37].

46. Ibid., p. 47, italics removed. Deleuze continues: "Attributes constitute the es-

sence of substance, but in no sense constitute the essence of modes or of creatures. *Yet they are forms common to both*, since creatures imply them both in their own essence and in their existence."

47. Ibid., p. 30.

48. Ibid., p. 64, italics removed.

49. Ibid., p. 33.

50. "Numerical distinction is never real; then conversely, real distinction is never numerical. Spinoza's argument now becomes: attributes are really distinct; but real distinction is never numerical; so there is only one substance for all attributes" (ibid., p. 34).

51. Ibid., p. 49.

52. Deleuze, *Difference and Repetition*, p. 36.

53. Ibid.

54. Ibid.

55. Ibid.

56. Ibid., p. 37.

57. Ibid.

58. Ibid., p. 39.

59. Most notably by Alain Badiou and, in a different vein, François Laruelle.

60. Deleuze, *Difference and Repetition*, p. 40. Also see Peter Hallward, *Out of This World: Deleuze and the Philosophy of Creation* (London: Verso, 2006).

61. Deleuze, *Difference and Repetition*, p. 41.

62. Gilles Deleuze, "Anti-Oedipe et Mille Plateaux," trans. Timothy Murphy, *Les Cours de Gilles Deleuze*, ed. Richard Pinhas, at www.webdeleuze.com. All citations are from this transcript.

63. Ibid.

64. Ibid.

65. Ibid.

66. Ibid.

67. Ibid.

68. Ibid.

69. If we can be allowed to extend Scotus' concept of univocity in this way, one question is how the implications of a univocal creature—an entity of a relation that is produced by the relation—is related to the mathematico-scientific definitions of self-organization in biocomplexity.

70. Duns Scotus, *Opus Oxoniense* I, dist. III, q. i, p. 23.

71. The term inexistence, and the logical conundrums it entails, is developed by Alain Badiou in the opening sections of *Being and Event*, trans. Oliver Feltham (New York: Continuum, 2005), specifically in relation to the concept of the void: "[I]f, in the immanence of a situation, its inconsistency does not come to light, nevertheless, its count-as-one being an operation itself indicates that the one is a result . . . To put it more clearly, once the entirety of a situation is subject to the law of the one and consistency, it is necessary, from the standpoint of immanence to the situation, that the pure multiple . . . be *nothing*. But being-nothing is as distinct from non-being as the 'there is' is distinct from being" (p. 53).

72. Gilles Deleuze, "Mathesis, Science, and Philosophy," *Collapse* III (2007), pp. 143–44.

73. Dōgen, *Shōbōgenzō*, trans. Thomas Cleary (Honolulu: University of Hawaii Press, 1992), p. 39.

74. Ibid., p. 38.

75. Ibid., p. 39.

76. Ibid., pp. 38–39. Dōgen later notes "it is *people eat food, food eats people* . . . it is the manifestation of the *nature of things* of good, it is the manifestation of the *nature of things* of eating" (pp. 39–40).

77. Ibid., p. 41.

78. Ibid.

CHAPTER 4

1. For recent scholarship on pantheism, see John Cooper, *Panentheism: The Other God of the Philosophers* (Ada: Baker Academic, 2006), and Michael Levine, *Pantheism: A Non-theistic Concept of Deity* (New York: Routledge, 1994).

2. In a sense, these three steps form part of a sequence, the third bringing us back to the first, for instance, in the notion of immanence as "nothing" or *nihil* in Eriugena.

3. Aquinas, *Summa Theologica*, vol. I, trans. Fathers of the English Dominican Province (New York: Benziger, 1947), pt. I, q. 18, a. 1. All citations refer to this edition unless otherwise noted. Other editions consulted include *Summa Theologiae, Vol. 4: Knowledge in God (1a, 14–18)*, ed. Thomas Gornall (Cambridge: Cambridge University Press, 2006).

4. Ibid.

5. Ibid.

6. Ibid., a. 2. Aquinas cites the *De Anima* II for the citation, but it is most likely the following passage, from III.431b20–22: "Now summing up what we have said about the soul, let us assert once more that in a sense the soul is all existing things" (ψυχὴ τὰ ὄντα πώς ἐστι πάντα). *De Anima*, trans. W. S. Hett (Cambridge: Harvard University Press, 2000). Interestingly, Heidegger also cites this passage in the opening chapters to *Being and Time* §4, though to demonstrate the "ontological priority of *Da-sein*."

7. Aquinas, *Summa Theologica*, a. 2.

8. Ibid.

9. Ibid., a.3, italics added.

10. Ibid.

11. Ibid.

12. On the divine nature in Scholasticism, see Marion, *God Without Being*, Alvin Plantinga, *Does God Have a Nature?* (Milwaukee: Marquette University Press, 1980), and Edward Wierenga, *The Nature of God: An Inquiry into Divine Attributes* (Ithaca: Cornell University Press, 1989).

13. Johannes Scottus Eriugena, *Periphyseon* I, 441A.

14. On the concept of *natura* in Eriugena, see Moran, *The Philosophy of John Scottus Eriugena*, pp. 241ff.

15. Eriugena, *Periphyseon* I, 441A.

16. Ibid.

17. Ibid.

18. We could have, certainly, conceived of a "cross" diagram that would resonate quite nicely with religious themes, but the "tilted" or "wobbly" cross has the advantage of suggesting more horizontal relationships, and it also emphasizes two other motifs that are repeatedly addressed in the *Periphyseon*: the circle and the wheel.

19. Ibid., I 441B.

20. Ibid., I 442A.

21. Ibid., II 528B.

22. Ibid., III 632B–C.

23. Cf. ibid., I 450D.

24. Cf. ibid., III 732B–733B.

25. Cf. ibid., III 732C.

26. Ibid., III 728A.

27. Ibid.

28. Ibid., III 728B.

29. Ibid., III 728D–729A.

30. Ibid., III 729A.

31. Ibid., III 729B.

32. Ibid., III 729B–C.

33. Ibid., III 729C.

34. Cf., I 452C.

35. Ibid., III 678D–679A.

36. Ibid., III 621D–622A.

37. Ibid., II 528B.

38. Ibid., III 679A.

39. Ibid., II, 529A, variant.

40. Cf. I 454C; I 468B; II 528B; II 579A; III 620B–621A; III 650C–D.

41. Ibid., III 687C.

42. Ibid.

43. Ibid., II 529A.

44. Ibid., I 518A.

45. Ibid., III 683A.

46. Gilles Deleuze, "Anti-Oedipe et Mille Plateaux," trans. Timothy Murphy, *Les Cours de Gilles Deleuze*, ed. Richard Pinhas, at http://www.webdeleuze.com.

47. Cf. John Duns Scotus, *God and Creatures: The Quodlibetal Questions*, trans. Felix Alluntis and Allan Wolter (Washington, DC: Catholic University of America Press, 1975), Q. 2, a. 2.

48. See the commentary in Allan Wolter and William Frank (eds.), *Duns Scotus, Metaphysician* (West Lafayette: Purdue University Press, 1995).

49. The existing edition known as the *Opus Oxoniense* is said to have been edited by Scotus' staff at the University of Paris, and in some cases "completed" from various student notes. While parts of the collected Paris lectures—known as the *Reportata Parisiensia*—do exist in a coherent form, and appear to have been authorized by Scotus himself, they are complicated by biographical facts: Scotus began his Paris lectures

around 1302, but was forced to leave Paris due to the ongoing disputes of the time between Pope Boniface VIII and King Philip the Fair. When he was allowed to return in 1304, he continued his lectures. However, modern scholars have noted a number of discrepancies in the *Reportata* between the original, written-down version (by an unknown scribe), an alternate version by Scotus' secretary William of Alnwick, and Scotus' own manuscripts and notes (in the *Liber Scoti*).

50. John Duns Scotus, *Reportata Parisiensia (Reportatio* IA*)*, in *Duns Scotus, Metaphysician*, d. 2, p. 41.

51. John Duns Scotus, *Opus Oxoniense (Ordinatio)*, in *Philosophical Writings*, I., dist. II, q. i, p. 35, italics removed.

52. A good account is given in A. W. Moore, *The Infinite* (New York: Routledge, 2001).

53. Duns Scotus, *Opus Oxoniense*, pt. II, third proof, p. 72.

54. We can provide a outline of Scotus' proof for the existence of God, as presented in the *Ordinatio* I, dist. II, q. i:

- Question: Among beings does one exist that is actually infinite?
- Replies Pro and Contra
- Body of the Question
  - Article I: The Relative Properties of God
    - Part I: The Triple Primacy
      - *Primacy of efficient causality*
        - Conclusion 1: "Among beings which can produce an effect one is simply first."
        - Conclusion 2: "Among those things that can produce an effect that which is simply first is itself incapable of being caused."
        - Conclusion 3: "Such a being actually exists and some nature actually existing is capable of such causality."
      - *Primacy of finality*
        - Conclusion 1: "The first conclusion is that some end is simply ultimate, that is, it can neither be ordained to something else nor exercise its finality in virtue of something else."
        - Conclusion 2: "The second conclusion is that the ultimate end cannot be caused in any way."
        - Conclusion 3: "The third conclusion is that the being which can be an ultimate end actually exists and that this primacy pertains to some actually existing nature."
      - *Primacy of preeminence*
        - Conclusion 1: "The first conclusion is that some eminent nature is simply first in perfection."
        - Conclusion 2: "The second conclusion is that the supreme nature cannot be caused."
        - Conclusion 3: "The third conclusion is that the supreme nature actually exists."

- Part II: The Interrelation of the Three Primacies
- Part III: The Unity of the Divine Nature
- Article II: The Absolute Properties of God
  - Part I: Intellect and Will
  - Part II: The Infinity of the First Being
- Solution to the Question
- Reply to the Arguments at the Beginning

55. Ibid., a. 1, p. 38.

56. Cf. I., dist. II, q. i, pt. I, pp. 39ff.

57. Cf. I., dist. II, q. i, pt. I, pp. 47ff.

58. In many ways Scotus' notion of preeminence goes against that of Aquinas, who, in the *Summa* I., q. 3, argues for the existence of God based on a hierarchy of perfection in the gradation of beings.

59. *Ordinatio* I, dist. II, q. i, pt. I, p. 48.

60. *Reportatio* IA, pt. I, p. 47.

61. Ibid., p. 49.

62. "[T]he first efficient cause does not act primarily or ultimately for the sake of anything distinct from itself; hence, it must act for itself as an end; therefore, the first efficient cause is the ultimate end" (ibid.).

63. "The first efficient cause is not a univocal cause with reference to the other efficient causes but rather an equivocal cause. Such a cause, therefore, is more excellent and noble than they" (ibid.).

64. "I say that since this triple primacy is found together (for where one is, there also are the others), it follows further that this triple identity is such that there is but one first efficient cause according to essence and nature" (ibid., pp. 49–50).

65. *Ordinatio* I, dist. II, q. i, pt. III, p. 50.

66. See *Nicholas of Cusa: The Catholic Concordance*, trans. Paul E. Sigmund (Cambridge: Cambridge University Press, 1996).

67. Scholarship on Cusa that has informed my own reading includes: Donald Duclow, "Pseudo-Dionysius, John Scottus Eriugena, Nicholas of Cusa: An Approach to the Hermeneutic of the *Divine Names*," *International Philosophical Quarterly* 12 (1972): 260–78; Dermot Moran, "Pantheism from John Scottus Eriugena to Nicholas of Cusa," *American Catholic Philosophical Quarterly* 64 (1990): 131–52; and the collection *Cusanus: The Legacy of Learned Ignorance*, ed. Peter Casarella (Washington, DC: Catholic University of America Press, 2006).

68. Nicholas of Cusa, *De Docta Ignorantia*, ed. and trans. H. Lawrence Bond (New York: Paulist Press, 1997), I.2.5. All citations refer to this edition.

69. Ibid., I.4.11.

70. Ibid., I.16.43.

71. Ibid., I.4.12.

72. Ibid., II.3.107.

73. Ibid., II.3.106.

74. Ibid., I.22.68.

75. Ibid., I.22.69.

76. Ibid., II.3.107.

77. Ibid., II.5.117.

78. Ibid., II.4.115.

79. Ibid., II.2.100.

80. Ibid., I.4.12.

81. Ibid., II.5.117.

82. Cf. III.2.194. This would be the place to explore in greater detail the role of Cusa to contemporary continental philosophy's engagement with Christology. See, for instance, Michel Henry, *I Am the Truth*, trans. Susan Emanuel (Stanford: Stanford University Press, 2002), François Laruelle, *Le Christ futur* (Paris: Exils, 2002); Jean-Luc Nancy, *Dis-enclosure*, trans. Bettina Bergo et al. (New York: Fordham University Press, 2008), and the collection *The Monstrosity of Christ* (Cambridge: MIT Press, 2009). I have elected not to engage with this discourse so as to focus on the latent non-anthropomorphism in Cusa's mysticism.

83. Gilles Deleuze, *Expressionism in Philosophy: Spinoza*, trans. Martin Joughin (New York: Zone, 1992), p. 18 [14].

84. Deleuze cites Gandillac's works on Cusa a number of times in *Spinoza et le problème de l'expression*.

85. Maurice de Gandillac, *Nicolas de Cues* (Paris: Ellipses, 2001 [1942]), p. 27, translation mine.

86. Ferdinand Alquié, "Nature et vérité dans la philosophie de Spinoza," in *Leçons sur Spinoza* (Paris: La Table Ronde, 2003 [1958]), p. 32, translation mine.

87. Ibid., p. 17, translation mine.

88. Deleuze, *Expressionism in Philosophy*, p. 16.

89. Ibid.

90. Ibid. The opening phrase reads: "Expliquer, c'est developer. Envelopper, c'est impliquer."

91. Ibid.

92. Ibid., p. 17.

93. Ibid., p. 333, italics removed.

94. Ibid., p. 322.

95. Ibid., p. 169.

96. Ibid., p. 170.

97. Ibid.

98. Ibid., p. 171.

99. Ibid., pp. 170–71.

100. Ibid., p. 171.

101. Ibid.

102. Ibid., p. 172.

103. Ibid., p. 175.

104. Ibid.

105. Ibid.

106. Ibid., p. 173.

107. Ibid.

108. Ibid., pp. 173–74.

109. Ibid., p. 180.

110. Ibid., p. 176.

111. Ibid., p. 180.

112. Gilles Deleuze, *Difference and Repetition*, trans. Paul Patton (New York: Columbia University Press, 1995), p. 35.

113. Duns Scotus, *Ordinatio* I, dist. II, q. iii.

114. Deleuze, *Expressionism in Philosophy*, p. 275.

115. Ibid.

116. Ibid., p. 278.

117. See, for instance, the chapter "The Geology of Morals," in Gilles Deleuze and Félix Guattari, *A Thousand Plateaus*, pp. 39ff. Deleuze also uses the Cuvier-Geoffroy debate in *Difference and Repetition*.

118. Deleuze, *Expressionism in Philosophy*, p. 278.

119. Ibid.

120. Ibid., p. 81.

121. See Alain Badiou, *Deleuze: The Clamor of Being*, trans. Louise Burchill (Minneapolis: University of Minnesota Press, 1999), pp. 19ff.

122. Ibid., p. 322.

123. I am indebted to Alexander Galloway for this coinage; he also uses it in his essay "Black Boxes and *Daimon* Code," *Perspectives in Speculative Computing* 9 (2009): 4–12.

124. Alain Badiou, *Logique des mondes* (Paris: Éditions du Seuil, 2006), p. 382, translation mine.

125. For a standard overview of Neo-Confucianism, see volume 2 of Yu-lan Fun, *A History of Chinese Philosophy*, trans. Derk Bodde (Princeton: Princeton University Press, 1983).

126. In *A Source Book in Chinese Philosophy*, ed. and trans. Wing-Tsit Chan (Princeton: Princeton University Press, 1969), p. 529.

127. "Day and night I was unable to understand the principles of the bamboo, until after seven days I also became ill because of having wearied and burdened my thoughts. In consequence we mutually sighed and said, 'We cannot be either sages or virtuous men, for we lack the real strength required to carry on the investigation of things' . . . I knew that there really was no one who could investigate the things under heaven. The task of investigating things can only be carried out in and with reference to one's body and mind" (*Record of Discourses*, in *The Philosophy of Wang Yangming*, trans. Frederick Goodrich Henke [Chicago: Open Court Press, 1916], p. 178).

128. "Instructions for Practical Living," in *The Philosophy of Wang Yangming*, trans. Frederick Goodrich Henke (Chicago: Open Court Press, 1916), p. 59.

129. *ad te omnis caro veniet*. Of the dark and sorrowful music of the *Tenebrae*, the one composed by Carlo Gesualdo, known as the *Tenebrae Responsoria* (1611), stands out in both content and form. Gesualdo—aristocrat, composer, depressive, and murderer—is equally known for his madrigals, a poetic and secular form of vocal music popular during the Renaissance. He wrote both the music and, it is thought, the words of his madrigals, which express with great intensity and subtlety the spectrum of affects dealing with love—ecstasy and agony, joy and sorrow. Gesualdo's *Tenebrae* pieces are in many ways madgrial-like; they contain formal experiments in chromaticism and

harmony that at times evoke a sense of spiritual dissonance. In a sense, by composing the liturgical *Tenebrae* in a way similar to the secular madrigals, Gesualdo also shifted this spiritual dissonance from musical form to its expressive content.

CHAPTER 5

1. In this way Kant's views on nature are significantly different from those of other philosophers working in and departing from the Idealist tradition. On the Kantian "two-worlds" physics (living vs. nonliving), and the critique of it posed by Schelling, see Iain Hamilton Grant, *Philosophies of Nature After Schelling* (London: Continuum, 2006), pp. 69ff. For a perceptive critique of contemporary biophilosophy and its relation to Kant, see Howard Caygill, "The Topology of Selection: The Limits of Deleuze's Biophilosophy," in *Gilles Deleuze: The Difference Engineer*, ed. Keith Ansell Pearson (New York: Routledge, 1997), pp. 149–62.

2. Immanuel Kant, *Critique of the Power of Judgment*, ed. Paul Guyer, trans. Paul Guyer and Eric Matthews (Cambridge: Cambridge University Press, 2000), §63–64. All references and citations are from this edition. Other editions consulted include Kant, *Critique of Judgment*, trans. J. H. Bernard (New York: Hafner, 1951), and Kant, *Kritik der Urteilskraft*, ed. Gerhard Lehmann (Stuttgart: Reclam, 1963).

3. Ibid., "First Introduction," II, p. 8. A more literal English rendering would be something like "appropriate end."

4. Ibid., §63, pp. 240–41.

5. Ibid.

6. Ibid., §64, p. 243.

7. Ibid., §65, p. 245.

8. Ibid. The phrase "an *organized* and *self-organizing* being" reads "als *organisiertes* und *sich selbst organisierendes* Wesen."

9. Ibid., §65, p. 246.

10. Ibid., §65, p. 246–47.

11. Ibid., §67, p. 249.

12. Ibid., §67, p. 250.

13. Ibid., §66, p. 248.

14. Quentin Meillassoux, *After Finitude: An Essay on the Necessity of Contingency*, trans. Ray Brassier (London: Continuum, 2008), p. 5.

15. Ibid.

16. Ray Brassier, Iain Hamilton Grant, Graham Harman, and Quentin Meillassoux, "Speculative Realism," *Collapse* 3 (2007): 409.

17. Ibid., p. 427.

18. Ibid.

19. Alain Badiou, *Logique des mondes* (Paris: Éditions du Seuil, 2006), p. 283, translation mine.

20. Ibid., p. 284, translation mine.

21. On the ontology of decay, see Reza Negarestani, "Undercover Softness: An Introduction to the Architecture and Politics of Decay," *Collapse* 6 (2010).

22. Brassier et al., "Speculative Realism," p. 308.

23. Ibid., pp. 308–9.

24. Kant, *Critique of the Power of Judgment*, §68, p. 253.

25. Ibid., §85, p. 303.

26. Ibid., §85, pp. 304–305.

27. Kant, *Lectures on the Philosophical Doctrine of Religion*, in *Religion and Rational Theology*, ed. and trans. Allen Wood and George di Giovanni (Cambridge: Cambridge University Press, 2005), p. 342.

28. Ibid., p. 347.

29. Ibid.

30. Ibid.

31. Georges Bataille, "Plans pour la somme athéologique," *Oeuvres Complètes* 6 (Paris: Gallimard, 1973), p. 367, Carnet 13. All translations from Bataille's *Oeuvres Complètes* are my own.

32. Bataille's use of the term atheology must be thought of alongside his earlier social experiments of the 1930s, of which the secret society Acéphale was exemplary. During this period the group published a journal, titled simply *Acéphale*. André Masson's drawings for the journal are emblematic of atheological thinking: a headless yet living body politic. Much of the contemporary secondary scholarship on Bataille tends to elide his indebtedness to Medieval philosophy and mysticism, despite its obvious presence in nearly all of Bataille's works. Notable exceptions include: Denis Hollier, *Against Architecture: The Writings of Georges Bataille* (Cambridge: MIT Press, 1995 [1974]), pp. 36ff; Bruce Hollsinger, *The Premodern Condition: Medievalism and the Making of Theory* (Chicago: University of Chicago Press, 2005), pp. 27ff; Alexander Irwin, *Saints of the Impossible: Bataille, Weil, and the Politics of the Sacred* (Minneapolis: University of Minnesota Press, 2002), pp. 124ff; Nick Land, *The Thirst for Annihilation* (New York: Routledge, 1992); Allan Stoekl, *Bataille's Peak: Energy, Religion, and Postsustainability* (Minneapolis: University of Minnesota Press, 2007), pp. 60ff. Hollier's book has become somewhat of a standard in Bataille studies, and offers an earlier treatment of the theme of atheology.

33. Bataille's plan for the *Somme Athéologique* went through numerous changes. For instance, around 1954, Bataille outlined the project as follows:

- *Inner Experience* (*L'Expérience Intérieure*)
- *Guilty* (*Le Coupable*)
- *On Nietzsche* (*Sur Nietzsche*)
- *Pure Happiness* (*Le Pur Bonheur*)
- *The Incomplete System of Non-Knowledge* (*Le Système Inachevé du Non-savoir*).

The title "Somme Athéologique" was first mentioned by Bataille in a letter to Raymond Queneau in 1949, and was advertised in the 1954 edition of *L'Expérience Intérieure*, then subsequently modified after 1961 to include only the first three volumes. Early outlines for the project included possible volumes such as "The Sanctity of Evil" (La Sainteté du Mal), "History of a Secret Society" (Histoire d'une Société Secrete), and "To Die from Laughing and to Laugh from Dying" (Mourir de Rire et Rire de Mourir).

34. Bataille, "Plans pour la somme athéologique." Another of Bataille's definitions runs as follows: "Define atheology: the science of the death or destruction of God (the

science of the thing being destroyed inasmuch as it is a thing" ("Aphorisms for the 'System,'" in *The Unfinished System of Nonknowledge*, trans. Stuart and Michelle Kendall [Minneapolis: University of Minnesota Press, 2004], p. 166).

35. "Plans pour la somme athéologique," p. 374, "Avertissement," boîte 12.

36. *Memorandum*, in *Oeuvres Complètes* 6, p. 261.

37. *Sur Nietzsche*, in *Oeuvres Complètes* 6, p. 48.

38. *L'Expérience Intérieure*, in *Oeuvres Complètes* 5, p. 111. Bataille's images of flow and light are frequent: "Furthermore, your life is not borne along this imperceptible, interior flowing; it also flows towards the outside and incessantly opens itself . . . The enduring whirlpool that composes you runs up against similar whirlpools with which it forms a vast animated form of measured agitation" (ibid.).

39. Ibid.

40. Ibid.

41. Ibid.

42. Georges Bataille, *Théorie de la Religion* (Paris: Gallimard, 1973), p. 54, translation mine.

43. Ibid., p. 64, translation mine.

44. Bataille, *Oeuvres Complètes* 6, carnet "M," p. 433.

45. Bataille, *Oeuvres Complètes* 5, carnet "B," p. 480.

46. Ibid., carnet "A," p. 464.

47. Bataille, "Plans pour la somme athéologique," p. 367.

48. William Hope Hodgson, *The Night Land*, volumes 1 and 2 (New York: Ballantine, 1973). This edition, though not the first, was included in the "Adult Fantasy" series edited by Lin Carter.

49. *Requiem æternam dona eis.* It goes without saying that there is no dancing during either the Requiem Mass or the *Tenebrae*. As a music of shadows, sorrow, and darkness, its very content would seem to mitigate against such a response. Nevertheless, one finds here and there passages of overflowing life—the Requiems of Brahms, Verdi, and Berlioz almost spill forth with their dazzling bright horns and epic choruses, sounding more like the *Carmina Burana* than a Mass for the Dead. Indeed, an earlier period might have attributed such contrasts to the influence of the devil's music. But beyond these contrasts of light and darkness, sorrow and joy, there is also the neutral plateau of a music that negates itself as music. Such describes the Requiem of the Hungarian composer György Ligeti. Ligeti's Requiem (1965) is an emptied music that pushes formal elements such as melody and rhythm into a background of nothingness. Not only do the voices of the chorus cease to be voices and become abstract sounds, but these sounds themselves dissipate seamlessly into a space above or below our sonic register that can be described only as empty sound.

INDEX